Musical Meaning and Expression

Also by Stephen Davies

Definitions of Art (1991)

MUSICAL MEANING

and Expression

Stephen Davies

CORNELL UNIVERSITY PRESS
Ithaca and London

First published 1994 by Cornell University Press.
First printing, Cornell Paperbacks, 1994.

Printed in the United States of America.

Library of Congress Cataloging-in-Publication Data

Davies, Stephen, 1950–
    Musical meaning and expression / Stephen Davies.
        p.   cm.
    Includes bibliographical references and index.
    ISBN 0-8014-2930-7 (cloth : alk. paper). —ISBN 0-8014-8151-1 (pbk. : alk. paper)
    1. Music—Philosophy and aesthetics. 2. Music—Psychology.
    I. Title.
    ML3800.D25   1994
    781'.1—dc20   93-39890

Cornell University Press strives to utilize environmentally responsible suppliers and materials to the fullest extent possible in the publishing of its books. Such materials include vegetable-based, low-VOC inks and acid-free papers that are also either recycled, totally chlorine-free, or partly composed of nonwood fibers.

Paperback printing   10   9   8   7   6   5   4   3   2

To Ruby Meager

Contents

Contents

< viii >

Preface

At the end of the film *Close Encounters of the Third Kind*, the extraterrestrials and humans attempt to communicate neither in Alienese nor in American English but in music. Apparently the aliens share the view that music is the universal language; perhaps they feel confirmed in this observation by the realization that many human musics are no less diatonic and triadic than their own. Music seems gravid with meaning. We talk not solely of a person's enjoying music but of his understanding or misunderstanding it. At times music seems to speak to deep human feelings and experiences, so that some works appear to possess not just content but profound content. A person with no understanding of music might strike us as impoverished in her existence. But what does music mean and how does it mean? Such questions are my subject.

This is a book about the meaning of music. As becomes apparent in the text, I do not believe that music is a symbol system that conveys a semantic, or quasi-semantic, content. But I am not embarrassed to use the term "meaning" here because I think both that music can and should be understood to be appreciated and that it is created to be so. That composers intend to make something that invites attention, engagement, and consideration rather than aiming to stimulate a mindless reflex, and that they succeed in producing works rewarding in just this way, suggests to me that we might reasonably talk of music's meaning what is grasped by the person who understands it.

Many of the arguments considered here focus on music's expressiveness or bear on issues related to that topic. That concentration might convey a

< ix >

Preface

misleading impression. I do not believe that all music is expressive. Neither do I believe that expressiveness is always the most important feature of music that is expressive. There is much more to appreciating most works than recognizing their expressive character, as I argue in Chapter 7. Nevertheless, the expression of emotion in music is bound to attract a philosopher's attention, for it raises philosophically perplexing questions. Given that music is nonsentient, how could emotions be expressed in it? Are musical phrases understood as utterances about emotions? or as pictures of emotions and the context in which they arise? or as symbols referring us to the world of human feeling? Or are they interpreted as gestures betraying the composer's or performer's emotions? Or are they expressive insofar as they move the listener? And, if the listener is moved, how could it be that the listener is moved by the music, which lacks life, thought, and sensation? Moreover, why would the listener seek out works that lead her to feelings she herself describes as ones of sadness? In considering these questions one runs up against others, no less difficult. How is it that we hear movement in music when nothing goes from place to place? Are descriptions of music usefully classed as metaphoric? Are the expressive elements of music natural or arbitrary, universal or merely cultural, in their significance? Other aspects of music, its works, and its practices are of concern to philosophers. The creative process, theories of musical analysis, the nature of musical works, the responsibilities and freedoms of the performer, the interpretation of historically distant works and conventions—all have provoked discussion in journals of philosophy. But, above all, it is music's expressive power that has proved to be philosophically intriguing.

As I say, musical expressiveness attracts more than its share of attention from philosophers because, as a topic, the puzzles it generates cry out for conceptual analysis. That lack of balance is perpetuated here. I have very little to say about the many delights and difficulties of composition, performance, and listening as these might be studied by practicing composers and musicians, as well as by the ordinary listener devoted to music. This is a book designed more for the philosopher of music than for the musicologist, the composer, the performer, or the listener. Music raises philosophical questions that have retained their interest not only because of their importance but also because of their undoubted difficulty. Difficult issues give rise to complicated arguments. If what I have to say, despite its detailed complexity, interests nonphilosophers, that is because many of those who discuss, listen to, analyze, compose, and play music share with the philosopher a fascination for the seeming improbability of the power of music to engage those

< x >

who attend to it. I hope that my discussion clarifies and articulates the puzzles experienced by musicians as much as by philosophers.

While I am making excuses I should add these. I write mainly about Western, "classical," instrumental music. I concentrate on Western music because I assume that most of my readers are less familiar with non-Western musics. I focus on "classical" music not only because my own preferences and knowledge lie in that direction but because that tradition provides a major part of the heritage from which other, popular forms of music draw. And instrumental music, aside from being central, if not dominant, within the Western "classical" tradition of the past two hundred years, seems most crucial for philosophical reasons: in respect of purely instrumental music philosophical questions are most acute, for such meaning as these works have belongs to the world of musical sound. The contribution music might make in song, opera, film, and the like are clear, I think, only if one is aware of the strengths and weaknesses, so to speak, of music in its most abstract setting.

If my focus is narrow, the scope of the arguments I consider is not. The theories discussed are of a generality such that, if they are successful, they should be applicable to many types of music. The reader is invited to attempt these applications where I do not do so.

It was as a student that I first began thinking about the issues discussed in this book. Indeed, I was prompted to pursue philosophy as a counterpoint to my studies in musicology and ethnomusicology by my interest in the questions I address here. In my early work on the expression of emotion in music I was guided by Ruby Meager, and I owe a great deal to her sage advice and sympathetic criticisms.

As becomes apparent in the text, my thinking has ben provoked, enriched, and stimulated by the philosophical literature, which has grown considerably in the 1980s. I have a special admiration for the writings of three philosophers—Malcolm Budd, Peter Kivy, and Jerrold Levinson. The reader should gauge my esteem for their work more by the number of times I return to their ideas than by the critical stance that I sometimes adopt in discussing their views.

Parts of the argument presented here first appeared in journals. My thanks to Oxford University Press, *Theoria*, and the University of Illinois Press for their permission to use and adapt the contents of "The Expression of Emotion in Music," *Mind*, 89 (1980): 67–86; "Is Music a Language of the Emotions?" *British Journal of Aesthetics*, 23 (1983): 222–233; "The Expression Theory Again," *Theoria*, 52 (1986): 146–167, and "Representa-

< xi >

tion in Music," *Journal of Aesthetic Education*, 27, no. 1 (1993): 16–22. Also I thank Oxford University Press for permission to reproduce part of Ralph Vaughan Williams's *Job: A Masque for Dancing* and Universal Edition A. G. for allowing the use of extracts from Franz Joseph Haydn's Symphony No. 98 and Johannes Brahms's Symphony No. 4.

I am indebted to many people for their advice and insightful criticisms. In particular, I thank Nick Beckingsale, Allan Beever, James D. Carney, R. E. Ewin, Stan Godlovitch, Kathleen Higgins, and Fred Kroon. I also thank Roger Haydon and Carol Betsch of Cornell University Press.

STEPHEN DAVIES

Auckland, New Zealand

Musical Meaning and Expression

O N E

· · ·

Music and Language

Looks, nudges, and winks can be meaningful, but our paradigm of the meaningful is linguistic utterance. It is natural, then, to commence the consideration of musical meaning with a comparison between music and natural languages. In this chapter, I argue that, for the most part, music is not usefully to be compared to language with respect to its meaning and that it is more misleading than illuminating to highlight such parallels as there are.

There are many respects in which our descriptions of music draw an analogy with language. We talk of musical grammar, of phrases, of one phrase as a question answered by the next, of statement, of quotation, of irony, of conversations and dialogues between instruments. Such ways of talking seem grounded in structural resemblances between music and language. Just as sentences are formed from the combination of words according to various rules or conventions, so too music comprises elements (such as notes and chords) combined in accordance with rules or conventions to make wholes (such as melodies). Like a sentence, a musical theme does not merely begin and end, it comes to a close. Just as sentences are combined to form paragraphs, and paragraphs are concatenated to create stories, musical themes are joined to form larger units—expositions, movements, symphonies. In these respects music is like a syntactic system. Like words, musical ideas retain (some of) their identity and significance within different contexts while contributing to the whole resulting from their combination; melodies introduced in the exposition remain recognizable as individuals when they return in the recapitulation, even if the altered method of their conjunction

< I >

lends a new significance to the result. With this in mind, we might wish to describe music as a syntactic system with a vocabulary. And finally, we talk of musical works as meaningful, as requiring understanding, as generating a content. So one might wish to take the analogy between music and language so far as to suggest that music is a syntactic system with a vocabulary used in such a way as to generate a semantics.

The comparison cuts both ways: if music has a linguistic character, language can have a musical one. The semantic content of spoken utterances can be affected by pitch, rhythm, tempo, accent, phrasing, attack, and decay. For example, the interrogative mood usually involves a rise in inflection. In some "tone" languages (such as are found in Asia and Africa), the relative pitch of a word is no less significant than its sound in fixing its meaning. Michael Butor (1968) goes so far as to suggest that language is rooted in music and that the most prosaic spoken language is always based on a musical structure. Sidney Finkelstein (1952) regards the "music" (inflections, accents, and intonations) of speech as adding to meaning "the essential human character" (also see Trott 1990).

If there are similarities between music and language, there are also striking differences. One could not learn Music as one's mother tongue. Moreover, whereas translation from Swahili to German admits of many difficulties— so that one might deny that meanings, in their fullest, richest sense, are transmissible between natural languages—such difficulties are as nothing compared to those facing the person who would try to translate the meaning of a Beethoven symphony into German prose. This is widely admitted. Ludwig Wittgenstein says: "Understanding a sentence is more akin to understanding a piece of music than one might think. Why must these bars be played just so? Why do I want to produce just this pattern of variation in loudness and tempo? I would like to say 'Because I know what it is all about.' But what is it all about? I should not be able to say. For explanation I can only translate the musical picture into a picture in another medium and let the one picture throw light on the other" (1974, sec. 4). Eduard Hanslick writes: "In music there is both meaning and logical sequence, but in a musical sense; it is a language we speak and understand, but which we are unable to translate" (1957, 50). Butor comments: "That music is a language is, I believe, evident to everyone; but one of the chief reasons for the obscurity and current impotence of musical criticism, the root of that prejudice which tends to make music an absolutely isolated and therefore inexplicable language, derives from the fact that we consider this language to be on the same level as the different spoken languages, as if there were English, German, French, Music,

< 2 >

and so on" (1968, 285). Fred Lerdahl and Ray Jackendoff, in adopting a Chomskian stance to the description of musical "grammar," say this:

> But pointing out superficial analogies between music and language, with or without the help of generative grammar, is an old and largely futile game. One should not approach music with any preconceptions that the substance of music theory will look at all like linguistic theory. For example, whatever music may "mean," it is in no sense comparable to linguistic meaning; there are no musical phenomena comparable to sense and reference in language, or to such semantic judgments as synonymy, analyticity, and entailment. Likewise there are no substantive parallels between elements of musical structure and such syntactic categories as noun, verb, adjective, preposition, noun phrase, and verb phrase. Finally, one should not be misled by the fact that both music and language deal with sound structure. There are no musical counterparts of such phonological parameters as voicing, nasality, tongue height, and lip rounding. (1983, 5–6)[1]

Now, the attitude one adopts to the comparison between music and language depends as much on the significance one attributes to the differences as it does on the number of similarities that might be identified. Three approaches are to be found in the literature.

The first approach regards the differences between music and natural languages to be so important that it treats reference to the similarities, at best, as a flowery conceit and, at worst, as misleading. The differences between the two indicate either that music lacks semantic content or that it does not acquire its semantic dimension in the way language does. Talk of vocabulary and syntax cannot help but draw on the notion that music has a semantic content produced as that of language is, for these notions come in the same conceptual package (see Scruton 1981b). So talk of music's possessing a vocabulary or a syntax is best avoided. I count myself among those of this persuasion.

The second approach treats the difference between music and the natural languages as significant in showing that music is not a language, but it also regards the force of the similarities as informing a useful analogy. For exam-

---

[1] These authors do uncover what they regard as deep similarities between music and language: some musical and linguistic rules operate in the same way (to produce time-span reduction and prosodic structure), though what the rules are applied to and most of the substance of the rules differ in the two areas (see Lerdahl and Jackendoff 1983, chap. 12). For critical discussion, see Peel and Slawson 1984.

< 3 >

ple, John Sloboda regards the analogy between music and language as "partial" but devotes more than fifty pages to its exposition (1985, 13–66). Diana Raffman claims that music undeniably has a syntax, "a rule-governed system of discrete and repeatable elements type-identifiable exclusively by physical shape" (1988, 690–691). She also reveals a relaxed approach to the notion of a semantics, so that she sees the possibility of describing music as possessing a semantics while denying that music is a language as such. She says:

> In the final analysis, then, do the musical feelings [feelings of tension and resolution, of metrical stress, and the like, but not emotions like sadness] constitute a semantics? The answer is: say what you like. If you require (e.g.) that a semantics specify truth-conditions for well-formed strings, then you'll be inclined to answer in the negative. If on the other hand you are impressed by the fact that the musical feelings result in systematic ways from grammatical operations, sustain robust notions of correctness and error, pass the so-called novelty test, underwrite a theory of musical communication [according to which performers convey their feelings of how the music should go to the listener], and play the teleological and guiding roles characteristic of meaning in the natural language, then you may well answer in the affirmative. (1991, 372)

For my part, I doubt that we should say just what we like on the issue. Raffman reaches her view by downplaying the truth-functional requirement that commonly is regarded as essential for a semantics and by placing the emphasis elsewhere. Her conditions for a semantics are these: that meaning be apparent (largely in the absence of contextual clues) to a native "speaker," that there be standards for correct and incorrect understandings, that it be possible to convey new meanings, and that there be communication. Were my disagreement with Raffman to be pursued, the debate would concern whether her conditions capture the concept in question, and, if so, whether they do not presuppose the relevance of truth conditions as governing such notions as correct understanding or successful communication.

The third approach to the comparison between music and the natural languages regards the similarities as more significant than the differences. In this view, the analogy between them runs so deep that musical meaning can be construed on the model of linguistic meaning (see Kurkela 1986 and 1988; Gärdenfors 1988). In its strongest version, the position held is that musical and linguistic meaning are species of the same genus, that music is no less a language than is English, and that both are languages for the same

< 4 >

sorts of reasons. I take this to be the stand of Wilson Coker (1972). Those who would adopt this position must explain away the differences between music and natural languages or must account for those differences. The standard approach to doing so is to suggest that, though music and languages are discourses of relevantly similar types, they deal with different areas of experience. Typically, music is said to be the language of the emotions. For example, Colin McAlpin observes, "It seems strange to raise such a question as [Is music the language of the emotions?], seeing how difficult it is to conceive of any one with a real love of music meeting it with a flat denial" (1925, 427). If natural languages also deal with the emotions, then music would be like an impoverished version of a natural language. On the other hand, if natural languages do not deal directly with the emotions, or are inadequate to their characterization, then music might better be regarded as an alternate language rather than as an impoverished one. This second view is the one most often favored. According to it, it is difficult linguistically to specify what music means, not because music is not a language, but rather because the language of music describes matters lying beyond the remit of natural languages.[2]

How is one to adjudicate between these two claims—that the differences between music and natural languages reveal that music is not usefully to be compared to a language with respect to its meaning, and that music derives its meaning much as natural languages do, with the differences between the two residing in discrepancies between the areas onto which their respective discourses are to be mapped? I do so by adopting this method: taking linguistic meaning as paradigmatic, I attempt to enumerate the conditions necessary for something's being a language or significantly like a language. For a listing of the relevant conditions, I turn to a useful article by Göran Hermerén (1988): a language must possess (1) discrete and repeatable elements (2) which, when strung together, suggest or evoke ideas or feelings (3) because they constitute a vocabulary; it must also possess (4) indexical and characterizing elements, (5) force-showing devices and modalities, as well as (7) logical connectives; in being thus, (6) it must admit the possibility of metalinguistic assertions about itself. Of these seven conditions, I suggest that music meets, at best, only the weakest three. Because every one of the conditions must be met if something is to be a language (whether one limited in scope or not)—for its having a semantics—I conclude that musical meaning is not a special kind of quasi-linguistic meaning. Since Coker (1972) argues that both music and natural languages attain semantic significance in a

---

[2] I discuss the subject of music's alleged ineffability in Chapter 3.

< 5 >

similar fashion, and because he appreciates much better than most that music could do so only if it meets conditions of the kind specified by Hermerén, I use his views as my main foil.

Conditions for Language-type Meaning

(1) Elements

The first of Hermerén's conditions for language is that there be "discrete and repeatable elements on several levels, analogous to letters, words and sentences—or morphemes, phonemes and utterances, depending on the level of analysis required in each particular case" (1988, 182–183). He believes that this minimal condition is met by music but is less sure that it applies to all paintings, for, in Nelson Goodman's terms (1968), the elements of paintings are syntactically dense rather than articulated.[3]

Minimal though the first condition is, Ann Clark questions whether music meets it. She doubts that in music we hear divisible, syntactically discrete parts such that one, as opposed to another, can be identified as exemplifying one mark in the score. We cannot (as the phonetician does for language) identify a musical element as the smallest unit of sound that makes a difference in meaning (1982, 201). Hermerén is not unsympathetic to the point: "From a phenomenological point of view it seems arbitrary to separate form, meaning and context," he says (1988, 184). I disagree. It is true that there may be many phenomenally detectable differences between different renditions of a given note, even where each rendition is consistent with the work's score. But this indicates that not all audible differences are significant in characterizing musical elements rather than that musical elements are not identifiable as such. In most of the Western tradition, the pitched tone is a musical element of identifiable (and reidentifiable) significance. The differences between particular instances of a given tone (for example, between performances on different occasions) need not affect its musical significance (as the leading note of the first subject theme, for instance). Musical meaning begins to operate at the level of the pitched tone, and not at some more finegrained level (see Davies 1991a; Raffman 1988). A similar point could be made regarding language itself: two utterances might have exactly the

---

[3] Hermerén is no less concerned with covering the presentational than the expressive arts in his essay. Because of its relevance in Chapter 2, I follow his lead in discussing depictive paintings, as well as music, in working through his account of the conditions for something's being a language. For further discussion, especially of painting, see Hermerén 1992.

< 6 >

same import even where there are subtle differences in timbre, pitch, and intonation between them. If spoken language can meet the first condition, it is difficult to see why music would not do so also.

(2) Suggestive of Ideas

Hermerén's second condition for language is that strings of elements suggest or evoke ideas, emotions, or feelings in those who contemplate these elements, though not necessarily the same ideas, emotions, or feelings in different readers or listeners. He accepts that all the arts satisfy this vague requirement. "The problem is that so does everything else" (1988, 183, 185). The condition is too weak to be interesting.

Coker (1972) follows Morris (1939) in characterizing semiosis as a five-way relation between (i) any stimulus that calls forth (ii) in some person or organism (iii) a disposition to respond in some way to (iv) another object or event (v) under certain conditions. He adds that the meaning of a sign is always affective (because the perception of its meaning involves the adoption of an "attitude" by the interpreter of the sign). He notes, as the foundation for his account of music as a language, that music functions as a sign in meeting these five conditions. Just as an armchair invites us to sit down, he writes, so music stimulates a response from us. Coker and Morris are inclined to see this definition as providing a sufficient condition, not merely a necessary one, for something's being a sign.[4] Given that one is prepared to construe "symbol" this widely, to say that music is a symbol is to be far (as yet) from saying that music is symbolic as language is.

(3) Vocabulary

"The third condition is that there be a semantics, i.e. a vocabulary, of X, assigning meanings to the elements of X, which may . . . be codified in books like *Oxford English Dictionary*." There must be discrete and repeatable elements with a standardized meaning; each element is used in different contexts with the same (sometimes more than one) meaning (Hermerén 1988, 183, 185). Elements not only should receive regular patterns of use or combination but also must refer (or denote). Musical elements do receive regular patterns of use or combination—and hence there are recognizable musical

---

[4] They have been criticized on this score by Stevenson (1958a). In a similar vein, Clark (1982) complains that Collingwood (1963) describes art as a language merely because it is a form of human activity.

< 7 >

styles—but Hermerén doubts that musical elements or their combinations are referential in character. In expressing sadness, say, the musical work does not (typically) refer to sadness. If music is not *about* anything, then it does not meet this third condition; it lacks semantic content.[5]

According to Hermerén, medieval paintings possess a vocabulary, as revealed by iconographers. This implies that, were it to have a vocabulary, music might be understood as a code. Of course, a musical code could be invented: one might assign conventional meanings to musical tones or rhythms, so that they could function as Morse Code does. But musical tones are not normally so used.[6]

In Western music it is not uncommon to find, if not a full-blooded code, then musical elements that seem to function like labels or names. The church hours and the church modes were associated, so a monk might reason thus: the plainsong mode is phrygian, so it is time for lunch. Such associations might be used intentionally by the composer; he might quote "Hail to the Chief" to refer to the president of the United States of America. In yet other cases, the composer creates the connection by a kind of stipulation rather than relying on cultural associations. This is the case with Wagnerian leitmotif. At the close of this chapter I consider such uses of music in some detail. Here it is sufficient to make these points: codelike elements may be found in music, but they are not found in all works; where they are found they concern only some elements within the wider musical context; and the use of such devices tends not to be systematic from work to work. In these respects, musical "vocabularies" are far more limited and disorganized than those of natural languages. And, unlike the words of a language, such meaning as is exploited by composers more often relies on widely shared but implicit associations than on public, arbitrary stipulation.

Musical elements would more readily appear to function as a vocabulary if it were the case that there was a consistent pattern to their use in achieving,

---

[5] The most vigorous defender of the view that purely instrumental music is not at all referential is Kivy (1980, 1989 and 1990a).

[6] The point is made by Sharpe (1970) and Scruton (1976). Perhaps one should not be too hasty in denying the existence of such codes. Some Australian aboriginal tribes "own" song cycles, consisting of many dozens of songs, in which events from the Dream Time are recounted: here a giant kangaroo stepped, creating a valley; there the ancestors paused to dine on honey ants; and so forth. These stories encode a map that might allow one to find one's way from waterhole to waterhole, food source to food source, across hundreds of kilometers of trackless desert. One objection to regarding these song cycles as a musical code might insist that the message lies in the text, rather than in the music. That objection would need to be treated carefully, given that the aborigines are not inclined to distinguish the meaning of the words from the singing of them.

< 8 >

for example, musical expressiveness. Deryck Cooke (1959) attempts to demonstrate that this is the case within Western tonal music, though he denies that his is an attempt to compile a musical dictionary of expressive elements (I consider Cooke's views later in this chapter). If such elements denote or refer to the emotions they express, one might suggest that music meets this third condition.

Goodman (1968 and 1978b) has argued that the arts are constituted by (different types of) symbol systems and thus are denotative; denotation is found not only in description but in representation and expression as well. Expression occurs when a property (or, in Goodman's nominalist terms, a label) is denoted through its metaphoric exemplification in the work. If a work is expressive, it is so by virtue of metaphorically exemplifying an expressive character. In Goodman's view, musical works are not descriptions or representations, but, to the extent that they are expressive, they are denotative (for details, see Chapters 2 and 3).

Despite regarding all the arts as denotative, and notwithstanding the title "Languages of Art," Goodman denies that music and painting are languages. Even if Goodman regards these arts as meeting the third condition in being denotative, he believes that they fail other of the necessary conditions for something's being a language. Painting lacks syntactically discrete elements and thereby does not satisfy the first condition; music fails the three conditions still to be considered. As I understand Goodman's position, it might be stated this way. Though music is denotative, the manner in which denotation is achieved in music (via exemplification) differs from the manner in which denotation is secured in language (via a semantic system). In language, denotation is a preparation for predication. Not only is this not so in music, it could not be so, given the differences between linguistic and musical symbol systems.

Goodman has his critics. Joseph Margolis (1987, also see 1974 and 1979) rejects Goodman's syntax-driven theory of symbol systems and the significance of the parallels between language and music Goodman draws. Monroe C. Beardsley (1979) sets out three objections to Goodman's stance: (i) an aesthetic understanding and appreciation of music and nonrepresentational paintings (usually) pays no heed to reference; we might delight in discovering the work itself, but not other things via the work's (possible) reference; (ii) natural objects are not characters in symbol systems, yet they have a value akin to that of artworks; (iii) rather than aiming at higher truths, artists bend the truth for the sake of aesthetic effect. Presumably (ii) and (iii) amplify (i) in indicating that, if denotation occurs (or is aimed at), it is peripheral rather than central to our understanding and enjoying such artforms. Goodman

< 9 >

(1978b) stresses the opacity of the symbolism involved, allowing that the focus falls on the symbol rather than on the signified, but then, Beardsley thinks, the cognitive, symbolic function of such works is not their primary (aesthetic) purpose.

As becomes apparent in Chapter 3, both these critics see musical expressiveness as a matter of possession and as not requiring denotation, thus rejecting the account of expressiveness proposed by Goodman. Now, they might be correct in denying that denotation is necessary for expressiveness but mistaken in denying that expressive properties are standardly used to achieve reference or denotation. If composers deliberately employ expressive features in their works, it might be that they aim to make their works expressive, thereby intending to refer more widely to the emotions exemplified in those works. By making the work sad, the composer might intend to denote sadness (and not merely to present an instance of it). As I have indicated, Beardsley not only denies that the act of denotation is necessary but also doubts that it is primary or common in music (and in this I suspect he is correct). Nevertheless, Coker (1972) cites Goodman with approval and accords a central place to the claim that composers use expressive materials denotatively. He goes further than Goodman, though, in claiming that music is like a language in meeting not only this condition but also the others I have listed.

Coker claims that music is referential. He says that many (but not all) musical signs are iconic, in that they refer through exemplifying features they share with their referents. By this means there is "extrageneric" reference to affective and mental states as well as to things (objects and states of affairs), though many qualities (for example, colors) and many objects (such as the moon) are not amenable to musical reference. According to Coker, music can say, for example, that fast-moving and complicated events are followed, on occasion, by simplification and calm. But, he continues, denotation is not confined to the extrageneric: it lies at the very heart of music. Many musical signs or "gestures" refer "congenerically," that is, to other parts of the musical work or musical style. One theme recalls another or "refers" to its own recurrences or treatment.[7]

Coker reveals what he takes to be the conditions for reference in the evidence he offers for his thesis: music not only is semiotic in character, like language it is formalized to the extent that it elicits similar responses from (educated) listeners, where these responses are thought-founded rather than

---

[7] Others who argue that music is self-referential in this manner are Kuhns (1978) and Price (1988).

< 10 >

instinctual. But these conditions are far too broad to capture a notion which parallels that of linguistic reference. Music is highly conventionalized, certainly, but it does not follow that the conventions are significantly analogous in form or function to those of language. Response to music shows considerable uniformity from listener to listener, agreed, but coincidence in responses might arise from factors other than the appreciation of referential import. People might concur that the level of the Dow Jones Index presages economic depression; such a recognition is thoughtful, rather than instinctual, and supposes a certain degree of educated sophistication, but we would not normally claim that the state of the Dow Jones Index *refers* to economic depression. People might learn (about emotions and other things) from music, surely, but it does not follow that they learn what they do because music asserts or symbolizes anything. I might learn what it is like to be poked in the eye with a burnt stick by being poked in the eye with a burnt stick, but this does not mean that the stick or the event refers to or denotes anything.[8]

In Coker's theory, sign and signified tend to collapse into each other (see Beardsley 1981; Clark 1982); a successful semiotic theory should be able to maintain their distinctness. Nowhere is this fault more obvious than in Coker's account of congeneric reference in music. A theme does not refer to itself simply because we recognize it when it recurs. That one musical gesture might lead us to think of another does not show that the first *says* anything about the second, or about gestures of that type, or about what might be done with such a gesture, and so on, though it might make us think on such matters.

(4) Indexical/Characterizing Parts

The fourth condition for a language is that there be indexical/characterizing parts in combinations of the elements; a subject is identified and something is predicated of it (Hermerén 1988, 183). Here, as we move nearer to the heart of language, the analogy between language and music collapses, says Hermerén (citing Beardsley 1958 and Scruton 1976). It is clear from Hermerén's treatment that this condition is intended to cover these facts: (i) the meaning of molecular sentences is a function of the meanings of the elements they comprise and of the manner in which those elements are combined; (ii) assertion is central to language; and (iii) assertions can be assessed

---

[8] Putman (1985) says that both music and touch are referential because we can learn from them. It is this vacuously wide notion of reference that I am rejecting, without also denying that music, or touch, can convey information.

< 11 >

for truth or falsity. The point might be developed this way: assertion is a foundational function of language, a function that must be performed by anything worth the name. The meaning of assertions, as with other grammatically complete linguistic units, depends on the meanings of the elements they comprise and the way the elements are ordered. Assertions take truth values. If musical works, themes, or phrases are not appropriately to be assessed for truth, then music performs no assertoric function: either it does not pick out a subject, or it fails to characterize the subjects it picks out in a way analogous to predication.

Before discussing music I consider depictions, because there is a firm tradition of regarding paintings as dealing with truths (see Korsmeyer 1989). Now, the word "true" has more than one sense: a true friend is a genuine or authentic friend; a lover who is true is faithful; a tabletop that is true is perfectly flat. One notion of truth, that of verisimilitude, obviously applies to paintings; a depiction might be "true to life." In this way a painting can be true without being true in the manner in which assertions are.[9] My concern, though, lies with the view that depictions take a truth value, just as assertions do. I wish to examine the view that *depicting X as Y* can be analyzed as *asserting that X is Y*. To reiterate a point made earlier, the question is not whether we might *learn* truths from paintings—of course we can—but whether they *state* those truths.

Many hold that paintings state truths.[10] John Bennett (1974) points out that pictures can be used within sentences. I might say, "The cat looked like <a picture of a, or the, cat>." This is true. That pictures can function sometimes as parts of sentences does not mean, however, that they are (in conjunction with their titles) sentences. Beardsley (1978) argues that this use of pictures requires the use of other predicate parts, such as "looks like," or a context in which their use might be presupposed. Even if a picture might contribute to an act of assertion, it does not follow that a picture can stand alone as an assertion, as a sentence can do. There are many ways in which the predicate parts of an assertion can relate to its subject: X is Y; X is not Y; X is partially Y; X always is Y; X never is Y; X is identical to Y; and so on. Even if pictures depict "Y-type" properties, the conventions of painting do not allow for the many copulations of Ys with Xs found in assertions.

[9] See Roskill and Carrier 1983 for a subtle account denying that paintings and photographs are propositional while arguing that they can be true or false in other senses—mainly by providing information from which truths or falsehoods might be inferred. Also see Schier 1986.

[10] For instance, see Bennett 1974, Kjörup 1974 and 1978, Scruton 1976 and 1981a, and Solt 1989. For an attempt to offer a semantics for pictures in terms of a three-valued, nonclassical logic, see Malinas 1991.

< 12 >

Depictions lend themselves to assertoric uses only where an essentially linguistic context is presupposed. They might play the role of a part of a sentence, but they could not stand as sentences in their own right.

Sören Kjörup (1974) anticipates this objection. He implies that no "utterance" stands alone: the context of the illocutionary act must always be understood, and usually we have no problem in doing this. We can imagine situations in which the illocutionary context is no less clear for pictures. These comments invite two counters: (i) Even if some pictures (advertisements, say) are presented in a context in which the illocutionary act performed with them is obvious, it is not so with art paintings. Though we might establish painterly conventions both for types of predication and to mark assertion, in fact there are no such conventions in use for art paintings. We do not view such paintings as purveyors of assertoric (or other illocutionary) speech acts. Kjörup attempts to parry this thrust (see also Scruton 1976). He concedes that an aesthetic interest in a painting is not primarily an interest in its truth, but he denies that this shows that paintings are not standardly used in the performance of speech acts, primarily assertoric ones. (ii) Where there is confusion about the illocutionary act being performed, we can always ask, for example, "Was that a promise?" Where there is doubt about a painting, the clarification always would have to be given in language; the pictorial medium provides no method for clarifying such confusions as does the linguistic medium. Kjörup admits this but suggests that it shows that paintings cannot be used to perform the illocutionary act of explaining which illocutionary act is being used, not that they are not used to perform illocutionary acts at all. I find this reply to be unsatisfactory. It opens the door to an infinite regress of questions about illocutionary acts. That door is closed in language, presumably, because there are illocutionary acts the function of which cannot be in doubt for someone who understands the language. Important here is the fact that the illocutionary act being performed can always be specified as part of its performance: "I swear that . . . ," "I warn that . . . ," "I promise that. . . . ." There are not in the same way fundamentally unambiguous possibilities for paintings. Paintings can play a part in illocutionary acts only because those acts can be integrated into a wider, essentially linguistic context. Paintings do not stand alone as painterly sentences (that is, within the painterly context) as sentences can stand alone within the linguistic context.

The replies to these worries suggest that depictions are limited in ways language is not, but they argue that this is not sufficient to show that depictions cannot function as assertions. In considering Hermerén's fifth and seventh conditions for something's being a language (that there be logical

< 13 >

connectives and force-showing devices), I suggest that no language allowing for an assertoric function could be restricted in these ways. For now I add just one other objection (which is developed in Chapter 2): A sentence with a conjunctive subject or predicate, or one that connects complete sentences with "and," can be determined to be true only if it comes to a close, only if it is completed. Open-ended, additive lists also cannot be shown to take the value "true." It is arguable that no depiction provides for the completion of the characterization of its subject; there is no end to the description that might be developed, because the elements of paintings are not packaged as discrete, separable units.[11] For this reason alone, it is difficult to see how depictions could be assimilated to assertions.

This discussion of depiction is beside the point if music is not representational as pictures sometimes are. The topic of musical depiction is discussed in Chapter 2. Many authors believe that music sometimes is depictive, and this is sufficient justification for my now pursuing the comparison between paintings and language. It is not only by claiming that music is depictive, however, that it has been argued that music is assertoric in character. How is it possible to argue that musical works (or themes, phrases, and the like) can be assessed for truth without linking that claim to the view that music is representational? I review several suggestions here.

Coker, in developing his account of music as language, recognizes the need to argue that music makes assertions that can be assessed for truth (though he allows that an aesthetic interest in musical statements is more concerned with how the truth or falsity is expressed than with what is asserted). He dismisses as "poppycock" the view that artistic assertions are neither true nor false and, adopting a correspondence theory of truth (an assertion is true if it correctly represents some state of the world), claims that musical works can make true assertions. He rejects the view that works, or parts of works, are true merely in the sense of being "true to life." Musical gestures are true because the composer created and presented them, and because others have accepted or assented to them in good faith. These are matters of fact, and hence of truth. The truths stated by music tend to be metaphoric ones (1972, 137–141, 196–199).[12]

Coker is confused on this point. As I have already indicated, that music expresses emotions, say, "as a matter of fact" does not mean that it asserts

---

[11] For a discussion, see Savile 1971; for a reply to Savile, see Carrier 1974.

[12] Also see Victor Bennett: "Against those who deny that music expresses truth . . . it is worth noting that these people thereby deprive music of its status as an art" (1936, 109), and Frank Howes: "The sort of truth that music knows is states of mind. We are discussing truth, you see, not beauty" (1958, 17).

< 14 >

such facts in a way that can be assessed for truth. As Douglas Morgan (1967) emphasizes, that music can be a source of knowledge about the world does not show that it asserts such truths; that it can convey truths does not entail that it can be assessed for truth value. Coker maintains that the iconicity of musical gestures with human ones is crucial to determining their truth value (1972, 139), but it is far from clear how iconicity goes beyond the notion of "truth to life" to that of asserted truth. He holds that music can make statements as some "object words" (that is, names) do (1972, 165).[13] But object words, names, do not make statements at all until combined with other words into sentences. It is only by taking musical gestures as equivalent to object words, and then by taking object words to be primitive statements, that Coker arrives at the conclusion that musical gestures state truths (as opposed merely to being "true to life"). These equivalences are obviously questionable.[14]

Are there no occasions on which object words perform the function of assertoric sentences? Must all assertions be reducible to subject and predicate parts? Though the answer to these questions is no, that answer provides little comfort to a Cokerian, for the questions are to be answered in the negative only where the full panoply of language comes into play, I think.[15] A sentence need not describe the subject it introduces. Some sentences do not function as subject-predicate sentences but rather as subject-introducing sentences. They are called by Strawson (1964, 202–217) "feature-placing sentences." The assertions in this subclass introduce neither particulars nor sortal universals (such as fall of snow); they introduce "feature-universals" or "feature-concepts" as does, for example, the sentence "It is snowing." Feature-placing sentences are not subject-predicate sentences; they introduce a universal or "stuff" and place it in space and time. It might be said that in feature-placing sentences the assertion is effected through the location of the subject.

Following Coker, it might be suggested that musical "sentences" perform the same function as this subclass of assertions found in natural languages. According to this view, the music's being sad can be analyzed as the assertion that "There is sound and sadness here." But such an approach fails on two counts: (i) It might be suspected that it is "particular-placing," rather than "feature-placing," that is required. By feature-placing the subject is trans-

[13] Perhaps that is why he holds that "basic gestures" are "true by self-ostensive definition" (Coker 1972, 196).

[14] For a similar equivocation, see Howard 1972, where there is a continual shift between naming and describing.

[15] In the following I rely on an argument I have presented in Davies 1983b, 225–226.

< 15 >

formed into a universal (or, sometimes, a "stuff"), so that "Sadness is here" is not equivalent to "The (bit of) sadness in which you are interested is here." That is, resort to the possibility that musical "sentences" are of the feature-placing sort loses the fact that our interest in the expressiveness heard in music is an interest in the particular expressiveness of a particular piece of music. (ii) A language's containing the possibility of feature-placing sentences presupposes that the language is one in which assertions introducing particulars and sortal universals are expressible (see Strawson, 1964, 214–225). There could be no language, such as Coker seems to envisage, in which all assertions were of the feature-placing type. Accordingly, the attempt to analyze music's expressiveness as the assertion of "There is sound and sadness here" fails. We are forced to conclude that what is involved in musical expression is not feature-placing but rather something like brute "naming." Then my former objection holds. Brute naming is a preparation for linguistic predication. Where predication is not possible, ostensive gestures have no point (so to speak!) and, in particular, establish neither truth nor falsity.

An interesting set of arguments favoring the view that music can be assessed for truth and falsity is that offered by Jerrold Levinson (1981). Levinson addresses a question posed by Douglas Morgan: "What, after all, could we literally mean by characterizing a sonata as true?" Levinson is trying to show how one might plausibly argue that a musical work is true. His doing so is consistent with his believing that musical works do not express truths (in which case, the plausibility of the argument would serve to explain how intelligent people might make such a mistake). He admits (1990a, 304–305) that his argument is speculative and hypothetical, and he denies that music is a language.

Levinson offers five suggestions for musical truth, which I formulate as follows: (i) The music expresses an emotion and does so because the musical structure corresponds to the morphology of the corresponding actual emotion. (ii) The music expresses X *as* Y; that is, expresses a Yish X; that is, expresses Y as qualifying X—and X is Y (sometimes).[16] (iii) The expressiveness achieved is the expressiveness aimed at. (iv) The music expresses X and Y as going together, and they do go together in that a person might experience the two emotions in close proximity (sometimes). (v) The music expresses Y as succeeding X, and the one might follow the other (sometimes). Levinson goes on to emphasize that artistic/aesthetic value does not derive from, and is not necessarily affected by, truth or falsity of the kind indicated.

---

[16] Note also the importance attached by Gombrich (1962) to the possibility in art of one property's qualifying another.

< 16 >

Levinson's first recommendation is that, if some aspect of the music corresponds to some aspect of the world that lies beyond the musical work, then the music is true (this is equivalent to Coker's claim about iconicity). The notion of truth invoked appears to be that of "truth to life," of matching.[17] Levinson's (iii) introduces a related notion of truth, equating it with success. Where the intention is carried through successfully, the musical result is "true to the intention." These notions of truth, as I have suggested earlier, are different from that of linguistic truth. Levinson acknowledges as much in allowing that musical works have "correspondence" truth rather than "propositional" truth, and that music brings properties to mind rather than asserting them.[18] Hermerén observes (1988, 200–202) that there is always the worry that such a use of the term "true" is more misleading than helpful, since it can be replaced so readily by "appropriate," "sincere," "successful," and the like; this is because music is lifelike in possessing certain properties found elsewhere in the world, not because it describes the world or asserts that the world has the relevant properties. Levinson (1990a) acknowledges the point but regards the criticisms as misdirected, for he did not claim more for music than truth to life.

There is one reason for thinking that Hermerén's criticisms have more bite than Levinson allows. Levinson holds that correspondence truth is referential; the notion of reference seems bound to take one beyond truth to life and nearer to the notion of linguistic truth. I take it that Levinson means not that reference is internal to correspondence truth but that, where the correspondence between the music and the world is engineered deliberately by the composer, reference is achieved. If this is his view, here he separates truth from reference, so that music might possess correspondence truth whether or not the correspondence is aimed at by the composer; that is, whether or not there is a successful attempt at reference.

The grammatical subject of a proposition may be compound (as in the construction "X and Y are . . .") and the predicate may be complex, with adverbial and other phrases modifying what is said. In languages, subsentential modifiers or structures distinguish among the many different possibilities for meaning. Levinson's (ii), (iv), and (v) claim not only that music expresses truths but also that the truths expressed are of the kind generated in language by subsentential operators. X and Y are expressed as going together (iv), or

---

[17] Ferguson (1960) also seems to appeal to this idea in claiming both that music can be true and that it can be used "for the utterance of false feeling."

[18] Casey (1970) argues that art presents neither propositional nor correspondence truth but rather truth as a sui generis (nontranslatable), symbolic insight into man; also see Reid 1964.

< 17 >

as succeeding each other (v), or with the one modifying the other (ii). A work that expresses two emotions is true if those emotions stand in the appropriate relation (going together, one succeeding the other, one qualifying the other) in reality and false otherwise. Levinson's example of (ii) is this: Nicolai Rimsky-Korsakov's *Scheherazade* expresses mysterious love, as opposed to mystery and love (or lovely mystery, or the succession of puzzlement by love). Thereby it is true, since love often is infected by mystery. A work that expresses eternal joy would, however, be false.

Now, even if we are dealing here with correspondence rather than propositional truth (with truth to life rather than with asserted truth), I doubt that music can be so specific as Levinson claims. Language can be used to express subtle, complex relations because it includes modifiers and constructions that operate in a regular fashion from sentence to sentence. It is through our knowledge of such operations that new sentences can be uttered and understood. So far as I can hear, however, musical works do not include modifiers and constructions which, in recurring from work to work, operate consistently to disambiguate the types of meaning Levinson distinguishes. For example, it is standard in first-movement sonata form that the second subject theme or group follows the first, and that these two are of contrasting emotional character. Sometimes the emotions expressed might go together in the world, or in another case they might succeed each other, or in yet further cases the one might qualify the other. How, though, could one distinguish among the countless works that employ this form those that truly show the relevant relations from those that do not? How, for example, does one separate a truth concerning togetherness from a falsehood about succession, or a truth about both togetherness and succession from a truth about either alone? The answer most likely to be offered is this: just as much of what is meant in linguistic utterance is apparent from the context rather than from the structure of the utterance as such, so too the rich complexity of each musical work establishes a setting so expressively specific that the use of standardized subsentential modifiers and structures is unnecessary. Yet I find this reply unconvincing, as should be apparent from my discussion of Kjörup's views. Much that is understood in conversation need not be stated directly; that it can be understood in context on a particular occasion might presuppose, however, the possibility of its being made explicit where doubt might arise about what was meant or about the context that holds. Where there is no way within the medium to distinguish one meaning from another, then the medium does not deal with those shades of meaning, or with meanings of that sort.

The worry I have tried to express here is not confined to the detail of

< 18 >

Levinson's (ii), (iv), and (v); in its more general version it returns under many guises. When I formulated my versions of Levinson's claims I appended the word "sometimes." I did so because it simply is not clear whether the relation between music and the world is truth-making only if it holds always, or often, or merely once. Levinson's suggestion that the relation must be psychologically possible, if not regular, provides little grip on hard cases—and in this area most of the cases are hard. If the music expresses X and Y as going together, it is not apparent how we could distinguish between its expressing these various relations: all Xs go with all Ys; all Xs go with some Ys; some Xs go with all Ys; some Xs go with some Ys; this X goes with this Y; and so forth. There are no quantifiers, or indicators of quantificational scope, within music, so distinctions of number are lost. Also absent from music are modal indicators, so there is no way of distinguishing between the music's expressing the thought that this X must be this Y, this X might be this Y, this X could be this Y if . . . , this X would be this Y if . . . , and so on.

(5) Force-showing Devices and Modalities

The fifth necessary condition for a language identified by Hermerén is this: "There are force-showing devices analogous to operators in ordinary language indicating the force of what is said ('I promise that', 'I warn that', 'I hope that', 'I predict that', 'I assert that', 'I imagine that' and so forth), which can be used to clarify how what is said or written is to be taken" (1988, 183; also see Margolis 1974). In addition, a language must contain modal indicators, so that it is possible to distinguish between "It must be the case," "It is possibly the case," "It would be the case," "It should be the case," and so forth. The devices Hermerén has in mind are ones internal to the mode of utterance, rather than those that might be given by elements in the context such as winks or shrugs of the shoulders (1988, 186).

Hermerén concentrates on representational paintings in discussing condition (5). The claim is that pictorial depiction fails this condition because ordinarily there are no conventions of painting that show force or modality in the representation of X as Y. In a pictorial representation of Napoleon, there is no established way of distinguishing between showing how Napoleon looked, how he would have looked if . . . , how it was hoped that he looked when . . . , how he might have looked if . . . , and so on. The painting might illustrate something that could be asserted, but it asserts nothing if we cannot tell the difference between its being used to assert, question, command, suppose, warn, or speculate. Since there is no method by which one can determine what speech act is performed in a musical work, there is no

< 19 >

ground for taking assertion as the "default" speech act. Even if assertion is primary in language, it is not obvious that there could be a language that does not make allowance for the possibility of the full range of speech acts (Davies 1983b). If that is true, then one can expect any language, or anything that can function as a language, to have force-, tense-, and modality-showing devices. Art paintings, when approached in the standard fashion, display no such devices. Where there is no reason to see paintings as performing any one speech act over others, there is no reason to think they perform speech acts at all.

Kjörup (1974) admits that there are some illocutionary acts that paintings cannot be used to perform, though he sees no reason why conventions might not be instituted to permit the possibility of paintings' being used in the performance of any illocutionary act (signing the painting on the lower-left might indicate a questioning attitude; signing it in the middle might indicate speculation). He does think, however, that it standardly is the case that a picture is used to perform some illocutionary act (asserting, warning, satirizing, criticizing). He specifies in a semiformal manner the conditions for paintings' performing different illocutionary acts (1978). His analysis comes to this: an illocutionary act is performed in a painting if and only if the artist intends to perform an illocutionary act through the production of the picture and believes that the audience will be able to recognize this intention as a result of knowing that certain conditions are met—for example, that the picture is seen clearly, that a subject is referred to, that the subject is represented as having a certain character. Kjörup allows that the subject might be picked out in a nonpictorial way.

Hermerén (1988) admits that advertisements, maps, and textbook illustrations are presented in a context in which they might be regarded as used in the performance of illocutionary acts, such as description, but he denies that this is the case in art paintings. The "meaning" of art paintings is far from clear given the situation in which they are normally presented. Moreover, he objects that Kjörup's examples rely too much on the quasi-linguistic functioning of nonpictorial indicators.[19] One way of developing Hermerén's points might take this form. Kjörup (1978) suggests that a picture might warn us against a particular object: poisonous toadstools might be illus-

---

[19] This objection recalls an earlier point: paintings might be incorporated into sentences, but the issue is whether they might stand alone as complete "sentences." The claims made on behalf of art paintings suggest the second, stronger view, whereas the evidence adduced supports only the former, weaker view according to which, rather than constituting a quasi-linguistic symbol system in its own right, painting provides elements that might be appropriated for use in linguistic contexts in which purely linguistic features do some of the crucial work.

< 20 >

trated in a text on fungi. But now, a picture of a toadstool could be used to illustrate many different kinds of warnings: don't eat this; don't inhale the fumes of this if it is ignited; don't think that this is an accurate illustration of a toadstool; don't think that every poisonous toadstool looks like this; don't fail to fry this toadstool in garlic to rid it of its poisonous qualities. There is no way of telling which warning is intended from the picture, or even from the context, without some specific indication in the text. If one cannot tell from the picture which of many possible warnings is being illustrated, neither can one say that the picture is, or contains, or states, or expresses a warning. And if one cannot say which of the many possible speech acts is being formed, one cannot say that any speech act is being performed. At best, the illustration can function as an element in, be a part of, a linguistic warning, but there is no reason for believing that it can perform that speech act function on its own, solely as a picture.[20]

Coker recognizes that music would be a language only if it could imply various moods of discourse: interrogative, exclamative, imperative, indicative, formative, performative, valuative (1972, 184). He asserts that it may do so but offers no argument (that I can find) in favor of this view beyond the claim that music might be emphatic or querulous in its "statements." That music may be emphatic does not demonstrate that what is emphasized is also asserted; that music might be querulous in character does not show it to be interrogative. Coker writes as if he can prove that music is primarily assertoric by arguing that it might be a bearer of meaning. Against this one can make the Fregean point that sense and assertion must be different. Though the antecedent of a conditional has a sense, that sense is not asserted; what is asserted is the whole conditional. So, that a thing can have a sense does not mean that the sense is asserted; it does not even mean that the sense could be asserted. I find that Coker fails to establish his claim that illocutionary acts are performed by or with music (and I note also that he does not show that music contains modal indicators).

(6) Metalanguage

It is a necessary condition for something's being a language that it permit metalinguistic assertions: it must be possible to use elements of the pur-

---

[20] A similar point applies to Levinson's (1981) account of how musical utterances might be true; that is, there is no reason to suppose that asserting, as opposed to other speech acts, is involved, and there is no way of distinguishing between the music's presenting necessary connections, possible connections, impossible connections, and the like.

< 21 >

ported language to refer to, or assert things about, other of its elements (Hermerén 1988, 183). Hermerén suggests that, if representational paintings and musical works cannot be used to assert, then they cannot be used to assert about themselves. Though one work may allude to, or quote from, or paraphrase another, this does not involve its asserting anything (which could be assessed for truth) about the other work.[21]

Coker accepts that a language presupposes a metalanguage and holds that the metalanguage of music is the language of technical analysis (1972, 128), that is the technical description in natural languages of musical effects. This is clearly different from what Hermerén has in mind and from what normally is understood by the idea of a metalanguage, which is that the very same language might be used in discussing the limits of what might be said in it, might be used in the analysis of meaning, reference, truth, and so on. In addition, Coker does allow for the notion of self-reference in music, which he calls congeneric musical meaning; it arises where, for example, the statement of a musical theme "refers" to its recurrences.[22] Just as an English sentence might call to mind another, or one use of an English sentence might call to mind the use of the same sentence in a different context, so too one musical gesture might lead us to think of another or to recall its earlier use. This analogy is far too weak, however, to sustain the claim that music possesses a metalanguage. That claim would involve showing not only that musical gestures may be assertoric in character and function but also that they take as their subject the topic of what it is to assert something in music.

(7) Logical Connectives

Hermerén's final condition for something's being a language is that it be possible to perform logical truth-functional operations—negation, conjunction, disjunction, implication, and quantification—on certain basic elements (such as sentences) of the putative language (1988, 183). Again, Hermerén concentrates on pictures in discussing this condition, presumably because he believes that music cannot negate, combine, distinguish, or quantify over what it cannot assert. He says that there are no pictorial devices for repre-

---

[21] As it happens, the notion of musical quotation cannot easily be construed on the model of linguistic quotation; see Goodman 1974 and Howard 1974.

[22] Also see Kuhns 1978 and Price 1988. Harold Fiske (1990) begins with a chapter titled "Is Music a (Meta) Language?" He argues there that music (like mathematics) is a metalanguage, "processing of which is controlled by a self-contained, information encapsulated, domain specific, modular cognitive system" (1990, 23). By this he means that music is "semantically closed," in that it must be understood in terms of its own logic, and that it is self-referential.

< 22 >

senting a negative.[23] A red slash is used as a matter of international convention to denote negation on public signs, as Hermerén is aware; his point is that, even if pictorial codes can be adopted for certain purposes, we do not appreciate the depicted content of ordinary pictures according to any such code.

True to form, Coker argues that music contains the semantic equivalents of logical connectives and devotes a chapter or more to their discussion (1972, 115–133). Disjunction involves "a shift to uncertainty" and is captured musically by the alternation of gestures—either vacillation in qualities (such as tonal relationships) or hesitancy in connecting passages. Conjunction involves succession, overlapping, or simultaneity in musically complementary gestures. Negation is implied in music by denial or disavowal (as in the interruption of a musical gesture, or by a sharp contrast in the character of themes). Implication in music involves the setting up of (melodic, rhythmic, or whatever) expectations; when a musical conditional is true, the expectations established by the antecedent are realized with the appearance of the consequent. The truth values of complex musical gestures are a function of their combinations (that is, of the connectives employed).

There are two important difficulties here. The first lies in the account of the connectives themselves. Where two contrasting themes are juxtaposed, what is the difference between negation and conjunction—between denying that the two themes go together and asserting that, despite their differences, they form a pair? Hesitation just is not the same thing as disjunction; one can be positive that there are only two alternatives, for example. Interruption is different from gainsaying. Entailment is not the same as expectation. The second point is that there seems to be no way in music to indicate the scope of logical operators. How would one distinguish between $\sim(p \vee q)$, $\sim p \vee q$, $p \vee \sim q$, $\sim(p \& q)$, $\sim p \& q$, and $p \& \sim q$? In treating the truth value of molecular musical gestures as arising from their combination, Coker slides over the issue of scope because he is never clear on the distinction between (i) basic musical gestures as names concatenated with predicates to form a statement with a truth value and (ii) basic musical gestures as assertions that might be connected into larger wholes the overall truth value of which is determined (truth-table-like) by the logical functions of the connectives employed, as mentioned under (4). In talking of the truth value of complex musical utterances and of the way connectives affect this, Coker does not make plain whether the connected elements are to be taken as statements or as words/names. He fudges the distinction between, on the one hand, the

---

[23] Danto (1982) is another who denies that art pictures standardly admit of negation.

< 23 >

relation of a grammatical subject to its predicate and, on the other, the relation between autonomous sentences and the various compound sentences that might be formed by their combination. Although Coker talks of logical connectives, more often he seems to have in mind rules of syntax connecting wordlike units into intelligible sentence wholes (for example, see his discussion of Stravinsky's *Orpheus* in 1972, 198–199).

Coker's failure to distinguish the creation of sentences out of subsentential elements from the creation of complex sentences through the combination of other sentences is no accident; his theory lacks the conceptual resources that would allow for that crucial distinction. Where the relevant difference cannot be traced, it is doubtful that music possesses a syntax that functions, like that of language, to generate semantic content.

Included under Hermerén's seventh condition is the topic of quantification: a language must provide for distinctions between "All Xs are Y," "Some Xs are Y," "A particular X is Y," "No Xs are Y," "Some Xs are not Y," and "A particular X is not Y." It should be apparent by now that music and representational artworks employ no clearly identifiable quantificational operators. I note that Coker does not attempt to argue for the actuality of quantification in music.

My goal in discussing Hermerén's conditions has not been to show merely that music cannot substitute for English as a natural language; that goes without saying. Rather, the aim has been to undermine the temptation to claim that the differences between music and natural languages might be accommodated by saying that music is an impoverished language (a language, say, merely of present-tense assertions) with a limited scope (a language of the emotions rather than of scientific fact). I have argued that music fails to meet most of the conditions crucial to something's being, and functioning as, a language. This is not to suggest that what music says is ineffable; instead, it is to deny that music says anything at all. Music might possess meaning in the sense that it presents a content that invites understanding. It might also be the case that, in one way or another, music draws attention to, and reflects on, extramusical phenomena, such as the world of human emotion. But its meaning is not stated.

Where music fails so many necessary conditions for something's being a language, there is no explanatory value to be gained from talk of music as an impoverished language, or as a syntactic system, or as possessing a vocabulary of terms and phrases. Indeed, if one were to persist in talking of vocabulary and syntax while attempting to analyze the nature of significance in music, one might easily mislead not only one's readers but also oneself. Such notions take their power from the intimate connection in language be-

< 24 >

tween semantic content and linguistic structure. The differences between music and natural languages suggest that extreme caution should be used in applying such concepts to music, for they carry misleading associations when transferred from the familiar to the new context.

The Theories of Cooke and Meyer

Whatever the inadequacies of his account, Coker appreciates what must be shown in making good the claim that music is a language of the emotions. Others are less careful in this regard. Two influential writers who may be guilty of the kind of equivocation deplored above are Deryck Cooke in *The Language of Music* (1959) and Leonard B. Meyer in *Emotion and Meaning in Music* (1956; also see 1957). The former talks of music as like language in having a quasi–vocabulary; the latter analyzes music as possessing a syntax. Their use of these notions suggests that music is, if not a full-blown language, a special, limited language. Their accounts of musical meaning trade on the way, in language, vocabulary and syntax take their importance in generating semantic content, but, to the extent that music is not a semantic system like a language, their analyses fail to account for musical meaning as they purport to do.

Cooke claims that music is a language of emotional expression. At no stage does he suggest that music is assertoric in character. Spoken/literary language and music are similar in elaborating the inarticulate cries of primitive humankind and in having a "logical" syntax used to make coherent statements. Music cannot express "concepts"; its expressiveness is restricted to the world of feelings. Cooke denies that a dictionary of musical meaning can be formulated, mainly because he accepts Felix Mendelssohn's claim that musical expressiveness is too specific to be put into words or captured in a simple formula, but he does catalogue the primitive elements of musical expression which the composer (unconsciously in his view) shapes and elaborates in the themes and forms of the musical work. Cooke does, then, describe a primitive musical vocabulary of the emotions, even if he denies that the meanings of musical terms are rigidly fixed. The expressive power of these elements is partly inherent, coming from the tensions between intervals as given in our experience of the natural harmonic series, and partly associative, in that their constant and consistent use in setting apposite texts reinforces their expressive power. The basic expressiveness of pitched intervals is shaped and articulated mainly by volume and time (tempo, phrasing, and movement), but texture and tone color also have their part to play in the process.

< 25 >

Cooke's achievement lies in his having identified figurations that reappear in similar expressive contexts across a wide historical spread of musical works.[24] The view that music's expressive character is natural at heart, but expanded and conventionalized through association, is suggestive, but it falls far short of a useful analysis of the nature of musical expression.[25] If Cooke seems to offer more than I have here allowed, he does so by exploiting the idea that music is a (special) sort of language illegitimately.

Cooke's critics draw implications from his account which they find unacceptable. Most authors take Cooke to be arguing that musical meanings might be compounded from units with more or less constant expressive import (like words) and, rightly, they deny that this is so (see Osborne 1983). The following are typical: Cooke forces a language theory onto an otherwise revealing analysis of quite unlinguistic mechanisms of musical expression (Howard 1978); musical meanings cannot be captured in dictionary form not because they are too specific to be put into words but because expression in music is more malleable and context-dependent than Cooke allows (Tanner 1985); Cooke generally underestimates the contribution to musical expressiveness made by instrumentation and large-scale form (Jones 1970 and Newcomb 1984); the meanings of emotion words cannot be taught to children exclusively from musical examples (Jones 1970); and music is more than a means for the communication of emotions (Jones 1970 and Sharpe 1970). Now, I suspect that Cooke would be puzzled by the suggestion that his view has the entailments these critics identify, but, whatever he may have intended, the search for counterintuitive implications of this kind is fueled by Cooke's proposing and developing the analogy between music and language.

Cooke implies that music has a vocabulary and, in that way, is like a lan-

---

[24] But critics were quick to point out that his theory does not apply readily to nontonal music; see Walker 1960 and, for a commentary on this view, Keller 1961. Jacobs (1960) notes Cooke's failure to consider the role of harmony. Ferguson (1960) objects to Cooke's treating enharmonically equivalent intervals—for example, a diminished sixth and an augmented fifth—as expressively equivalent.

[25] Both Leahy (1976) and Scruton (1983) point out that the regular association of a musical figure with words expressive of a given emotion does not explain the expressive result as residing in the music. Hoaglund (1980) defends Cooke against the point, claiming that the expressive elements Cooke identifies involve conventions of expression, not merely mechanical associations. It might be noted, however, that Cooke does not make sufficiently clear where he stands on the issue. Though Cooke denies offering a dictionary of musical meanings, his tendency to identify expressive elements with great precision and without sufficient regard to context invites the charge, which is made in Ferguson 1960, Scruton 1983, Tanner 1985, and Evans 1990. There are other respects in which his account is unclear: for example, as Beardsley (1981) notes, it is never obvious if he thinks expressiveness is a property of the music or an emotional state to which the music refers.

< 26 >

guage. Meyer (1956) adopts an information-theoretic approach in arguing that music has a syntax. He describes this syntax in terms suggesting that it generates an informational (semantic) content.[26] Meyer bases his theory on Prägnanz's law: that we strive to establish and maintain completeness and stability in perceptual forms and shapes, desiring completion and closure in their treatment. So long as a musical work fulfills the listener's expectations immediately, it conveys no information. Where it (temporarily) defeats the listener's expectation, a response is produced, a response seeking a return to predictability. This reaction may be "affective" (a feeling) or it may be intellectual (a thought), but on Meyer's view it cannot be both. The eventual fulfillment of the original expectation gives sense and resolution to the departure from the expected course. So, music has informational content both because it is structured according to stylistic rules by reference to which one predicts the future course of the work and because composers sometimes defeat or delay these expectations, generating informational content in doing so. If this content is to be conveyed, there must be sufficient redundancy of information (repetition) that interference caused by "noise" does not obscure the course or flow of musical information to the listener. Also, the listener must be familiar with the stylistic rules that govern the work (otherwise the message is obscured by "cultural noise").

Many of Meyer's claims can be challenged: for example, that it is both necessary and sufficient for "affect" that a tendency be blocked or thwarted, or that "undifferentiated affect" is emotion, or that the process of the generation of affect as he describes it amounts to expression.[27] Here, though, my concern lies with the way Meyer's terminology and analysis invoke a misleading analogy with language.[28] Meyer's "information" is not at all like information as the notion is commonly understood; it is not like the idea of a semantic content. Semantic information can be paraphrased, whereas the information conveyed by music through its syntactic structure cannot be paraphrased readily; it is not apparent that the syntax of music says anything (Vermazen 1971). Further, Meyer's account suggests that, the better one knows a musical work, the less information it conveys and the less meaning-

---

[26] The information-theoretic approach is also propounded in Youngblood 1958, Coons and Kraehenbuehl 1958 and 1959, and Moles 1966. A similar view is presented, specifically concerning dodecaphonic compositional style, in Carpenter 1966 and Adorno 1973. For the application of the approach to nursery tunes, see Pinkerton 1956.

[27] One or more of these points is made in Laszlo 1968, Scruton 1983, Budd 1985a, Kivy 1987, and Hansen 1989.

[28] Note that Meyer (1959) compares musical utterances directly to English sentences in which content depends on semantic, not solely grammatical, factors.

< 27 >

ful it becomes, and this is not what we would normally say about information or meaning.[29] Meyer's is (at best) an account of why we find *some* musical passages more interesting (or boring) than others and is not, as he implies, an account of musical meaning as such. For example, in exclusively emphasizing the importance of the musically unexpected, he ignores the significance of repetition, of performance skills, and of the work as a whole.[30] Although Meyer (1959) holds that at least part of the value of great music resides in its high informational content, it cannot be seen clearly that his kind of information has value as does semantic content—as a source of knowledge and of the power that goes with knowledge.[31] Keil (1966) accepts the outline of Meyer's theory but sees it applying mainly to notated, Western music, and thereby as failing to explain value in much non-Western and improvised music, but for a contrary view, see Palmer 1992. Budd (1985a) makes a stronger claim: that Meyer's theory accounts neither for the value of music nor for its expressive powers and that, because of this, the theory falls.

The information-theoretic approach is syntax-driven and attempts to include a quasi-semantic dimension in music by describing the relation between syntax and semantics as that of a stimulus to a response elicited in conformity with basic, psychological laws.[32] But, as Margolis (1987) notes, the stimulus-response relation is too crude to explain the notion of semantic content and its communication, because it is automatically triggered and does not count the importance of the responder's understanding of the situation or the cultural background of knowledge he brings to it. Wollheim (1980) suggests that redundancy and expectation apply not to the meaning of a sentence but to the readability of its notation. The mechanisms given prominence by Meyer's approach no more explain the ways music strikes us as meaningful or expressive than they explain meaning and communication in natural languages. Forest Hansen (1989) attempts to retrieve Meyer's theory by modifying it to be less mechanistic and more contextual, but Budd (1985a) predicts that such alterations cannot save the theory, and I believe he is correct in this.

Meyer's talk both of information and meaning relies on the place of these

[29] See Sherburne 1966, Vermazen 1971, Howard 1971a, Dipert 1983, Budd 1985a, and Hansen 1989. For a reply to Vermazen and Sherburne, see Titchener and Broyles 1973; and for Meyer's discussion of the topic, see Meyer 1961.

[30] See Keil 1966, Taylor 1974, and Dipert 1983.

[31] The point is made in Vermazen 1971, Sparshott 1987, Hansen 1989, and Goldman 1992.

[32] Note that Moles acknowledges a debt to Pavlov and Watson and sees the theory's "mechanistic character" as counting for, rather than against, the information-theoretic analysis of meaning (1966, 194–195).

< 28 >

notions in an account of the semantic content of language, but the information-theoretic approach can explain the place of neither. As an analysis of the nature of some musical styles and their use by composers, Meyer's is an important contribution.[33] The terms in which his analysis of music is couched must imply a connection between syntax and meaning such as is found in natural languages, however, and there can be little doubt that Meyer takes himself to be offering some such story. Claims of that kind, I have argued, are importantly misleading because they invite the thought that music has referential meaning as linguistic utterances do.

Types of Meaning

So far I have compared music to natural languages, taking these as paradigm repositories of meaning. To take the inquiry further, a typology of meanings would be useful. In this section I outline five types of meaning. First, some preliminary, crude remarks are in order. Meaning involves a directional (usually nonreciprocal) relation between two things, signifier and signified.[34] As I employ the term, "reference" involves or implies the intentional use of the signifier to pick out an instance of the signified. Not all meaningful connections are referential. At the nonreferential level, to say that X means Y is to indicate that X provides a reason for one's taking Y to be the case. Where the signified is deliberately and sincerely used—that is, where reference is involved—its use provides grounds for the judgment that the signified is meant. Different types of meaning might be characterized in terms of the relations involved between these elements: intended/unintended; natural/arbitrary; meaning within a symbol system/stand-alone meaning.

Meaning A: Natural, Unintended Meaning

The connection that generates meaning might be natural.[35] Dark clouds mean rain; smoke signals the presence of fire; the fresh droppings of lions

---

[33] Observe, however, that, like Cooke's, Meyer's account is not readily applied to nontonal music; see Sherburne 1966 and Sharpe 1971.

[34] This is not to say that the signified must be a material object, or even that it must exist; neither is it to equate the meaning of a term with its referent, should it have one; neither is it to rule out the possibility that in some cases meaning runs in both directions.

[35] The term "natural" has many possible uses and meanings. I apply it mostly to properties or relations that are not stipulated arbitrarily from within a cultural setting. Distinctions between the natural and the non-natural are pursued on pp. 36–39.

< 29 >

signify the recent passing of lions. In these examples, there is a causal connection between the signifier and signified, allowing a secure inference from the one to the likelihood of the other. The connection does not depend on its use or recognition by anyone. Smoke does not *refer* to fire. Neither does the significance of smoke depend on a context provided by a symbol system.

Causal connections are not the only natural relations that secure meaning A. Constant conjunction might suffice. Snow at sea level might mean that it is winter; lightning might mean that thunder is to follow. Relations of constitution, of part to whole or whole to part, might also give rise to meaning A. I take this to be the case where tears signify unhappiness and spots signify measles. These might be thought to be cases of causal connection. But if the sadness is constituted in part by an inclination toward tears, so that a person has never felt sadness if he has never been inclined to cry, then the relation is constitutional rather than merely causal. Similarly, if it cannot be measles that one has if one does not display spots of the appropriate kind, the relation is not merely causal.

In cases of meaning A, the directionality of the relation might be suggested by temporal order, as is true with lightning and thunder. A more important factor in determining the directionality of the relation, usually, is the relative importance of the interests we take in the connection or in the elements connected. If we are interested in the presence of lions, and fresh lion droppings are seen to be connected to the presence of lions, then a sighting of fresh lion droppings is noteworthy. Because we are concerned with the lions, rather than with their droppings as such, we take the fresh droppings as signifying the presence of lions, but we are not similarly inclined to take the presence of lions, when we come across them, as signifying that the area contains fresh droppings.

The relation of resemblance might sometimes secure meaning A, but resemblance, as an absolute relation, lacks the selectivity and directionality on which meaning depends; resemblance is a symmetrical, reciprocal relation. Moreover, anything might resemble any other in some respect. Elephants resemble unicorns in that none of either is in my study at the moment. That two things resemble each other is not, therefore, a reason for treating either as signifying the other. Nevertheless, resemblance standardly is relativized to our interests. Where the interests to which resemblance is relativized are widely shared, so that the resemblance is commonly recognized, and where the one element is of special importance to us, resemblance might give rise to meaning A. The nature of our interests might sometimes lead us not only to recognize resemblances but to see a directionality in the relation. The world of human emotion and the forms of its expression might be of such

< 30 >

importance to us that we cannot help but see willow trees as recalling the bearing of sad people, due to the resemblance between the two. Because the forms of trees do not normally interest us in the same way, we do not think in terms of the reverse relation: we do not generally see the comportment of sad people as signifying the form of willow trees. To the extent that such resemblances seem to force themselves to our attention and are directed by interests we share, they can be a source of meaning A.

Meaning B: The Intentional Use of Natural Significance

Meaning B involves the intentional use of meaning A, or of a natural relation with potential for meaning A, to secure reference. A person with the spots of measles might be shown to a class of medical students as an instance of the measled condition: "Those spots mean measles." If you ask me how I feel, I might, instead of telling you, intentionally adopt the expression of someone who feels sad. Like an actor, I might pull a sad face, or I might point to the expression of someone who is feeling sad and showing it. These are cases in which meaning A is appropriated and intentionally used. In others, a natural relation that lacks directionality (such as resemblance, constitutionality, or identity) might have directionality imparted to it through its intentional use, so that meaning B is generated. I might, for the purposes of a classroom illustration of the disposition of heavenly bodies, stipulate that an orange is to be the sun. Oranges do not mean (A) suns, but they do resemble suns in respects salient to the use to which I put the orange in the classroom. This is to be contrasted with the case in which I specify that a metal paperclip is to be the sun or I use the word "sun" to refer to the sun. Here the connection is arbitrary, whereas, where meaning B is involved, some prior, natural connection is employed. Prior, natural connections of the kind envisaged, I have allowed, presuppose shared interests in terms of which, in this case, shape and color are viewed as features with a potential for significance.

Where a relation not having meaning A is invested with meaning B by its intentional use, the audience must be able to recognize the use being adopted. This might be made possible simply by the announcement of the use: "Let this orange stand for the sun." Alternatively, the use might be apparent from the context of action, so that the intention can be read off without its being announced. In the absence of these conditions, there must be some convention that reveals the relevant intention. Such conventions as are

< 31 >

used point to the intentional use of a natural element or relation on which meaning B depends in part.

Meaning C: Systematized, Intentional Use of Natural Elements

Natural relations might take on meaning in a way that depends on their intentional use within a conventional schema or system. Suppose (for the sake of the argument) that there is a natural ordering between two-note intervals, so that fifths and fourths are more tense than octaves, thirds and sixths more tense than fifths and fourths, seconds and sevenths more tense than thirds and sixths.[36] Suppose also that the two-note intervals available for use and their relative frequency are governed by the conventions of the stylistic schema within which the composer works. Now, are thirds tense or not? The answer to that question depends on how the use or range of intervals is structured by the style schema. If the style allows only for thirds, sixths, seconds, and sevenths, the thirds mark points of repose. On the other hand, if the style allows only for octaves, fifths, fourths, thirds, and sixths, the thirds are highly tense. Meaning C (like meaning B) takes its significance from a natural element or relation; that significance is affected, however, by the rules of a symbol system, so that it is apparent only to someone familiar with those rules. The rules structure a natural potential for significance rather than generating significance entirely on their own. This goes part of the way to explaining how meaning might depend on a natural potential for significance while being used in a culture-bound fashion; not all culturally relative meanings are entirely arbitrary. Even if some musical intervals are naturally more tense than others, a person cannot assign to them a significance deriving from their natural features until she knows something of the conventions by which these natural features are structured. In medieval music the major third is a discord, because it is the most tense of the intervals used. In Wagner's music the major third is, relatively speaking, a point of repose, because tritones, major and minor seconds, major and minor sevenths, and augmented and diminished sixths are common.

This kind of point has been emphasized by E. H. Gombrich (1962 and 1980, chap. 11). He is inclined to go so far as to deny that any elements are naturally expressive in a void. The expressive element natural to the items in question becomes apparent only where there is a fixed range of elements

---

[36] I ignore the obvious complications—for example, that thirds played two octaves below middle C are more tense than those played above middle C, or that tenths need not have the same tension as thirds.

< 32 >

forming a comparison class; an artist's choosing green, say, has a meaning that is a function of the colors that were available and not chosen. In art, we can appreciate the expressive significance of the painter's choice only if we know what was on his palette and are familiar with the medium employed and the traditions against which he worked. Expressiveness is context-dependent, and the conventions within which or against which the artist works provide the context without which natural expressiveness cannot exist.[37]

Richard Wollheim (1980, secs. 30–32) has objected to Gombrich's line that the relation between expression and context precludes independent knowledge of conventions, such as Gombrich's account presupposes, for our recognition of expressiveness: "Confronted with the *oeuvre* of a given artist, how are we to decide, on the Gombrich argument, whether this is the work of an artist who within a narrow repertoire expressed a wide range of inner states, or of one who within a much broader repertoire expressed a narrow range of states? Internal evidence is indifferent as to the two hypotheses: and it is unclear what external evidence the argument allows us to invoke" (1980, sec. 30, 62). Wollheim goes on to suggest that what is missing from this story is an account of the artist's style and its formation, for it is the artist's style that sets the limits of the repertoire. At best, Gombrich's view makes implicit appeal to a wide notion of style "in which it is something akin to a language," or like a method of projection in cartography.

If he means to make more than an ad hominem point, Wollheim's objection seems to be surmountable. If he is correct, then it seems that Gombrich's theory is incomplete rather than plain wrong. If an account of the individual's style can be given, as Wollheim (1979) thinks is possible, then Gombrich's view is strengthened. And, though Gombrich's argument appeals to aspects of the experience of color that are general, there is nothing to suggest that Gombrich believes the artistic conventions structuring these aspects allow for the mechanical production of expressive works; obviously the expressive potential of color is only one of many factors contributing to the emotional tone of the complete work. Even if he does not place so much emphasis on the individuality of the artist as would please Wollheim, Gombrich's implicit appeal is to a notion of style of the type recognized by Wollheim as relevant to the issue: it is the genre, category, or school of a work

[37] I take it that in the nonartistic case it is the known repertoire of human behaviors and situations that provides the context against which natural expressiveness emerges, whereas, for art, where something much more complex is involved if the communication of emotion is attempted, it is only against the setting of artistic traditions and conventions that the natural potential for expressiveness can be realized.

< 33 >

that establishes the repertoire from which the artist chooses in producing a particular work. To the extent that a genre can be described in a way allowing that new works might be recognized as belonging to it, so that its description offers criteria for membership and not merely a list of its instances, then the expressive character of the elements found in a particular work is revealed in the context of an appreciation of the work's genre (see Walton 1970). The range of elements constituting the comparison class is given within an account of the style or genre within which the artist works, and the character of that style or genre can be specified independently of our merely cataloguing what is found in the artist's works.

Meaning D: Intentional, Arbitrary Stipulation of Stand-alone Meaning

With meaning D, a meaning is stipulated or given solely by conventions. The connection between signifier and signified is arbitrary rather than naturally based. For example, a bell might be sounded to signify that supper is to be served, or a paper clip might be used to stand for the sun. If nods, winks, and nudges have import, they have meaning D. In these cases, the connection is not only conventional, it is arbitrarily so. Meaning D depends on conventions, but the conventions on which it depends do not constitute a symbol system. Meaning D is an analogue of meaning B in that both might be described as involving association or conditioning. Note that meaning is neither less deeply secure nor less powerful in the case of meaning D than in that of meaning B, despite the fact that meaning D relies on arbitrary rather than natural connections. People salivate if they hear the dinner bell no less than if they smell dinner, and salivation might also occur when a similar bell is heard in another context, though the person knows that dinner is not being served.

Meaning E: Arbitrary Meaning Generated within a Symbol System

For meaning E, a symbol or sign has meaning as an element or "character" in an arbitrary symbol scheme that provides rules for the generation of meaning by the appropriate uses of these elements. Linguistic meaning is of meaning E. As with meaning D, elements are given meaning (originally) by acts of stipulation, baptism, ostension. But, whereas (given the context) this is sufficient to establish meaning D, the corresponding process establishes meaning E only against the background of a symbol system that prepares a semantic use for the elements thus identified. There is a tendency to think of naming as a preparation for language—memorizing vocabulary is an im-

< 34 >

portant part of learning a second language, for example—but Wittgenstein (1953) points out that naming is a linguistic, rather than a prelinguistic, process. Naming makes sense only for people who know what names are and what they are used for. Naming assumes a great deal of stage-setting; there must be a place, a use, for names of the relevant sort within the symbol system.

We do talk of the meanings of words apart from their context of use in a particular utterance (hence, it is possible to compile dictionaries), but "timeless word meaning" presupposes consistent use in accordance with the conventions of the relevant symbol system. The word "sun" has its timeless or contextless meaning only against the background of the English language. The use of the language, and of this word in it, sustains the word's meaning and, divorced from that context, from its home in the symbol system, the vocable (or the marks on paper) have no meaning. The same is not true of signifiers with meaning D; their import is similarly arbitrary and conventional, but they do not possess their meaning as a result of the application of principles for combining elements to generate a semantic content.

Within languages there may be elements that stand in some natural relationship to what they signify. This is the case with onomatopoeic words— slurp, crash, whisper, murmur, bang, tinkle (a notational equivalent is the Roman numeral III). Because the sound (and notation) of language is primarily arbitrary, and because meaning depends on the conventions of a symbol system, we recognize the resemblance in these cases only after having grasped the meanings of the terms. The resemblance presupposes the meaning rather than explaining it, though it might explain why the person who coined the neologism chose that vocable rather than another. "Uuuu-urrrrggghhhh" means nothing, because it is not a word in the English language, even if it does sound like the noise made by a person who is dying. Resemblance might lend itself to signification (as in meaning B), but the occurrence of resemblance need not indicate that signification depends on its use. In language, resemblance, even where it occurs, plays no major role in securing meaning or reference. This is an important point in distinguishing meaning E from meaning C. Although meaning is effected by the context of the element within a symbol-scheme in both cases, and although a natural relation may hold between an element and that to which it refers in both cases, in meaning E the generation of meaning does not rely in any way on the presence of a natural relation (even where one exists), whereas in meaning C the natural element plays a crucial role in contributing to the meaning of the element in its context. The point might be put this way: in the case of meaning E, it is the function of the symbol system to create semantic content,

< 35 >

whereas, in the case of meaning C, the symbol system affects, without arbitrarily imposing a significance on, something having meaning A, or having a potential for meaning B, independently of the symbol system in which it is located.

Natural versus Non-Natural Meaning

The distinctions drawn between meanings B and D and between meanings C and E suppose that there is a sense to talking of natural relationships (relativized to interests); it supposes a distinction between natural and arbitrary connections. The latter are established by stipulation and conventions of use and might vary from place to place and time to time. The former might depend on interests and modes of perceiving that have a biological basis and thereby are common to all people (and perhaps also common to human beings and some nonhuman animals).[38]

Obviously there are different ways of grouping and contrasting these types of meaning. Natural elements are important in meanings A, B, and C but not in meanings D and E. Meaning A is entirely "natural," but this is not true of meanings B, C, D, and E. Meaning is entirely arbitrary in meanings D and E but not in meanings A, B, and C. Intentions and reference are involved in meanings B, C, D, and E but not in meaning A. Meanings C and E depend on the context of a symbol system, whereas meanings A, B, and D involve "stand-alone" meaning (in not depending on a symbol system). If one attends to only some of these differences, or to only a limited range of examples, as one attempts to distinguish natural from non-natural meaning, that distinction might appear to be clearer than it is.

One account that suffers from this defect is that of H. P. Grice (1957). He attempts to distinguish natural from non-natural meaning, using "Those three rings on the bell of the bus mean that 'the bus is full'" as his example of non-natural meaning (meaning$_{NN}$) and "Those spots mean measles" as his example of natural meaning (meaning$_N$). He notes five points of difference between natural and non-natural meaning: (i) "x means that p" with meaning$_N$ entails p, but with meaning$_{NN}$ p is not entailed (the bus conductor can be mistaken). (ii) With meaning$_N$ we cannot argue from "x means that p" to "by those spots *it* is meant that he has measles," but with meaning$_{NN}$ we can argue from the sentence to what is meant *by* it. (iii) With meaning$_N$ we cannot argue from the sentence to the conclusion that someone meant by the

---

[38] Some writers, such as Goodman, would deny that there is any such distinction to be drawn, that there are any nonarbitrary connections. I return to that issue briefly in Chapter 2.

< 36 >

spots so-and-so; but with meaning$_{NN}$ we can argue to the conclusion that someone meant that the bus was full. (iv) With meaning$_N$ the sentence cannot be restated so that "mean" is followed by a sentence or phrase in reported speech (we cannot say "Those spots mean 'he has measles'"), but with meaning$_{NN}$ we can do this. (v) With meaning$_N$ the sentence can be restated beginning with "the fact that" (as in "The fact that he has those spots means that he has measles") without changing its meaning, but with meaning$_{NN}$ a restatement of the sentence in this form does not preserve the meaning of the original version, though both statements may be true.

Grice's first condition appears too strong. Black clouds do not entail rain, though if they have meaning it is meaning$_N$ rather than meaning$_{NN}$. Grice's treatment of the example suggests that he takes meaning$_N$ to deal with sufficient conditions (x means$_N$ y just in case x is a sufficient condition for y), but weaker connections, such as causal ones, might suffice to establish meaning$_N$. This point aside, though, Grice hits the target at which he aims: whatever problems stand in the way of inference in the case of meaning$_N$, they are not problems of opacity generated by an intensional context, as is true with meaning$_{NN}$. The difficulty a person has in drawing an inference to meaning$_N$ is not that another person might be making a mistake. Revised in this way, it looks as if Grice's distinction between meaning$_N$ and meaning$_{NN}$ corresponds, in my terms, to a distinction between meaning A and meanings B, C, D, and E. This appearance is strengthened by a consideration of Grice's second through fourth conditions. To the extent that intentional use is required in securing meaning, meaning$_{NN}$ rather than meaning$_N$ is involved. His fifth condition implicitly appeals to intentions in allowing that, typically, with meaning$_N$ there is a fact of the matter that is independent of the context of utterance.[39]

If Grice's criteria are decisive then, as I have noted, his distinction corresponds to one between, on the one side, meaning A and, on the other, meanings B, C, D, and E. But his choice of examples suggests that his concern is to distinguish meaning A from meanings D and E. His failure to consider the possibility of meanings B and C explicitly leaves in doubt his attitude toward their classification as natural or non-natural. If meaning$_N$ excludes meanings B and C, Grice's five conditions must be intended to be decisive. But if meaning$_N$ includes, as well as meaning A, meanings B and C, Grice's five conditions cannot be more than indicative, serving to distinguish only some (paradigmatic) instances of meaning$_N$ from meaning$_{NN}$.

I do not believe that meanings B and C are more naturally to be grouped

---

[39] For further discussion of these conditions, see Davies 1983b.

< 37 >

with meanings D and E than with meaning A. A person who intentionally adopts a sad expression to show how she feels appropriates, rather than arbitrarily creates, a meaning. A person who uses an orange to represent the sun relies on a natural relation between the two in doing so, whereas a person who stipulates that a paper clip stand for the sun does not. If "natural" means nonarbitrary, as often it does, then meanings B and C are no less natural than is meaning A. There is all the world of difference between the tears to which one gives way and the sad expression one intentionally adopts, but the difference revealed is that between one's betraying one's feelings and one's employing a natural meaning to reveal them, so I see no reason to distinguish the one as non-natural and the other as natural. The intentionally adopted expression is not non-natural in the arbitrary way in which one's saying "I am sad" (as opposed, say, to "Je suis triste") is.

My aim is not so much to undermine the distinction between natural and non-natural meaning as it is to suggest that the distinction is more complex and multidimensional than Grice's discussion allows. If the terms "natural" and "non-natural" are used by Grice not as technical terms but as terms paying heed to ordinary usage, his analysis is too simplistic to be helpful. This is especially obvious in the musical case, where effects are usually intentionally contrived by composers but in which the elements seem to have meaning A, or to involve natural relations exploited by the composer, as often as they have the arbitrary character of linguistic or quasi-linguistic signs. In the case of musical expressiveness, the composer is like someone who reveals her feelings by holding to her face a mask of the sort used to indicate tragedy rather than comedy, or holds the mask not to indicate her own feelings but instead to present the appearance of tragedy rather than of comedy. To the extent that the use is intentional, Grice's account suggests that the meaning is non-natural as opposed to natural. But, to the extent that a meaning is appropriated rather than arbitrarily created, the music presents elements with a natural, rather than a non-natural, significance or potential.

Many theories of musical expressiveness regard music as involving meanings A, B, or C rather than meanings D or E. One such is Susanne Langer's, according to which artworks are iconic symbols of the forms of feeling (iconicity is a matter of resemblance in formal properties). There is a suggestion in Cooke's theory that music is naturally meaningful, as I noted earlier. Much that is of import within music appears to rely on such meaning. It also is clear, however, that musical expressiveness is usually intentionally contrived by the composer, and that it is conventionalized to a considerable degree so that the expressive character of a piece might not be apparent to a member of a different musical culture. It is these considerations, I think, on

< 38 >

which the parallel with language has been thought to depend. Because of them, I believe, writers such as Cooke and Coker have thought it appropriate to argue that music is a (sort of) language. There is an unfortunate tendency to treat "conventional" as equivalent to "arbitrary" and to regard all conventions as structuring symbol systems dedicated to generating semantic content. To do so is to obscure the distinctions between meanings A, B, C, D, and E; it is to see (wrongly) meanings B and C as more intimately allied to meanings D and E than to meaning A, or it is to assimilate (wrongly) all intentionally used meanings to the model of linguistic meaning, or it is to assume (wrongly) that music might possess only one type of meaning.

If (some) musical meaning is of the A, B, or C type, it relies at least in part on the significance accorded to natural connections, and in that respect it differs from language. Some account of those connections are necessary to an explanation of musical meaning, whereas no such account is required in a discussion of linguistic meaning.[40] And if (some) musical meaning is of type D, then, though musical meaning is arbitrarily created in the way linguistic meaning (originally) is, still music differs from language in not requiring a symbol system for the generation of its meaningful content. Music is highly conventionalized and might be described as constituting a symbol system (or symbol systems), but if this is the case the arguments offered in the first part of this chapter suggest that music does not constitute a symbol system comparable to that of natural languages in having the function of generating semantic content through the application of rules of combination to elements with specifiable meanings.[41]

Examples of Meaning D in Music

Most of the theories I consider in subsequent chapters stress the extent to which musical meaning involves natural elements, even if their protagonists

---

[40] For a sensitive and subtle account of musical meaning, in my terms, of type C, see Lippman 1977. Lippman holds that musical meaning is shaped and controlled by historical, social, and cultural factors but also that this shaping draws on "archetypally" significant elements or forms invariant between those cultures which provide for a conceptual distinction between music and raw sound.

[41] One finds in the literature debate about the relation in music between expression and reference. A range of views is presented: that reference rarely occurs (Kivy 1989); that it is irrelevant where it occurs (Beardsley 1958 and Margolis 1974); that it is relevant in promoting expressiveness where it occurs, but also that expressiveness, not reference, takes precedence in aesthetics (Kaplan 1954); that it is central to expressiveness, at least when weakened to the notion of denotation, as in Goodman's (1968) view. Underlying these disagreements, it seems to me, are commitments to different views about the kind of meaning involved in artworks' being expressive. In cases of meaning A, reference does not occur and is irrelevant to meaning; in some cases

< 39 >

also take care to point out the degree to which the use of such elements is deliberate and is structured by conventions familiar only to those at home with the relevant style. It would be a mistake, however, to ignore the extent to which musical meaning sometimes depends on arbitrary associations and stipulations—to ignore the prevalence of meaning D in musical works. Because meaning of this sort approximates the type of meaning found in full-blown languages (meaning E), and because musical instances of meaning D are not difficult to analyze and explain, I devote the remainder of this chapter to a consideration of musical examples of meaning D and to distinguishing such examples from outwardly similar ones.

In Camille Saint-Saëns's *Danse Macabre* a solo violin represents Death (or a violin played by Death). The highest string (which usually is tuned to E) is tuned to E-flat. A two-note chord, A–E-flat, is often played on the two, top, open strings. The interval of three whole tones (of which A–E-flat is an example) was forbidden in plainsong and in early polyphonic music under names such as "the devil in music" (*diabolus in musica*). Although the tritone is respectable in twentieth-century music, Saint-Saëns's use of the interval involves a subtle pun on its name.[42] I take this to be an example of meaning D.

A case deserving special mention is the final, unfinished, triple fugue of *The Art of Fugue*, in which the composer "spells" his own name in the first four notes of the subject of the second fugue: B(-flat)–A–C–H (B-natural). In his use of the motive, Bach created a private reference of meaning type D. In homage to Bach, other composers—for instance, Albrechtsberger, Schumann, Liszt, Reger, and Busoni—have used the motive, especially when writing fugues. The tonal ambiguity of the motive lends it a distinctive character, so that it can be recognized easily by a listener who first has made the connection. Short though it is, the composer's deliberate use of the motive is likely to be noticed, so that he can expect his reference to be widely recognized. It is interesting to note that, because most people lack perfect pitch, what is recognized is the pattern of intervals rather than a series of pitches (to my ears, F–E–G–G-flat spells BACH). In other words, though "B," "A," "C," and "H" are labels for particular notes, the listener appreciates the reference usually by taking "BACH" to be a label for the entire motive comprising a

---

of meaning B, reference may occur while being irrelevant to the element of natural meaning employed; in other cases of meaning B and of meaning C, it is relevant but perhaps not essential; in cases of meanings D and E, it is crucial.

[42] One can easily imagine other examples of musical puns: a song about betrayal by one's family using "false relations"; a canonic setting of the word "law."

< 40 >

falling minor second/rising minor third/falling minor second. Again, this is an example of meaning D in music.

Much more common than punning is reference between works (or within works) through quotation or the evocation of styles. Mozart (*Die Schauspiel-Direktor*) and Antonio Salieri (*Prima la Musica, poi le Parole*) satirized the excesses of the opera singers of their day. Mozart's *Ein Musikalischer Spass* makes a joke of the clichés of the prevalent style. In Dmitri Shostakovitch's ballet *The Age of Gold*, twelve-tone music is parodied; in Béla Bartók's Concerto for Orchestra, a theme from Shostakovitch's Seventh Symphony is lampooned for its banality.[43] I regard these cases as best to be classed as involving meaning B. The quotation of a theme or invocation of a style refers to the theme or style by recreating it. The device is akin to that of including a person in a movie, not by having an actor play the part, but by having the actual person play a cameo role. What more intimate, natural relation is there than identity? By quoting a theme, where the audience will recognize it as mentioned rather than as freshly composed, the composer can get that theme to mean itself, or to mean the work in which it appears. And by self-consciously invoking a style or genre (by parodying the current fashion or by recalling a style or genre now passed), a composer can refer to a musical type without thereby producing merely another instance of that kind of music.

Meaning B is soon transformed to meaning D, however, when the point of the musical quotation is not to refer to the music as such (to the theme, style, or genre) but is to evoke what is associated with the music quoted. I take the following to be examples of meaning D: Beethoven quotes "God Save the King" in *Wellington's Victory*, relying on the audience's prior knowledge of the significance of this theme as a national anthem. Similarly, Piotr Tchaikovsky quotes the "Marseillaise," the tsarist anthem, and the Russian hymn "God Preserve Thy People" in the *1812* Overture. The open-

---

[43] Cases such as these should be distinguished from others in which themes are quoted (as in themes and variations, such as Beethoven's *Diabelli* Variations), or "borrowed" (as in the overture to Mozart's *Magic Flute*, which takes its theme from a Clementi piano sonata), or in which accidental similarity occurs (as in the scherzo theme from Beethoven's Symphony No. 5 which famously recalls the opening melody of Mozart's Symphony No. 40). In these cases no reference is intended, or if it is intended the reference is not musically important. By contrast, the examples indicated previously take their point from the intended reference, and an appreciation of the music is impossible or inhibited if the reference is missed. Similarly for quotation within a work, the recapitulation of a theme involves its repetition, its use rather than its mention, so it is not usually appropriate to talk of mutual reference in such cases (which is not to say that a recognition of the repetition is unimportant). By contrast, when Beethoven reviews and rejects the themes of the earlier movements at the start of the last movement of his Symphony No. 9, reference is involved.

< 41 >

ing notes of the plainsong "Dies Irae" are quoted in many compositions, such as Saint-Saëns's *Danse Macabre*, Franz Liszt's *Todten-Tanz*, Hector Berlioz's *Symphonie Fantastique*, as well as in several requiems, which exploit the connection between the melody and the words it sets.[44] Works in which this device is employed are not always overtly programmatic. Johannes Brahms's *Academic Festival* Overture contains what were well-known student songs. Franz Joseph Haydn's String Quartet Op. 76, No. 3 contains variations on the theme given by Haydn to his country as its anthem.[45] Sometimes the reference has a significance private to the composer: the third movement of Gustav Mahler's First Symphony is based on the German nursery song "Brother Martin, Are You Sleeping?" cast in the minor key and a solemn style, apparently in reference to the death of his younger brother, Ernst, when Mahler was fourteen.

Composers also play on the fact that certain instruments have (or had) associations with particular social contexts and countries. Horns accompany the hunt; the oboe, cor inglais, and panpipes invoke rustic settings; muffled snare drums suggest state funerals and executions; fifes and drums go with marches; bagpipes are bound to call Scotland to mind; organs now have religious connotations. Composers have imported these associations to their works in their use of instruments (especially where the instrument is not one standardly found in orchestras of the type for which the work is written). In programmatic works, song, ballet, opera and film music, such associations are not only invoked but also reinforced where the dramatic context or words call for such effects (few composers would pass by a mention of the chase in the words of a song without providing the French horn with a fanfare). In some cases, rather than use the instruments, their effect is created by orchestration; Igor Stravinsky conjures from the orchestra in *Petrushka* the sound of an organ, such as would be heard on the streets, in

---

[44] Nicolai Paganini quotes the "Dies Irae" in his *Caprices*. In this case, the reference has no musico-dramatic point but exploits and promotes the rumor that the violinist's amazing skill was vouchsafed as a result of his entering a Faustian pact with the devil. Although this case is like the others in using the "Dies Irae" to achieve reference, it differs in that an appreciation of the reference is not important to an understanding of the musical work as such.

[45] Again, examples of this type should be distinguished from others in which a theme that later acquired associations is used without the intention of evoking those associations. I take this to be the case with the finale of Felix Mendelssohn's Trio Op. 66, in which the "Old Hundred" appears. This also is true, I take it, when tenor parts of a mass are based on secular themes (as in the Parody masses of the fifteenth and sixteenth centuries); here the theme is usually unrecognizable. The aim of the distinction, now as previously, is to contrast importantly referential from nonreferential (or only incidentally referential) uses.

< 42 >

creating the atmosphere of the Shrovetide fair. Again, the examples are ones of meaning D.[46]

Social contexts are associated not only with instruments but also with types of music. Fanfares recall the hunt. In *Don Giovanni*, when at the close of the first act the on-stage orchestras simultaneously play various dance pieces, Mozart gives the courtly minuet to the aristocrats and the cruder, duple-time dance to the peasants, exploiting the social significance of the dance types to a dramatic purpose. Dances can mark particular social occasions (waltzes go with balls, as in Giuseppe Verdi's *Un Ballo in Maschera*), and they are associated with countries (reels, tarantellas, hat dances). To bring a country to mind the composer might make use of an appropriate folk idiom; bagpipe-like drones and "Scotch snaps" are suggestive in Mendelssohn's Scottish Symphony. Once more, these are examples of meaning D.[47]

As yet I have not stressed one of the more common and obvious methods for securing reference in music, the exploitation of associations between words and the themes to which they are set. If a song is familiar, one need only hear the theme to have the words brought to mind. This motivates the use of thematic quotation on many occasions. Usually attention is drawn to

[46] These cases should be distinguished from the following: in Ralph Vaughan Williams's ballet *Job: A Masque for Dancing*, the unctuousness of Job's comforters is captured by the use of an E-flat saxophone; in Sergei Prokofiev's *Peter and the Wolf*, the French horn represents the wolf. The appropriateness of the characterizations here depends on the timbral qualities of the instruments and not on any prior associations. These would be examples of meaning B, since what is quoted or recalled is a sound, or the synaesthetic feel of a sound, and not an arbitrary connection between an instrument and something else. Intermediate, difficult-to-classify cases are not hard to find: the tinkling of tuneful bells is associated with the character of Papageno in Mozart's *Magic Flute*, but, given that Papageno is a birdlike bird-catcher, and that the songs of some birds are bell-like, the significance of the sound of the bells in calling Papageno to mind is not easily classed as meaning B as opposed to meaning D.

[47] As before, these uses for securing reference should be distinguished from those works in which the idiom is employed not for the sake of a reference but as part of the composer's style (a style influenced by folk music, say); that is, it is appropriate to distinguish the use of a folk idiom from its mention. Bartók's music, for example, is permeated by folk influences, but it does not for the most part refer to folk music. Darius Milhaud's ballet *La Création du Monde* and Stravinsky's *Ebony* Concerto use jazz styles, but they do so without referring to smoky cafés and the social context from which jazz arose naturally. To the extent that Milhaud and Stravinsky are self-conscious in their use of the techniques of jazz as a musical style, intending thereby to refer to jazz, their music has meaning B. If the rhythms and modalities of Hungarian music flow from Bartók's musical pores, so that he is no more aware of his "accent" than is a person speaking the dialect natural to her, his music lacks "Hungarian" meaning, though it has a Hungarian style or flavor. On the other hand, if he relishes the Hungarian sound of his music and means us to do the same, meaning B is involved (even if the "intention" to write in that style was not one he could control).

< 43 >

the quoted theme (if it is not already stylistically distinguishable) by the way it is presented. I mention just one example: Alban Berg's Violin Concerto quotes (and varies) the chorale "Es ist genug!" from J. S. Bach's cantata "O Ewigkeit, du Donnerwort" as well as giving prominence to the opening notes of the chorale throughout the work. The claim that this "is surely a kind of internal evidence that Berg planned the work with the vague premonition that it was to be his own requiem" (Reich 1965, 100) is fanciful in my view, but it is likely that Berg intended that his audience bring the words of the chorale to mind, complementing, as they do, the emotional mood of the latter half of the concerto.[48]

Associations between music and words might be established within a song, choral work, or opera rather than being brought to the work from outside. One example: in Stravinsky's opera *The Rake's Progress*, Anne Trulove prays when her heart's love, Tom, has left for the city under the charge of his diabolical servant, Nick. She sings: "O God, protect dear Tom, support my father, and strengthen my resolve." Later, Tom, diseased, corrupted, and sick at heart, is deceived (yet again) by Nick into believing that he has at his disposal a machine that turns stone into bread. He hopes, by rescuing humankind from starvation with his machine, to qualify again as worthy of Anne's love. To the tune of Anne's prayer he sings: "O may I not, forgiven all my past, For one good deed deserve dear Anne at last?" Anne's prayer and the circumstances of the lovers' separation are thereby recalled.

Perhaps the most famous systematic use of this device is Richard Wagner's adoption of leitmotif technique in his operas. Typically a theme is associated with a character, an object, a mood, or an event; at the reappearance or mention of the character, mood, or event, its "signature" tune is played or

---

[48] Again, unintended associations must be distinguished from those that are meant. A famous Verdi chorus was once used with suitably changed words in a television advertisement for toothpaste. I cannot avoid recalling the words when I hear the chorus, and this destroys the music for me, because the words of the advertisement are irrelevant to Verdi's opera. Similarly, I find it impossible to hear Paul Dukas's *Sorcerer's Apprentice* without also seeing in my mind's eye the Disney studio's famous cartoon animation of the work. Archibald Davison attacks music educators who provide "easy little jingles" to help students remember themes from instrumental works. He notes that what is recalled is not the theme but the silly patter: "It is a melancholy experience to glance around a concert hall during the performance of a certain familiar orchestral work and to see numbers of persons soundlessly and resentfully moving their lips to that lethal bit of doggerel, 'This is the symphony that Schubert wrote and never finished'" (1954, 22). If these are examples of meaning D, which is doubtful, they are examples of meanings not intended by the composer as well as of meanings not supported by the composer's work.

< 44 >

sung.[49] Leitmotifs can be established only if that with which they are associated can be presented clearly. People and objects can be presented clearly in operatic contexts, as can be emotions (through action and dramatic context). Ideas or emotions might also be mentioned or described in the text sung when a leitmotif first makes its appearance, but, where the object is abstract and is not referred to, I am skeptical that it can be indicated by a leitmotif.[50] I am skeptical, that is, of some claims made for the referential power of leitmotifs, especially as these regard complex, abstract notions not directly enacted or discussed on stage.

Leitmotifs operate like labels. The musical statement of a leitmotif can indicate that Amy is thinking of Brad, though she says that it is Colin who is in her thoughts, because her words are accompanied by Brad's rather than Colin's theme. This use of themes as labels or signatures has a long musical history, but Wagner is more systematic and tenacious in his commitment to the approach than others. The use of the technique presupposes a programmatic, or textual, or dramatic context, because it relies on the presentation or description of the object in conjunction with its musical label. For that reason, leitmotif should be distinguished from other repetitious or cyclic uses of themes. The recurrent theme in César Franck's Symphony in D minor is not a leitmotif and it creates no reference.

The reference established by leitmotif technique is usually confined to a single work (or collection of works), but the ostentatious quotation of a well-known leitmotif, such as the sword theme from *Der Ring des Nibelungen*, would secure a reference in another composer's work both to *Der Ring* and to the sword (this method might be used for comic as well as dramatic effect). In Richard Strauss's *Ein Heldenleben*, many major themes of his symphonic poems are recalled, and with them a reference to the dramatic programs of the earlier works is established.

Leitmotifs and their equivalents aim to create an association rather than adopting an association established outside the musical/dramatic context (such as that between the "Marseillaise" and the French). The connection must be established within the musical work and, if possible, it must be drawn to the attention of the audience at first hearing. It is understandable,

---

[49] For a useful discussion, see Brown 1948, 93–98; also see Howes 1958 and Lippman 1966. For a more detailed account of Wagner's technique, see Newman 1933–46 and Donington 1963.

[50] Howes (1958) claims that the leitmotif is an example of "conceptual thinking" in music, but he seems to mean by this that the reference secured by the technique for music is often unusually specific and concrete.

< 45 >

then, that a natural element is often prominent in the use of the technique: Wagner's sword motive is assertive, powerful, and up-thrusting; the love music swells yearningly and throbs passionately; the fire motive has a leaping effervescence. The expressive or dynamic quality of the music, thus, commonly suits it to the character of that with which it is associated and to which it refers. Often, then, meaning B rather than meaning D is involved, though this is not always the case.

I have said that the association established between a leitmotif and what it signifies might rely on a natural element, but I have also noted that meaning B is sometimes transformed into meaning D. In the first instance, an expressive or dramatic flourish—one that derives its character from some natural element—might be introduced in a work. This device is taken up within the style, becoming standardized and stylized through time. Because it is used consistently where the appropriate expressive or dramatic effect is called for, it continues to signify that effect, but the connection no longer sounds natural. So it is, one suspects, that the minor third retained a (tenuous) connection with sadness, although changes in musical style transformed it from a discord to a relatively concordant interval. An especially fine example of this process is described by Edward Lippman (1977, 270–283): the chromaticism of the leitmotif indicating Amfortas's wound in Wagner's *Parsifal* draws on the role of chromaticism in centuries of music portraying the crucifixion. Elsewhere Lippman describes a similar process as lying behind the development of musical symbolism: "In a rationalistic setting, the conventional element of this symbolism becomes dominant. Direct response recedes in favor of symbolism in its restricted sense—knowing, or conscious recognition of meaning. The conventional nature of the figures explains their efficacy even in non-programmatic instrumental music" (1953, 564–565).

I have yet to discuss "word-painting" (*Wortmalerei*). The device is a common one when texts are set. No baroque composer passes by the opportunity to set the word "resurrection" to an ascending phrase, "water" to an undulating motive, and so on. Bach's settings are replete with examples (Haydon 1948). At its crudest, the technique gives rise to meaning A or B. But where things become more complex, such natural elements as there are become shaped and altered by the context of musical conventions, and meaning D is involved. In Josquin's motet *In pauperum refugium*, the words "via errantium" (the life of the erring ones) are set to aimless, harmonically uncoordinated music; at the start of Haydn's *Die Schöpfung*, tonal and rhythmic disintegration provides a purely musical illustration of the absence of order that precedes God's act of creation. But what counts as stylistically erroneous is governed by the conventions of the style rather than by natural rela-

< 46 >

tions as such, so that Haydn can anticipate the "Tristan" chord at the close of his portrayal of musical chaos but cannot give it the significance it acquires in Wagner's *Tristan und Isolde*. At times in musical history, theories of the musical settings of words have attempted to specify and codify the possibilities of the current style: Maniera and Musica Reservata in the late sixteenth century; Affektenlehre in the late eighteenth century.[51] To the extent that the natural element became highly stylized and the reference was established as much by the terms of the widely known theories as naturally, meaning D rather than meaning B was in question; such movements dealt in a sort of musical code.[52]

The previous examples of musical reference are mostly instances of meaning D (though straightforward musical quotation and parody of themes not associated with words or ideas suggests meaning B rather than meaning D). It is contingent that a country has the particular national anthem it does, or that shepherds play oboes rather than violas. The associations are of the part-for-whole variety, but the elements associated stand in a socially established, arbitrary relation. Leitmotifs, because they are to be fixed as names or labels within the work, rely heavily on natural connections, but they are best viewed as instances of meaning D rather than meaning B because the natural connection is not sufficient to serve the referential function that is the leitmotif's role.

The aforementioned cases are ones in which reference is made within a musical work, and the reference is such that the fullest appreciation of the work depends on its recognition. Sometimes the reference relies on an association established outside the musical or dramatic context; in other cases the association is established within the work itself. Where the latter is the case, the basis of the association is likely to involve a strong natural element, and it is the intentional use of this natural connection that generates reference. Except for reference to purely musical themes, works, or styles, the successful generation of reference relevant to the appreciation of the work presupposes either a connection clearly established outside the work or the presence of nonmusical elements in the work—titles, stories, spoken or sung words, or dramatic action. It is significant, I think, that, to the extent that music is to be appreciated as operating like a code (meaning D), it does so in fulfilling

---

[51] For comment on these movements, see Lippman 1966 and Barry 1987; for a fuller treatment, see Winn 1981 and Neubauer 1986.

[52] The most famous attempt to analyze music as a code is that offered by Schering (1941) in his account of J. S. Bach's music. For analysis of the way formalized elements of spoken rhetoric are imitated in Handel's setting of John Dryden's *Ode to Saint Cecilia*, see Thom 1983, and for more on rhetoric and music, see Winn 1981 and Neubauer 1986.

< 47 >

its role within dramatic genres in which it is not the sole element: program music, song, choral music, opera, ballet. Music is not a code in the way Morse is; it does not provide a translation schema for natural languages. Musical "signs" stand alone and do not depend for their significance on their place within a wider symbol system. As observed earlier, we might talk of the meaning of words as if they stand alone, as when we compile a dictionary, but ultimately words get their meaning only as characters within a symbol scheme providing for the generation of sentences with semantic content. By contrast, musical signs stand alone in a more radical way—without presupposing the background context of a symbol system.

If the significance of musical ideas were exclusively formal, there would be no temptation to argue that music is a language. To understand a musical work would be to understand how it is put together; musical meaning would consist in the coherence of the structure of the work, and the significance of elements would derive from their contribution to the creation of this structure. Most theorists hold that, mostly, musical significance is "internal" and formal in this way, but they also hold that music refers to, or denotes, or brings to mind nonmusical ideas, events, or things—in particular, that music expresses emotion. Recognition of the fact that the significance of music is not solely formal motivates the comparison of music to language, for the most striking feature of language is that it refers beyond itself.

Nevertheless, I have argued in this chapter that music is not usefully to be compared to natural languages with respect to its meaning. Music fails most of the conditions necessary in a symbol system capable of generating meaningful utterances, as language does. Theories that rely too heavily on the comparison between music and language in discussing what music means and how it gets its meaning are, I have suggested, empty of explanatory power. Because superficial similarities mask crucial differences, it may be more misleading than helpful to emphasize the analogies between the two.

One might preserve the view that the significance of music is not purely formal, while avoiding the temptation to analyze music as a kind of language, if there were ways of securing meaning not like those central to the function of language. If language is not the only possible symbol system, or type of sign, or bearer of meaning, one might deny the parallel with language without depriving music of its extramusical content. I offered a typology of kinds of meaning with the aim of outlining some of the possibilities for an account of musical meaning as nonlinguistic in character. Accepting that music is not a language, one might explain how it might possess extraformal significance by arguing that it comprises a nonlinguistic symbol system that

< 48 >

does its thing in its own way, or that it is a sign (if not a symbol within a symbol system), or if not a sign that it has the power to bring extramusical matters to mind.

I closed the chapter with a discussion of ways in which some musical meaning often has the arbitrarily conventional character of linguistic meaning, though the conventions applying in these musical cases do not constitute symbol systems such as can be compared with languages. The approach to music in terms of such meanings is not unlike the iconographic study of paintings, as a collection of signs not integrated within a generative symbol system. Though few would deny that music offers possibilities for use as a limited, nonlinguistic code, possibilities clearly recognized by many composers, most would feel that such a technique by no means exhausts the potential for nonformal meaning in music. Music operates at its best as a code when its primary function is dramatic, vocal, or programmatic, for it is in these contexts that the significance of particular musical symbols is most easily established; usually the meaning of a particular musical idea is unique to a given work and must be fixed within that work. Musical symbols have been systematized and stylized so that they might be used across a range of works sharing a common style, but the more sophisticated musical codes are poor in their narrative potential. Meanwhile, the expressive power that so often seems to give music its significance apparently does not depend on the operation of formulaic codes. It is not surprising, then, that the attempt to explain the meaning of music looks beyond its potential for use as a nonlinguistic code. Two possibilities, explored in the following chapters, recommend themselves: perhaps music has meaning by depicting, as pictures do, rather than by describing, as language does; or perhaps music is a symbol system of a distinctive type, doing its own thing in its own way.

< 49 >

T W O
• • •

Music and Pictures

In the previous chapter I considered whether music is meaningful as linguistic utterances are, and the conclusion was negative. I began with language because questions of meaning arise most naturally in that connection. In this chapter I compare music with pictures, for we regard pictures as meaningful. They are said to be worth a thousand words and, if this is false, it is so not because pictures are without significance but because their significance is not structured as is that of linguistic utterances. The idea is this: perhaps, rather than asserting or describing, as language does, music represents or depicts, as nonabstract paintings and sculptures do. Such a view has obvious attractions. Music often is used—in song, film, opera, and ballet—not merely to accompany the action and text but to illustrate them. Moreover, one genre of instrumental music—program music—purports to be representational and uses literary titles and accompanying texts to focus the listener's attention on the subjects supposedly depicted. There is no doubt that many composers have believed they could paint pictures in sound and, hence, that their music is representational.

The notions of representation/represent/representative are extremely complex, so I begin with some points of clarification. "Represent" can mean "assert" or "intimate," as in "He represented to John the danger of the situation." It can mean "speak for" where it refers to lawyers, guardians, and so on. It can mean "typical of," as in "a representative sample." It can mean "stand for," "symbolize," "denote," or "refer to." And it can mean "pic-

< 51 >

ture" or "depict." My concern here lies with this last use, with the suggestion that music pictures or depicts things as do some paintings.

A terminological point: One author, Kendall Walton (1990; also see 1973 and 1974), offers a general account of representation as covering descriptions and narrations as well as pictures. In Walton's view something is a representation if it serves as a prop in a game of make-believe. It is also the case that anything that is a fiction is a representation in his theory. As he notes, this account is broader in some respects, and narrower in others, than ordinary usage. For example, in his view all paintings are representational and no photographs are representational.[1] Now, Walton distinguishes depiction from representation, regarding the former as a species of the latter.[2] If Walton's approach were to be accepted, my concern in this chapter would lie with depiction rather than representation. But I use "depiction" and "representation" as synonyms, despite Walton's (idiosyncratic) terminologies. I say very little about Walton's general, wide notion of representation, but later I consider his views on musical depiction.

I approach the topic first by defining and discussing pictorial representation. I do so because I take paintings (drawing, silhouettes, also statues, dolls, puppets, masks) to provide our paradigms. The point of starting with them is to discover the central conditions governing the notion. Music, if it were representational, would be representational in its own way, so the argument is not about whether music might represent the same subjects as may be depicted in paintings, or whether the techniques of representation are the same in the two cases. Nevertheless, whatever differences there are between pictures and music, if music is representational it must satisfy the general conditions for representation and those conditions are most readily elucidated through a consideration of cases from the visual arts, where claims to representationality are not in dispute. I focus on two main types of theory: the "semantic" and "seeing-in" accounts of representation. In addition, I discuss Walton's views on depiction. Then I argue that, for the most part, music fails to meet analogous conditions. The differences between painting and music, rather than marking a distinction between types of representation, are such as to suggest that music is not a depictive artform.

---

[1] See Walton 1984 and 1990; and, for discussion, Currie 1991b.

[2] Others draw similar distinctions; see, for example, Pleydell-Pearce 1967, and for criticism, Elliott 1968. Peacocke (1987) is typical in reserving "depicting" for picturing and "representing" for the broader notion of symbolizing.

< 52 >

Music and Pictures

Necessary Conditions for Pictorial Depiction

What are the necessary conditions for pictorial representation? I list four such, none of which is sufficient alone. Protagonists of both the seeing-in and semantic theories of depiction would agree to the second and fourth of the conditions I outline; most would subscribe to the first also. It is the necessity of the third condition that is disputed. As I interpret it, the seeing-in theory endorses the third condition whereas the semantic theory (in its main version) rejects it. Because I am inclined to support the seeing-in account, I include and defend this third condition.

(1) *Intention:* It is a necessary condition for X's representing Y that X be intended to represent Y.[3]

If, as a result of an explosion in an artist's studio, a canvas were covered in paint so that it looked exactly like da Vinci's *Mona Lisa*, it could not be the case that the woman represented in da Vinci's painting would be represented in the paint-covered canvas. If da Vinci pictorially represented a woman who looked identical, as we now can see, to Marilyn Monroe, the painting could not represent Marilyn Monroe. Also, if an artist painted one of two identical twins, it would be her intention that determined which of the twins was represented, or if neither was represented. (The painting might represent someone other than one of the twins, such as Billy Bunter; or it might represent Fred even if Tom, Fred's identical twin, was used as the sitter.) These cases show that mere resemblance is not sufficient for representation and that the absence of the relevant intention defeats the claim that the piece is depictive, or is depictive of this rather than that.

Three objections might be raised to this first condition for representation:

(i) It might be thought that there is a circularity in analyzing representation in terms of intention, since the relevant intention is an intention to represent.[4] The reply to this point could take this form: There are noncircular ways of specifying the intention—for example, as an intention to produce an X in which Y can be seen. Additionally, note that artists work within historically established traditions rather than inventing new systems of rep-

---

[3] Among those who subscribe to this condition are Hermerén (1969 and 1977), Wollheim (1980, 1987 and 1991), Kivy (1980, 64, and 1990a, 18), Wolterstorff (1980), and Peacocke (1987). Among those who reject or question the condition are Beardsley (1958), Ziff (1960), Black (1972), Novitz (1975 and 1977), Robinson (1979), and Schier (1986).

[4] See Black 1972; for versions of the reply that follows, see Hermerén 1977 and Peacocke 1987.

< 53 >

resentation for each painting. Indeed, it is arguable that conventions of depiction could no more be unique to each work than that each utterance could be in a different language. Consistency in the use of the relevant conventions is important for the possibility of representation, and that consistency presupposes the intentionality of their use.

(ii) A camera might be triggered by accident and produces a representation, despite the absence of the relevant intention. For the camera, the reliability of the causal mechanism renders image-making intentions unnecessary. Different responses to this objection are available: (a) One might argue that, just because the relevant intentions are absent, photographs are not depictions. Mechanical devices, like photocopy machines, generate copies rather than representations in reproducing an image. Perhaps cameras should be regarded in the same light (see Walton 1984 and, for comment, Warburton 1988). (b) Alternatively, one might accept that photographs are depictions but attempt to save this disputed condition for representation by arguing that intentions of the relevant sort remain in play. For example, one might suggest that the designer's or manufacturer's intention to produce an image-making device satisfies the condition. But this approach is unconvincing, since the intention to make such a device is far from equivalent to someone's intending that a depiction result from every activation of the mechanism. Or, if a print is developed by hand, one might argue that what is revealed on it owes much to decisions taken by the developer, so that the intentions of the print maker are crucial even where the camera is activated by accident.[5] (c) Or, finally, one might accept that, even if photography is a representational artform, the causal mechanisms involved in determining the character of the photographic image distinguish this artform from painting (see Novitz 1975, Currie 1991b), so that it is not implausible to hold to the necessity of the condition under discussion for painterly depiction while accepting that the counterexample shows that a freer approach should be taken to photographic representation; *drawings*-as-depictions, then, might be treated as a distinct subclass of representations.

[5] If the aim of this argument is to establish the credentials of photography as an artform, then it may go further than is required. A case could be made for the view that such freedom as is exercised by the developer affects not the basic representationality of the photograph but the artistry present in the details; that is, photography might qualify as an art not because it achieves representation but instead because of the artistic treatment given to the depicted image. Scruton in (1981a) argues that photography is not a representational *art* (for further discussion, see Black 1972), whereas Wicks (1989) disagrees though he accepts that, as an artform, photography is limited. Snyder and Allen (1975) and Snyder (1983) challenge the claim (presented in Arnheim 1974 and elsewhere) that photographs reproduce reality (as we normally perceive it) more obviously than do paintings; see also Roskill and Carrier 1983.

< 54 >

I have done little more than indicate the lines that might be taken in reply-ing to this alleged counterexample, for I regard it as peripheral to my con-cerns. If music is representational, it is so by analogy with painting rather than with photography. Such musical image-making as is achieved relies on the composer and not on a mechanism.[6] If artists' intentions are necessary for painterly depiction, then composers' intentions also are necessary for the usual case of musical representation, notwithstanding the possibility that the equivalent intentions can be dispensed with where photographic depiction is concerned.

(iii) The third objection against regarding relevant intentions as necessary for representation might be put this way: One can easily imagine the case in which a scene is pictured and it is known that the artist did not intend to represent that scene. Suppose in drawing his *Liberation* of 1955, M. C. Escher is unaware that the gaps between the birds clearly can also be seen as birds. Or imagine a person who draws Jastrow's duck-rabbit figure while intending to represent (only) a duck. What are we to say in these cases?

Usually we do not have access to a painter's intentions independently of what is painted. We typically see what the painter intended to represent in the painting itself. This is possible because there are conventions for repre-sentation, and painters make their intentions public through their use of those conventions.[7] There is an intimate relation between painters' having the intention to depict and their succeeding, more often than not, in using the conventions for representation to the appropriate effect, so that the viewer is licensed to infer the intentions directly from the painting.

This said, the conventions for pictorial representation have a life of their own, and sometimes they continue to do their work in the absence or failure of the relevant intentions.[8] A painting can look like, and function as, a repre-

---

[6] If the composer's score specifies that the tuning nob of a radio be twiddled at random, or if the work includes wind machines or the playing of tapes that were recorded at random, then the parallel might be with accidental photography rather than with painting. But, whether or not photographs are representations, I deny that parts of radio programs are *represented* in John Cage's *Variations IV*, as opposed merely to being included within a performance of the work. I would say the same of a painting employing collage and thereby including prints of photographs taken at random.

[7] See, for example, Wollheim 1970 and 1980, sec. 13; and Hermerén 1977. Wollheim (1987) takes a broad view of intention; for further discussion of his position, see Levinson 1990c and Wollheim 1990. In the same way, one generally knows what a speaker intends to say from what he does say and the context of utterance. A person's mastery of English amounts to a mastery of the conventions for saying what he means.

[8] Again, the same is true of utterances. We can talk of the unintended meanings of an utterance and can concern ourselves with the meanings that might be put on an utterance rather than with what the utterer meant to say.

< 55 >

sentation of something it was not intended to represent. A painting intended to represent Churchill as thoughtful might look like a depiction of Churchill as worried. In light of this, if one sees representation as carried through by the conventions, one might claim that a painting can represent something it was not and could not have been intended to represent.

To my mind, this view forces an unnatural break between the conventions for representation and their intentional use. It is only because the conventions are used successfully for the most part that they are sustained, even if it is true that they are not destroyed by occasional lapses such as those just mentioned. With this point in mind, I prefer to stand by condition (1) and to accommodate counterexamples of the type envisaged by distinguishing, where appropriate, what is represented from what I call the "representational character" of the picture. The representational character of a picture is determined by the painterly conventions for representation, without regard to their intentional use. A painting depicting a dead person might have the representational character of a painting of a wax statue. A painting that fails to represent anything successfully might yet retain a representational character.

Now, I believe that an artistic/aesthetic interest in a painting is typically an interest in its representational character (as given by the conventions of the time at which the artist worked) rather than in what it represents.[9] So I also believe that philosophers who are inclined to dismiss the relevance of painters' intentions as not determinative of an artistic/aesthetic appreciation of those artists' works are on the right track. But I stress that an artistic/aesthetic interest focusing on the representational character of a work presupposes the possibility of pictorial representation in general, because it is only through their being used intentionally and successfully that the conventions for representation are sustained, and it is only where those conventions are a living force that works can be viewed for their representational character.[10] A concern with the representational character of music assumes that there are established conventions for musical depiction, and that in turn supposes that musical representation is possible.

The approach I advocate provides some grip on arguments used by Walton (1990) in defending an anti–intentionalist stance. Walton holds that there can be "natural" (unauthored) stories and pictures. A sentence or de-

[9] Equally, I think that an artistic/aesthetic interest in a literary work is typically an interest in the meanings that can be put on the words in the light of the literary conventions applying to the work, rather than an interest in what the author meant to say.

[10] A more detailed discussion of these matters may be found in Davies 1982 and 1991b, chaps. 8–9.

< 56 >

piction might be produced on the surface of a rock as a result of weathering; a cloud might represent a camel. Because such things lend themselves to use as props in games of make-believe, they are representations in his view: "A thing may be said to have the function of serving a certain purpose, regardless of the intentions of its maker, if things of that *kind* are typically or normally meant by their makers to serve that purpose" (1990, 52).[11]

Walton's critics have objected to his anti–intentionalism, with its tendency to downplay the artist's act of making a depiction. As Jerrold Levinson (1993) puts it, even if such things as weathered rocks might regularly be used as representations are, this is not sufficient to show that they have the function of being representations. Peter Lamarque (1991) suggests that Walton misses the point that those who use such things as props *make* them props (not by painting or fashioning them but by employing them as they do).[12]

In replying to Richard Wollheim (1991), Walton (1991) maintains that, whereas intentions have a determinative role in communication, pictures are not (or need not be) approached as communications. An interest in using something as a prop in a game of make-believe need not presuppose its being intended for that use. This view is correct, I think, while one takes a case-by-case approach. Where the concern lies with the possibility of representation in general, though, it would be a mistake to underrate the social context in which, typically, representations are made, presented, and appreciated. The *practice* of appreciating representations relies—centrally if not exclusively—on conventions and the recognition that they are employed by those who create depictions for appreciation. This is not something Walton is inclined to deny, I think, given the extent to which he stresses in his theory the importance of rules and metarules (these may be implicit and accepted naturally, but often they are not) and also given the place accorded in his account to the importance of socially authorized games of make-believe. So, ultimately, I see his anti–intentionalism as designed to stress the extent to which, as I have put it, the conventions of representation take on a life of their own, allowing us to see a representational character in things not necessarily designed to have that function. That type of anti–intentionalism is compatible, I have suggested, with the account of the first condition I have offered. In my terms, Walton puts the weight on representational character rather than on representation as such. His doing so is compatible with the narrow view of representation as requiring intention, so long as one allows

---

[11] Note that the point is made by Walton about his special class of "representations," but clearly he takes it to apply also to the narrower sphere of depictions.

[12] For similar claims, see Wollheim 1991 and Wolterstorff 1991a and 1991b.

< 57 >

that a concern with representational character presupposes and is founded on a concern with intended representation, for the conventions permitting that concern arise from and are sustained by the narrower sphere in which such intentions are crucial. In Walton's terms, the specification of "kind" in "a thing may be said to have the function of serving a certain purpose if things of that *kind* are typically or normally meant by their makers to serve that purpose" is likely to reintroduce the importance of the intention to represent in general while allowing that, when the kind is established, we might in particular cases relate to it objects that were not intended to instance it.

(2) *Medium/content distinction:* It is a necessary condition for X's representing Y that there be a distinction between the medium of representation and the represented content.

Most writers on the subject of depiction recognize a condition of this sort. To appreciate a representation as such is to acknowledge the painter's achievement in rendering the firm softness of flesh, or the hardness of metal, or the near-transparency of glass, or whatever, in paint. Representations are to be distinguished from mere re-presentations of their subjects. If I copy a chair in making a replica, then I produce another instance of the same type of thing rather than a representation of that type of thing. The chair I make might be representative in the sense of being typical as a token of the type, but that sense of the word is not the one at issue. It is, as it were, the job of the medium, the mode of depiction, to separate the representation from what is represented.

In the case of an ordinary representation, the medium might be transparent to the represented subject. In the old family snapshots we see the people photographed and pay no special regard to the sepia color that is an accident of the process of production. But for art, argues Arthur Danto (1981), the medium of representation is more crucial in that what is represented is never indifferent to the mode of depiction; the use of the medium of representation not only separates the representation from the subject, it allows the depiction to comment on its subject in presenting a way of seeing that subject. An architect's plan of a building does not comment on its own style, but a painting in the style of an architect's plan draws attention to the means of representation. Artworks are "about" the mode of representation as much as they are "about" the subjects represented. Were we to learn that the medium of representation was not what we supposed—that a statue was worked in soap rather than marble, say (Kivy 1984)—the artistically/aesthetically relevant properties of the work would be seen to change.

< 58 >

This point suggests that the subject/medium distinction must be treated with considerable care. Danto is much concerned with the way "mere real things" take on a significance when they become artworks which prevents their collapsing back onto reality. Marcel Duchamp could turn a urinal into an artwork and, as such, *Fountain* comments on the tradition of sculpting in marble in a way a mere urinal (from which *Fountain* might be perceptually indiscernible) does not. An artist might appropriate a "mere real thing" and, through his use of it as an artistic medium, separate it from its real counterparts. Or, to take a different example, John McEnroe might play himself in the film of a fictional story.

Danto's claims might be thought to be exaggerated. If one thinks of the medium of representation as the stuff of representation—paint, stone, and the like—then the use to which Danto puts the subject/medium distinction appears not to sustain the force of his claims. If, however, one accepts that the notion of the medium of representation pays heed not only to the material qualities of the stuff used but also to the histories and traditions of the use of that stuff, or similar stuff, within a particular social context (for example, an art-making as opposed to a urinal-making context), his claims appear to be more plausible. I am sure that it is the latter view he intends. Note that, on this broader reading, the distinction between subject and medium might be established as effectively by the context of presentation as by a difference (if any) in the material natures of subject and medium.

(3) *Resemblance between perceptual experiences:* It is a necessary condition for X's representing Y that there be a resemblance between a person's perceptual experiences of X and of Y, given that the person views X in terms of the applicable conventions.

According to Wollheim, the attempt to represent a man in a painting is successful only if a man can be *seen in* the painting.[13] This position, which I call the seeing-in theory, distinguishes between representational and abstract paintings by reference to the content of the visual experiences to which they give rise. If a likeness of Churchill cannot be found in a painting, then the painting does not depict Churchill. A painting of a blue square with the title "Churchill" does not represent Churchill; a painting of a lamb looking just

[13] Wollheim (1980, essay 5) prefers an account using seeing-in rather than seeing-as; see Hyslop 1986, Schier 1986, and Peacocke 1987 for discussion of the differences and relative merits of the two views. Seeing-as accounts of representation can be found in Aldrich 1963, Scruton 1974, and Hermerén 1969 and 1977; for wider discussion, also see Wilkerson 1973 and 1978, and Hyslop 1983. I pass by the niceties of distinguishing between seeing-in and seeing-as.

< 59 >

like a lamb and with the title "Christ" does not depict Christ, though it might symbolize Christ.[14] A painting of a bulldog with Churchillian facial features and the title "Churchill" would represent Churchill as a bulldog.

Wollheim is wary of "resemblance" accounts of representation, because often these appeal to the idea that representation involves the creation of an illusion, whereas he (rightly) emphasizes that the viewer should remain aware of the painted surface as she has the experience of seeing a represented subject in it. In addition, Wollheim makes no attempt to explain the cause of this experience,[15] so he does not appeal to underlying similarities of structure, light reflection, or whatever, as grounding the resemblance in perceptual experiences. Nevertheless, I do regard Wollheim as insisting on a resemblance between perceptual experiences as a necessary condition for representation, though he holds that this resemblance is apparent only to a viewer familiar with the appropriate conventions for representation, and that usually there are also differences between the perceptual experiences, so that the viewer is unlikely to mistake the one for the other.

Of course, any thing resembles every other in some respect; two paintings resemble each other in being paintings. Resemblance is a three-place, rather than a two-place, relation; resemblances hold between two things within a particular context or framework. In what respect do paintings resemble their subjects rather than each other? It is tempting to say the resemblance lies in the *look* of the painting (as does Blinder 1986) rather than in the features that might concern, say, a physicist. As it stands, this reply will not do, because there are visual respects in which paintings resemble each other more than they resemble their depicted subjects. The relevant resemblance is visual, but it is one that forces itself to our attention as a result of our having a point of view leading us to give salience to some visual features over others. Pictures have roles and functions in our lives; they have a place in certain forms of life, and we view them from a context set by our interest in them as pictures (Novitz 1975; for comment, see Schier 1986). It is through our approaching them in their roles and functions as pictures that we find resemblances between them and what they picture, while we pass over other rela-

---

[14] The point is made in Wollheim 1970, Harris 1973, Novitz 1975, and Hermerén 1977.

[15] This is a point James D. Carney has raised with me in querying whether my view of the seeing-in theory of representation accords with Wollheim's. I go further than Wollheim in this respect, I think: where, for qualified viewers, there are interpersonal standards governing the resemblances that should be experienced, I would be happy to talk of resemblance in some aspect or degree as holding between the depiction and its subject; that is, I see the resemblance between the perceptual experiences of a depiction and of its subject as warranting the attribution of a resemblance between the things themselves, so long as the perceptual experiences are controlled by public conventions, such as those for depiction, and are not merely idiosyncratic.

< 60 >

tions and properties, such as those common to any two pictures, that might strike us as resemblances were our concerns different. As a way of acknowledging this point, one might insist that the resemblance be pictorial, not merely visual. Usually, claims of resemblance presuppose the relevant context. The context depends not just on the physical properties of the painting (and its subject) but also on the role paintings play, or are made to play, in our daily lives.

Though theories of representation according a central place to resemblance often go far beyond this crude account, the basic points made here are widely accepted. It is also generally acknowledged that resemblance is a symmetrical relation, whereas representation is not, and hence that resemblance is not sufficient for representation, even if it is necessary.

A painting might represent a unicorn, but it cannot resemble a unicorn since there are no unicorns.[16] The seeing-in theory might deal with such cases counterfactually: a pictorial representation must resemble the appearance of its subject, were its subject to exist. We can know how unicorns would/ should look from descriptions (and depictions) that lead us to form mental images of them.[17] This leaves a problem, though, for underdescribed objects, for nonexistent subjects having no fixed visual appearance (such as Martians), and for Escher-like impossible objects. For underdescribed objects, any representation consistent with what is specified could picture the object described.[18] Underdescribed nonexistent objects could be dealt with in the same way. But a stronger line of reply may be available, one dealing with depictions of Escher-like impossibilities as well as with unicorns and Martians. If the same brainware is used in perception as in visual imagery, there need be no epistemic difference between our recognizing things we see, our recognizing pictures of things we see, and our recognizing pictures of things we might imagine seeing or have not seen. As Karen Neander puts it, "Our epistemological position is the same whether we are looking at a picture of a unicorn, or a picture of a mammoth, or of our great-grandmother" (1987, 224; see also Danto 1982).

The seeing-in theory might adopt a similar solution to the problem posed by genre paintings (in which, for example, a peasant is represented though

---

[16] Of course, it might present a perceptual experience significantly like those presented by other *pictures* of unicorns.

[17] The point is made in Ziff 1960, Hermerén 1969 and 1977, Novitz 1975, and Danto 1982. For further discussion, see Schier 1986.

[18] Any drawing of a man would serve to illustrate a passage in a novel in which all that is indicated is that a man called (Novitz 1975). For further discussion, see Novitz 1982, and for a critique, see Pollard 1984; also see Peetz 1987.

< 61 >

no actual, live or dead, person is depicted). The notion of pictorial similarity would be overworked, though, if it were used to explain how a painting might depict Cleopatra while it more obviously resembles Ellie Denood, the artist's model who posed for the work. In these cases the work's title, along with the artist's intention, performs an important function in disambiguating the subject of representation as the Queen of the Nile rather than as the artist's model in fancy dress. Even if the seeing-in theory gives crucial emphasis to the place of an experience of perceptual resemblance where representation succeeds, it must also allow the relevance of elements not perceived in the work, such as the work's title. With this conceded, it also can be allowed that the title might function in determining what is represented in a genre painting or in illustrations of mythical stories and fantastic creatures. So there is no reason, I take it, to think that the cases described by Danto (1981, 1–2) are counterexamples to the seeing-in theory of representation.[19]

Two types of case might be thought to raise special problems for the seeing-in theory's adherence to condition (3): (i) that in which a subject is realistically depicted but in which no subject can be seen, either because (a) the subject itself is abstract (for example, a closely cropped photorealistic depiction of a jumble of polystyrene beads) or because (b) the subject is unrecognizable (for example, a view of the fibers of a piece of cloth as they appear through a microscope);[20] (ii) that in which the artist abstracts from the subject depicted to the point at which the subject can be seen in the painting only if one has knowledge of the process of creation or other "external" information. A work in which the process of abstraction can be seen directly is Henri Matisse's bronze statues of a woman's back (*The Back*, 1929): the first statue is realistic, the second less so, and the third is yet more abstract and idealized. The process of abstraction might be recorded, if at all, in the finished work or, more likely, in sketches and studies for the fin-

---

[19] His cases are ones in which visually similar, uniformly red-covered canvases are pictorially distinct in that some represent different subjects (the minimalist work titled "Red Square;" "Red Table Cloth," by an embittered disciple of Henri Matisse), others refer to different subjects without representing them ("Kierkegaard's Mood" by a Danish portraitist; a clever bit of Moscow landscape, "Red Square;" another work represents the Red Sea after it has closed over the Egyptians pursuing Moses and his tribe; "Nirvana," a metaphysical work based on the idea that the Samsara world is called red dust by its deprecators), another is abstract (with the title "Untitled"), and a final one is not yet a painting (Giorgione's canvas grounded by him in red lead as a preparation for his work).

[20] I mean (b) to be distinct from "hidden man pictures," for example, in which the lines that together depict a man are lost among many similar lines having no depictive function. In type-(b) cases, the difficulty of recognition results more from the oddity of the perspective, shading, magnification, or coloration than from the obscuring effect of irrelevant doodles or other representations.

< 62 >

ished work. A good example, perhaps, is Piet Mondrian's *Broadway Boogie-woogie*. The painting can be seen as a stylized ("jazzy"), bird's-eye view of city streets, but someone ignorant of the work's title, or not knowing that "Broadway" names a street, might easily take the painting to be abstract, especially given Mondrian's stylistic predilections.

Such cases appear to be problematic for the seeing-in theory of representation for this reason: the theory appears to equate in condition (3) the production of a representation with the possibility of its being recognized as such, and cases like the ones given suggest that we might always prise these two apart by presenting examples in which something is depictive but is not immediately or easily seen to be so. The same difficulty might also be indicated by a third case, (iii), in which a person finds a likeness to her beloved in a pattern of lines which, to everyone else, seems abstract. How can one admit under the theory cases such as those of the first two types while excluding fantasies of the third kind?

As a first line of defense, appeal can be made to condition (1) as a way of excluding many cases of the (iii) type, and some cases of the (i) and (ii) types can be met by allowing the title of the painting to be considered as identifying a subject that then shows in the painting. Not only can the title of a work disambiguate the subject represented, it can also sometimes disambiguate the type of painting, allowing it to be seen (correctly) as representational rather than as abstract. Mondrian's title is not something independent of the work, it is part of the work and invites one to see a jazzy drawing of streets if one can. Also, it can be pointed out that the stipulation in condition (3) need not be read as requiring that a depictive painting be seen as representational on every occasion or by every viewer. These strategies, however, are unlikely to dispose of all the cases that are problematic in the ways listed here.

A more successful approach to the indicated difficulties might argue that resemblance is a natural, primitive relation between perceptual experiences. Were this not so it would be difficult to explain the success with which very young children are taught the meanings of words through the use of picture books, or to explain the perceptual abilities of nonhuman animals faced with images. That said, though, resemblance is a relation that might be generated within all sorts of contexts and sets of conventions. For example, there are many systems of cartographic projection. Whether a person sees a resemblance between the world and any given map of it depends not only on what that person knows of the world but also on his familiarity with the system of projection employed. In the same way, what a viewer can see in a painting depends on her grasp of the conventions for depiction as employed in the

< 63 >

given work. This grasp need not always be readily describable, since it is usually founded on practical skill and experience rather than on discursive explanation and analysis. Nevertheless, it is through such conventions that we see of a painting of a horse in motion that it is just that, and not a painting of a statue of a horse in motion, or a painting of some unknown horselike creature only one centimeter tall, or a painting of a stationary horse magically frozen in mid-gallop. A painting must be viewed in light of the conventions of representation applying to it, and these are determined by many factors: its period, the individual style of the artist, and so on.[21] When we know that a painting is, say, cubist in style, we may be able to see in it things that otherwise we would not see and thereby come to observe that it is depictive.

This reply does much to explicate the notion of seeing-in in a way that removes the force of many of the aforementioned counterexamples. The seeing-in theory, as I present it, need not hold that all resemblances are immediately given to perceptual experience as such. When viewed in light of the appropriate conventions (including ones taking account of the circumstances of production), subjects can be seen in (i)- and (ii)-type paintings after all. Or, if subjects cannot be found when the work is viewed in terms of the conventions and rules that apply to it, the painting is revealed as abstract. A work such as Theo van Doesburg's *Cow* might carry the process of abstraction so far that it properly is to be seen as abstract, even if the artist worked from a cow and began with representational sketches. Most of the mistakes made by viewers can be explained as involving a lack of knowledge of the appropriate conventions. Examples of type (iii) differ from type (i) and (ii) examples because, in their case, the relevant conventions do not reveal a depicted subject (or do not reveal the subject the cross-eyed lover finds there).

To deal with all the problems that might arise, it is necessary that the theory allow as sometimes relevant to a work's appreciation information beyond a familiarity with the history of art, traditions of representation, traditions of choice of subjects, and idiosyncrasies of individual style and of the artist's psychological makeup. Considerations of these sorts leave untouched some type (i) examples, such as that in which the artist's photorealist style is applied for the first time to a beach subject, which happens to be a square meter of sand, depicted on a square meter of canvas. To cover such cases, the history of production of the particular work must also be counted

---

[21] Some, such as Grigg (1984), who argue for the cultural and historical relativity of depictive realism, see their claims as rejecting the idea that resemblance is natural. I am suggesting that this conclusion is not entailed by the relativization of standards for resemblance to periods and styles.

< 64 >

as relevant to the recognition of its depicted content. Those who hold to the seeing-in theory would be happy, I think, to concede the place of a knowledge of such factors as sometimes necessary for the proper categorization and appreciation of a painting.

Walton regards his own theory of depiction as compatible, even complementary, with the seeing-in theory (1991; for detail see 1992). He objects that Wollheim leaves the notion of seeing-in unanalyzed and implies that his own account of the role of make-believe in the perceptual experience of paintings might supply the kind of analysis he finds lacking in Wollheim's thesis. But Walton is inclined to reject resemblance, or "matching," as a necessary condition for depiction (see 1990, 108–109, 298–324), though the notion retains some importance in his account.

I find Walton's views on these matters to be obscure. He is inclined to regard conventions as arbitrary and matching as entirely nonconventional, so he does not appear to allow for the position I have just sketched in which natural tendencies might be structured by conventions while retaining a nonarbitrary character. He stresses (1990, 304–307), as I think he should, similarities between the way we look at paintings and the way we might look at their (actual) subjects rather than similarities between the subject and its depiction. Sometimes, though, he relies on similarities of the latter kind in developing his view: for example, in explaining the possibility of mistakes about what is depicted by reference to visual resemblances between a thing and a depiction of it (1990, 309) and in discussing one type of realism (1990, 328).

Some of Walton's critics think that his notion of make-believe fails to capture the irreducibly perceptual experience that is central to the notion of depiction in the seeing-in theory.[22] The objection comes to this: the suitability of depictions for serving as props in games of make-believe usually depends on a recognition of their depictive character, so depiction cannot be analyzed as a thing's serving as a prop in such a game. Even if the recognition of a depiction as such involves the imagination no less than does the playing of games, the role of the imagination is not identical in these two cases. Moreover, Walton's theory does not explain, as the seeing-in theory claims to do, our ability to "transfer" the skills involved in appreciating representations as such. If a person can see what one picture represents, then she also can see what many other pictures with different subjects represent.[23] The

[22] See Hyslop 1983, Peacocke 1987, 391–392, Wollheim 1986, 1987, and 1991, Currie 1991a, Novitz 1991, and Budd 1992. For discussion of Novitz, see Burton 1991.
[23] See Wollheim 1991; also see the discussion later in this chapter on "umbrella" conventions.

< 65 >

recognition of depictions relies on a fundamental, generalizable skill that cannot be explained by reference to any tendency we might have to engage in games of make-believe structured by rules or conventions inclining to the arbitrary.

Because I tend to agree with such criticisms, I do not see Walton's theory as replacing, or even as rounding out, the seeing-in theory. If the seeing-in theory is flawed, Walton's theory will not rescue it. I argue later in this chapter that the distinctive element in Walton's theory—his analysis of the experience of art in terms of the notion of make-believe—does not have the explanatory power for music he claims.

I turn now to the semantic theory of representation, which I regard as the major rival to the seeing-in theory. The semantic theory, through the person of Nelson Goodman, the advocate of its strongest version, appears to reject condition (3), and it is primarily the disagreements between the theories over the necessity of this condition for depiction that distinguishes them.

Goodman characterizes representation as involving denotation in accordance with the conventions of a (pictorial) symbol system. Pictorial depiction involves denotation (X represents Y) and description (X represents Y as Z). In other words, pictorial representation serves the same function as is primary within language. Pictorial description is distinguished from language by reference to features of the types of symbol schemes they employ. In paintings, by contrast with spoken and written languages, the symbol scheme is dense (syntactic elements and semantic units are not discrete in that they always admit of intermediates) and relatively replete (every element might have significance) (see 1968, 225–226).[24] But these two different types of symbol schemes, each in its own way, can be used to the same purpose—to denote and to characterize what is denoted.

Goodman's concern lies with a broad conception of representation—standing for, or symbolizing, as well as depicting. In the context of that broader concern, it would be quite reasonable that he reject resemblance as a necessary condition for representation. Many symbols do not depict what they denote. Goodman also aims to characterize the narrower sense of the term "representation" as it is used concerning paintings, however. He says, "What I am considering here is pictorial representation, or depiction, and the comparable representation that may occur in other arts" (1968, 4, n. 1)

---

[24] Peacocke (1987, 405–406) presents a counterexample to suggest that these conditions are neither necessary nor sufficient for picturing. Bach (1970) offers a different account of the characteristics of picturing symbol schemes and is criticized by Harris (1973). Howard (1975) discusses challenges, such as Bach's and Harris's, to the view that density is a characteristic feature of pictorial symbol schemes.

< 66 >

and adds, "If pictures in a commandeered museum are used by a briefing officer to stand for enemy emplacements, the pictures do not thereby represent these emplacements. To represent, a picture must function as a pictorial symbol; that is, function in a system such that what is denoted depends solely upon the pictorial properties of the symbol" (1968, 41–42). Goodman notes (1968, 30) that, if Wellington is a soldier, a picture that represents Wellington also represents a soldier, but it need not pictorially represent Wellington as a soldier, since Wellington might be pictured in civilian dress; the point is missed in Harris 1973. When he focuses on pictorial depiction, on the narrower sense of representation, Goodman remains adamant in denying that resemblance is a necessary condition for representation. He holds that Christ might be pictorially depicted as a lamb (and not merely be symbolized by a pictured lamb). He concludes:

> This all adds up to open heresy. Descriptions are distinguished from depictions not through being more arbitrary but through belonging to articulate rather than to dense schemes; and words are more conventional than pictures only if conventionality is construed in terms of differentiation rather than artifactuality. Nothing here depends upon the internal structure of a symbol; for what describes in some systems may depict in others. Resemblance disappears as a criterion of representation, and structural similarity as a requirement upon notational or any other languages. The often stressed distinction between iconic and other signs becomes transient and trivial; thus does heresy breed iconoclasm. (1968, 230–231)

At first glance it appears that Goodman equivocates between the narrow and broad senses of the term "represent" in holding, for example, that Christ can be represented as a lamb (see Harris 1973). It might appear that Goodman presupposes, rather than analyzes, the notion of pictorial content and is concerned instead with the use of that content in a symbolic manner. In this vein, David Novitz (1975) suggests that Goodman does not distinguish clearly or often enough between one thing's picturing another and its being used in a way not depending on its pictorial character to denote that other thing. Some such view leads to the claim (in Beardsley 1978 and Margolis 1981, for instance) that a picture might represent quite independently of its being used to denote. These criticisms misrepresent Goodman's position, however.

Goodman's concern lies with pictorial elements, construed neither as a represented subject nor as paint marks but as elements in pictorial symbol

< 67 >

systems—pictorial symbol systems being those marked by syntactic density and repleteness. He presupposes, not the semantic *content* of a painting, but the *syntactic features* that secure denotation in pictorial symbol systems. For any painting, there is a pictorial symbol system that maps features of the painting onto almost any subject. A painting representing a lamb under one pictorial symbol system could, under another, represent Christ. The mayor of a village might be represented as the village idiot. Just what is represented is relative to the symbol scheme applying to the work, and whether or not the representation is a pictorial one depends on the syntactic character of that symbol scheme (see Goodman 1978a, 160). In considering such cases as Christ's being represented as a lamb, after all, Goodman is concerned with the narrow sense of representation as applied to pictures. His point is that a painting might pictorially represent Christ, or represent a lamb, depending on the pictorial symbol scheme under which it was created.[25] Where the pictorial symbol scheme maps the picture to its subject in a non-standard fashion, the representation is not a realistic one. The realism of a picture is a function of (no more than) the familiarity of the pictorial symbol scheme it employs.

> Almost any picture may represent almost anything; that is, given picture and object there is usually a system of representation, a plan of correlation, under which the picture represents the object. How correct the picture is under that system depends upon how accurate is the information about the object that is obtained by reading the picture according to that system. But how literal or realistic the picture is depends upon how standard the system is. If representation is a matter of information, realism is a matter of habit. (Goodman 1968, 38; endorsed in Manns 1971 and Grigg 1984)

Although Goodman can avoid the allegation that his theory deals only with the wider notion of representation, his treatment of the narrower notion is unclear in many respects. Because he is reluctant to discuss the details of the symbol systems actually used by artists, he often seems to make claims about what might be the case as if they are claims about what is the case. For example, in the picture (apparently) of a lamb, Christ is not pictorially

---

[25] So a picture might represent X under one pictorial symbol scheme, whereas it appears to depict Y when viewed as if falling under a different pictorial symbol scheme. Where the latter scheme is dominant, but we know that the former was used, we might feel inclined to say that the picture depicts X as Y.

< 68 >

represented unless the pictorial symbol scheme of the work is nonstandard.[26] Moreover, Goodman does not discuss how many pictorial symbol schemes are in common use, or how they are established. According to Richard Martin (1981), Goodman sometimes writes as if they are unique to particular works, sometimes as if they are very general. It is not clear if Goodman thinks each style or school employs a distinctive pictorial symbol system, or that individual artists do, or that symbol schemes are unique to particular works, or that there are common features to a wide spread of pictorial symbol schemes, and so on. In fact, according to James Ackerman (1981; also see Carrier 1974), he tends to ignore both artists and viewers.

Given his account of pictorial realism, it is perhaps not surprising that Goodman rejects the relevance of resemblance in pictorial depiction. What can be "seen in" a picture is far from clear, he says (1970a). He attacks the notion of fidelity in perspectival representation (1968,10–19).[27] His nominalism leads him to reject the idea of resemblances that might exist prior to, and independently of, any arbitrary symbol scheme.[28] For Goodman, the connection between a painting and what it pictorially represents is no less arbitrary than is that between a word and what it denotes (Carrier 1974), because, as a nominalist, he treats talk of properties as no more than a shorthand way of referring to "labels" (that is, predicates).

Goodman attacks the "absolutist" account of resemblance as a two-place relation: "An object resembles itself to the maximum degree but rarely represents itself. . . . A Constable painting of Marlborough Castle is more like any other picture than it is like the Castle, yet it represents the Castle and not another picture—not even the closest copy" (1968, 4–5). Some commentators remark unfavorably on Goodman's "essentialist" approach to resemblance.[29] No doubt they do so because it is plain that most of those who argue for the central place of resemblance in representation recognize that it is to be treated as a three-place relation, as relative to a context. I have allowed that a proponent of the seeing-in theory of representation is likely to

---

[26] Bach (1970) suggests that Goodman "slipped" in saying that *what* is represented depends on the pictorial properties of the symbol. According to Bach, Goodman should say that *how* the subject is represented depends on this.

[27] For criticism, see Presley 1970; also see Peacocke 1987, 408–409. For another version of the Goodmanian argument, see Wartofsky 1978; for a reply to Wartofsky, see Goodman 1978a; and for further comment, see Gibson 1971 and Carrier 1980.

[28] For discussion of the way Goodman's nominalism affects his theory of representation, see O'Neil 1971, Arrell 1987, and Goodrich 1988. For Goodman's rejection of Arrell's own theory, see Goodman 1988.

[29] See Manns 1971, Harris 1973, Pole 1974, and Novitz 1975.

< 69 >

agree with Goodman that there is no "innocent eye"[30] and that resemblance is apparent only to someone familiar with the relevant conventions of representation. Equally, such a theorist will agree with Goodman that representation is an asymmetric relation, and hence not reducible to resemblance, and that the directional quality of representation arises from the operation of conventions that might define a symbol scheme. So it is not surprising that these writers regard many of Goodman's critical comments as beside the point.

Goodman does appeal to the notion of resemblance, if mainly in a negative fashion, as the quotation in the previous paragraph testifies. Sometimes he suggests that a suitably relativized view of the resemblance relation would be congenial to his position: "The most we can say is that among pictures that represent actual objects, degree of realism correlates to some extent with degree of similarity of picture to object. But we must beware of supposing that similarity constitutes any firm, invariant criterion of realism; for similarity is relative, variable, culture-dependent" (1970b, 20); "To Beardsley's proposal to distinguish depiction—or what we usually consider to be 'naturalistic' or 'realistic' depiction—in terms of resemblance between picture and pictured, I have little objection so long as we bear in mind that resemblance is a variable and relative matter that as much follows as guides customs of representation" (1978a, 169). These remarks suggest that Goodman's target is not solely an absolutist view of resemblance but also an account of resemblance (or pictorial realism) that conceives the relation as somehow natural, not as purely conventional. If "X resembles Y" is supposed to indicate a nonarbitrary relation natural to our mode of perception, then Goodman denies that any such relation exists. If, on the other hand, "X resembles Y" indicates a relation established arbitrarily and depending on a symbol scheme, Goodman can countenance it. He might, that is, allow a conventionalist, as opposed to a naturalist, account of resemblance.

One author who has written on the subject of musical representation is Jenefer Robinson. She approaches the topic through a consideration of the two theories I have been discussing. She suggests that "the semantic and seeing-in theories, far from being rivals, require and support each other" (1987, 178). Is it the case, then, that the seeing-in and semantic theories are reconcilable after all?

On one analysis of the term "resemblance" (what I have called the conventionalist reading), the two theories might be seen as complementary, but on the other reading (what I have called the naturalist reading) they are not.

---

[30] As do Hermerén (1969 and 1977), Wollheim (1970), Manns (1971), and Pole (1974).

< 70 >

Someone who accepts that resemblances are achieved within, and only within, the confines of an arbitrary symbol scheme might assimilate the two theories.[31] On the other hand, someone who sees resemblance as involving a natural relation, albeit one often (or perhaps always) subject to structuring by conventions, so that it might not be automatically recognizable as such, could not accept the semantic theory of representation as presented by Goodman.[32] Such a person would believe that the recognition of resemblance might depend on perceptual abilities and skills, and on interests that direct those abilities, while denying that resemblance is purely arbitrary.

In defense of this second view, the following point is made: for some systems, no amount of familiarity with the system will allow one to see the subject in its "representations." To reverse the point, even if resemblance is always structured by conventions to some extent, and even if the immediate recognition of resemblance often presupposes familiarity with those conventions, some sets of conventions might engage more directly and readily with our natural (perhaps biologically determined) interests and modes of perceiving; the required familiarity might be governed by nature rather than nurture, hard-wired rather than acquired. Some conventions for mapping depictions onto subjects will be transparent, as it were, whereas others cannot but be opaque, no matter how often they are applied and examined. Nonhuman animals can recognize resemblances sometimes (not only between objects but also between photographs and their subjects), though their modes of perception do not encode arbitrarily established symbol schemes of the kind envisaged by Goodman. For human animals, it might be held that the difference in significance and response between an encounter with the words "naked man" and with da Vinci's famous anatomical representation of a naked man cannot be explained solely by reference to the amount of information presented or to differences in the symbol schemes employed. One might argue that a painting or photograph can be pornographic, as a detailed verbal description of what it depicts is not, in virtue of the natural power and immediacy of the visual over the verbal.

One way of approaching the distinction between the semantic and the seeing-in theories of representation might be as follows: We discriminate

[31] For discussion, see O'Neil (1971), Manns (1971), and Arrell (1987), all of whom object to the inconsistency in Goodman's apparent rejection of resemblance when a conventionalist account is possible.

[32] Such a view is presented in Rogers 1965, Hermerén 1969, Presley 1970, Blocker 1974, Pole 1974, Novitz 1975 and 1977, Wollheim 1980, essay 5; Danto 1982 and 1986; Blinder 1983 and 1986, Schier 1986, Neander 1987, and Peacocke 1987. Also see Maynard 1972, Gombrich 1981, and, speaking for Wittgenstein, Carney 1981.

< 71 >

between representational depictions and abstract paintings. In the seeing-in theory, according to which the experience of a resemblance is natural (if conventionally structured), this distinction marks a difference in kind.[33] By contrast, according to the (purely) conventional view of resemblance, as in the semantic theory, the difference, if it is to be acknowledged at all, is merely one of degree; at best there is an arbitrarily divided continuum, and not a difference in kind.[34] Now, the borderline between abstract and representational paintings is indistinct, but from that it does not follow that no boundary exists. It does not seem merely to be a reflection of arbitrary conventions and historical accident that we teach children with pictures of one kind rather than another—that we show them man-looking pictures, not lamb-looking pictures, when we first teach them that Christ was a man.

A theory of pictorial depiction that cannot provide a distinction between abstract and representational paintings is likely to be unsatisfying (however illuminating is its discussion of the broader sense of the term "representation"). Now, the semantic theory cannot draw that distinction by appeal to a notion of (natural, but structured) resemblance. It does so by reference to the familiarity of the symbol system employed, though I doubt, for the reasons indicated earlier, that this approach can sustain the explanatory burden placed on it. The difference between the two cases is marked in the semantic

---

[33] It must be admitted that sometimes instances of these different kinds might *look* identical. I discuss some examples later but here mention one drawn to my attention by James D. Carney. Accept (if only for the sake of the argument) that Kasimir Malevich's *Suprematist Painting* depicts gravity-free, geometrically shaped objects in absolute space. Both Wollheim (1973) and Walton (1990, 54–56) claim of the representationality of this work that it shows that most "abstract" paintings are depictive. I disagree. Not all look-alikes share the same artistically significant properties; a work might be seemingly identical in its appearance to Malevich's and yet be abstract, I hold. What the case shows, I maintain, is the role played by conventions of style and genre in securing representation. A look-alike painting properly to be located in a different style or genre need not be depictive. It might be the case that, in such a work, one plane or surface is experienced as in front of another. But whether the work depicts, as well as exhibiting, this relation, as does Malevich's, depends on its meeting *all* the conditions for representation, and there is no reason to assume that it must do so. I would make this further point: depictions that are sophisticated in this manner presuppose and call on conventions for "realistic" representation that must already be well established through the creation of works unequivocably representational of their nonabstract subjects.

[34] Carrier (1974) sees it as a virtue of Goodman's theory that it eliminates the "tiresome and difficult" distinction between abstractions and depictions, but Carrier's seems to be a point about the broad notion of representation. As a possible inconsistency on Goodman's part, Carrier notes that Goodman sometimes seems to acknowledge a distinction between the abstract and the depictive, as when he says "a passage or picture may exemplify or express without describing or representing, and even without being a description or representation at all" (Goodman 1968, 92). Like Goodman, Carrier doubts that conventions can be explained by reference to innate characteristics of the human organism; see Carrier 1980.

< 72 >

theory by ways the elements of the symbol scheme are used, or by the way different elements within the symbol scheme come into play. But even if this were to be accepted, the distinction thus allowed must be arbitrary, and there remains a problem in explaining just why we are inclined to draw it where we do. Even if different cultures employ different conventions for representation, so that it might not always be possible for a person from one culture to recognize another culture's depictions as such, I suspect that most cultures recognize a difference between abstract and depictive art and, more to the point, draw that distinction at roughly equivalent points.[35] If this, admittedly speculative, claim is true, it is difficult to agree with the semantic theory's analysis; it is difficult to deny that some nonarbitrary type of relation, the relation captured by the notion of resemblance in the naturalist version of the seeing-in theory, underpins the distinction.

The difference between the two theories might now be glossed this way: The semantic theory allows that representation is possible wherever there are rules mapping elements of a picture to a scene, whether or not those rules are such as to generate a perceptible likeness; the perceptibility of a likeness is said to be merely a function of the viewer's familiarity with the rules in question. By contrast, the seeing-in theory holds that it is crucial for representation that a likeness between the perceptual experience of the picture and its depicted subject be generated, even if it is true that this likeness need be apparent only to someone familiar with the rules in question. For some sets of rules, no amount of familiarity would help one to perceive a likeness between the appearance of the depiction and of the depicted subject, though familiarity might make it easier to work out what it is that the rules map the picture onto. In this case, the rules are not those of a representational symbol system. The symbol system shares its syntactic structure with representational ones, but that, in common with its intentional use, is not sufficient to generate depictions. Abstract paintings might be produced from the application of symbol-systems of the same syntactic types as those giving rise to depictions (though not all abstractions need be created in accordance with the conventions of some symbol system). The border between representations and abstractions cannot be established by reference to the syntactic character of the symbol systems under which they are produced. The borderline between representations and abstractions is hazy and disputed, because not all viewers have the same experience and education in recognizing like-

---

[35] Sparshott (1974) notes that we can study Indian literature in translation but not Indian painting. Whatever the difficulties of understanding Chinese paintings, they differ strikingly from the greater difficulties of learning the Chinese languages.

< 73 >

nesses. Nevertheless, that vague borderline marks a distinction of importance to us, and no amount of familiarity with some symbol systems would allow us to remove the border altogether or to shift it to a radically different place within the continuum of depictions/abstractions.

So far I have ignored some problems that might be posed for the semantic theory: (i) the representation of nonexistent subjects, (ii) the representation of subjects other than those modeled, (iii) possible mismatches between the represented subject and the title of a work, and (iv) clarification of the central appeal to denotation.

(i) How does the semantic theory of representation deal with those cases in which something is pictured (a unicorn, say) but nothing is denoted since what is depicted does not exist? It does so by allowing that "X represents Y" does not entail "there is a Y that X denotes." Where there is null denotation, rather than construing "represents" as involving a two-place relation, one should treat it as an unbreakable one-place predicate or class term, like "desk" or "table" (Goodman 1968, 21).[36] In the case of pictorial representations of nonexistent subjects, we should speak of the type of picture—"unicorn-depicting picture," for instance—rather than of representation of the kind that implies denoting. "A picture must denote a man to represent him, but need not denote anything to be a man-representation" (Goodman 1968, 25).

Now though, it seems after all that denotation does not lie at the heart of representation. Goodman attempts to retrieve his theory as follows. Where a picture denotes a man and depicts him, denotation runs from the picture to the man. Where a man-picture does not denote a man, there is "converse denotation." In such a case denotation runs from the description ("man-picture") to the picture (Goodman 1970a). Denotation lies at the heart of representation, but it does not always move from the picture to its subject (for critical discussion, see Dempster 1989).

(ii) What of the case in which a painting represents Cleopatra though it bears the likeness of Ellie Denood, the model who sat for it? The semantic theory accommodates this case much as the seeing-in theory does, by giving a central place to the picture's title (see Bennett 1974, n. 16) as specifying what a picture denotes. Very often the title is a guide to the symbol system employed.

(iii) It is always possible that there be a mismatch between the title of a

---

[36] Later, Goodman concedes that it was a mistake to characterize the predicate as unbreakable, for the predicate is friable if, as he accepts, "X is a Pickwickian-clown-picture" entails "X is a clown-picture" (1970a, 564; also see 1978a, 154).

< 74 >

depiction and its content. A painting that is unambiguously depictive might have a title suggesting that it is abstract: for example, James Whistler's portrait of his mother, *Study in Gray* (see Savedoff 1989). Or an unambiguously depictive painting might have a title suggesting that it is depictive, yet the title and the subject depicted do not match in any recognizable way: for instance, René Magritte's *L'Arc de Triomphe* plainly depicts a tree. Or a painting might be abstract and yet have a title implying that it is depictive: for example, Franz Kline's *Cardinal* or Jack Smith's *Sea Movement* (see Robinson 1987). The seeing-in theory of representation deals with such cases by giving representational primacy to what can be seen in the painting over its title and, in doing so, would appear to reflect the way such paintings are properly to be approached and appreciated. By contrast, to the extent that the semantic theory of representation accords primacy to the title, it appears to be at a loss to explain the experience provided by such paintings and the descriptions offered of them.

Goodman might be able to account for such cases by suggesting that they arise from a tension between the pictorial elements of the symbol system of the painting and the nonpictorial role played by the work's title. John Bennett (1974) develops such a line: a picture is a predicate conjoined with a label; whether a picture is a so-and-so-representing picture is a matter of whether its extension (as a predicate) contains so-and-sos, and this may be entirely independent of what is designated by the label (in this case, the title of the picture). Now, titles, even if they contribute to the function of the pictorial symbol, do not do so entirely on their own. The semantic theory, even if it allows an important place to a painting's title, accords that importance only as something conjoined with the painting's pictorial content, as given by the pictorial symbol system employed in the picture.[37] So, many of the aforementioned examples could be accommodated by the semantic theory. It need not claim that the title always takes representational preeminence.

It might be thought, though, that this reply is inadequate. It does not explain why the contents of the paintings in question should be more important than their titles. The reliance in the seeing-in theory on the central place of resemblance between perceptual experiences allows for an account of the prioritization occurring in such cases. The semantic theory can offer no explanation of that sort. Even if it explains (in terms of the elements and function of the relevant symbol scheme) why titles alone do not secure pictorial

---

[37] Even if, usually, the title is a guide to what is depicted within the symbol system employed, it does not determine which symbol system that is, and so the two might come into conflict.

< 75 >

representation, it does not explain the basis for any such ranking of elements with regard to their importance in contributing toward pictorial representation. But at this point an advocate of the semantic theory might employ an ad hominem argument against his opponent. In at least one type of case the seeing-in theory gives primary (if not exclusive) importance to the title of a painting: that in which the painting represents Cleopatra rather than Ellie Denood, though it bears the likeness of Ellie, who may not have looked at all like the Queen of Nile. On the matter of the relation between a work's pictorial content and its title, then, each theory allows dominance to the former over the latter in some cases and each reverses this order in others.

(iv) There are larger and deeper problems faced by the semantic theory of representation, which I mention without discussing. As many writers have observed, Goodman does not analyze the crucial notion of denotation; it operates as a primitive in his theory.[38] The failure to analyze the notion of denotation becomes problematic because the use made of that notion in the discussion of representations of fictions is so unconvincing. It looks as if there must be a prior grasp of the sense of a term such as "unicorn" from which derives our ability to classify pictures as "of a unicorn," yet Goodman is committed to denying any such prior semantic content.[39] Goodman's nominalist commitments lead him to reject analyses appealing to semantic considerations in general, and to intensional concepts in particular, but it is debatable that this permits him to provide a satisfactory account of the concepts in question.[40]

I have additional reservations about the claim—that depictions primarily serve an assertoric function—made by some who subscribe to the semantic theory. In a development of Goodman's theory, Bennett (1974) characterizes pictures as sentences or speech acts that may be true or false. Sören Kjörup (1974 and 1978) offers a speech act analysis, arguing that pictures can be and are used to make various illocutionary acts such as asserting or warning.[41] The relevant objections to this approach were indicated in the previous

---

[38] See Presley 1970, O'Neil 1971, Pole 1974, Beardsley 1978, Robinson 1979, Martin 1981, and Walton 1990, 121–125. One writer who discusses the Fregean, Quinean, and Kripkean notions of reference and denotation within the context of Goodman's theory of representation is Robinson (1978 and 1979). She suggests that Goodman's account of depiction can be accommodated to none of these theories.

[39] The issue is raised in Wollheim 1970 and discussed in O'Neil 1971, Savile 1971, Peltz 1972, Scruton 1974, and Peetz 1987. For a defense of the Goodmanian perspective, see Carrier 1974. For comment on both Goodman and Peltz, see Dempster 1989.

[40] See Presley 1970, O'Neil 1971, Beardsley 1978, and Dempster 1989.

[41] Goodman, it should be noted, does not present the theory in this way. He denies that paintings are usefully to be compared to sentences except in respect of denotation. They are nonde-

< 76 >

chapter. In brief, pictures provide no clear distinction between moods and parts of speech—between asserting that Napoleon looked worried, asking if Napoleon looked worried, musing that Napoleon looked worried, denying that Napoleon looked worried. And it is doubtful that a symbol scheme can properly be described as functioning to denote and describe unless it marks such distinctions. There is no basis for assimilating "X represents Y as Z" (as in, The picture represents Napoleon as worried) with "X asserts that Y is Z." Neither can one easily assimilate the notion of truth to life to that of linguistic truth. That the former might apply to pictorial representation (as a measure of the realism of the depiction) does not show that the latter might do so also.

The arguments offered here in favor of condition (3) are suggestive rather than decisive. I suspect that the semantic theory could be made more attractive by a much more detailed analysis than is usually offered of the elements of the symbol schemes used, their relations, the point of their use, and their connection to the perceptual equipment and interests of those who use them. All in all, I am inclined to prefer the version of the seeing-in theory that treats as a necessary condition for representation a resemblance between one's seeing X in a representation and one's seeing X, provided that it also allows that the "naturalness" of this element is tempered, structured, doctored, and shaped by conventions that have varied in their detail from place to place and time to time.

The fourth condition for representation concerns the recognition of a representation as such. This is appropriate if we accept the seeing-in theory, since in that view there is an intimate connection between something's being a representation and its being perceptible as one.

(4) *Conventions:* Commonly (perhaps always), X represents Y within the context of conventions (that might be regarded as constituting a symbol system), so that the recognition of Y in X presupposes the viewer's familiarity with those conventions and his viewing X in terms of them in perceiving Y in X.

---

clarative; they cannot be assessed for truth, though they are subject to a more general notion of rightness; they cannot be resolved into wordlike elements that make up sentencelike sequences (1978a, 169, 178–179). That is, though Goodman holds that language and depiction might serve the same function—denotation and the characterization of the subject denoted—he describes the respective kinds of symbol schemes through which this function is realized as importantly different. In particular, pictorial elements must be "dense" and "replete," whereas the elements of language are "articulated." Because pictorial elements are dense, there is no equivalent to the sentence's full stop; depictive significance flows from top to bottom and side to side across the entire picture, and every element might have pictorial significance.

< 77 >

Enough has already been said concerning conditions (1), (2), and (3) to show that, even if representation results from the intentional creation and use of resemblance filtered through a medium, in most (perhaps all) cases the success of this use supports, and relies in its turn, on conventions with which the viewer is expected to be versed. For example, the conventions for spatial representation differ between Chinese and Western art traditions, the latter relying on projection toward a vanishing point and the former depending more on the vertical extension of the pictorial plane. Moreover, the conventions in questions must be sufficiently broad to encompass not only differences and changes in traditions and styles between places, cultures, and times but also the idiosyncratic features of the individual artist's personal style, as well as the particular circumstances of creation relevant to the piece in question, as was made apparent in the discussion of condition (2). The viewer's familiarity with the relevant conventions is normally grounded in direct acquaintance with appropriate works and genres rather than in "book knowledge." As a result, it is not always the case that the viewer is skilled in articulating the knowledge she possesses of the conventions; the important test of her knowledge is the degree of her practical skills in identifying depictions as such, in her discriminating between apparently similar depictions, and so forth.

Accounts of the relevant conventions are offered by L. R. Rogers (1965), H. Gene Blocker (1974), and David Novitz (1976). They characterize general "graphic," "blanket," or "umbrella" conventions for representation. These amount to a rule-governed method for producing pictures which, when applied or grasped, allows for the production and recognition of any object drawn this way.[42] Rogers and Novitz (following Gombrich) also allow for the possibility of schemata (a method for depicting a particular object) and allow that some (most, in art paintings) schemata might also be conventional. Both argue that umbrella conventions for depicting not only are more basic than schemata but also are necessary for depiction. Both point out that umbrella conventions mark pictorial styles and that different pictorial styles each are characterized by their commitment to different umbrella conventions—for example, those of impressionist, Western realist, Chinese, and Egyptian modes of perspective.

With respect to the discussion presented in the previous chapter, umbrella

---

[42] The "recognition" requirement perhaps begs the question in favor of the seeing-in theory if it is taken to imply that the recognition be perceptual; an intellectual realization that the image maps onto its subject in accordance with the umbrella conventions is all that is required according to the semantic theory.

< 78 >

conventions are of a kind that generates meaning C or E. On the account of representation offered by the semantic theory, depiction is analyzable as involving meaning E. Depiction is distinguished from description not by the type of meaning involved but in terms of the conventions and the elements combined according to them. Constraints inherent to both the elements and the conventions mark the vital differences between language and pictures. Schemata are likely to be seen under this theory as generating meaning D. On the account of representation offered by the seeing-in theory, in which a natural relation lies at the heart of representation, depiction involves meaning C. Schemata are likely to be seen under this theory as generating meaning B.[43]

The Argument against Musical Representation

With the preliminary discussion of pictorial representation now complete, I turn to the topic in hand, musical depiction. After presenting a few caveats, I consider how applicable to the musical case are the semantic and seeing-in theories, since I take those to be the most plausible of the accounts of representation on offer. For the most part my conclusions are negative. I take this not as evidence of the extent to which musical depiction differs from pictorial representation but rather as indicating that music is not (primarily) a depictive art.

An aside: Sometimes composers have drawn "pictures" in their scores, pictures created by the disposition of notes on the page. Mozart wrote "rounds" on circular staves in his letters. Edward Lippman (1966) mentions a chanson of about 1400 by Baude Cordier notated in the form of a heart and points out (1953) that, where words about the sea are set to undulating, fast passages, the appearance of the notation, as well as the sound, suggests the sea; for other examples of "eye music," see Dart 1980. In Stravinsky's *Petrushka*, as the blackamoor paces in his cage the orchestra's regular chords punctuate the theme played by three bassoons; in the score, the chords appear as vertical *bars* "behind" which the line of the bassoons' melody stalks. Effects of this sort are not common. More to the point, whatever their interest, such notational effects are not examples of *musical* depiction. For music, the connection between the identifying properties of the work and of its

---

[43] I regard the elegant theory developed in Schier 1986 to be consistent with the view I have defended. Schier stresses the naturally generative character of picturing and emphasizes that the resemblances that ground representation are subject to conventions unlike those of language.

< 79 >

score (should it have one) are weak ones.[44] Further, it is not normally assumed that the appreciator's access to the work comes through a reading of its score. For these reasons, I do not believe that such pictures as might appear in the score of a musical work are a part of it.

A point about scope: Few would deny that opera or ballet is depictive, but the argument about music's representational powers concentrates not on the contribution made by music in such artforms but on its capacity to be depictive in its "pure" form.[45] Most of those who argue that music can be representational, or programmatic, make the claim only on behalf of *some* instrumental works.[46] For example, Peter Kivy believes that "a small but not negligible amount of instrumental and vocal music, in the modern Western tradition, is representational" (1989, 255).[47] So, for many, musical representation is a regular and persistent aspect in music, but it is not common in instrumental music in general. The types of music most often identified as depictive are the genres of song and of program music (works with "literary" titles and, sometimes, an accompanying text).

Contrary to this view, some other writers appear to hold that all music is to be understood as programmatic, and hence as depictive. One such is J. W. N. Sullivan (1927), who describes all great music as involving a program about human spirituality. Another is Jacques Barzun (1980), who argues that musical works involve three kinds of programs: a matching of the rhythms and accents of words, if there are any; their own musical forms; and their expressive character. A very broad notion of "program" is required to give such views plausibility. Barzun writes, "To cover all cases, it seems necessary to define as programmatic any scheme or idea, general or particular, that helps to determine the course of the composition" (1980, 3). He continues: "The program does not preexist in any clear sense; it is simply the maker's intention at any given moment of composition" (1980, 11). Barzun repeatedly describes the program as "hidden" and as evading detailed de-

[44] Notwithstanding the interpretation of my view offered by Higgins (1991, 41), I think that musical works are distinct from their scores (where they have them). The score is a specification for the production of an instance of the work and is not itself an instance of the work.

[45] By the terms "pure music," I mean in this book music without words, accompanying text, illustrative title, or dramatic context. Many instrumental works of the late eighteenth century, such as Franz Joseph Haydn's String Quartet in C, Op. 74, No. 1, or his Symphony No. 102 in B-flat major, conform to this type.

[46] As do Cazden (1951), Cooke (1959), Butor (1968), Howard (1972), Urmson (1973), Kivy (1980 and 1984), and Walton (1990, 334).

[47] Kivy (1991) goes further, suggesting that, apart from the period 1550–1650, when the goal was the representation of human expressive utterance, music is a decorative and not a fine—that is, representational—art. For discussion, see Alperson 1992.

< 80 >

scription. In his writings, the notions of meaning, reference, representation, and expression are constantly conflated. In this theory, any human action (and any artifact) is programmatic and, to that extent, self-referential and self-representational. Clearly this involves an expansion beyond the ordinary of the concept of representation. Is there any point to treating the notion this way? Kivy (1990a), who discusses Barzun and the similar position of Richard Kuhns (1978), thinks not, and rightly so in my opinion.[48] He rejects as unfalsifiable Barzun's view that music represents itself. He observes that musical representation is important precisely because it is enjoyed, and that to be enjoyed it must be perceivable, so the appeal to hidden, inexpressible programs is devoid of explanatory power.

Though Kivy thinks that some music is depictive, he objects to an approach treating all music as of this type. Someone who hears a "story" in a work of pure music treats the experience of listening merely as the occasion for indulging her imagination, allowing the music to prompt her thoughts where their own lack of vivacity or interest do not make them self-propelling, as it were. Kivy says that this approach goes beyond what "good musical analysis and sound musical practice will allow" (1989, 221–222). A person who substitutes fantasy for attention to the work reacts (at best) to an idiosyncratic amalgamation of the music and an imaginatively generated program not connected to the work; the response is not to the work itself but to some private, personal object of fantasy. To the extent that her response is shaped by the detail of the imaginatively invented program, that response is not to something depicted in the work.[49]

Perhaps Kuhns and Barzun would object that I mischaracterized their views. Despite their talk of programs and representation, I think they mean to make this point: Sometimes if one listens to a work as illustrating a story, one can be led deeper into the music itself, noticing details and structures one might otherwise overlook. Many people might best be prompted to understand music by approaching all works programmatically (as if they were programmatic), and where can the harm be in that? The "program" is

[48] For another critique of Kuhns's thesis, see Robinson 1979; for a denial that Kuhns's position is similar to Barzun's, see Price 1992.

[49] Lippman (1977) reminds us that programmatic works range from those attempting to represent particular objects, actions, or events to those doing no more than expressing a mood that complements the narrative supplied by the program. If the advocacy of programmatic listening has in mind "program" music of the latter type, it amounts merely to the suggestion that one should hear the expressive character of the music. Kivy would have no objection to this, but I suspect that he would challenge the idea that music is expressive only in conjunction with a program, or that the particularity of its expressive character always depends on the detail of a program, or that expressiveness is to be equated with, or explained as, programmatic depiction.

< 81 >

a prosthetic device and could always be put aside when its purpose is served. This seems to be what Barzun has in mind. He says that literature and music summon up and shape the stuff of human experience; it is this that prompts us to "tag" music with programs; programs are useful analogies but should not be taken literally; they are to be put aside when understanding has been achieved by means of them (1953, 16–17, 21).[50]

But, if this reading is correct, I doubt that any claims are being made about musical depiction as such. The idea is that programs and titles, whether supplied by the composer or the hearer, might always be helpful in promoting musical understanding. This is not because music must be appreciated as depicting as pictures do but because music is something to be understood mainly on its own terms, and a "program" might provide the prop making this possible. If I need to be drunk to appreciate Wagner's music, then the consumption of alcohol makes this appreciation possible, but it does not follow that Wagner's music depicts a few stiff brandys. No more is it reasonable to suppose that a musical work depicts the story that helps a given listener to understand that work. After all, there might be as many such stories as there are understanding listeners.[51]

Which of the Theories of Depiction Better Fits the Musical Case?

Robinson (1987) considers both the semantic theory and the seeing-in theories of depiction in relation to music. She suggests that much music is representational according to the former, so long as it has a suitably literary title and complements that title with some apt mood, and that little music is representational according to the latter, because we cannot usually hear definite subjects in music without knowing in advance the title of the works in question. All this strikes me as too fast.

Even if the semantic theory gives priority to the work's title, it also insists

---

[50] Callen (1982a) argues that we can and should make sense of all music by listening to it programmatically, that is, by inventing and reacting to a story of emotions and their progression suggested to us by the music. Also see McMullin 1947.

[51] This discussion indirectly raises two issues that I cover elsewhere: (i) If the current topic were pursued, it might be claimed that "programmatic" listening must be involved in recognizing music's expressiveness, for the emotions expressed in music are presented without "owners" or contexts. Later in this chapter I suggest that it would be an error to assimilate the notions of expression and representation. And in Chapters 3 and 5 I am inclined to deny that the recognition of expressiveness in music depends on the type of imagining that goes into the appreciation of paintings or of literature. (ii) This discussion also raises questions about what it is to understand a musical work and about the manner in which this understanding is to be pursued. I discuss the subject of musical understanding in Chapter 7.

< 82 >

that the title can contribute to representation only where the elements are systematized in a way that might allow them to combine appropriately with the title to secure denotation and a characterization of the subject. A semantic theorist might deny that the elements of music are of a type that permits them to conjoin with the work's title in producing a depiction. Goodman himself does so. Because he describes the elements of music as articulate rather than as dense and replete (an exception being electronic music), Goodman doubts that they have the requisite character to allow for depiction: "If a performance of a work defined by a standard score denotes at all, it still does not represent; for as a performance of such a work it belongs to an articulate set. . . . electronic music without any notation or language properly so-called may be representational, while music under standard notation, if denotative at all, is descriptive. This is a minor curiosity, especially since denotation plays so small a role in music" (1968, 232). According to Goodman, if music is denotative (which often it is not), it has the character of a linguistic utterance rather than of a depiction. I note later, however, that Goodman 1981 shows a change of heart.

And even if the seeing-in theory places more emphasis on what can be seen or heard in a work than on its title, the theory by no means treats the title of the work as irrelevant. To the extent that the title might mark a work as of a particular type (say, program music) or contribute to the disambiguation of subjects that a musical work can be heard as resembling, and if the resemblance is deliberately produced, the theory might allow that many musical works with literary titles or texts are representational.

Matters may not be so straightforward as Robinson implies, but perhaps she is correct, anyway, in thinking that the semantic theory of representation can be applied to music, showing it to be capable of representation. Kivy appears to think so. He compares his own view with the semantic theory and claims to find significant parallels between the two. Provided that non-notational elements can be counted as part of the work, provided that one regards most (notational) elements as depictive rather than descriptive, and provided that one accepts (as Kivy is reluctant to do) that representation is essentially denotative, then the spirit, if not the letter, of Kivy's own account of musical representation is consistent with Goodman's analysis, he thinks. Kivy notes (1984, 122) that "little" in Goodman's account needs to be modified to fit his own account of musical representation. I doubt this, as does Levinson (1985b). Kivy will have no truck with the notion of denotation central to Goodman's account both of depiction and of expression. Moreover, Kivy does not see the need to argue that music constitutes a representa-

< 83 >

tional symbol system, yet this must be a crucial element within the application of Goodman's theory to the musical case.

One who explicitly sets out to apply the semantic theory to the musical case is Vernon Howard (1972). He disagrees (as does O'Neil 1971) with Goodman's (1968) denial that much music is denotational. Howard argues that some music is representational under an application of Goodman's theory. Music shares some features of both notational (that is, linguistic) and pictorial symbol systems. To the extent that it can be scored it is notational; that is, it is articulate, nonreplete, and so on.[52] But to the extent that tempo, volume, phrasing, and the like are syntactically and semantically undifferentiated, music is like painting. Because Goodman assumes no ambiguity between the music as sound event and what it denotes, he treats it as descriptive, but in doing so he neglects the part that might be played in the work by its non-notational elements.[53] Howard suggests that music might be representational because of its non-notational features, since paintings are representational in virtue of similar features. A crescendo followed by a diminuendo might represent the approach and departure of a rider. The diminuendo of a Wagnerian leitmotif on the death of the character "named" by that motive would transform the "name" into the representation of the event.[54]

Howard's argument is ingenious, but it dilutes the notion of musical representation. Those who would argue that music may be representational standardly make the claim not only for non-notational elements (such as tempo, dynamics, and phrasing) but also on behalf of melodies, harmonies, voice relations (such as imitation), and instrumentation. The musical representation for which Howard argues is far too impoverished to be acceptable to such theorists.

Howard revises his view to sidestep this objection. He notes that a notational element in one system need not retain this character within another: "Music is no more prevented from representing in one system because of its notational compliant-status than a poem about a fish typed out in the shape of a fish is prevented from being a fish-*depiction* because it happens also to be a fish-*description*" (1975, 212). "We may choose to ignore [notational] properties altogether as we do with digital pictures and interpret the total

[52] What matters is not that a score preexists the work's first performance but that a score determining the class of compliant performances be recoverable from any performance. The point is made in Howard 1972 and Tormey 1974.

[53] Goodman 1981 concedes this criticism and accepts the view Howard develops.

[54] See Howes 1958 for a relevant description of the way Siegfried's leitmotif is manipulated in like manner by Wagner in *Der Ring des Nibelungen*.

< 84 >

sound-configuration as a dense scheme relative to musical forms, expressive properties, or something denoted by the music" (1975, 210). This new approach dodges the aforementioned difficulty in suggesting that, if *any* musical features can have representational significance, then *all* might do so. Howard's argument does not, however, establish the truth of the antecedent. To do this one would have to prove that music is denotational, and that it is so just as pictures commonly are. This demonstration involves showing not only that music shares some properties with pictorial symbol schemes but also that it constitutes a scheme or schemes amenable to the same (depictive) use, that is, that there are musical conventions systematizing the elements of music so they can be combined to form a representational whole. I doubt that this could be proved, and I note that Howard makes no attempt to do so.

The issue here is whether music meets condition (4). If it does not, this counts against its being representational on both the semantic and seeing-in theories. Are there musical conventions for depiction of the umbrella type mentioned earlier? Are there general methods for musical depiction such that, when they are followed, many different sounds, objects, or states of affairs might be depicted? Are there conventions (as there are for perspective in various styles of pictorial depictions) for mapping musical features onto the world in a systematic fashion? I think not. Richard Strauss aims to depict the glitter of the rose in *Der Rosenkavalier* and perhaps succeeds in doing so, given the full dramatic context of the operatic work. But there seem to be no conventions which, for pure music, would allow one to distinguish the glitter of a silver rose from that of a diamond. Neither are there conventions allowing one to distinguish glitter from glare, or from palsy, or from shivering. If we cannot detect a relevant difference between works aiming to depict these respective subjects, then none is depicted. Moreover, it is suggestive that there are not within music markedly different styles or schools of (alleged) representation, as there are within painting. To deny that there are umbrella conventions for musical depiction is not to deny that music is a highly conventionalized artform. There are many distinctive musical styles within Western music, each of which can be characterized mainly through rules governing the combination, or frequency of combination, of the musical elements. The conventions of musical style do not, however, function as do those of a representational symbol system: namely, to project an image of some part of the world into the music, so that image might be perceived (or at least be demonstrable) within the sound of the work.

There may, however, be musical equivalents of schemata. These apply in cases where the attempt is to represent a sound, or something intimately associated with a sound. It is standard that the cuckoo is suggested by a

< 85 >

falling minor (or sometimes major) third and, if the work uses the instrument, the interval is played on the clarinet. The formula for schemata of this type seems to consist, rather crudely, in reproducing the relevant sound in as high a fidelity as is possible without the use of tapes of the actual sound. Also, synaesthetic puns of the type mentioned in the previous chapter are used so regularly that they probably qualify as schemata: notes comparatively long in duration are used to set the word "long," melodies that evenly rise and fall illustrate the word "rainbow," atonalism in a tonal context is often used to stand for chaos. Now, if Rogers (1965) and Novitz (1976) are correct, the existence of such schemata in the absence of a background of umbrella conventions would not show that music is representational. It would show instead that music might function symbolically (like iconographic symbols in paintings, for example) rather than depictively. If music employing these schemata were to be called representational, it would be representational in a way which, by comparison with the depictive power of pictures, is extremely impoverished.

I have suggested that it is less easy than Robinson supposes to reconcile cases of alleged musical representation with the semantic analysis of depiction. Now I turn to her view that the seeing-in theory does not reveal music to be a depictive art. Though I agree with Robinson that this is so, I am inclined to question the reason she offers for her conclusion. As I have noted, the seeing-in theory sometimes allows that titles are important in determining the represented content of a work, so it could not with consistency debar reference to them in the musical case. So the problem, as I see it, lies not with the vagueness of alleged cases of musical depiction but with the nature of what it is that is said to be represented. The seeing-in theory, as its name implies, emphasizes that a perceptual experience is involved in recognizing depiction where it is successful. In the case of paintings, this experience is visual. If a man is depicted, this is because people familiar with the relevant conventions have a visual experience as of a man while looking at (and being aware of looking at) the picture. For music, one would expect the relevant perceptual experience to be aural, but, whereas music sometimes is said to represent sounds, so that one hears the sound as of a hand knocking on the door in hearing the repeated drumbeats, more often it is said to represent things having no sound. It is often said that, above all, music depicts love and yearning, motion, and the phenomenal qualities of emotions and moods. It seems to me that the appeal and force of the seeing-in theory is removed if the perceptual element of the experience is lost or underplayed, and that this must result where one attempts to accommodate the musical

< 86 >

depiction of the phenomenal, nonperceptual qualities of emotional states and the like to a hearing-in account of musical depiction.

Robinson declares herself in favor of an account that "embodies insights from both" the seeing-in and semantic theories in characterizing depiction (1987, 167). She does not develop the idea, but the line of her thought perhaps is indicated when she distinguishes "visual" from (more purely) "cognitive" types of seeing-as (1979). Seeing a cloud as a camel is an instance of the former and seeing the Vietnam War as a threat to Western civilization is an instance of the latter. She continues: Wollheim is wrong in treating representation exclusively in terms of the first kind of seeing-as: Christ can be represented as a lamb. Goodman is wrong in treating representation exclusively in terms of the second: pictorial realism is not arbitrarily created but has something to do with ways of seeing, even where those ways of seeing are subject to conventions.

I find these remarks opaque. I take it that Robinson means to comment on the narrower meaning of "represents," since it is the discussion of this sense, rather than the broader one, at issue between Wollheim and Goodman. I have allowed that a person holding to the seeing-in theory can and should accept that perception is often informed and affected by cognition, and that this is regularly the case in the perception of visual likenesses between depictions and their pictured subjects. Because one's understanding can be grounded in one's perceptual experiences, it is not surprising that "see" can mean "understand." But to see that the Vietnam War threatened Western civilization (and Eastern ones as well, I would have thought), or that a pictured lamb stands for Christ, is to have an experience from which the perceptual component has been expunged or in which the content of the perceptual experience does not bear immediately on what one understands. So I do not see that Wollheim can concede much to Goodman on cases of this type without abandoning his theory. Equally, I do not see that Goodman can allow to Wollheim that the conventions for realistic depiction are not arbitrary without his being forced also to abandon his view that the analysis of representation can be given solely in terms of the syntactic structure and element types of a symbol scheme. That further concession would break the back of his theory. So, as I see the two theories and the issues dividing their protagonists, there simply is no middle ground to which both might retreat in the spirit of reconciliation Robinson recommends.[55]

One author whose theory of pictorial representation combines elements

[55] Also see Gibson (1971), who holds that Goodman's theory cannot be combined with visual accounts of representation.

< 87 >

of the semantic and seeing-in theories is Roger Scruton (1976).[56] Scruton outlines five conditions for representation—or, more accurately, for the appreciation of a representation as such (the point being that, if one cannot appreciate something purported to be a representation as a representation, then the intention to produce something representational must have failed): (i) a person must be aware of what is represented; (ii) there must be a distinction between medium and subject; (iii) an interest in a representation must require an interest in its subject; (iv) thoughts (he also says "definite thoughts") must be expressed about the subject; (v) where the concern is an aesthetic one, the interest in the representation is an interest in its lifelikeness perhaps, but not in its truth. Scruton also accepts as a necessary condition of representation that the work be intended to be representational. He applies his theory to music and concludes that it fails the conditions he enumerates and, therefore, is not a representational art.

The seeing-in component of Scruton's theory is apparent in his development of (i) and (iii). The semantic element can be seen in (iv): a representation must introduce a subject and express a complete thought about that subject. Here Scruton seems to model depiction on assertion; in an assertoric sentence there is a subject, a predicate, and (importantly) a full stop. Another, related echo of the semantic theory is apparent in Scruton's fifth condition. In suggesting that an aesthetic interest in a representational painting need not involve a concern with its truthfulness, he implies that pictorial "assertions" can be assessed for truth.

I am inclined to challenge the aspects of the semantic theory found in Scruton's account. Scruton argues that music does not meet his (iv), thereby failing a condition of representation. He says that there is no definite thought expressed by Strauss's music for the rose in *Der Rosenkavalier*, except that the rose glitters, and that there is no point to developing a description of the sea as one listens to Claude Debussy's *La Mer*. This strikes me as false. One can develop a description of the sea in terms of the unfolding of Debussy's music. There is, however, no definite end to the description one might offer, no full stop provided by the music with which to end the characterization of its subject. In that respect musical depiction is unlike assertion (where the predicate is completed in that the sentence comes to a grammatical close), but so too is pictorial representation. Where is the thought expressed in a painting completed? Pictures are said to be worth a thousand words just because there need be no end to the description of the way a subject is repre-

---

[56] This, though, cannot be the kind of theory Robinson has in mind, since she (1981) rejects Scruton's views.

< 88 >

sented. More correctly, there is no exact number of words equivalent to a picture, because pictures do not describe as language does (Davidson 1978). Therefore, that music fails Scruton's fourth condition can hardly count against music's being depictive, since representational paintings fail the same condition in a similar manner. Accordingly, Kivy (1984) replies to Scruton with the following conditional: if paintings are able to meet this condition, then so too are musical works. If Scruton believes that paintings can meet this condition (as presumably he must), it is difficult to find the argument that shows that music could not do so also. I conclude that Scruton is mistaken in identifying (iv) as a necessary condition of pictorial representation.[57]

Music and the First Two Necessary Conditions for Representation

In the remainder of this chapter I consider in some detail Scruton's attack on the view that music is representational and the replies, especially those by Kivy, this has provoked. I interpret Scruton's conditions (i)–(iii), which I count as the seeing-in component of his theory, as versions of conditions (2) and (3) given earlier in this chapter. I ignore as mistaken Scruton's conditions (iv) and (v), the semantic component of his composite theory. Levinson (1985b) regards Kivy's response to Scruton's points as largely successful. I argue that this reading is overly optimistic; Kivy's criticisms are less damning, and Scruton's position might be defended more vigorously, than this critic seems to appreciate.

Scruton subscribes to my conditions (1) and (4). He insists that a representation must be intended as such and that, in understanding a depiction, due place must be given to tradition and convention (1974, 198–200). He observes (1976) that representation can be begun only where it can be completed; that is, condition (1) can be met in the musical case only if the other conditions might also be met; otherwise one has the expression of a futile hope rather than the expression of an intention as such. Many composers have believed that their music can be representational and have intended that it be so, but that the intention can be formulated does not show that it can be executed. Scruton doubts that conventions of the sort needed to bring such an intention to fruition are available for the composer's use. As I see it, Scruton takes himself to be showing that condition (4) is not met in the

[57] The semantic element in Scruton's theory appears to go beyond that proposed by Goodman; see note 41 above. Scruton commits the semantic theory to too strong a parallel between depiction and language, and that is why depictive paintings, not just musical works, fail to meet his condition (iv).

< 89 >

musical case when he claims that music is not appreciated as a code; that is, he denies that music contains a translation schema by which it could be mapped onto a symbol system permitting reference and description, such as language is, or a pictorial map, such as a picture, or directly onto the world. In my terms, he seems to hold that music displays neither meaning C nor E, whereas both natural languages and standard depictions do so.

I have already suggested that music does not satisfy condition (4). More-oever, given the intimacy of the connection between intention and action, one might hold that condition (1) is met only where there are public conven-tions that reveal the composer's intentions to the listener through her experi-ence of his work. It might then be inferred from the notoriously high level of disagreement about what music represents that condition (1) also fails to hold. In any event, how one feels about music's success or otherwise in meet-ing conditions (1) and (4) is likely to be determined by its fate in meeting conditions (2) and (3). Only if a case can be mounted for saying these condi-tions are satisfied by music is it appropriate to revise the reservations ex-pressed about music's meeting condition (4), and only where (4) is met is it plausible to suggest that condition (1) is also realized. I move on, then, to the discussion of conditions (2) and (3), and of Scruton's (i)-(iii).

Scruton's condition (ii) corresponds to condition (2) outlined earlier: there must be a distinction between medium and subject. He holds that music fails even this minimal condition for representation, arguing as follows: If music can represent anything, then it ought to be sounds it can represent. The can-nons in Tchaikovsky's *1812* Overture do not, however, represent the sounds of cannons; they make them. One might argue similarly, the sound of anvils in Verdi's *Il Trovatore* is made by the striking of anvils; the cowbell sound in Mahler's Fourth Symphony is simply the sound of a cowbell. Matters are no better when the sounds issue from musical instruments. When music, as an art of sounds, attempts to represent an X by copying the sound X's make, what we get is an instance of an X-sound and not a representation of an X, says Scruton (1976 and 1980c). This is because sounds exist for us as indi-viduals rather than as properties of individuals; Scruton cites Strawson 1964 on this point. A composer might try to represent a hammer by copying the sound of a hammer's blows, but the listener's tendency to reify the sounds would defeat the attempt at representation, for what would be heard would be (instances of) bangs, not the sound of a hammer striking something. When Beethoven attempts to represent the cuckoo in his Sixth Symphony, we hear a sound (as of a cuckoo) but no bird. We hear a ticking sound in the slow movement of Haydn's Symphony No. 101 *(Clock)* but not the tick-ing of a clock. And we hear the sound as of a train in Arthur Honegger's

< 90 >

Pacific 231, but no train is represented as making that sound. Where the attempt is made to represent sounds in music, the medium/content distinction evaporates.

I disagree with the claim that attempts at musical representation fail for the want of a distinction between the medium of representation and the nature of the subject for depiction. There is usually a detectable difference between the sound of musical instruments and the sound of the thing the music is intended to represent. Most people can distinguish the sound of a clarinet from that of a cuckoo, despite the similarity in timbre. No one familiar with the sound of a steam train is likely to be fooled by *Pacific 231*; only someone with defective hearing would mistake the flutes of Bedřich Smetana's *Ma Vlast* for the bubbling spring that forms the headwaters of the river Moldau. J. O. Urmson (1973) notes that, because nature is not very musical, musical representations of nonmusical sounds are generally rather unlike what they are supposed to represent.[58] But, even if there were no detectable differences between musical sounds and the sounds of the things they are intended to represent, it would not follow that music fails the requirement for a distinction between the representational medium and the depicted content. Four observations are relevant:

(a) Often the subject of depiction plainly is meant not to be a sound as such but the sound as made by a given type of sound maker. Surely Beethoven does not intend merely to represent the sound as of a cuckoo but to represent the call of a cuckoo. The composer aims to produce sounds recognizable as representations of those made by a nonmusical source, and to represent those sounds as arising from that source. To counter such tendency as we have to reify the sounds we hear, the composer deals with sounds distinctive to a given source or imitates a sound in such extended detail as to bring to mind a given source. Sounds may be regarded as individuals in their own right in some contexts; so many things can make loud, sudden noises that we can talk of bangs and crashes without mentioning what made the noise. Often, though, we identify a sound with what makes it (Carpenter 1966): the cry of a baby, or the noise of a stylus scraping across a vinyl record as it is being played.

(b) Not all differences are perceptible: the visual experiences of a train, of a hallucination of a train, of the image of a train reflected in a mirror, of a photograph of a train, and of a miniature model of a train might be phenomenally identical. How do we know that a painting producing such an experience represents a train, not a hallucination, a reflection, a photograph,

[58] The point is made also in Cazden 1951, McLaughlin 1970, and Hanslick 1957 and 1986.

< 91 >

or a miniature model, or merely a visual experience as of a train, or even a visual experience as of a picture of a train? The default assumption is that, when a picture is viewed in terms of the conventions of representation applying to it, the resulting perceptual experience is an analogue of the experience that would result were the conditions standard and the perception veridical. Explicit clues should be offered where it is appropriate to reject this assumption, given that standard tests of size, reflection, and perspective (such as moving the head, walking nearer for a better look) do not apply in the orthodox fashion to the content when it is a picture one is examining. If the clue is not given in the title, or in the place of the given work within a series of works, or whatever, then some perceptible indication should be, and usually is, provided.

If music is representational as pictures are, similar conventions can be expected to hold. If the ticking sound is as of a clock, then, if it represents anything, the music depicts a clock's ticking. If Honegger represents anything in *Pacific 231*, he represents the sound of a steam train and not, say, the sound as of a steam train or the sound of a magnetic tape (of a steam train) played on a tape recorder.

(c) Because of their similarity a person might mistake the sound of a clarinet for a cuckoo. Equally, though, a person might take a painting on a wall as of a door for an actual door. The possibility of one's being fooled shows the failure of the content/medium distinction in neither case. The standard conditions under which paintings are viewed, and music is heard, allow one to test the character of the sight or sound against the evidence of other senses. Being in a gallery, I can feel for the doorknob. Being at a musical performance, I can see that clarinets, rather than cuckoos, are used; even when I listen to a recording, it is understood that I can know what would have been seen by a witness to the live performance.

(d) That I might see the musical instruments in use is not a fact of merely incidental relevance. An interest in music involves a concern not only with sounds as such but also with the means of their production, for artistically important properties of musical works depend on such considerations. For example, whether a passage is difficult to play, rushed, or unusual depends on the instrument for which it is written.[59] So, even if a sound is duplicated exactly (for example, by a sound synthesizer), the fact that a concern with music takes note of the means of sound production inhibits our tendency to reify the sound. Sound synthesizers are not exchangeable for the instruments

[59] For a useful discussion of a range of cases, see Levinson 1980 and 1990a, chap. 16.

< 92 >

the sounds of which they faithfully reproduce; see Godlovitch 1990a and 1990b.

The final point comes to this: Quite independently of whether music may be depictive as paintings are, and hence independently of any appeal to conventions for representation as in (b) above, the relevance of the means of production (as well as of the resulting sound) to the appreciation of the artistic properties constitutive of musical works guarantees that it is inappropriate to reify sounds in musical works as one might tend to in other contexts. To aim to understand and appreciate most musical works written after 1750 is to consider the effort and skill that goes into coaxing sounds from the instruments for which the composer wrote. In that case, though, if the sound is one distinctive to some nonmusical cause or arises from one instrument's imitating another (as where a string drone recalls a hurdy-gurdy or the bagpipes, or where pizzicato strings stand proxy for a guitar or mandolin), then the coupling of a concern with the means of production with the thought that that sound typically has a different source secures the distinction between medium and content (or signifier and signified).

The remarks made so far do not deal with the admittedly unusual cases in which cowbells, cannons, and the like are added to the orchestra in the attempt to represent the sound of cowbells, of cannons, and so on. Even in instances such as these, one might argue that a distinction between subject and medium is preserved. It is possible for something to depict itself. For example, John McEnroe could play himself in a film (with a fictional story). Knowing that the film is a fiction, the viewer takes McEnroe's cameo to be a representation of himself (and she knows, for instance, that the opinions he states in that role ought not to be taken as his own). The cannons in the *1812* Overture and the cowbell in Mahler's Fourth Symphony seem to be used to impersonate themselves in a similar manner. Knowing that one is at a concert performance, one takes the sound of the cannons and the sound of the cowbell to be standing for the sounds of cannons and a cowbell. As I indicated in the earlier discussion of condition (2), it is a mistake to conceive of the content/medium distinction solely by reference to the stuff of the medium. Account must also be taken of the circumstances of production and of the traditions within which composers work.

If the subject/medium distinction fails anywhere, it should fail where the subject is itself a musical idea or work. Some writers maintain that self-representation is common in music. Robert P. Morgan (1977), describes post-1950s music as program music that is about itself. Kuhns (1978) attacks Scruton (1976) on the grounds that musical works, as well as quoting each other and imitating natural sounds, are self-referential and, to that extent,

< 93 >

self-representational. We hear in a theme a reference to its subsequent use and development, he says.[60] As noted, Barzun (1980) argues that the form of a musical work is a program for it. As I have presented them, either these views involve a broad notion of representation (which is more concerned with reference than with depiction) or they are mistaken. Generally, the musical repetitions within a work involve the use, not merely the mention or quotation, of the materials. Of course, we are supposed to bring to mind the earlier occurrence of a theme when it is repeated, but this does not mean that the earlier occurrence is *referred to* by the later one. Anyway, even if it is true that one instance of a theme refers to its earlier appearances, reference is not depiction. Where material is repeated within a movement or work it is clear, I think, that depiction is bound to fail for want of a distinction between the medium of the subject and the medium of representation.

The subject/medium distinction also fails, I think, in the majority of cases in which one musical work alludes to, or refers to, or quotes from another. Here reference is achieved through quotation/mention rather than by depiction. This is the case when Mozart quotes "Non Più Andrai" from his own *Marriage of Figaro*, an aria from Vicente Martín y Soler's *Una Cosa Rara,* and another from Giovanni Paisiello's *Fra i due Litiganti il Terzo Gode* in *Don Giovanni,* and also when Beethoven announces Diabelli's theme before launching into his variations on it. If these examples fail the content/medium distinction, as I believe they do, it is because the idiom or dialect is unchanged, so one takes the notes (or themes) at face value rather than as note depictions (or as theme depictions). But in music there is a range of styles and, where a style atypical for the composer or context is used self-consciously, it may be that it is depicted. Scruton (1974 and 1976) himself offers a very suggestive example: In a dance scene set in a tavern in *Wozzeck,* Berg writes a waltz that recalls (and is intended to represent) the Viennese waltzes of an earlier period (that in which the opera is set). He does so in the prevailing atonal mode of the work. Nevertheless, he uses this idiom in a way that brings to mind the robust tonalities of Johann Strauss. So one might argue that the style of Berg's opera (the medium) and the style of Strauss's waltzes (the subject) provide for a content/medium distinction such as that on which representation depends.

The practice to which Scruton has drawn attention is not uncommon in music. Eighteenth-century Viennese composers wrote "Turkish" music, just as those of the late nineteenth century were prone to "Chinoiserie." The use

[60] Also see Carpenter (1966) and Price (1988), both of whom regard musical tones as referring to each other.

< 94 >

of drums and cymbals in the one case and of pentatonic scales in the other readily distinguished such styles from those that prevailed more widely at the time. Stravinsky invokes Mozart's *opera buffa* in his *Rake's Progress*, but the harmonies of the work retain an edge locating it unmistakably in the twentieth century. Benjamin Britten uses the resources of the modern, Western orchestra to recall the sound of Indonesian gamelan in his *Prince of the Pagodas*.

I described Scruton's example from *Wozzeck* as suggestive. Scruton seems of two minds about the case. He implies that the attempt at representation succeeds, though we should "regard genuine representation in music as a rare and peripheral phenomenon" (1974, 211). Elsewhere, though, he claims that "the representational character is not an autonomous property of the music, and can be fully understood only through theatrical conventions that are entirely non-musical in their origin" (1976, 284); there he concludes that depiction fails in this case not because the medium/content distinction is violated but because his (semantic) requirement—that the music convey a definite thought about the subject—is not met.[61] The opera is depictive, but these musical passages within it are not representational. Now, I am unconvinced by this semantic requirement and suspect that in these cases representation, or something very like it, succeeds, so I prefer Scruton's earlier (1974) conclusion. Sometimes, though not commonly, music can represent music. The important point for the present context is this: if music is sound, then it is not always the case that the subject/medium distinction is violated by the attempt to depict sound in sound.

So far, in discussing whether music respects the requirement of a distinction between subject and medium, I have concentrated on the possibility of music's depicting sounds—for example, the sound as of a clock, or the sound of a clock's ticking. I have done so because it is in just such cases that music's success in meeting that requirement is in doubt. Often it is claimed that music depicts subjects so different from sounds that the subject/medium distinction is guaranteed. I turn now to a discussion of those cases. To anticipate the conclusions that follow, though I think that music can depict the source of a sound if it can depict that sound (so that it can depict a clock if it can depict a clock's ticking), I am skeptical of some further claims made for music's representational powers, such as that it depicts movement or emotions. I am skeptical because I believe that music often possesses properties of movement or expressiveness without its also referring to such properties, and that,

---

[61] Urmson (1973) is another who denies that music can represent music.

< 95 >

where its possessing those properties *is* used referentially, reference is secured via association rather than by depiction.

If the context of music appreciation allows us sometimes to move from "sound as of a cuckoo" to "sound of cuckoo's call," as I argued previously, then I cannot see why that same context would not license the move from "sound of cuckoo's call" to "presence of cuckoo," conceding (of course) that the presence of the cuckoo is entertained rather than believed. Beethoven intends to depict in his Symphony No. 6 not merely a quail-like sound but a quail as the source of that sound. I regard this type of case as analogous to that in which a painting both depicts a kangaroo as peering over a thick bush (so that the legs and feet cannot be seen) and depicts a kangaroo with feet, or in which the same painting depicts a kangaroo with a heart though it does not show its heart. It strikes me as odd to insist that the feet and the heart are not depicted, whereas the bush and the chest are, on the grounds that the former are not shown whereas the latter are. For the seeing-in theory of representation I have endorsed does not require for the representation of a kangaroo with all its body parts that all the body parts of a kangaroo be visible in the picture. What is required is that one be able to see some subset of body parts which, along with the conventions of pictorial style governing works of that sort, and in the absence of contrary indications as discussed under (b), allow one to deduce that a kangaroo (with all its body parts) is depicted. If the appropriate conventions are realist, then the kangaroo has feet and a heart; if the feet show then nothing obstructs the view, and if the heart can be seen the creature's chest is open.[62] As already implied, the appeal here is to considerations mentioned under (b). In discussing (b) I suggested that, if the conventions do not disallow it, one should move from "the sound as of an X" to "an X's sound." To this I now add that, if the conventions do not disallow it, one should move from "an X's sound" to "the presence of an X."[63]

A similar approach can be taken to Tchaikovsky's cannons, Mahler's cowbell, and Verdi's anvils. One can move from the sound of a cannon (in the

---

[62] By contrast, according to the conventions employed by some Australian aboriginal artists, if one could not see the kangaroo's heart then the heart must have been removed from the animal's body; in this tradition, one is offered an "X-ray" view of the skeleton and of the vital organs of the living creature.

[63] Walton believes that cross-modal depiction rarely is possible for music, which typically represents auditory phenomena (1990, 334–345). As an example of musical depiction he offers the passage in Beethoven's *Missa Solemnis* in which we hear the nails being driven into the cross. I note that nails are not sounds and that Walton means to claim that nails-being-driven are depicted, not merely sounds as of nails-being-driven, so I assume that his dismissal of cross-modal depiction is aimed at some other type of case.

< 96 >

orchestra, firing blanks) to the sound of a cannon (in battle, firing live shells) to the cannon (in battle). And, just as one might say of a lump of coal, "let this lump of coal represent next year's coal production," so in this case the wider context says "let these firings stand for barrages, and this cannon first for the artillery of the French, then for the artillery of the Russians." An instance of a thing (or a tag for it) may be used to represent a collection of such things, as in the figures of speech metonymy and synecdoche. Tchaikovsky's cannons do not merely reproduce the noise of cannons, they represent the barrages of the artillery used by both sides in Napoleon's invasion of Russia. Verdi's anvils depict anvils in general and further symbolize the self-sufficiency of the gypsy life.

More ambitious claims are made on behalf of musical representation than those considered so far. Frequently it is alleged that music represents things other than sounds or their sources. Music is experienced as possessing a dynamic/spatial character, and often composers claim to depict dynamic, non-musical processes without reference to sound as such.[64] Honegger claimed to be representing not the sound of a train in *Pacific 231* but the character of its motion. Rising scales and plummeting intervals indicate ascent and fall. Sometimes it is suggested that music represents the emotions we hear given expression within it, and that it does so not always by imitating the sound of the human voice. It is also said that music can represent with great specificity objects having no distinctive sound, usually by imitating their dynamic or expressive character. For example, Wagner is said to depict the flickering of fire in *Der Ring des Nibelungen*; in his *Nocturnes* Debussy characterizes the clouds with floating, ethereal music; Saint-Saëns, in attempting to represent the swan in his *Carnival of the Animals*, writes music expressive of languor, nobility, and gentleness.

---

[64] I have heard some women say of different musical pieces that orgasm is depicted therein. I have assumed that men are silent on this matter because the vast majority of musical works are of more than a couple of minute's duration. But perhaps their taciturnity signifies a conspiracy. Susan McClary (1991, chap. 5) maintains that tonal, classical music is patterned on male orgasm and is an expression of patriarchal culture. She says, "When musicians describe a compelling performance, they commonly describe it as 'balls-to-the-wall' or say that it had 'thrust,' and they accompany these words with the gesture of the jabbing clenched fist and the facial grimace usually reserved for purposes of connoting male sexual aggression" (1991, 130). This extraordinary behavior is not confined to musicians, apparently; in an earlier essay she writes this: "*Musik in Geschichte und Gegenwart* characterizes masculine themes as 'thrusting' and aggressive, and effective readings of Beethoven symphonies or Strauss tone poems are guaranteed to have male audience members pumping their fists in the lobby as they describe how the performance had 'balls'" (1990, 13). The musicians and audiences of her acquaintance seem to be not at all like those I know, so I cannot help wondering if the attitudes she sees as gender-based are not influenced as much, or more, by cultural factors.

< 97 >

In sum, composers have often attempted to represent much more than could be captured through the mimicry of sounds. Scruton has arguments that suggest to him that such attempts at depiction are doomed to failure. I have already denied that there are umbrella conventions in music of a kind allowing for the depiction of flickering fires and the like, and I consider the arguments against the idea that music depicts process or expressive properties in what follows. The point to make here is this: if music is not depictive of such things, this is not for the want of a distinction between medium and subject in these cases; if music cannot depict motion or emotion, this must be because music fails some requirement other than condition (2).

Music and the Third Condition for Representation

I turn now to a consideration of the crucial third condition for representation lying at the heart of the seeing-in theory—that there be a resemblance between the perceptual experiences of the depiction and of what it depicts. Scruton's first condition for representation—that it must be possible to see in a representational work the subject represented—derives from the seeing-in theory and corresponds to condition (3). Scruton stresses that the subject must be recognizable without the aid of the title of the work. His third condition draws out what I take to be implications of condition (3): the viewer must take note of the represented subject, for one could not (fully) understand a (successfully) representational work if one failed to recognize that it was representational.[65] Scruton concludes that music fails his first and third conditions, whereas he believes that representational paintings satisfy them; that is, music fails, and painting meets, my condition (3) in his view. A listener can (fully) understand Debussy's La Mer without realizing that it is intended to be representational.[66] Without reference to the title of the piece one would have no reason to hear Debussy's work as representing the sea, whereas in the case of a painting the viewer standardly can see what is represented without recourse to the work's title. Therefore music is not representational in Scruton's view.

I regard these points as laying the foundation for a powerful attack on the claim that music can be depictive. They invite a detailed consideration of a

---

[65] A person might look at a representational painting as if it were abstract, concentrating on the formal features of line and color, say, and thereby come to a heightened understanding and appreciation of the work, but this would be a sophistication, albeit a common one, on the response to the work as depictive.

[66] John Sloboda writes, "Musical reference is special because the music 'makes sense' even if the reference is *not* appreciated by a listener" (1985, 60).

< 98 >

range of issues: What is involved in understanding paintings and music? Is the title part of the work that should not be ignored, or is it merely a label? Is the disanalogy between the appropriate approach to paintings and to music as marked as Scruton supposes?

Must we be able to see depiction if we are ignorant of the title?[67] Earlier I mentioned three kinds of cases suggesting this question is to be answered in the negative. A painting might represent Cleopatra, though it is a likeness to Ellie Denood that can be discerned in it; a painting might appear abstract to someone unaware of its subject, though it is a photorealistic depiction of part of a sandy beach; the creation of the work might involve a process of abstraction that fragments the subject to a point at which it is perceptible only to a viewer who has an inkling of what the artist intended to represent. In these cases what is depicted is not directly perceptible, for the key to an awareness of what is represented is some piece of knowledge not conveyed in the appearance of the painting. The point might always be made by reference to paintings identical in their appearance. Three paintings that look the same might depict different subjects, namely, Cleopatra, Ellie Denood, and Flora Denood (Ellie's identical twin sister). Or another painting might be abstract while its look-alike depicts a beach. Or yet another painting might be abstract while its twin is a jazzy representation of a bird's-eye view of part of Manhattan by Mondrian. Now, as I suggested when discussing how such cases are to be handled by the seeing-in theory, the crucial bit of information settling what is depicted is provided by the work's title, the conventions that apply to its style of representation, or the artist's intentions.

The problem posed by Debussy's *La Mer* is not a difficulty in deciding whether it is the Atlantic, the Pacific, or some fictional sea that is represented,[68] and the problem is not that the sea is an inherently abstract subject. Rather, it is that the "image" inevitably is abstracted in being transposed to sound. For this reason the third of the examples just offered is the one most pertinent to music.[69] In objecting to Scruton's theory, it is the third case—in particular, the counterexample of *Broadway Boogie-woogie*—on which Kivy (1984) focuses.[70] Mondrian's work and Turner's later paintings are

---

[67] In this section and those that follow I develop arguments introduced in Davies 1993.

[68] Neither is the problem that of deciding whether Lake Geneva qualifies as a sea when considering the legitimacy of the interpretation offered by L'Orchestre de la Suisse Romande.

[69] The point could be made this way in connection with the first two cases: if music cannot clearly represent an individual, it cannot represent abstract-sounding individuals or abstracted-from individuals.

[70] For further discussion on the representational character of this piece, see Gombrich 1980, chap. 11, and Vermazen 1986.

< 99 >

likely to be seen (wrongly) as abstract by someone unaware of their titles, but they can and should be seen as depictive. The process of abstraction has gone far enough that one might not immediately recognize the depictive character of such works, but not so far that the image is destroyed. The person who knows to look for it, and how to do so, can find the likeness.

Let us accept that Kivy establishes that it is not always the case that what is depicted in a representational painting must be immediately apparent. Can one conclude, as he does, that musical representation might be equivocal in an analogous fashion? I think not. It is plausible to suggest that equivocal instances of representation in paintings are parasitic on the standard case in which the representational character of the work is immediately apparent to anyone familiar with the relevant painterly conventions; the notion of depiction might be extended to cover cases such as *Broadway Boogie-woogie* only because unequivocal depiction is both possible and primary. There is an unclear borderline to be recognized just because there is something on either side of it—unequivocal representations and pure abstractions. The situation may be crucially different for an artform (which music usually is admitted to be) in which most alleged instances of representation are equivocal. Most people could agree about some of the things depicted in the majority of representational paintings without consulting the titles of the paintings, but when the title is ignored it is a commonplace that music "depicts" nearly as many things as there are listeners. It is not obvious, then, that it is legitimate to argue from the fact that musical works might be heard as if they are representational when their illustrative titles are known, just as Mondrian's work can be seen as representational when its title is known, to the conclusion that depiction succeeds in the musical case, as it does in *Broadway Boogie-woogie*. Even if some pictorial representations are not immediately recognizable as such, Scruton is not wrong to insist that music could be representational only if composers' attempts at representation give rise much more often than is the case to immediately recognizable subjects.

Kivy believes he can reply to this point, because he thinks that in a few cases musical representation is unequivocal. He says, "No one fails to recognize the bird songs in Beethoven's *Pastoral* or, I believe, the steam engine in *Pacific* 231" (1984, 147). But I am skeptical of the claim. In Beethoven's work, the clarinet's "cuckoo" and the oboe's "wet my lips" (as the European quail is supposed to "say") are plain enough, but the subtle complexities of rhythm and timbre marking the nightingale's song are mostly lost to the flute, so those familiar with the voice of this prince among passerines might fail to recognize it in the music. Others who realize that a bird's call is being imitated might wonder whether the aim is to depict *Luscinia megarhynchos*,

< 100 >

L. svecica, *L. luscinia*, or *L. calliope*. (Were *L. megarhynchos* and *L. luscinia* distinguished as separate species in Beethoven's day? Can one rule out the possibility of *L. calliope* on the grounds that it is unlikely to have been known to Beethoven?) Stravinsky tries to represent the nightingale realistically in his setting of Hans Andersen's tale, but the music he writes is quite different from Beethoven's. As for *Pacific 231*, in my experience students are as likely to hear dinosaurs as they are to hear trains in this work, and they are no less content after hearing it when told that the music comes from a horror film about giant spiders as when told that it represents a train.

Can we understand music if we do not know what it represents? I accept the view that someone who fails to notice that a representational painting is depictive cannot understand the work. Such a person could note and appreciate aspects of the artist's technique and of the work's form and sensuous properties, but, provided the representational character of the work is not disguised (as in a "hidden man" drawing), one would question the depth of understanding gained by such a person. The point is not that the most important thing about a depictive work is always its representational character but that someone who overlooked the representational character of a work might have defective sight, or insufficient knowledge of the conventions applying to the work, and either of these failings counts against his comprehension of the work. We would not feel the same way about a person who claimed to understand a musical work and could describe the way it is put together but did not realize that the work purports to represent the actions of a Byronic hero in Italy, for instance.

Robinson (1981) and Kivy (1984) argue against Scruton's view by pointing out that there are many musical works intended to be representational which make no musical sense when treated as if they are pure music, that is, if one ignores the work's title or the accompanying program. What would one make of the sudden appearances of the "Marseillaise" and the "Hymn for the Czar," of the cannons, and so forth in Tchaikovsky's *1812* Overture if all one knows of it is that it is an overture? Or what would one make of Richard Strauss's *Till Eulenspiegel* or Berlioz's *Symphonie Fantastique*, both of which introduce a march to the scaffold toward the end? In these cases there is no *musical* reason for the use of the material, and the musical structure is governed by that of the story being illustrated rather than by purely musical paradigms of form. Robinson (1981) adds that the work's expressive properties are affected by its program; the humor and wit of *Till Eulenspiegel* are qualities determined in part by the representational content of the music.

A reply to these points might take a bipartite form: (i) Episodic and free

< 101 >

structures (as in the fantasia or impromptu), as well as the frequent use of quotation and allusion (as in Rachmaninov's obsession with the "Dies Irae"), are common in the world of pure music, so one should not be too quick to assume that the aforementioned works do not stand scrutiny when stripped of their literary cloaks. (ii) But, even if it is true that such works are musical nonsense when the story is ignored, one cannot show that a musical work is representational where the composer was directed by a story merely by demonstrating that the piece makes no musical sense otherwise. Suppose that composers believe that musical representation is possible when it is not. This might explain why their works take the form they do (and, in that sense, allow us to understand why those works are as they are), but that we can understand what was done in such terms does not prove that we are properly understanding the works in question as depictive. Rather, what might be understood thereby is an otherwise inexplicable departure from musical sense; the reason for the failure to write a musically satisfactory work is understood.

As for the expressive properties alleged to depend on a concern with the represented content, such as wit and humor, several lines might be taken. One might deny that the music possesses such properties or deny that it needs to be understood as possessing them. Or one might suggest that such properties might be expressed by the music without their being represented, since nothing is.

A consideration with an importance confirmed by its pervasiveness in musical history weighs in favor of the argument just offered. Most allegedly depictive works make perfect musical sense when their titles are ignored; the composers of such music have consistently attempted to create musical structures with a viability not depending on their illustrative role. For example, Tchaikovsky's *Romeo and Juliet* Overture is in sonata form and Debussy's *La Mer* "works" musically when treated as pure music, despite its departing from textbook models of musical form. The implication is this: titles and programs may guide the composer and help the audience, but most composers, most of the time, have acted as if such things are ancillary to their works. If program music almost always aspires in this way to the condition of pure music, then the attempt at depiction is incidental in the musical case, as it is not for the art of painting.

Many writers emphasize the point that programmatic music should possess the integrity of purely symphonic music. The view is expressed by Robert Schumann and other composers; Barzun (1980) suggests that this position is shared even by Berlioz. Calvin Brown notes that Richard Strauss moved from free forms in the early tone-poems to more traditional structures

< 102 >

in the later ones (1948, 227). He identifies a widespread commitment to musical integrity as a common ground on which "programmatists" and "absolutists" generally agree:

> The advocates of the program will admit that music without verbal aid cannot convey an external idea with any precision or certainty, and that program music is still essentially music. The absolutists, on the other hand, will admit that the following of a program may add a certain interest to the hearing of a piece of music, though they may deny that this extra interest is really musical. Thus the compromise is reached: the composer must write something that will stand on its own feet from a musical point of view, something that *can* be satisfying if considered as absolute music; but he has every right to include subject-matter outside the range of "pure" music—to attach as much or as little of a program as he desires. (Brown 1948, 243; also see Epperson 1967)

Cazden (1951) seems to make this a condition of what he calls musical "realism" (that is, depiction, which he distinguishes from "naturalism," "pictorialism," and "symbolism"); for criticism of Cazden's terminology, see Frank (1952).

The arguments just offered count, if at all, only against the view that music might depict specific events or actions. Earlier I noted that music might be thought to depict spatial and dynamic properties, or the expression of emotions. I doubt that anyone would hold that an appreciation of these is irrelevant to musical understanding. If such things are represented in music, one could not in this case stand by the claim that a person could understand a musical work while ignoring its representational character. How could he appreciate the tonal, harmonic, and melodic structures of musical works if he could not hear patterns of tension and release? How could he claim to understand Tchaikovsky's Symphony No. 6 if he could not give some account of its expressive mood?

The response is this: one could not understand musical works if one ignored their dynamic and expressive characters; this does not show, however, that the depictive character of music must be grasped if the music is to be understood, for the properties that must be noted are ones possessed by, rather than represented in, the music. I argue in Chapter 3 against the tendency to assume that attributions of spatial and expressive properties to music must be metaphoric, and in Chapter 5 I attempt to explain how music could literally possess such properties. Literally possessed properties may be used to symbolize (or represent, using "represent" in its broad sense) those

< 103 >

same properties—as in the earlier example of a lump of coal's being used to stand for the year's coal production—but if a property is literally possessed it is not also depicted (or represented, using "represent" in its narrow sense). A stone does not picture or depict its weight, it has it.

Scruton (1976; also see 1980a, 1980b, and 1980c) warns that it is an error to assimilate the notions of expression and depiction; pure music expresses emotions rather than depicting them.[71] The two concepts are distinct, and this must be respected in any discussion of the topic here under consideration, however loose ordinary parlance may be. Even where a program is to be counted as part of a musical work, we should not take the intimacy of the cooperation between music and text as a sign that the two do the same job in the same way. Music's contribution to the combination is expressive rather than depictive or narrational.

Others have stressed the need for a clear distinction between depiction and expression (see Howard 1972; Kivy 1984, chap. 7). The view that music complements the meaning of words with the (nondepictive, nondescriptive) expression of emotion or mood is widely held. Brown says, "Thus the best course would seem to be for the poet and the composer to work as a team, the poet in general conveying those particularities the composer cannot indicate, and the composer producing those states of mind that the poet cannot so adequately or directly communicate" (1948, 67; also see 83–86.) Many writers allow that music needs words if it is to attain more than vague expression.[72]

Howard (1972) attempts a Goodmanian analysis of the distinction between musical depiction and expression. He argues that the former involves denotation whereas the latter does not, though it does involve exemplification. But this view mistakes Goodman's position. In Goodman's account, both depiction and expression involve denotation: in expression, the denotation runs from the predicate to the exemplifier; in the representation of an existent subject, denotation runs from the picture to the subject. At first sight this implies that Goodman draws the distinction not in terms of the presence or absence of denotation (as Howard proposes) but by reference to the directionality of denotation. Though such an account seems to be presented by

---

[71] In opera, the emotion expressed in the music might represent or indicate the feelings experienced by a character; similarly, in a painting, a person might be depicted as sad. But the emotions expressed in music and painting are not always those of a depicted person and, in this case, it is a mistake to equate expression with depiction. In pure music, the emotions expressed are not the feelings of any person.

[72] See Rieser 1942, McMullin 1947, Brown 1948, Lippman 1953, 1966, and 1977, Davison 1954, Cazden 1955, and Howes 1958.

< 104 >

Goodman (see 1968), later (1970a) he rejects it. According to him, where a fiction is depicted, denotation runs via exemplification from the predicate to the (type of) picture—that is, in the same direction as is involved in expression.[73] Wollheim (1970) points out that there is not, as one might have hoped and expected, a neat distinction between representation and expression in Goodman's theory. So, though Howard recognizes the importance of the distinction, it is not obvious that it can be made in the Goodmanian line he adopts.

Common usage sometimes treats "express" and "represent" as synonyms, and philosophers do not always see the need to keep the notions distinct. Donald Ferguson (1960) recognizes that mere similarity between, on the one hand, the forms of feelings and their expressions and, on the other, the fluctuations of musical movement and tension could not explain the attribution to music of expressive properties. In acknowledging that more is needed, he suggests that music represents, and does not merely resemble, the experience of emotions. But he denies that music can represent *things* as pictures may do, so his notion of representation seems to collapse into that of expression. Urmson (1973) is another who runs the two together. Such talk of representation, rather than explaining and analyzing the notion of musical expressiveness, seems to presuppose that notion and recasts it in misleading terms.

The temptation to treat musical expression as a species of depiction arises this way, I think: Music seems to have dynamic and expressive qualities it could not possess, since it does not literally move anywhere or feel anything. Attributions of such qualities to music must be metaphoric. Rather than possessing such properties, it must be that music refers to them. But the listener's experience is not like that of hearing such things described, so the type of reference is not like that of language. Instead, the listener's experience of the properties seems immediate; it is, as it were, the experience of directly perceiving such qualities. Depictions also seem to give us immediate perceptual access to their subjects, despite the literal absence of those subjects. So musical expression is a kind of depiction.

My own approach is to attack this argument at its root. If it can be shown that music literally possesses the relevant properties, the temptation to wander down the path of reference to the haven of depiction is removed. By contrast, many of the writers who might query the argument of the previous paragraph agree with its initial premise, so they must dispute one of the later claims. Walton (1988 and 1990) is one who does so. He is aware of the

---

[73] But note that Goodman (1981) seems to return to distinguishing representation from expression by the direction of denotation.

< 105 >

attractiveness of the view but is inclined to reject it, defending the distinction between expression and depiction in doing so. He believes that depiction is possible in music, but that it is largely confined to the depiction of sounds. Cross-modal depiction is unlikely to be possible, he suggests (1990, 335).[74] Important though they are in the listener's experience and understanding, emotions are not depicted by music.

In challenging the argument given previously, Walton (1988; 1990, 63, 335–336, 340–341) proceeds by questioning the analogy between the experience of depictive works and of music. We do not have perceptual access to emotion and movement in the world of the musical work, for it does not present a determinate person or subject who feels or moves. Moreover, point of view (the perspective from which, fictionally, we perceive what is depicted) tends to be absent in music; if a stream allegedly is depicted, we hear it from neither upstream nor down.[75] Point of view (both first- and third-person) might also be absent from the presentation of emotions in music. And struggle might be depicted without there being any indication of whom is struggling or why. When we make-believe instances of movement or emotion in music, we do not make-believe *perceiving* such instances (neither do we make-believe that such things are reported to us). Whereas indeterminacy distances the reader from the story in literature, or the viewer from the subject of a painting, in music it permits and encourages an intimate relation between the listener and the work. The music seems to portray the phenomenal character of emotion or tension directly, rather than as a person's actions or feelings. By make-believedly engaging with the music, we can make it fictional that that action or emotion is our own (see Elliott 1966/67; Levinson 1982).

Walton regards music as representational—in his sense of the word this means that it is a prop in a game of make-believe—and it is part of his view that all representations are fictions (1990, 70). In Walton's view, "seeing/hearing in" involves the imagination, and in doing so it marks the listener's experience as one of make-believe. Make-believe is involved not only in hearing emotion in music but also in hearing a work's themes, since the listener

---

[74] Recall that, though he commonly describes music as representational, Walton regards depiction as a subspecies of representation. In holding that music is usually representational he means that it is properly to be used as a prop in a game of make-believe. Except where it deals with auditory phenomena, the game to be played with the music is not that to be played with a depiction; that is, it is not the game of making believe that one's auditory experience of the music is an auditory experience of what the music allegedly depicts.

[75] As I understand it, this particular disanalogy between music and painting does not count decisively in Walton's view against musical depiction; a stream might be depicted by the musical recreation of its distinctive sound.

< 106 >

hears the theme in the succession of notes. Besides, the recognition of movement in music clearly depends on make-believe in Walton's view (1988), and a person who could not appreciate movement in music could hear neither the theme as such nor its expressive character (since that movement makes these what they are). Moreover, the attempt to hear the theme and its expression is one authorized and prescribed for music, so the listener engages in a *game* of make-believe in hearing these things, according to Walton.

Is it true that I engage in a game of make-believe when I hear the theme of a symphony? I doubt this, because I doubt that hearing the theme involves the type of imagination that must be central to Walton's thesis.[76] I hear the theme in the notes, as opposed merely to hearing a succession of tones, and perhaps it does take imagination to organize the perceptual manifold. But, if so, the type of imagination involved is one found in veridical perception rather than the variety motivating games of make-believe. I do not hear the notes *as if* they are a theme, I do not *entertain* the thought that they constitute a theme—for I would make no mistake in taking them for a theme. In this case imagination is required (if at all) not in taking something for what it is not (paint for a barn) but to constitute it as it is. It is not fictional that those notes make up the theme, and it is not fictional of me that I hear the theme. As I understand it, the kind of imagination lying at the heart of make-believe, as described by Walton, is not involved in the experience of hearing the theme.

Neither is it clear to me that make-believe is involved in perceiving motion and expressiveness in music. There is no definite individual presented in the music who moves or feels, but that does not mean one makes-believe that there is such an individual or that one is that individual. I argue in Chapter 5 that we are familiar with motion that is not the movement of any individual in space or time, and that we widely acknowledge an expressive character in appearances that are not the appearances of persons. So I am inclined to reject the assumption that attributions to musical works of movement or expressive character must be fictional, and hence I resist the move that finds explanatory power in resort to talk of make-believe where such attributions are to be analyzed.

Is it proper to dismiss the titles or programs of musical works as irrelevant to understanding them? The argument of the previous section claims that most programmatic musical works are comprehensible in purely musical

---

[76] The observations made here apply equally to the discussion of the place of the imagination in hearing a theme outlined by Scruton (1974 and 1983). Indirect comments along similar lines can be found in Savile 1986 and Wollheim 1986.

< 107 >

terms even when their allegedly representational character is ignored. A critic of the Scrutonite line might allow this while denying that it is appropriate to take no account of the work's title or story: Someone who knows the titles of Debussy's *La Mer* and of its movements can hear in the piece a striking depiction of the sea; a person knowing the story of the operas can also hear the sea in Britten's *Four Interludes from Peter Grimes* and Wagner's *Der Fliegende Holländer*. That an experience of the representational character of these works depends on a knowledge of the story or title does not distinguish them from depictive works, such as Mondrian's *Broadway Boogie-woogie*. Now, if the title is part of the work, it should not be ignored. The listener who disregards the title cannot fully understand the work, even if that person finds the work to make musical sense while dismissing its title as irrelevant. If the title is part of the work and a knowledge of it adds something to the work—namely, a depictive character—then that something also is part of the work and should be appreciated as such by the listener who is motivated to understand the work. Just as one should consider the title of Mondrian's work in appreciating the piece as a representation, so too, it is suggested, the literary titles and programs of musical works intended to be depictive should be counted. When this is done, the representational character of those works becomes manifest.

The subject of titles has attracted some attention from John Fisher (1984), Jerrold Levinson (1985a), Hazard Adams (1987), and S. J. Wilsmore (1987). These authors agree in denying that it is appropriate to treat titles or accompanying texts as irrelevant to an artwork's proper appreciation. Various points are emphasized: (i) The title must be conferred by the artist, even if she does so at the suggestion of someone else (Fisher is criticized by Adams for missing this point). Neither "Moonlight" nor "Appassionata" was bestowed or sanctioned by Beethoven, so appeal cannot be made to the association of those labels with the works in claiming that Beethoven's sonatas are representational. (ii) The title is part of the work and not merely a label attached to it. (iii) Designatory titles, such as "Symphony No. 6 in B minor," have more than a classificatory significance, because they locate the work within a tradition—in more than one tradition in this case, because "symphony" has meant different things at different times in musical history—and within the artist's oeuvre (again, Adams complains that Fisher misses the point). (iv) Both (ii) and (iii) follow from the fact that a work's title affects the work's properties, including those that are artistically important. The title is relevant not simply because it directs attention to properties that are present but might easily be overlooked but, further, because it establishes a context in which the work takes on its properties. The smile on the face of

< 108 >

the woman depicted in da Vinci's *Mona Lisa* is often described as enigmatic. Had the painting been titled by da Vinci "Woman Observing the Entry into the Room of Her Secret Lover" or "Woman Gloating as Her Loathed Enemy Is Cruelly Tortured before Her," the character of the smile would be seen to change. Not only would it cease to be enigmatic, in the one case it would take on a sly, sensual character, and in the other it would become malicious. The same point can also apply to designatory titles, for example, insofar as they reveal the work's chronological position. Haydn's first symphony has features that depend on its being written as a youthful work when classical style was in its infancy, so the absence in it of a slow introduction has a quite different significance from the absence of a slow introduction in his Symphony No. 95.

Urmson (1973) apparently accepts that the title and program are parts of the work in arguing that music is representational. He explicitly accepts the four conditions for representation I set out earlier. He advocates that resemblance is a natural relation not depending on any knowledge of the artistic medium involved, but he also argues that the specificity of musical representation assumes the listener's knowledge of musical conventions. Even in comparatively simple cases of the representation of sound, some extramusical evidence is normally necessary to make clear exactly what is represented, and the evidence is usually supplied by the work's title (or by the words, if the piece is a song). It is only with an awareness of the nature of George Frideric Handel's orchestra and the conventions of musical composition of the time that we can hear the fall of a Philistine temple in *Samson*, but with that knowledge the resemblance is there, plainly to be heard. Urmson might suggest, then, as does Robinson (1981), that Scruton does not pay sufficient regard to extramusical considerations as contributing, with resemblance, to the success of representation.

Are programmatic titles and texts among the constituents of musical works? It is accepted for opera and song that the text is part of the work and that the work has depictive elements. But the debate about musical representation has always concentrated on program music, and this is because there is a genuine doubt here if the accompanying story is part of the work as such (Brown 1948, 229). I do not pursue this line, however, because I can concede the importance of titles and programs in such works while denying that program music is representational. I accept the points made above about the importance of titles and programs, but I think that they do not count so forcefully against Scruton's antirepresentational line as might at first be thought. One can allow that, as part of the work, the title might affect some of the artistically important properties, while denying that the title could

< 109 >

make the difference between the work's being depictive and nondepictive. As I read it, Scruton does not recommend that the title be ignored and he does not insist that it is irrelevant. Rather, his point seems to be that the importance of the title does not usually consist in its making the piece depictive where otherwise it would not be.

The representational character of a depictive work might be affected by the discovery that it had a different title from what was supposed. As noted previously, paintings that are identical in their appearance might represent different subjects if they have different titles. It rarely is the case, though, that a nonrepresentational painting would be made depictive had its title been different, or vice versa. A white-painted square titled "Abstract" would not have been representational had it been titled "Grass."[77] And James Whistler's paintings of his mother and of Carlysle are plainly representational, despite titles suggesting otherwise. If van Doesburg's *Cow* (which, despite its title, does not represent a cow, though its form was derived by abstraction from sketches in which a bovine beast can be discerned) had been titled "War," the painting might have had different properties, but it would have been no less abstract. Even if the title and accompanying programmatic text are properly to be regarded as part of the work, that fact alone could not count as evidence for the representational character of the works in question.

A reply to this point allows that the title can secure depiction only where it receives suitable "cooperation" from the work. The title does some but not all the work of depiction. In some cases, such as *Broadway Boogie-woogie,* the title's contribution would make the difference between the work's being abstract and its being representational.

Is this response convincing when music is said to be representational by analogy with *Broadway Boogie-woogie?* I doubt this. For painting, the title, if it helps, plugs into conventions for depiction that operate independently of the title's contribution. Usually a viewer familiar with the conventions can see that a man, say, is depicted, even if resort to the title is needed to be sure which man that is. For music, however, it is the existence of such conventions that is at issue. Stressing the importance of the title does not settle the matter, since (on both theories of representation discussed previously) the title is not sufficient on its own to make a work representational. The effect of a knowledge of the work's title on the listener's experience of the sound might

[77] The trick might work if the title of "Abstract" had been "White Square," or "Representation of a White Square," or "Representation of an Abstract Painting." Of course, self-reference is a distinctive feature of these special cases.

< 110 >

be explained as depending on association or the like rather than on the activation of conventions for depiction as such.

As I pointed out before, a person might approach a work with a story in mind the better to understand the music: "Hear this not as someone pushing a very heavy weight uphill, say, but as someone pulling a heavy weight downhill." The phenomenal experience of the music, and the terms in which he would be inclined to describe it, alter accordingly. But the point of using the story (supposing in this case that the work is musically as pure as the driven snow) is to help one understand the work. The listener might reveal this understanding through a description that develops the story, or by talking of tunes, tensions, and the like, or by discussing modulations and thematic inversions. Different stories might lead to a common understanding; descriptions of the work mentioning these different stories might reveal the same, equally deep appreciation. We should not be inclined (given that the work in question indisputably is pure) to regard any of these stories as depicted by the music. Rather, we would regard the various descriptions as significant since they reveal a recognition of relationships and patterns of tension and release—no matter that the relations hold between gnomes in one account and between international bankers in the other.

Like Scruton, I do not see program music as significantly different from pure music in this respect. A person who knows that Debussy's work is titled *La Mer* will be inclined to develop a description of the work in suitably watery terms—ebb and flow, currents, waves, spume. That person, naturally enough, seems to hear such things in the work, but this need not be evidence of the work's representationality, even if the title is part of the work. Another person, too stingy to buy a program at the concert, takes the work for a symphonic suite and talks instead of the power of the bass line, harmonic clashes, and so forth. A third listener mistakenly believes that the work is supposed to depict Debussy's mother. This person offers an account of the piece in terms appropriate to the description of a person: the mother is sometimes moody, but she displays deep inner strength, even when outwardly calm. The character of the mother comes to the mind's eye of the third listener no less clearly than does the sea come to the mind's eye of the first listener. Now, it seems to me that the first listener's description might easily reveal her lack of understanding—she hears calm ripples where she should sense a threatening undertow—and that the second and third listeners' descriptions might reveal a level of understanding such that, if they were conductors, those listeners could elicit strikingly convincing interpretations of

< 111 >

the work from a competent orchestra.[78] That one can relate a story supplied by the composer to the passage of the music is not a necessary skill for musical understanding in the way that it is necessary that a person see that thirteen people are depicted in da Vinci's *Last Supper* if we are to take seriously his prognostications on the work's significance.

It might be complained that I have argued that, as part of the work, the title or program makes a difference that makes no difference. Awareness of the title is likely to affect the phenomenology of the hearing experience and the terms in which one might develop a description of the work, but, important as these things are in the experience of the individual, I have denied both that they are directly implicated in the listener's understanding and that they show the work to be depictive. Earlier, though, I accepted that the work's title might affect its properties. Which qualities, if not representational ones, would be altered were we to discover that a musical work had a different title from what we thought? How does the title create a difference that makes a difference?

A reply to these questions is indicated by a consideration of the discovery that an abstract painting had a title other than what one had thought. If the title were found to be "Study No. 15," one might expect to locate it in a series, and it might take on properties depending on that placing. If the title were found to be "Girl and Boy" and the painting features pink and blue, the associations of these colors might become important. If the title were discovered to be "War," one might find in the work expressions of violence. In these cases the qualities one newly finds in the work are not properties one overlooked formerly but properties effected by interaction between the work's title and other of its parts. And in these cases, though the viewer brings to mind different ideas in considering the work's title, never does the title name a subject depicted in the painting.

The discovery that a musical work had a title other than one believed might produce results similar to those just described. (i) If the work is now known to be a "Suite," not a "Symphony," then it takes on some new properties while others that were important formerly no longer are so, for the title establishes it as belonging to an unsuspected comparison class; for example, its containing five movements is no longer an exceptional feature. (ii) If the work is now titled "Peace," not "War," one hears not conflict ending

---

[78] Fisher (1984) recounts that Schumann was tricked into thinking he was listening to Mendelssohn's "Italian" Symphony when it was that composer's "Scottish" Symphony he was hearing. He had no difficulty "seeing" in the work Italian landscapes and vistas with incredible detail. Obviously there is a sense in which Schumann's description of the work is inappropriate, but we should be reluctant to say that a composer of his powers misunderstood it.

< 112 >

with exhaustion but a working through of mutual differences in the success-ful pursuit of compromise or common ground. (iii) Just in case we might mistake satire for incompetence, Mozart titled one work *Ein Musikalischer Spass*. Had it been written by Carl Ditters von Dittersdorf and played by the local band, aspects of the work and its performance would be laughably bad, not witty.

Given Scruton's emphasis on a distinction between musical expression and depiction (1976, 1980a, 1980b, 1980c), he might be happy to allow that a work's title could affect its expressive character. The sadness of a work might be an objective property of it not dependent on its title, but the title "Piece Composed on the Death of a Dearly loved Canary" might reveal the sadness as that of mourning. Music is expressive in character, rather than representa-tional as pictures are, and sometimes the title of a musical work can be rele-vant to an appreciation of the detail of its expressive character.

Lippman suggests that there is a continuity between abstract and program music, noting that some symphonic movements derive from dances, such as the minuet, waltz, and *Ländler* (and from other types of functional music, such as the march). The dance form that is the movement's ancestor leaves a "deposition or impression" of the significance it derives from its social function and place (1977, 268–270). A similar and compelling account is presented by Norman Cazden (1955). Wilson Coker (1983) points out that verbal indications ("vivace," "with passion," and so on) are standard within scores and should be regarded as no less a part of the work than are notes on staves. Allowing this, there need be no special difficulty, he observes, in recognizing titles and other discursive, programmatic indications as integral to the work. Now, I am sure that these observations are correct, but I inter-pret the absence of a clear distinction between pure and program music, not as showing that a story should be read into pieces such as Stravinsky's Symphony in Three Movements, but rather as emphasizing the extent to which the human aspect of emotional expression is present in all kinds of music. This seems to be Lippman's own view. And it is Cazden's: "Nowhere do I suggest a hidden 'programme' in the naïve nineteenth-century sense or a verbal 'meaning' that ought to be translated out of the work during lis-tening" (1955, 35).

Is it proper to treat program music as a subspecies of pure music rather than as a distinct genre? It might be objected that I have missed the full significance of discursive titles. Not only are they relevant in determining directly some of the work's properties, they also indicate that the work be-longs to the genre of program music and, hence, that it is not to be ap-proached as an instance of abstract, pure music. To ignore the title and to

< 113 >

attempt to understand the piece in purely musical terms is not to understand it better or somehow more correctly, it is to approach the work incorrectly, to treat it as something it is not. Just as it would be perverse to ignore the words of a song or the action of an opera and to treat the work on purely musical terms,[79] so it is perverse to treat program music in this fashion. Walton (1970) indicates that one could not understand a work while mistaking or ignoring its genre, for the work's genre determines some of its artistically important properties. The arguments offered earlier give insufficient weight to the distinction in genre between pure and program music.

In this view, program music is an artistic hybrid between music and words. Representation might be achieved by music in its marriage with words, though depiction is not a feature of pure music. After all, music is an important element in many hybrid artforms—opera, ballet, song, and film—that are undoubtedly held to be representational.

The hybrid (or composite) nature of (some) artforms has attracted little attention in the literature, an exception being by Levinson (1984).[80] Levinson argues that hybrid status is primarily a historical thing, not merely a matter of the use of more than one medium. Hybrids arise from the combination or interpenetration of earlier artforms and should be understood in terms of, and in light of, their historically autonomous components.[81] The media of hybrid artforms are historically prior artforms rather than stuff, such as paint. For example, the media of (Wagnerian) opera are song and drama.[82]

Levinson describes the relation between the combined artforms in a hybrid as of three possible types: the *juxtapositional*, in which the components re-

---

[79] As Anton Bruckner is said to have done during *Der Ring des Nibelungen* when finally he tore his gaze from the pit, noticed the events on stage, and asked "Why are they burning that woman?"

[80] For a useful discussion of the musical case, see Lippman 1977, though Lippman is concerned mainly with the cross-fertilization between abstract music and hybrid forms in which music plays a role.

[81] Complex, multi-media affairs with no historical roots in other artforms—*Gedanken* hybrids—are distinct from true hybrids in his view.

[82] If composite artforms are always to be viewed in terms of the character and properties of their historical ancestors, is one to approach an artform that results from decomposition in a similar fashion? Pure instrumental music arose historically from practices that mixed music with words, action, and ceremony, but we treat it as distinct from song, ballet, and the like; in this case, the historical approach recommended for hybrids seems not to apply. It could be argued, however, that pure music has lost touch with its ancestors in a way that is not so for a hybrid artform such as opera, which must be understood as drawing on the character of its antecedents. Pure music may have emerged by abstraction from song and dance, but the songs and dances from which it emerged are now lost to us, it might be said, and should not be confused with much later sophistications, such as lieder and ballet.

< 114 >

tain the identity they possess in their pure manifestations—for example, mime accompanied by a flute; the *synthetic*, in which the individual components lose some of their individuality through mutual modification involving a merging or dissolving of their original identities—for example, Wagnerian opera; a type intermediate between the juxtapositional and the synthetic, the *transformational*, in which one artform retains its primary character but the others are modified—Levinson offers as an example kinetic sculpture, which is sculpture in movement, not sculptural dance.

Juxtapositional artforms might be described as involving a *mixture* of their components, whereas synthetic artforms might be described as involving a *compound* of their components. A mixture has properties neither of its components possess. A mixture of equal quantities of H_2 and O_2 in a test tube has a density differing from that of a test tube containing solely either one of these elements. The properties of a mixture result from the summation of the properties of the individual components according to their proportion. By contrast, a compound is a new entity, not merely a composite entity, with properties of a different order from those of its constituents. H_2O, for example, is a liquid at room temperature in which one can drown for lack of oxygen. Of course, this talk of chemical compounds and elements is analogical only. In the sense of "compound" relevant here, a cake is a compound (or synthesis) of its constituents and not a mixture (or juxtaposition). In the case of a synthetic artform, the constituents remain recognizable as such: the music in an opera does not disappear and an instrumental suite might be drawn from the work, such as Pablo Sarasate's fantasy on Georges Bizet's *Carmen*, or Wagner's *Siegfried Idyll*. So, a better analogy than that of a cake or chemical compound is that of a gestalt. Dots and dashes might be disposed to picture a face, but in seeing the face one remains aware of the dots and dashes. In a similar way, then, synthetic (and transformational) artforms are perceived as gestalts generated from the combination of their constituent artforms.[83]

[83] There is an issue not considered by Levinson (since he discusses genres rather than individual works): It is not uncommon for independent musical works, or parts of musical works, to be appropriated for use within hybrid artforms. Ballets have been based on symphonies and concertos. Familiar orchestral or choral music accompanies television advertisements, so that, for example, Handel's "Hallelujah" chorus from the *Messiah* becomes the "Aluminium" (pronounced in the British, not North American, manner) chorus. Musical works also find their way into the soundtracks of films, as happened to the slow movement of Mozart's Piano Concerto in C, K. 467, which was used in the film *Elvira Madigan*. (The victims are not always the composers. Verdi's *Otello* is adapted from Shakespeare's play, and both Gioacchino Rossini's *Barber of Seville* and Mozart's *Marriage of Figaro* come from Pierre de Beaumarchais's trilogy.) How are these cases to be described? Because part of the work is appropriated, it might be thought

< 115 >

In discussing whether and how the genre of program music might differ from that of pure music with respect to its representational character, I consider two matters. First, I attempt to classify some musical genres, and other genres in which music features as an element, with respect to the kind of hybrid they involve. Then I argue that music is not representational, whether as an element in a synthetic or in a juxtapositional hybrid—that, whatever the difference in genre between pure and program music might come to, the difference is not such that music could be depictive in the one unless it were so in the other.

Music is conjoined with many other elements, and in many different proportions, to create hybrid artforms. There is a gradation of cases, from musical works with literary titles for the whole and its movements, such as Gustav Holst's *The Planets* or Modest Mussorgsky's *Pictures at an Exhibition*; through works with an accompanying text supplied or indicated by the composer, such as Johann Kuhnau's *Biblische Historien* or Liszt's *Mazeppa* (after Victor Hugo); through works with a narrated story, such as Prokofiev's *Peter and the Wolf*; through song, choral music generally, oratorio, the mass, and the passions; through opera and ballet; through film music, such as Prokofiev's famous work for S. M. Eisenstein's *Alexander Nevsky*, not to mention the efforts of composers such as Dmitri Tiomkin and Elmer Bernstein and the improvisations of those who accompany silent films; through incidental music for plays, such as Bizet's music for Alphonse Daudet's *L'Arlésienne* and Edvard Grieg's music for Henrik Ibsen's *Peer Gynt*; to cases in which a musical accompaniment is a more or less optional supplement to the main artistic fare. With so many types of example to choose from, it is not surprising that music figures in hybrids of all three types identified by Levinson.

I think that works with titles (and no more) are best thought of as juxtapositional hybrids (if they are to be thought of as hybrids at all). Program works with an associated text or story are transformational hybrids in which the music is dominant if they were intended (as most were) to make musical

---

that these works should be regarded as juxtapositions, but it seems plain silly to treat Mozart's *Marriage of Figaro*, for example, as a nonsynthetic mixture of music and play. On the other hand, if such works are regarded as synthetic hybrids, it looks as if, through no act of Mozart's and with no alteration of its notes, the music from K. 467 can be transformed into part of a representational whole. Even if at least one artist carefully combined the parts into a satisfactory whole, we have some grounds for discomfort because another artist's work was treated as it was not intended to be treated. There are fewer classificatory problems if the appropriated piece is modified to suit it to its new use (for example, in Stravinsky's light-handed recomposition for *Pulcinella* of Giovanni Pergolesi's music), because then it is easier to see that a synthesis is achieved.

< 116 >

sense when judged by the standards of pure music, or they are transformational hybrids in which the narrative is uppermost if they are works in which the music makes no sense when separated from the narrative context. I believe that song, opera, ballet, and film should be viewed as synthetic artforms. It is significant, perhaps, that these artforms are not called "music" (as one has orchestral music, choral music, chamber music, and so on), music being but one element in the whole. I note, however, that music and words are sometimes described as manifesting an antipathy so great that, shake them as one will, like oil and water they result in a juxtapositional hybrid. I regard this view as exaggerated but mention some who have held it. Brown (1948) treats song as juxtapositional, with subjects picked out by the text and emotions presented in the music. He mentions (1948, 84) Franz Schubert's *Erlkönig* as an ideal and very rare example of music and literature combining to form one indivisible artwork. Lippman (1977, 252–253) takes a similar position, seeing a potential incompatibility between the concrete definiteness of words and the expressive character of music, an incompatibility only great skill can overcome. Archibald Davison (1954) indicates many ways musical settings can fail to respect the integrity of the words and meanings they set. He concludes that: "words and music certainly are fundamentally unlike in their nature" (1954, 3), and Gordon Epperson agrees: "The alliance of words with music, no matter how successful it may be, is an association of disparate elements" (1967, 1).[84] Opera, as well as song, is sometimes characterized as a juxtapositional hybrid, despite its dramatic content. Brown (1948, 88–90) says that the different artforms involved often tend to get in each other's way rather than fusing into a satisfactory whole. Lippman (1977, 254–255) is more charitable, allowing that the temporal nature of music allows it to fuse with dramatic action, but he too sees problems in melding all the elements. Kivy (1988a) distinguishes between "drama made music" and "opera as drama" and suggests that, in the former, "opera cannot do what music cannot do." That is, he treats some operas (Mozart's *Così Fan Tutte* is his main example) as transformational, with music as the primary element, rather than as synthetic. In doing so he downplays the representational and dramatic character of such works; for criticism, see Levinson 1987b. In the case of cinema, Lippman (1977) distinguishes the role of music in silent films, in which it is an integral element, from its place in contemporary films. He implies that, whereas the silent film is a synthetic hybrid, contemporary film is usually a transformational hybrid, so much does the drama dominate the music.

---

[84] For a discussion of the problems that arise in marrying words and music, see Winn 1981.

< 117 >

Earlier I noted that, whereas opera, song, and ballet are regarded as depictive, the argument about musical representation centers on program music. I also observed that most composers and commentators think that programmatic works should be capable of standing on their own, as it were, as if they were pure music. I am inclined here to interpret the difference in the attitude expressed to opera and ballet, on the one hand, and program music, on the other, as evidence that we regard these as examples of different kinds of hybrids. Then, program music must belong near the juxtapositional end of the continuum, with opera and ballet as synthetic. So I disagree with the attitudes expressed in the previous paragraph. Whether I am correct in this classification may not matter, for I now argue that the place of music within a hybrid of any kind does not make it depictive if pure music is not itself depictive.

If the hybrid is juxtapositional, music retains its autonomous character. It contributes no more and no less than it would possess as pure music. If pure music is not depictive, then the juxtapositional hybrid in which music is an element is depictive, if at all, only because another element has a representational character. This is not to deny that the music has a contribution to make to the whole; it might express appropriate emotions, generate a complementary mood, and so on, and in doing so it could considerably enhance the overall effect. But it cannot contribute what it does not independently possess. Levinson's example of a juxtapositional hybrid, mime accompanied by flute, is also an example of a representational hybrid. It is so because the mime depicts actions, such as that of encountering an invisible wall. Where the juxtapositional hybrid combines narration with music, as in Arnold Schönberg's *Pierrot Lunaire*, the hybrid is narrational rather than depictive. Depiction and narration can be combined, as in the cartoon strip, or where speech or action is acted out and not merely described, but the whole arising from the combination of music and words is not automatically a depictive one.

I suspect that programmatic musical works, as hybrids, are narrational rather than depictive and, in any event, that it is the text, not the music, that does most of the describing or picturing. If depiction of a crude and subsidiary kind is possible in music, such "sound painting" as occurs ("He knocked on the door," followed by staccato chords) is likely to be a comparatively small factor in the whole. Music can and does contribute "sound effects," but this does not show that the music changes the character of such works from narrational to representational. Given that the musical element retains its autonomous character within a juxtapositional hybrid, and also given the dominance of the musical element in programmatic works, Scruton is not

< 118 >

wrong to insist that such music be judged by standards set by pure music, notwithstanding the difference in genre.[85]

If the hybrid is synthetic (or transformational, with a nonmusical artform as the primary one), it would be fallacious, as Scruton (1976) points out, to argue from the properties of the whole to the properties of the constituents. The cake may be sweet but this does mean that the salt going into it is sweet. Opera, which I take to be a synthetic hybrid, is representational, but one cannot argue validly from this fact to the conclusion that the music within it is depictive.

Robinson (1981) objects: it is not music's playing a role in dramatic contexts that makes it representational, it is the nature of the role it plays. Her point might be this: One cannot reason from the depictive character of opera to the representationality of any of the elements the opera comprises; nevertheless, some of those elements do have a depictive function. For opera, where the elements are not transformed out of existence in the process of being combined, one can examine the contribution made by each, just as one can see in a picture made up of dots and dashes that a particular dash marks the mouth, a dot the pupil of the eye, and so on. When one looks, one can *observe* that music serves a representational role within opera. A sforzando chord signifies the sound of the hero's thumping the table; the sadness expressed in the music depicts the sadness felt by the character; the pursuit of an ever-receding, changing tonic represents the lovers' yearning for the consummation of the relationship.

I accept that, in opera, the music contributes significantly to the depictive character of the whole rather than merely accompanying the depictive function of other elements. It plays this role, however, only because of its place in the wider context. Therefore, even if one talks loosely of the representational character of the music in an opera, it is not proper to hold that such music could be depictive when divorced from its dramatic context. It makes sense to talk of music's representational place only within the context (actual or assumed) of the whole to which it contributes. The music in the opera is like the dash which, in context, is the mouth of the depicted face, or is like a gray patch which, in the given painting, depicts the shadow of the nose, or is like the word "this," which takes a reference only within a broader setting.

Is an orchestral suite abstracted from an opera, film, or ballet representational? If one is ignorant of the plot, or of the significance of the music within the plot, it probably sounds like pure music. This, at least, is how I hear

---

[85] Lippman (1977) reaches a similar conclusion; that is, program music is a composite artform in which music is dominant, so standards for abstract music apply.

< 119 >

Prokofiev's suite from *Lieutenant Kije*. I know the story of the film but am familiar only with the suite and do not know in detail how it relates to the plot's presentation. On the other hand, if one is so well acquainted with the work that one hears the suite as if it were a replay of dramatic highlights, with every note bringing to mind the words sung to it, or spoken as it was played, the context of action, and so forth, then the music sounds representational just because it serves as a mnemonic for the work from which it derives.[86] Now, even if one believed that the suite could be understood only by someone so much at home with the opera itself that she needed no more than is supplied by the suite to bring the work to mind—and that belief strikes me as far too strong to be justified—this would not establish that the music of the suite is representational as such. It would show instead that the non-musical context on which representationality depends might be recollected, rather than synthesized at the time of the performance. It would not prove that pure music—or music contiguous with, but not interactively combined with, other elements—is depictive.

Hence, whether the hybrid in which music features is synthetic or juxtapositional, there is no straightforward argument allowing a move from the representational character of a hybrid artform to claims about the representational character of the music it includes. And, if the hybrid involves juxtaposition, we should be inclined to deny that the music is depictive since the musical element retains its autonomous character and, as such, is best viewed as nonrepresentational. If the hybrid involves synthesis, then, howsoever the music contributes to the total depiction, there is no way of isolating the contribution of the music in a way that licenses claims about the representational character of music as such (that is, of "unsynthesized" music).

Even if we allow that music does its own thing, that "thing" can usefully be described as depiction only if music satisfies the most general conditions for representation. These general conditions are most clearly to be seen through a consideration of picturing. I have discussed pictures not because music would be representational only if it could deal with the same subjects by employing analogous techniques but because a consideration of paintings reveals the background conditions without which any representation would be impossible. I have suggested that, for the most part, music does not satisfy

---

[86] The trumpet call in Beethoven's *Leonore* No. 3 cannot help but recall the dramatic significance of its occurrence in *Fidelio* to someone familiar with the opera. Though the overture is not directly extracted from the opera, its connection with *Fidelio* is crucial, I think, if we are to hear more than usually is associated with such martial flourishes. In this respect, compare *Leonore* No. 3 with the allegretto of Haydn's Symphony No. 100 (*Military*).

< 120 >

these conditions. So I see no virtue in holding to the view that music achieves a special variety of representation, a distinctive species within the wider genus. The differences between paintings and music are not attributable to the specific character of their modes of depiction. Those differences tend to be generic ones: painting can be depictive, music usually cannot be.

It has not been my aim to argue that music is incapable of depiction but rather to show that its capacities in this regard are severely limited, though sometimes of interest. Sounds might be depicted in music, I think. The same is true of dynamic processes with a distinctive phenomenology, though there may be few such. Under rather special circumstances, musical passages or styles might also be depicted in music. But, for the most part, the richness of music does not arise from its depictive powers. Emotions are often expressed and complex dynamic structures are presented, but to regard music as *depicting* such things usually requires such a weakening of the notion of representation as to render it uninformatively colorless. Equally, reference to things lying beyond the music is often possible—it would be difficult to quote the "Marseillaise" without referring to the French—but there is no virtue in assimilating reference of this type to that of depiction. The meaning and importance of music (whatever those might involve and come to) do not depend primarily on music's possessing a depictive character.

In Chapter 1 I rejected the view that music is significantly like a natural language, though I allowed that some musical symbols are purely conventional in the way the meanings of most words are. In this chapter I have rejected the view that music is representational as pictures often are, but I have allowed that there may be a degree of depiction in music (like that in pictorial representation) based on natural (but conventionally structured) resemblances. An obvious possibility to explore next is that music employs a symbol scheme that is sui generis. On this theory, music shares with language and representational pictures a symbolic content secured in a systematic fashion, but it differs from both in establishing this content in terms of the distinctive (nondiscursive, nonpictorial) conventions of its own distinctive symbol system. I also have suggested that music's power lies more with its expressive than with its limited representational possibilities. I turn, then, in the next chapter to an account of music as a symbol scheme devoted to the symbolization of feeling.

< 121 >

T H R E E

· · · · ·

Music and Symbols

Underlying some of the theories discussed in the previous chapters is the idea that music, depictions, and linguistic utterances all partake of a level of symbolism, each type being formalized in its own way. Perhaps one might take up that idea and, rather than push the analogy between music and language, or between music and depiction, argue that music achieves its expressive effect as another, distinctive type of symbol. Music might comprise a symbol system (or systems) that differs in structure or operation from those of language or pictures; in being expressive, music might be doing its symbolic thing in its own way. Versions of such a view are presented by Susanne Langer and Nelson Goodman, and it is their positions on which I concentrate in this chapter.[1] Though both philosophers present their theories as applying to expressiveness in the arts in general, I focus on the application of their views to music.

Langer's Theory: Presentational Symbols

According to Langer (especially 1942, 1953), music (and art in general) is an iconic symbol of mental states identifiable as emotions. She regards the

---

[1] In terms of the typology of meanings outlined in Chapter 1, Langer regards musical meaning as of type A or B, whereas Goodman's antinaturalism leads him to regard it as of type E. Such differences have little effect on the criticisms I consider. It is not uncommon for antinominalists to accept the general shape of Goodman's theory.

< 123 >

meaning of music as relying importantly on a natural element, iconicity, and she denies that, as a symbol, a musical work depends for its significance on its place within a general symbol system.

Langer's position always has attracted support.[2] "Semiotic aesthetics," of which Langer's theory is a prime example, had its heyday in the 1940s and 1950s. This style of theory no longer is much in vogue among Anglo-American, analytic philosophers of art (see, though, Tarasti 1987), but the ghost of Langerian theory survives in the European concern with hermeneutics.[3] The hermeneuticist most likely differs from Langer in seeing music as culture-bound rather than as natural in its significance.

According to Langer, works of art are "presentational" symbols of feelings. Her account of presentational symbolism is developed by contrasting this mode of symbolism with the discursive symbolism of language. She accepts the account of significance in language known as the "picture theory of meaning," offered by Ludwig Wittgenstein in his *Tractatus Logico-Philosophicus*. In this view, sentences function as pictures of the logical form of reality. A sentence is true when its logical form accurately models the logical form of reality. Empirically unverifiable statements are meaningless. At the time of writing the *Tractatus*, Wittgenstein held that many statements of ethics and aesthetics are nonverifiable and he concluded, "Whereof one cannot speak, thereof one must be silent" (1922). By contrast, Langer thinks that there is much to be said about possibilities of meaning that cannot be

[2] Her followers include Howes (1958) and Epperson (1967). She is cited with approval by Ballard (1953), Meyer (1956), Jacobs (1960), Schaper (1964), Hansen (1968), McLaughlin (1970), and Petock (1972). For recent work on a Langerian wavelength, see von Morstein 1982 and 1986. Piechowski (1981) offers the research of the psychologist Clyne as empirical confirmation of Langer's views and provides a gem of his own: each composer's work is marked by an inner pulse, and we like the music of a composer if the inner pulse in his music chimes with our own inner pulse. For a more circumspect attempt to salvage the nuggets from Langer's works, see Slattery 1987.

[3] For example, Henry Orlov says this: "If music is to be considered a sign system, then it is a very strange one: an icon which has nothing in common with the object it presents; an abstract language which does not allow for a prior definition of its alphabet and vocabulary, and operates with an indefinite, virtually infinite number of unique elements; a text which cannot be decomposed into standard interchangeable items. These discrepancies can be reconciled if music is approached in terms of semiotics but without its preconceptions. Music is an icon on the surface, by appearance; it is perceived as an icon. The icon is peculiar, however, since it does not and cannot resemble the object it presents, which is ideal and unattainable to the senses. Therefore, what appears as the icon on the surface acts, behind the surface, as an abstract sign—a symbol, but a special kind of symbol which is unique and otherwise indefinable. . . . The reason for this strangeness is that the reality so symbolized is that of preverbal experience—the reality of immediate mental, emotional, and sensuous life in the human being" (1981, 136–137). For similar observations, see Charles 1988.

< 124 >

captured by the discursive mode of symbolism analyzed by Wittgenstein. She holds that such meanings are the provenance of presentational, nondiscursive symbols, and her theory offers an account of this mode of symbolism. She argues that it is above all the arts, and in particular music, which trade in presentational symbols. Garry Hagberg neatly summarizes Langer's view, capturing the way it differs from Wittgenstein's: whereof we cannot speak, thereof we must compose, paint, write, sculpt, and so forth (1984, 127).

Presentational symbols derive their meaning from their picturing the logical form of reality, writes Langer, and in this respect they are like discursive symbols. In other ways the two types of symbol differ significantly. Discursive symbols (linguistic utterances) are created from a vocabulary, the units of which have conventionally assigned meanings that are interdefinable. Sentences are built from the elements of the vocabulary in a rule-governed way. The meaning of a proposition is a function of the meanings of its constituents. Propositions can be translated from one language to another. They can be true or false. These features of language are definitional; these are the requirements of discursive "forms," of the use of language to assert, question, command, and so forth. By contrast, a presentational symbol is neither true nor false; it does not have an assertoric function. The meaning of a presentational symbol (its significance) is necessarily altered if the elements constituting its form are removed, altered, or replaced. A presentational symbol cannot be translated. A presentational symbol lacks reference, though it has import. Whereas a language is a symbol system, each presentational symbol is autonomous and, together, presentational symbols do not constitute a symbol system.[4] Because of their differences, these two modes of symbolism deal with exclusive areas of meaning. As a result, we cannot *say* what the meaning of a presentational symbol is, though we can know its import through direct acquaintance with it.

In Langer's view, a presentational symbol is a vehicle for the conception of a subject; it evokes a conception of the subject symbolized. The appropriate response to a presentational symbol is a thought—not a thought about the subject, but an idea or conception of the nature of that subject. Langer is keen to reject expression and arousal theories of musical expression.[5] Accordingly, she emphasizes the idea that music symbolizes not occurrences of

---

[4] For a similar account of the differences between these types of symbol, also see Körner 1955.
[5] These views are discussed further in Chapter 4. In brief, the expressionist claims that the emotions expressed in music are feelings experienced by the composer, whereas the arousalist claims that music's expressiveness consists in its power to move the listener to an affective response. Schaper (1964) argues that Langer continues, rather than displaces, the romantic tradition in which such views find their home.

< 125 >

feelings but the concept of them. In addition, she stresses the importance of the adoption of an aesthetic, disinterested attitude as a condition for appreciating art's symbolic character, as does the Langerian Gordon Epperson (1967).

One thing can be a presentational symbol of another because the form of the first is iconic with the form of the second. The form of a thing is a function of the relation between its parts or elements. No feature of a thing can be dismissed a priori as irrelevant to its form. The form of a thing can be abstracted from it in experience, but it cannot be described, except ostensively; neither can it be depicted, except by the reproduction of the object in all its detail. The form of a thing is unique to it; we experience the uniqueness of the form even though we cannot give a uniquely identifying description of that form. Where the forms of two things are iconic, the *essential relation* between the elements of the two things is one of qualitative identity, despite differences between the "materials" constituting the elements and consequent differences in the descriptions we might be tempted to offer of the relationships within the two sets of elements. So, the spatial form of a painting can be iconic with the temporal form of a feeling, because the essential relationship between the elements of the painting can (be known to) correspond to the essential relationship between the elements of the feeling. Similarly, the relationship between the aural elements of a musical work can be the same as the relationship between the thoughts and sensations that constitute a feeling.[6] When an artist or composer symbolizes some feeling in his work, he "transforms" the relationship between the elements of that feeling to a relationship between visual or auditory elements. The "laws of projection" mapping the one to the other are unique to the particular case and, anyway, could not be stated.[7] These laws of projection are applied unconsciously and intuitively by the artist. And when his audience recognizes his work as a presentational symbol of feeling, it does so as a result of a process that also is unthinking and intuitive. The abstraction and comparison of forms is a constant, unconscious process. We can only report *that* it is done; for any particular case we cannot say *how* it is done. The directionality of

---

[6] Langer (1953) explains the distinctions between the arts as depending on differences in their "primary illusions." Bufford (1972) argues that this aspect of her theory is distinct from her general theory of expressiveness. Scholz (1972), Agarwal (1973), and Carter (1974) criticize her accounts of literature, architecture, and painting, respectively. Alperson (1980) rejects her account of virtual time in music.

[7] Langer writes of these laws as unique to each work; also, she does not consider them to be stipulated or arbitrary. For these reasons, it would be a mistake, I think, to interpret her as claiming that presentational symbols operate within the context of symbol systems.

< 126 >

symbolism is governed not by intentions but rather by the manipulability and accessibility of the forms compared for iconicity. Where one form is appreciated as a transformation of another with which it is iconic, we become aware of the first form bearer as a presentational symbol of the second.

Sometimes Langer intimates that what is symbolized by artworks is the form common to all feelings. At other times she implies that what is symbolized is the form common to the various instances of a particular feeling. This ambiguity (which also can be found in Epperson 1967) arises, perhaps, because she realizes that different feelings, even contrary feelings, might share the same form, while she also believes that some feelings have their own, distinctive forms.

As modes of symbolization, discursive and presentational symbols are quite different. In Langer's view, therefore, it is not surprising that we cannot provide an adequate account of the one in terms of the other. We cannot describe the laws of projection involved in the creation of presentational symbols. We can describe the form of an object not in terms of its essential relations but only by reference to the elements whose relations constitute the form. Hence, in describing the form of a painting, we describe a configuration in space; we characterize musical form as a pattern in aural space; we describe the form of feeling as articulated in mental space. The descriptions we are able to offer of different objects obscure, rather than expose, the isomorphism their forms may display. Nevertheless, we are aware of the iconicity of the forms through our *experience* of them; we experience a sameness between the forms of works of art and of feelings. As a result, we are aware of works of art as symbols of feelings. Works of art bring to mind conceptions of the nature of emotions; works of art are experienced as sharing the forms of feelings despite the difference between their respective materials and the realm of the mental. The process of symbolization and the resulting iconicity cannot be demonstrated or described. But from our experience of works of art as symbolizing emotions we can infer the outline of the procedure by which the symbolization is brought about, even if we cannot fully describe this procedure.

A first move in criticizing Langer's theory would be to query the tenability of the account of the emotions it presupposes. Most emotions involve, as well as feelings with a dynamic character or form, objects toward which these feelings are directed, certain types of beliefs about the nature of those objects, behavioral expressions (some of which may be distinctive), and typical causal contexts. Langer tends to regard such things as merely contingent concomitants of emotions, which she seems to conceive as agitations of the inner, animal, vital spirits. Like Descartes, then, she tends to treat emotions

< 127 >

as if they are (complex) sensations. Her theory clearly implies that feelings are identified with (not just that they can be individuated by) their forms "in the mind": one can know that X symbolizes some feeling because of the iconicity of the form of X with the form of that feeling only if one can identify that feeling by its form. Such a view is unattractive, to say the least. Emotions are conceptually much richer than Langer allows. When all the "concomitants" are ignored, it seems not so much that we are left with the essential form of feelings as that the feelings themselves have been dispensed with.

Langer's critics have seized on this point. Although Michael Piechowski (1981) holds that emotions (construed as complex sensations) have the multiplicity of articulative elements necessary for a logical form susceptible to representation, Harold Osborne (1982) denies this. Moreover, Osborne (1955) doubts that there is sufficient uniformity among responses to music to support the view that music symbolizes feelings. Others note that Langer's attempt to neutralize this criticism—by suggesting that different emotions might share the same form—creates more difficulties for her theory than it solves. Revised this way, the view implies that it is form, rather than feeling, that is presented in music.[8] Besides, a given morphology might be common not only to quite different emotions (for example, bursting with joy and blowing one's top) but also to other events or processes (such as the departure of a train) which, usually, we would not take the music to symbolize.[9] Hagberg (1984) develops the theme: whether one takes the forms to be of large scale (for example, sonata form), medium scale (themes, phrases), or small scale (intervallic relations), it always seems to be possible to find works that share the same form but do not symbolize the same emotion. He concludes that the notion of form central to Langer's account of presentational modes of symbolism is not merely indescribable, as she would have it, but incoherent: "Within the theory the word 'form' is being employed in some unrecognizable or systematically elusive way. . . . The doctrine of unsayability, at least when given the theoretical formulation, conceals at its core an element of impenetrable mystery" (1984, 338).

As a second line of attack one might criticize Langer's theory of discursive symbolism and thereby call into question her account of presentational symbols, since she develops her view of the latter mainly by contrast with her

---

[8] See Nagel 1943; also Wilkinson 1992. The point lies behind Clark's (1982) contending that the referent disappears into the symbol in Langer's theory, so the distinction between the two is lost; also see Evans 1990.

[9] The point is made in Beardsley 1958, Binkley 1970, and Budd 1985a.

< 128 >

account of the former.[10] The "picture theory of meaning" has been rejected, most notably by Wittgenstein himself. In brief, the problem is that the meanings of sentences depend more on the context of their use than on their form; many sentences sharing a superficially similar form operate in different ways within the various social practices in which they find their homes. The force of such worries cannot easily be avoided by distinguishing "surface" from "logical" form, because the notion of logical form (divorced from any context of use) is fraught with difficulties. These include those of giving an account of names such that sentences might be regarded (as the theory does) as concatenations of simple names, and of finding the atomic facts that are said to be named by logically simple sentences. In addition, there is room to doubt that Langer's account of Wittgenstein's *Tractatus* theory of language reveals a correct understanding of that doctrine.[11] With the "picture theory of meaning" abandoned, one might be inclined to deny that Langer establishes the distinctness of discursive and presentational symbols.[12] Her account makes much of the exclusivity of these two modes of symbolism in explaining the indescribability of the symbolic relation typically found in musical works. If they are not exclusive, her inability to describe in detail how musical events and relations are iconic symbols of the form of feeling no longer seems excusable.

Rather than pursue the lines of criticism indicated above, I confront the notion of a presentational mode of symbolism more directly. The issue that interests me can be drawn from a discussion of the notions of reference and symbolism as these have been considered by the theory's critics and presenters. Langer denies that presentational symbols are referential and characterizes them as "unconsummated."[13] Some critics regard reference as a necessary condition for symbolization.[14] They accept, as does Langer, that artworks do not refer to feelings, or that, if they do refer to feelings, this is not relevant to their *aesthetic/artistic* appreciation. Such critics wonder why

[10] See Weitz 1954, Welch 1955, Beardsley 1958, Kennick 1961, Monelle 1979, and Hagberg 1984.

[11] The point is made in Welch 1955, Scholz 1972, and Budd 1985a.

[12] See Welch 1955, Dorfles 1957, Kennick 1961, Hansen 1972, Carter 1974, Budd 1985a, and Higgins 1991.

[13] Howes, (1958, 15) expresses reluctance in following Langer's rejection of reference, which leaves only the "ghost of meaning," but he is consoled by her claim that music has import: namely, the pattern of life itself as it is felt and directly known.

[14] See Nagel 1943, Szathmary 1954, Rudner 1957, Beardsley 1958, Hospers 1964, Binkley 1970, Margolis 1974, Clifton 1983, Budd 1985a, and Stambaugh 1989. Price (1953) allows for nonreferential symbols, but he also argues (against Charles Morris rather than Langer) that artworks do not operate as symbols. Alternatively, it is argued that Langer should regard music as referential, despite her contrary view; for example, see Scruton 1983.

< 129 >

Langer insists that artworks involve a mode of symbolism while denying that they are referential. The answer is suggested by the following argument: if music is not a symbol of the emotions, then it is meaningless (or has purely internal, formal significance); but it does have emotional import; therefore it must be symbolic. So, Epperson claims (1967, 136–139, 237–242) that music is not meaningless, and that there is more to meaning than can be captured in language, in arguing against the suggestion that music is not primarily referential. Musical meaning of the sort in question is taken to presuppose symbolization. What lies behind that assumption, I take it, is this idea: emotions cannot literally be in music, so, if musical import involves emotional expression (and the relation is not a causal one between the composer's feeling and the music, or between the music and the listener's feeling), then some feature of the music (its form) must make a connection to the world of human feeling (if not to occurrent feelings) that lies beyond the work. That relation, since it involves the music's reaching beyond itself, is properly described as symbolic, even if not referential (since the connection does not depend on anyone's intending it to hold).

Two reasons for challenging these arguments might be offered. The first points out that iconicity, as a symmetrical relation, lacks the directionality presupposed by symbolism/meaning and doubts that Langer's account of the source of this directionality—as arising from the manipulability and accessibility of the forms compared for iconicity—is convincing.[15] Now, if this criticism presupposes that the directionality of symbolic meaning necessarily depends on intentional use (which, in turn, should make the meaning referential), I find it unattractive. In discussing kinds of meaning at the close of Chapter 1, I suggested that, where natural relations such as iconicity are involved, the directionality of meaning might be generated by the priorities of our interests (instead of always relying on someone's intentional use of the conventions of a symbol system). Perhaps this is what Langer has in mind in holding that presentational symbols can be meaningful independently of their being used to refer.

I find a second approach to the rejection of the previous arguments more interesting. If expressed emotion is possessed by the musical work, then one can allow that the work has import without seeing that import as deriving from the music's symbolizing something lying beyond it.[16] The previously

---

[15] See Nagel 1943, Beardsley 1958, Stevenson 1958a, Howard 1971b, and Kivy 1980. The problem comes up in C. S. Peirce's original account of iconic symbols; see Burks 1954.

[16] This is not necessarily to assume that the emotions expressed in music are sui generis, with no connection to the world of human feeling. It might be to say that the connection is one

< 130 >

offered argument to the view that music must be symbolic supposes that music could not directly present a conception of (the form of) sadness, say. If this supposition might be rejected, the temptation to see music as deriving its significance through its symbolizing subjects that fall outside its boundaries would be removed. This rejection of the Langerian theory need not entail, as the theory's advocates assume, a denial that music has an import and significance that derives from its expressiveness. Denied here is the assumption that music attains this import as a result of standing in a symbolic relation to something external to the work.[17]

Although I have set out the issues discussed above as arising from a puzzle generated by Langer's denial that presentational symbols are referential, the argument does not depend strictly on that aspect of Langer's account. At heart she sees musical import as being, in my terms, of meaning A and, hence, as nonreferential. But one might always allow that, with an appropriately intentional use, the element of natural meaning leads to reference (that is, becomes a matter of meaning B). In such a case, not only does the musical work express sadness, say, but its doing so is exploited by the composer to secure a reference to sadness in general.

The introduction of reference and symbolism in the manner just suggested would not, however, remove the previous objection to Langer's theory. In the first instance it is reasonable to deny (see Laszlo 1967; Howard 1971b) that much music is symbolic and referential in this manner. Composers usually intend their works to have the expressive properties that they do have, but this does not mean that it is also usual that composers intend those properties to refer to emotions in general. In some works, such as *The Magic Flute*, some such reference is probably intended. The point, however, is this: the intention to make the work expressive need not, and often apparently does not, include a referential intention. In the second instance, the introduction into the story of referential intentions does not avoid the aforementioned difficulties, because the intentions in question rely on the appropriation of a natural meaning, and the analysis of musical expressiveness must be an analysis of how music possesses that meaning rather than of its potential for referential use. The issue, as Langer seems to recognize, is not the possibility of a referential use as such but rather an account of how the

---

between, say, musical sadness and human sadness, rather than between purely musical form and the form of sadness. I address the issue mentioned here in Chapter 5.

[17] This, I think, is the view in Price 1953, Szathmary 1954, Beardsley 1958, Howard 1971b, Margolis 1974, Shiner 1982, and Budd 1985a; also see Clifton 1983. Some of Langer's critics seem to deny not only that music is symbolic of emotions but also that it has emotional import; see Nagel 1943 and Hospers 1964.

< 131 >

music possesses a natural meaning, where this natural meaning is such that it might be employed by the composer to create a general reference in the absence of the conventions that distinguish a symbol system.

Langer attempts to explain music's natural meaning as symbolic in character. The alternative view regards this meaning as a matter of possession rather than of symbolization. Obviously the notion of possession is problematic and requires explanation, given that the meaning in question is supposed to be a matter of emotional content and also given that music is nonsentient. How such a theory might be developed is the subject of Chapter 5. The point to make here is this: much as Langer might seem drawn to such an account, she could not abandon her view of music as a presentational symbol of feeling without also abandoning her claim to analyze the nature of musical expressiveness, for, insofar as she succeeds in explaining what a presentational symbol is, it is that explanation that supposedly accounts for music's expressive power.[18] If her theory of presentational symbolism is incoherent, she acknowledges that emotions are expressed in music but fails to explain how this is possible.

Is Langer's theory capable of sustaining the explanatory burden she places on it? I do not believe so. The central ideas of Langer's theory—indescribable forms, undemonstrable iconicity, and unstatable laws of projection—are unintelligible. If "unintelligible" means here "cannot be explained fully in language," Langer would agree.[19] She seeks to immunize her theory from the criticism that it fails convincingly to describe the nature of the presentational symbolism which, in her view, is involved in music's expressing emotion. She does so by suggesting that no theory stated in language could fully explain the symbolic connection between works of art and emotions. The statement of her theory is, as it were, a rickety scaffold which, though not leading directly to the truth, gives a view of the truth hidden behind the theory's statement. We might continue, though: the problem her theory is meant to answer is such that it demands an explanation that can be given in language, and therefore the unintelligibility of her theory is a crucial weakness (Davies 1983b).

I have already suggested that the exclusivity of discursive and presentational modes of symbolism is questionable, so the defense of denying the possibility of a discursive analysis of the operation of presentational symbols

---

[18] Contrast this with Hansen (1968), who regards Langer's talk of symbolization as inviting the misinterpretation of her position; also see Harrell 1986.

[19] Monelle (1979) believes, however, that Langer does not take the notion of transcendence far enough, in that she does not celebrate the semireligious mystery that he sees as occupying the heart of musical experience.

< 132 >

is not obviously available to Langer. Putting that point aside, her excuse for the incoherence of her account is not established by her own theory. As Hagberg puts it:

> At this point one may begin to suspect that the unsayability doctrine has got out of control. This suspicion derives from this fact: it is one thing to be limited in what we can say about the expressive or emotional content of particular works of art, and it is quite another thing to be limited in what we can say to explain the *theory* designed to provide an explanation of the way in which those works possess meaning. What can be discursively captured may have limits, but this fact—if it is a fact—in no way justifies the ultimately obscurantist and very different claim that the "logical resemblance" between work and feeling, the resemblance that must be understood if the theory is to prove illuminating, need not itself be explained. (1984, 332–333)

The difficulties faced by the view that music is an iconic symbol of the forms of feelings are caused not by the alleged inadequacies of language (that is, of discursive symbols), as Langer would have it, but by the question-begging confusions that plague her theory. By denying the possibility of a full explanation, Langer deprives her theory of significant content. Rather than analyzing the nature of musical expressiveness, as it purports to do, Langer's theory restates the apparent fact to which the nature of aesthetic discourse testifies—that we hear emotions in music—in new and misleadingly technical terms.[20] That Langer's theory, her answer to the problem posed by the expression of emotion in music, cannot be stated in a perspicuous fashion indicates that her theory is mistaken.

Langer would claim, I suppose, that the ultimate and only real test of her theory is an empirical one, given in the experience of music. Once we have understood what presentational symbols are like, we should recognize that, in appreciating musical works as expressive, we are appreciating them as presentational symbols; that is, as conveying conceptions of emotions. When her claims are tested against our experience of the expressiveness of music, however, they prove to be false. The expressiveness of musical works sometimes seems to demand an emotional response from the listener. By Langer's theory, works of art express or signify not emotions but conceptions of emotions. Now, though it may be obvious that the presentation of an emotion

---

[20] The point is made in Weitz 1954, Kennick 1961, Hoaglund 1980, Davies 1983b, and Hagberg 1984.

< 133 >

sometimes compels an emotional response from the listener, it is not at all obvious that the presentation of the conception of an emotion would ever call forth an emotional response. Langer's theory removes emotion from art, replacing it with conceptions of emotions. In so doing, her theory undermines the basis for emotional responses to musical works and makes mysterious the power of art to evoke such responses.[21] An account of musical expressiveness that fails to explain why we find music moving must be significantly flawed, and Langer's is such a theory.

Pratt's Theory of Musical Expression

The difficulties identified in the previous section are the more apparent in theories resembling Langer's but not relying on the complex terminology that cloaks her thesis. One such is the account of musical expressiveness offered by the psychologist Carroll C. Pratt (see especially 1931, 1938, and 1952). Note that Pratt and Langer cite each other's writing with approval. Pratt is not of the view that music is a (nonreferential) symbol, but he does hold that it possesses an objective, emotional character due to the formal similarity between musical motion and the organic or kinaesthetic sensations that are the correlates and determinants of emotions. "Music at its best is not symbolic at all. . . . tonal design stands for nothing beyond itself. It does not suggest mood and feeling. It *is* mood and feeling. The qualities of auditory perception are not iconic signs, nor do they by themselves represent or imitate or copy anything" (Pratt 1954, 290). "The emotions and strivings of the will and desire are embodied in music not directly, but indirectly by way of tonal designs which closely resemble in formal outline the inner movements of the spirit. . . . But here at last it may indeed be true that music becomes symbolic, for it seems to stand for and express the joy and sorrow of all mankind" (1954, 300).

According to Pratt, emotions are "subjective" (that is, experienced as within the body): "The material of emotion is bodily process, an elaborate pattern of muscular and visceral disturbance" (1954, 291). Music cannot embody or contain emotions, but because of its dynamic character music

---

[21] She does this, presumably, as part of her rejection of arousal theory, but, as I argue in the next chapter, one can hold that music produces an affective response without also holding that musical expressiveness is to be analyzed as residing in its power to produce such responses. The objection is made in Szathmary 1954, Reid 1965 and 1968, Kivy 1980, Davies 1983b, and Higgins 1991. Epperson (1967) claims that the response to a presentational symbol might be an emotional one, but it is not clear to me how he squares this with his commitment to Langer's position.

< 134 >

possesses properties that are so similar to those of the emotions that it can be said to possess or present an emotional character. Such attributions are figurative, metaphoric. Music does not "mean" (that is, refer to) emotions; rather, it possesses formal properties with an objective (that is, "external to the body") character strikingly similar to that of the emotions. "Agitation is both an organic feel and an auditory perception, but in the former case it is an emotion and in the latter it is a tertiary sensory impression—two quite different psychological modes of experience, which nevertheless, because of the similarity in form between them, are called by the same name. The verbal confusion is largely responsible for the confusion in theory" (Pratt 1952, 18).[22] Listeners might respond emotionally to music, but the expressiveness of music is independent of its effects. In brief, Pratt is a formalist who complains that other formalists, such as Eduard Hanslick, have had too limited a notion of what form can convey. Music presents forms that strike the senses as so similar to those of feelings that we call the music sad, happy, and so on.

Many of the criticisms applied to Langer's theory also are invited by Pratt's approach. He tends to treat emotions as vibrations of the viscera that can be individuated by virtue of the character of their motions. Such a view ignores the distinctive intentionality of most emotions and their dependence on standard types of causal circumstances. In discussing the dynamics of emotions, Pratt sometimes mentions, as well as somatic patterns, public, behavioral expressions. I doubt that this inclusion saves his case, because I doubt that the emotions listed by Pratt are individuable in terms of the conjunction of these inner and outer motions.[23] If they are not so, music could not be expressive because of sharing with these feelings their dynamic form. Mere similarity between the forms of musical works and the forms of the emotions cannot fully account for the inclination to describe music in such terms, given that music resembles in its dynamism many other events and processes which it is not usually said to express or present, and also given that we are not similarly inclined to describe these events and processes as possessing or expressing emotion; for development of the point, see Budd 1983, 1985a, and 1989b. Further, one might wonder if Pratt, like Langer,

---

[22] Also see Pratt 1954, 295, where the same example, that of agitation, is used. Pratt claims that all words used to describe mood and feeling could be illustrated with analogous examples. For a similar view, see Zink 1960.

[23] In his various writings, Pratt mentions music as possessing the character of being agitated, calm, wistful, dramatic, seductive, restless, pompous, passionate, sombre, triumphant, erotic, exhilarating, martial, pensive, languid, yearning, stately, majestic, lugubrious, ecstatic, sprightly, and aspiring. Of Pratt's examples, I find agitation, restlessness, and vacillation to be those most plausibly to be regarded as possessing a distinctive dynamic character. But I wonder if these are properly called emotions, and if they belong with joy and triumph.

< 135 >

separates the listener's emotional response from the music's expressiveness to an extent that renders inexplicable the power of music to call forth such responses.

Pratt encapsulates his theory in the famous slogan *"Music sounds the way the emotions feel."* To this I am inclined to respond both with "of course" and with "what is that supposed to mean?" Pratt's view, like Langer's, testifies to the phenomenal character of the experience of music's expressiveness, but in doing so it fails to answer the puzzle that leads one to ask "how is this possible?" The suggestion that music is only figuratively to be described as sad does not, as I argue later in this chapter, hold out the promise of a solution to the puzzle by an analysis of metaphor. Also, the phenomenal similarity between the sound of music and the "form of feelings" seems inadequate to the explanatory task. The difficulty is not, say, that grief hurts whereas the music does not sound hurt (though problems of that sort might be compelling enough to lead one to challenge the claim of similarity). Rather, even if the phenomenal similarity is conceded, one still wants to know how such disparate things could share a similarity of that sort; one wants to know how, among inanimate, nonsentient things, we are so strongly inclined to experience music as suited to the expression of human feeling.

Reason giving must end somewhere. At some point an explanation comes to a halt with the bare assertion of some (allegedly) brute fact of which one can say no more than "that's the way things are."[24] Where the reasons run out, there are no further reasons to be given. The brute facts, the givens of experience, are hoped to lie near enough to the epistemic foundations that they can be widely accepted as grounding the explanation. If this is not so, then the dispute as to the facts remains unresolved or must shift to another order of reason giving.[25] So, my objection to theories such as Langer's and Pratt's does not rest on their appealing to irreducible similarities in our experiences of music and of emotions. At some point one is bound to exhaust the reasons that can be offered by running against some such irreducible, brute fact. My complaint is that, in their theories, this happens too early to provide a solution to the puzzle posed by music's expressive powers. If theories such as theirs are the best we can come by, this shows that music's expressiveness retains an element of insoluble mystery. Many of those who write on music's expressiveness might accept that this is the case. Indeed, they might embrace

[24] Brute facts of this sort are, for the cultural relativist, socially bound; they are the way things are for the given culture. For the objectivist, they indicate the way the world is for everyone, and perhaps also the way the world is independently of anyone's existing.

[25] For example, the topic of the debate might shift from the conceptual to the physiological, provided that some appropriate connection between the two can be accepted.

< 136 >

the idea and celebrate this triumph of the heart over dry intellect as a sign of music's glory. Others, including myself, find the absence of analytical content in such theories deeply unsatisfying and frustrating. At this stage of the enquiry I am inclined to doubt that Langer's and Pratt's are the best explanations that might be offered of music's expressiveness. I choose to look further in the hope of plucking the heart from this mystery.

Goodman's Theory: Exemplificational Symbols

Goodman (1968) analyzes artworks as "characters" in symbol systems. The arts differ in the elements of their symbol systems with respect to notational/syntactic features such as repleteness and density. These differences affect manifest features of the works produced within each artform, so that the various arts differ in being descriptive, depictive, expressive, and so forth. The arts have in common some features reflecting their general symbolic nature—denotation, in particular—but they are distinguishable from other symbol systems in inclining to opacity, turning their symbolic function in on themselves (1978b). This follows from five symptomatic features of their symbol systems (the fifth being added in 1978b): (i) syntactic density, (ii) semantic density, (iii) relative repleteness, (iv) exemplification, and (v) multiple and complex reference.[26]

Let us begin by considering some of Goodman's key notions: possession, denotation, and exemplification. Something, such as a piece of cloth, possesses many properties, such as that of being blue. Usually the cloth does not denote or refer to blueness; simply, it possesses and displays an instance of the quality without denoting the property it possesses. There is, however, a use of the cloth that leads to its denoting blueness and does so by exploiting its possession of the relevant property. The cloth is employed in this manner

---

[26] In the 1950s, when semiotic aesthetics was a hot issue, it was argued that artworks could not be symbols because, whereas artworks interest us for their own sakes as autonomous objects/events and an appropriate experience of them is "immediate," symbols direct attention away from themselves toward that to which they refer and therefore are valued merely as means; see Garvin 1947, Rudner 1951 and 1957, Osborne 1955, and Reid 1965. Others argued that this objection fails or is not decisive; see Ballard 1953, Copi 1955, Vivas 1955, and Stevenson 1958b. Nowadays artworks and their properties are likely to be seen as context-dependent, so there is little inclination to vigorously defend the thesis that artworks are autonomous in standing apart from their social and historical settings. Nevertheless, it remains true that the appropriate experience of artworks is often described as immediate and that this might be thought to count against theories in which it is argued that artworks must be understood as performing a symbolic function. Goodman's approach counters this difficulty in that he argues that artworks are symbolic in a way that renders them opaque rather than transparent, that is, in a manner that makes them, and not some distant "signified," the object of attention.

< 137 >

when it is treated as a sample. Goodman's example is that of a salesperson who uses a book of sample swatches to illustrate texture, weave, hue, and the like. The color of the piece of cloth in the booklet denotes the color of the bolt of material to which it stands as a sample, and what makes reference possible in such a case is not any semantic connection but rather the fact of the sample's exhibiting the property in question. In Goodman's terms, the swatch (literally) *exemplifies* the color blue, or blueness; it denotes the color, and its being used to do so depends on its possessing the relevant property. Exemplification is distinct from mere possession in that it involves denotation.

The notion of exemplification can perhaps be made clearer by considering words. The word "red" refers to a quality (or universal) but does not display the quality to which it refers. If the word were printed in red, it not only would refer to the color red, it would exhibit the quality to which it refers. Similarly, the word "multisyllabic" is multisyllabic, the word "word" is a word, the word "short" is comparatively short, and so on. Of course, that the word in question exhibits the property to which it refers does not mean that its displaying the property in any way contributes to its referring. Nevertheless, because it possesses the quality in question, it might be used to illustrate the property, and thereby a reference apart from the word's semantic reference might be achieved: "An example of a multisyllabic word? Well, the word 'multisyllabic' is one such." The quotational device shows that the word is mentioned without being given its usual semantic reference; nevertheless, denotation occurs through the literal exemplification of the relevant feature.

Now, exemplification in these examples depends on the literal exhibition of the property in question. Nevertheless, according to Goodman, this method of generating denotation might be metaphoric sometimes: "How does the sun shine? Juliet's smile shines like the sun." Juliet's smile possesses the metaphoric property of shining like the sun. Or, a shaggy-dog story might be used (metaphorically) to exemplify some aspect of shaggy-dogged-ness. Vernon A. Howard (1971b) presents as an example of metaphoric exemplification the case of a tall story's being offered to illustrate tallness.

In summary, Goodman's theory of expression is this: X expresses Y if and only if X possesses Y metaphorically and X exemplifies Y. Although X does not denote Y, denotation is present within this relation—it runs from "Y" (the predicate) to X. An artwork is expressive when it metaphorically possesses a property it exemplifies. Goodman offers this as a general analysis of expression in the arts, applying to painting, for example, as well as to

< 138 >

music.[27] A musical work is sad just in case it has the metaphoric property of being sad and this property is exemplified (presumably the property is supposed to be metaphoric in this case, since music does not literally feel emotions).

First Criticisms of Goodman's Account of Expression

We typically distinguish what a painting expresses from what is expressed in it by a depicted character, but it is not obvious that Goodman's theory can allow for this important distinction. Moreover, it is not clear that a depicted character's expression is a matter of *metaphoric* exemplification; one might, afterall, deny that Macbeth's horror is any more metaphoric than the horror expressed by a real person in an actual situation. Where expressions are depicted, it is not apparent whether what is metaphoric is the denotation achieved through possession or the possession itself, but neither alternative is a happy one. If the *possession* of an expressive character itself is metaphoric, then it is difficult to see how to preserve a connection between the metaphoric label "sad," as applied to the fictional act of expression, and the literal meaning of the word when it is used to denote actual occurrences of the emotion. Goodman's nominalist rejection of intensional explanations leaves his theory of metaphor open to this problem. On the other hand, if the *denotation* is metaphoric, the notion of denotation is rendered yet more obscure than it is already in Goodman's theory.[28]

Another criticism, which applies specifically to the application of Goodman's theory to musical expressiveness, also deserves to be noted. In Goodman's view, the properties of a musical work must be properties common to all its correct performances.[29] If correct performances of a given work may differ in their expressive characters, as seems true, then it is not obvious that

[27] This theory is widely accepted. For just a few examples of its use, see Howard 1971a, 1971b, 1972, 1974, and 1975, Kulenkampff 1981, and Newcomb 1984. Lammenranta 1988 and 1992 shows qualified acceptance of the view. For critical discussion, see Peltz 1972, Jensen 1973, and Dempster 1989.

[28] Both O'Neil (1971) and Savile (1971) have queried the applicability of Goodman's theory to the expressiveness of pictorial representations on these grounds.

[29] Goodman's account of the standards for correct performance is unusual in that he holds that a correct performance is one compliant with signs in the score which are definite and discrete in their significance. Pitch indications are signs of the appropriate sort; tempo specifications, such as "allegro," are not. It is part of Goodman's view that the work lacks specified tempo. For critical discussion, see Boretz 1970, Savile 1971, Webster 1974, Wolterstorff 1975, Price 1982, Carrier 1983, Kivy 1984, Margolis 1987, and Pearce 1988b. For a defense of the Goodmanian line, see Harrison 1975.

< 139 >

Goodman should regard expressiveness as a property of musical works, as he does. He should instead regard the expressiveness as a property of the given performance (see Clark 1982 and Pearce 1988a).

Exemplification

The obvious objection to Goodman's theory is this: Exemplification involves the *use* of a property already possessed by the artwork, a use that (on Goodman's account) secures denotation. But if the work already possesses the property of being sad, say, then expressiveness is a matter of possession rather than exemplification. Goodman's concern lies with the symbolic use of art's expressiveness, with a speech act using that expressiveness, but the work could possess the expressive property without its being used to denote the property it possesses (that is, without the property's being exemplified). Expressiveness is not then a matter of exemplification; exemplification is a necessary condition not for expressiveness as such but for referring, via the use of the relevant property. As Monroe Beardsley (1981) observes, exemplified properties are noteworthy or good-making independently of their being given an exemplifying function, so we need not concentrate too much on their being exemplificatory; instead, we should focus on the properties in question, not on their referring; the musical work need not denote anything, since merely presenting its own aesthetically notable qualities is sufficient for its playing its role in helping us to understand our world and cope with it. So, Goodman's analysis presupposes, rather than explains, expressiveness in art. His concern lies instead with the referential use to which the expressiveness of art lends itself.[30]

Insofar as he attempts to reply to the objection, Goodman seems to adopt a two-pronged approach. On the one hand, he argues (i) that exemplification does not require an agent's intentional use of an item (and, hence, that deno-

---

[30] Versions of this objection are to be found in Sparshott 1974, Margolis 1974, 1979, and 1981, Beardsley 1975 and 1978, and Vermazen 1986. Kulenkampff (1981) makes the same point but seemingly does not regard it as critical. Lammenranta (1992) argues that Goodman might avoid the objection only if exemplification is restricted to the case in which a work's referring to its own properties serves a cognitive purpose. He denies that nonrepresentational art is typically used for "knowing oneself and other people better," so he believes that the notion of exemplification can be retrieved only if one rejects Goodman's claim that artworks necessarily function as symbols. Note: The problem does not come up in the same way in Goodman's account of representation. In that case, the story of the symbolic use is the story of how the property of being representational is acquired. But, where expression is concerned, possession is conceded as something *prior* to the symbolic use.

< 140 >

tation is distinct from reference as that was characterized in Chapter 1).[31] He suggests that denotation arises from the place of a work or its properties within a symbol scheme independently of its being placed there deliberately. He indicates that exemplification depends on denotation coming not through the deliberate use of the property but through its context within the relevant symbol scheme. On the other hand, he emphasizes (ii) that a work possesses many properties only some of which are aesthetically/artistically significant. There must be some way of sorting aesthetically/artistically important properties from those that are merely possessed. To explain a feature's artistic importance as residing in its expressive character, appeal must be made to something more than the fact of the work's possessing the feature in question. According to Goodman, that "something more" is the exemplificatory nature of the feature. These two lines of argument, if they succeed, do much to defuse the objection just raised, but I doubt that they succeed.

Goodman's first reply is this: denotation does not presuppose deliberate use; neither, then, does exemplification. Goodman denies that he is confusing a claim about use with one about nature. For the most part, he does not talk about the uses made of artworks; indeed, he discusses neither artists nor their application of the symbol schemes he describes. In reply to Kjörup's (1978) complaint that he underplays the communicative use of art, Goodman (1978a, 78) notes that the function of symbols can be studied apart from the beliefs or motives of any agent that may have brought about the relationships involved. He says we need not ask who bounced the ball, or whether it just rolled off the shelf, to know the way the ball bounces. I take the point to be this: where the conventions of a symbol system are established, they do their work independently of their being used intentionally. A picture might have what I called in the previous chapter a representational character when viewed in terms of the relevant conventions for representation, whether or not those conventions were deliberately employed. And we might concern ourselves with the meanings of words or sentences without regard to what was or might have been meant by them on any particular occasion. Significance arises within the context of a symbol system and is generated there whether or not someone aims to create or draw attention to that import.[32]

---

[31] Beardsley (1981) thinks that, in emphasizing denotation as he does, Goodman regards the intentional use of the property in question to a referential end as a necessary condition for exemplification. This mistaken assumption no doubt lies behind most versions of this objection.

[32] This seems to be the point Arrell (1990) has in mind when he argues that a work exemplifies its expressive or aesthetic properties if it constrains us to perceive it by a particular system of categories—as a symphony, say. He holds that the category of a work sets the context within

< 141 >

Joseph Margolis (1981) objects that Goodman's disregard of the place of the artist in the symbolizing process has the unfortunate consequence of his anthropomorphizing the work, as if it alone succeeds in exemplifying some of its properties. I agree. Goodman implies that, just by functioning as a character within a symbol system, the work uses its own properties to achieve denotation and, thereby, exemplification. The extended notion of "use" to which appeal here is made cannot, however, sustain the explanatory burden placed on it, as is apparent when one considers Goodman's reply to Margolis's objection. He counters (1981) that we can say that the work selects its properties for exemplification, just as we can say that a colored surface selects the light it will reflect. If, as I suspect, we should be wary of talk of selection in both cases, then the reply does not convince.

The strain of preserving the analysis of exemplification as involving denotation, realized not by a person's deliberate use but automatically, through the workings of the symbol system, emerges clearly in the view of Goodman's disciple, Sören Kjörup. The latter suggests (1974, 225–227) that, when we ask of a stone why it possesses its properties, it *tells* us why and in doing so exemplifies the relevant properties. He comments: if we make the appropriate presuppositions, the stone can tell us not only what red (redness) is (a property it primarily exemplifies) but also that most of Scandinavia was once covered by glacial ice (a property it secondarily exemplifies). Kjörup retains the idea that exemplification involves denotation and thereby is distinct from mere possession, but he does so at the cost of diluting the idea of exemplification to the point at which X exemplifies Y if, with the appropriate presuppositions, Y can be learned from X.

Now, I have already allowed in Chapter 2 that conventions (or, if one prefers, the rules and practices structuring a symbol system) do their work of conferring meaning even in cases where they are not used to do so, but I deny that this justifies the dismissal of intentions, uses, or practices as irrelevant to establishing the context for Goodmanian exemplification (neither do I believe that it licenses the suggestion that the piece itself is responsible for using its own features in an exemplificatory manner). It does not follow from the fact that we can concern ourselves with symbolic content without regard to intentions on particular occasions that we could do so always. That we can consider symbolic content without regard to intentional use does not show that a symbol system, such as Goodman has in mind, could generate exemplificatory significance without its ever being used, or being understood

---

which some of its properties take on aesthetic significance and, in doing so, become exemplificational.

< 142 >

correctly to be employed, to effect communication. Goodman's analogy of the bouncing ball is misleading; balls bounce independently of the use we make of them, whereas Goodmanian symbol systems would not exist unless there were a connection between their intentional use and the public import secured through that use. Symbol systems are established and sustained only through their deliberate use—in general, if not on each occasion. That a particular work can exemplify an import it was not intended to have as a result of its belonging within a symbol system does not establish that we might sever the intimate connection that usually holds between exemplification and use. In particular, it does not show that it is possible to give an account of denotation as underpinning Goodmanian exemplification without mention of such matters.[33] So, Goodman's reply does not defuse the objection.

The second string to Goodman's bow, (ii), points out that expressiveness, as an artistically significant property, must go beyond mere possession, since the vast majority of possessed properties are of no significance. A work possesses many properties it does not exemplify, such as that of being performed when rain is falling in Timbuctoo (Goodman 1981). Exemplification involves not just predicability but the "selection" of a property for attention. Goodman's theory purports to explain this process of selection as the harnessing of a possessed property to achieve a kind of denotation (all this being made possible by the work's location within a symbol system).

This sounds very fine, but what in Goodman's theory is the mark that distinguishes exemplified from merely possessed properties? In *Languages of Art* (1968, 93) Goodman gives the impression (perhaps inadvertently) that the prominence of a property might indicate its being exemplified. Subsequently in (1978a) he concedes that Beardsley (1978) establishes the crude inadequacy of this view. In that case, however, it appears that Goodman has no criteria that might be applied in distinguishing merely possessed from exemplified properties. Jensen (1973) complains that Goodman seems to dis-

---

[33] In chapter 2 I pointed out that many of Goodman's critics deny that he has a *theory* of denotation and that they regard this fact as sometimes important in disguising the implausibility of crucial parts of his account. In this context we can see just one instance of the worry that lies behind the complaint: Goodman, in protecting his view of expressiveness from attack, denies that the denotation resulting from exemplification relies on someone's intending to refer, but so underanalyzed is the notion of denotation on which his theory relies, and so apparent are some of the difficulties it faces, that the alleged reply muddies the waters yet further rather than clarifying matters. But if one were to abandon talk of denotation, or to dilute the notion beyond recognition, as both Kjörup (1974) and Arrell (1990) come near to doing, one could not hope to salvage *Goodman's* theory of expression, so central does he make the notion of denotation to his account of exemplification.

< 143 >

claim responsibility for explaining how and why the distinction between merely possessed and exemplified properties operates.

Goodman's failure to make clear how in practice one might distinguish the two types of property does seems a serious oversight since there is a huge disparity between his prime example of exemplification, the swatch displayed by a salesperson as a sample of the suit that might be made from similar material, and the artistic context of expression. If expressiveness is to be distinguished from mere possession by its being essentially exemplificatory, Goodman should show in what senses and why it is appropriate to see expressiveness in art as relying on exemplification. He could do so only if he could explain the appropriateness of our regarding artworks as standing (metaphorically) to the expression of an emotion as a salesperson's swatch stands (literally) to the material of a suit that might be made from the bolt of cloth of which it is a sample. The parallel between the two cases is far from clear. It is not easy to see how a concerto grosso by Handel serves as a *sample* of the qualities it expresses.[34] Goodman (1978a) responds that a birthday cake in a baker's window can serve as a sample, even if no birthday cakes are baked. This reply misses the point, which I take to be this: the place filled by samples in our lives is as preparation for other things. Goodman suggests that the promise of a sample need not be fulfilled in any particular case. That is true, but it does not meet the challenge of proving that Handel's work functions, in virtue of its expressiveness, as a sample. There is no reason to regard the expressive properties of artworks as a promise of anything, or to see their importance as deriving from their playing such a role. Seemingly, Goodman characterizes expression as an ongoing game of ostension, of labeling, as if such a game could have a point as something other than a preparation for . . . what? The failure to spell out both what exemplification amounts to in an artwork and what is sampled in exemplificatory contexts calls into question the success of Goodman's theory in its claim to distinguish expressive from other, merely possessed, properties. He seems to take aesthetic/artistic importance as the sole criterion for identifying exemplified properties (whereas he should regard the aesthetic/artistic importance of a property as explained by, and hence as distinguishable from, its being exemplificatory). Where expressiveness and exemplification are not independently identifiable, the importance of expressive features cannot be explained as a matter of their being exemplificatory.

Goodman is correct in holding that not all a work's properties are aesthetically relevant in the way that its expressiveness usually is, in maintaining

---

[34] A point made in Beardsley 1975 and 1978; also see Kivy 1980.

< 144 >

that there must be some way of sorting aesthetically relevant from irrelevant properties, and in acknowledging that a property's being possessed does not distinguish that property from infinitely many others, most of which are of no aesthetic importance. But there is no reason (beyond a prior commitment to a theory that gives a central place to denotation and founds an account of exemplification on this) to suppose that it is the denotative function of some properties which marks them for attention. Indeed, so Goodman's critics claim, there is no reason to believe that aesthetically/artistically important properties need have any denotative function. On the one hand, it is not always obvious why we would regard denotation or exemplification as an aesthetically significant feature where it does occur (see Budd 1989a; Beardsley 1981). On the other hand, there are available many other ways to account for the aesthetic importance of some possessed properties over others without resort to the notions of denotation or exemplification.

To deny that expressiveness depends on denotation leading to exemplification is not also to deny that artists sometimes employ the expressive potential of their works in the service of reference; for example, the sadness of the music in an aria might obviously refer to the particular sadness about which the protagonist sings. Nor is it to deny that the importance of art might derive in part from the possibility of just such a use. In noting these points, Beardsley (1981) sees room for a conciliatory approach to Goodman's theory. Similarly, Peter Kivy (1980, 49, 61) writes that Goodman's is consistent with his own account of musical expressiveness, a version of which I discuss in Chapter 5, and Jerrold Levinson (1990a, 340) nods approvingly in the direction of Goodman's theory of musical expression. Nevertheless, the impression that Goodman might share with these theorists some middle ground is misleading at best. These authors explicitly regard expressiveness as involving possession rather than reference or denotation and, if they allow for the possibility of a referential use of expressive properties, they regard such a use neither as necessary nor as sufficient for expressiveness in music. By contrast, Goodman insists on the centrality in his analysis of the notion of denotation. The concessions and acknowledgments made to his theory by these other authors should be seen as falling far short of acceptance.

Metaphoric Exemplification

It might be thought that I have taken unfair advantage when criticizing Goodman's theory of expressiveness in art in that I have ignored the central claim that the exemplified features are metaphoric. In seeking an analysis of musical expressiveness from Goodman, the attention should fall on the no-

< 145 >

tion of *metaphoric* possession, perhaps, rather than on the further claim that music's exhibiting expressive properties involves denotation. It is instructive, therefore, to consider if the theory of expressiveness is made clearer or more plausible when one considers what Goodman has to say about metaphor. I hope to show that this is not so. The argument has these parts: I suggest that Goodman is correct in thinking that he needs a distinction between a musical property's being metaphoric and a musical property's being described metaphorically; I clarify that distinction; I indicate that the idea of music's being a metaphor cannot usefully be approached via the model of linguistic metaphor; and I conclude that Goodman's notion of metaphor as employed in the theory of metaphoric exemplification is no less obscure than is the notion of exemplification used in that same theory.

Goodman's analysis of expression as metaphoric exemplification suggests that its being metaphoric is a feature of the manner in which music possesses or presents the property in question, whereas standardly we think of metaphor as a figure of speech, as a use of language.[35] It is not obvious what it is for exemplification, as distinct from attribution, to be metaphoric; it is not obvious, in other words, what it is for music, as opposed to descriptions of music, to be metaphoric, especially since Goodman resists the view that music is to be compared to a language in respect of its meaning.

Is it necessary that we distinguish between the case in which the music's possession of a feature is metaphoric and that in which a description of the music is metaphoric? Were one to think the answer is yes, one might reason as follows: *Any* musical feature might be characterized metaphorically. For example, I might say of their entry in the first movement of Mozart's Symphonia Concertante for Violin and Viola, K. 364, that the soloists are homing pigeons, first perceived as dots in the distance, which, on drawing near, flutter to their dovecote. In this example, my use of the metaphor might be regarded as gratuitous, since there are many other, equally informative accounts I might offer of the passage. At other times, the use of a particular metaphor seems mandated by the nature of the music itself. Some musical features seem to *require* metaphoric descriptions in expressive terms, for they cannot be indicated readily except by such words as "sad." For this reason, there is an important difference between the metaphors involved in saying "the soloists are homing pigeons" and saying "the music is sad."

Goodman's musical acolyte, Howard, suggests (1971b) that Goodman's

---

[35] For an odd exchange, see that between Lipman (1970a and 1970b) and Goodman (1970c). Goodman says, "All properties exemplified, whether the exemplification is literal or metaphorical, belong to the symbol itself" (1970c, 415).

< 146 >

has the advantage over other theories of musical expression (such as formalist ones) in that it acknowledges a need for this distinction and attempts to ground it by reference to the notion of exemplification. Whereas the sadness of the slow movement is exemplified, the homing pigeonness of the soloists' entry in the first movement is not. I doubt that Howard's can be the best account of Goodman's position for the following reason. The entry of the soloists in Mozart's K. 364 possesses the features that are metaphorically indicated via the homing pigeon story: the soloists enter, almost imperceptibly, high (in pitch) above the orchestral tutti, which drops away as, with a gentle crescendo, the solo parts descend lightly in tandem to confirm the tonic prior to the reaffirmation of the first subject. Now, not only are these features possessed, but I suspect that Goodman would regard them as exemplified (given their artistic significance in the work). In that case, however, these features are no less exemplificatory than is the sombre character of the slow movement. Therefore, appeal to exemplification does not distinguish metaphoric properties of the music from other of its properties that might be described metaphorically. The difference (if there is one) is not indicated by the presence or absence of exemplification; rather, the difference appears to be indicated by whether a literally exemplified property is described in metaphoric terms or, instead, a metaphorically possessed feature is described in literal terms. In the latter case, such metaphoricity as the account contains derives from what is described rather from the manner of the description's use. Both the homing pigeon story and the sadness story are metaphoric (and the musical properties in either case might be exemplificatory), but the metaphor in the former case lies in the character of the description rather than in the nature of what is described, whereas in the latter case the metaphor lies not in the nature of the description but in the character of the property described. I assume that is why Goodman recognizes a distinction between exemplification simpliciter (that is, literal exemplification) and metaphoric exemplification.

As indicated earlier, I regard the appropriate gloss on the difference between our saying that it is the music, rather than a description of it, which is metaphoric as follows: for musical metaphor the use of the metaphor is ineliminable, which is not so for (merely) metaphoric descriptions of music. Whereas talk of homing pigeons might be dismissed as a redundant, literary flourish, mention of the slow movement's expressive tone is not something that can be dispensed with so readily in favor of an equally informative but more prosaic alternative. In the latter case it is as if the music forces the metaphor on the describer, whereas in the former the use of the metaphor is not required, or even invited, by the music. One might dramatize the differ-

< 147 >

ence as that between the metaphoric description of a literally possessed property and the literal description of a metaphorically possessed property. Talk of homing pigeons is a metaphoric gesture toward features that might be described literally, whereas talk of the slow movement's sadness is a direct indication of something belonging to the music which, nevertheless, cannot be a literal property of it, apparently, since the music is not sentient. In Goodman's nominalist terms, in the former case it is the label that has the metaphoric character rather than that to which it attaches, whereas in the latter the label derives such metaphoric character as it has from the nature of that to which it is appended.

If there is a distinction to be drawn between metaphor in music and metaphor in descriptions of music, as Goodman's account supposes, then one cannot expect theories or definitions of literary metaphors to be revealing of the former, though they should illuminate the latter. It is not surprising, then, that Goodman's (1968, 69) metaphoric definition of (literary) metaphor, as an affair between a predicate with a past and an object that yields while protesting, is unhelpful in making clear the nature of musical expression.[36] The definition is unhelpful not because it is metaphoric but because it deals with predicates and the like. "Predicate," as used in the definition, is literal, and there are no predicates in musical works. So there is no obvious way of applying the definition perspicuously to the case of music's possessing a property metaphorically.

Goodman is not alone in claiming that music itself is metaphoric. Donald Ferguson (1960) suggests that music has an almost unique aptness for metaphoric utterance. He offers the suggestion that a metaphor is an inflection (tone of voice in utterance) that adds a "poetic increment" to the standard meaning of a word. Now, even were we to accept this unusual account, it is doubtful that Ferguson can make good the claim that music is suited to metaphoric utterance. His observation that music is largely a matter of inflections of the voice does not establish the case, for it is not apparent how such inflections add a "poetic increment" to the "standard meaning" of a wordlike unit. Daniel Putman (1989) is another who writes of music as metaphor. The highness and lowness of notes, and musical motion, are metaphoric features of musical works, he holds. He suggests that, when music becomes a dead metaphor, people begin to hear not music but a succession

---

[36] Goodman does not offer an analysis of metaphor, nor does he indicate where one is to be found. It is arguable that it is impossible for him to be illuminating on the subject, since metaphor seems to require an intentionalist account and Goodman's nominalism prevents him from going in that direction; see O'Neil 1971 and Beardsley 1975. For an attempt to analyze music as metaphor, see Grund 1988.

< 148 >

of sounds. To the extent that these writers subscribe to a model of metaphor relying on semantic/syntactic features distinctive to natural languages, their claims about music obscure, rather than clarify, the distinction between music's being metaphoric and the use of metaphor in the description of music, since there is no explanation of how remarks about the one kind of metaphor are to be interpreted when applied to the other.

The difficulty faced by any attempt to characterize music as metaphoric when one starts from a literary model of metaphor is revealed by Steven Krantz (1987), who projects some of the more prominent theories of metaphor onto the musical case. Krantz's conclusions are largely negative. He decides that only on an interactional theory of metaphor, and only with music that relies on cultural associations to secure reference—for instance, where trumpets connote power—is there some similarity with (linguistic) metaphor. But musical expressiveness does not always trade on associations, so not even the feeble similarity identified by Krantz holds for all the cases Goodman would regard as metaphoric. And where the similarity does hold, it is tenuous at best. The interactional theory describes metaphor as arising from the interplay between the meanings of sentence parts, such as subjects and predicates, and I have argued in Chapter 1 that musical elements do not have comparable syntactic/semantic functions. Under those circumstances, saying that music is metaphoric (in being like linguistic metaphor) is simply to employ an unilluminating metaphor.

The moral I draw is this: the nature of metaphoric exemplification can be clarified neither by contrast with (literal) exemplification nor with linguistic metaphor. I have turned without success to the notion of music's being metaphoric in the hope of elucidating the idea of (metaphoric) exemplification.[37] All this suggests that metaphoric exemplification operates in music not as a property standing on two legs—metaphor and exemplification—but as a complexly unitary type of property: to adapt terminology introduced in Chapter 2, "metaphoric exemplification" names a feature resting on synthesis, not juxtaposition. This explains, I think, why analyses of literal exemplification and of linguistic metaphor fail to adequately support or clarify the notion of metaphoric exemplification, which is something other than their sum. Perhaps this much would be accepted by Goodman, but I also contend that the result creates more puzzlement than it resolves. For it leaves the notion of metaphoric exemplification, a notion that is far from self-explanatory, unanalyzed and, ultimately, beyond analysis. Goodman's theory

---

[37] Howard (1971b) adopts the reverse approach, but with no greater success.

< 149 >

of metaphoric exemplification, rather than explaining how music is expressive, draws a dark shroud about the subject.

Metaphor

Earlier I noted that one might be tempted to claim that the metaphor resides in the music where its use seems essential in conveying the nature of the music. In discussing Mozart's K. 364, I suggested that the description of the slow movement as sad is ineliminable, whereas the description of the first-movement entry of the soloists as homing pigeons is dispensable in the sense that many other descriptions would be no less informative of the music's character. So, as I see it, talk of the music as metaphoric is best interpreted as a way of distinguishing among metaphoric descriptions of music those that are central in seeming not to be eliminable in favor of other literal or metaphoric descriptions. Rather than locating the metaphor in the music as opposed to the description, I implied that the distinction might be drawn as one between two kinds of description: the unavoidable versus the gratuitous. If both descriptions are metaphoric (an assumption I question), then it would be reasonable to analyze the expression of emotion in music by considering what grounds the relevant kind of metaphor. Since the question is one about the basis for a distinction between two kinds of nonliteral *description* (the ineliminable versus the rhetorical), we can turn to a consideration of linguistic metaphor with the hope of understanding more about the character of musical expressiveness, for the focus now lies on the idea that it is descriptions of music that are metaphoric (rather than on the far from clear notion that the music possesses some of its properties metaphorically).

Linguistic metaphor is difficult to analyze; the literature on the subject is enormous. So I take the approach of defending the view I favor instead of reviewing all the available alternatives. I endorse the account of metaphor offered by Donald Davidson (1978), and follow the application of Davidson's views to descriptions of music made by Malcolm Budd (1985b and 1989a). In this position, to understand a metaphor is to grasp its point. The point of a metaphor can be given in a paraphrase of it; someone who understands a metaphor must be able to paraphrase it (thus passing a public test of understanding). The paraphrase eliminates the metaphor but expresses the sense contained in (intimated by) the metaphor.[38] Because it is a neces-

---

[38] Budd (1985b) suggests that the paraphrase must be literal. Perhaps this goes too far. A paraphrase might itself contain metaphors, but it cannot contain the metaphor to which it stands as a paraphrase.

< 150 >

sary condition for something's being a metaphor that it be paraphrasable, an utterance that cannot be paraphrased cannot be a metaphor.

Budd first claims (1985b) that, even if "the music is sad" is a metaphor, a recognition of this fact is no substitute for what stands in need of analysis. Metaphors can be used to do many things. What we need for a helpful analysis of musical expressiveness in terms of metaphoric description is an account of the point of this type of metaphor. The analysis of musical expression should explain the attraction of descriptions of music as sad and the like, should explain why this type of description seems to be forced on us. As Cavell notes (1977), what is needed is an explanation of why we describe artworks in terms usually confined to the description of sentient creatures (more specifically, persons). To say that the description is metaphoric and to say no more is to stop short of giving the analysis required. There is no reason, then, to think that reference to metaphor can be a substitute for an analysis of the phenomenon standing in need of explanation.[39]

Budd (1989a) then goes on to deny that the ascription of emotion terms to music involves metaphor. He argues that no analysis of musical expressiveness as metaphoric could be forthcoming; that is, nothing would count as filling out the point of the description of the music as, say, sad. To explain the point of a metaphor one must paraphrase it, but a claim such as "the music is sad" cannot be paraphrased in the required manner. The point of saying "the music is sad" cannot be captured without reference to the emotional character of the music's expressiveness; "sadness" or its cognates cannot be eliminated from the description if one is to be saying the same thing in other words. In Budd's view, this shows that the ascription of emotion to music is not metaphoric.

A version of this argument is presented in Budd (1985b). There he attacks a claim made by Scruton (1983) that the metaphors used in describing music are ineliminable. Budd holds that ineliminability and metaphoricity are exclusive. In some cases (including ones presented by Scruton) the terms are eliminable and metaphoric; in others they may be eliminable and not metaphoric; in yet others they are ineliminable and then cannot be metaphoric. Budd is criticized by Putman (1989), who seems to misunderstand the argument. Putman takes Budd to imply that descriptions of music as expressive must be eliminable. In fact, Budd accepts the ineliminability of expressive

---

[39] This charge might be leveled at Scruton (1983), Putman (1985 and 1989), and Evans (1990). Budd (1985b) notes that Scruton seems to think that no such analysis is necessary or available.

< 151 >

terms in descriptions of music (see Budd 1980, for example). He denies not that expressive terms are ineliminable but that they are metaphoric.[40]

Is Budd right that, where music is appropriately described as sad and the like, the use of emotion terms is not eliminable in favor of a paraphrase using other terms but saying the same thing? And is he correct in holding that it is a necessary condition for metaphoricity that paraphrase always be possible?

Are Emotion Terms Eliminable?

If the word "sad" can be eliminated without loss of sense in a paraphrase of "the music is sad," the most likely candidates for the paraphrase are descriptions of the music in terms of purely sensible features (such as slowness, quietness, and lowness in pitch) or descriptions in more abstractly technical terms (such as "minor key" and "falling minor sixths"). Does "the music is sad" lose anything in its translation to descriptions of either of these two types?

The first of these candidates is defended by Hanslick (1957 and 1986), who holds that "expressive talk" about music is eliminable in favor of descriptions of sensible features of the music (see Bowman 1991). Emotion terms used in descriptions of music are figurative. We might always substitute for them terms from a different order of phenomenon. Instead of describing music as happy or sad, we might characterize it instead as sweet, fresh, cloudy, cool, and so on. Nothing would be lost by way of description of the music if we were to make such substitutions. Hanslick thinks that emotion terms are used figuratively to stand for, or refer to, technical musical features and, therefore, that no substitution preserving the reference would involve a loss of sense. "The melody is sad" and "the melody is dull" both would be ways of saying that the melody is in a minor key (or has a dynamic character shared by dullness and sadness); the one description might do duty for the other.

Budd (1980 and 1985a; also see Howard 1971b) considers Hanslick's

---

[40] For further discussion of Budd versus Scruton, see Zangwill 1991. Zangwill holds that a realist account of musical expressiveness must maintain that there is a causal connection between the use of "sad" as an aesthetic predicate and its standard use, even if, at the level of the "language of thought," the two uses have different contents and are tested for appropriateness by different criteria. Earlier I drew a distinction between homing pigeon descriptions and sadness descriptions of Mozart's K.364 by noting that the latter, unlike the former, seem not to be eliminable in favor of other descriptions saying the same thing. In the discussion of Goodman's views, that distinction was presented as one between two kinds of metaphor. If Budd is right, as I think he is, those descriptions that are ineliminable are not metaphoric. The distinction properly to be drawn is, then, one between a literal and a metaphoric use of language.

< 152 >

views and objects. Even if sad music always displays the relevant sensible properties, not every work possessing the properties (slowness, quietness, and the like) is properly described as sad. Moreover, many other things display the same qualities (sloths, for example, might move slowly and call quietly at a low pitch), yet the description of music in terms of these other things seems not to be equally appropriate. Often, the use of the emotion term appears to be integral and essential to capturing the quality of the music we find interesting; no paraphrase using other terms can be substituted without changing the meaning. The meaning of what is said seems essentially to involve reference to the emotional quality attributed to the music; neither a figurative replacement nor a technical account retains the sense. The point of characterizing the music as sad is lost in such a paraphrase. Even if descriptions of the music as sad or as slow and low equally succeed in drawing attention to a given (technical) feature of the musical substrate, the meanings of the two descriptions differ, so that a move from one to the other involves a change of sense.

The second possibility for an adequate paraphrase—that descriptions of expressive qualities can be replaced without loss of sense by musically technical descriptions—is widely held; for example, a version of it is presented by R. A. Sharpe (1982).[41] Sharpe maintains that descriptions of music in emotion terms are a beginner's way of drawing attention to significant features of the music. By "significant features" he seems to mean properties such as chromaticism and modulation. A person should outgrow the tendency to describe music as sad and the like with the maturation of her musical understanding and appreciation. Emotion words are eliminable in favor of technical descriptions (or of other ways of drawing attention to the treatment of musical materials). The listener, by mastering the technical vocabulary of musical analysis, not only can, but should, seek to eliminate her use of emotion words in describing music.

I regard this second approach to paraphrasability as a variant on the first, so I believe that Sharpe's view is mistaken for reasons just rehearsed. Even if a technical description correctly identifies the musical substrate of the expressive property, a reductive account of the latter in terms of the former loses the baby as well as the bath water (the reductionist in this case mistakes a causal relation for an identity). A person can appreciate the expressiveness

---

[41] Also see Boretz 1970. Evans (1990, 38–39, 88–89) holds that "the music is sad" is a dead metaphor indicating the presence of a formulaic, technical effect. Subtle shades of expression, rather than "sadness" or "happiness," are of aesthetic interest. These retain metaphoric power in not being governed by rules or criteria, he holds.

< 153 >

of the music without recognizing the nature of the musical substrate of its expressiveness. Equally, he might recognize, in technical terms, what is happening without also appreciating the expressive character of the work. The technical description offers (if anything) the cause of the expressive property, and an account of the cause is not the same as an account of the effect, so the technical description fails to capture the point of the expressive description of the musical work.

Budd (1985a, 35) allows that a person might mean no more by "the music is sad" than that the melody contains leaps to dissonant intervals; that is, he allows for the case in which "sad" functions merely as a codeword understood by initiates as shorthand for a longer, technical description. In such a case, "sad" is used metaphorically (or, at least, is not used in its standard literal senses) and is eliminable in favor of the technical description. But, quite rightly in my view, Budd doubts that this is what most people mean when they talk of musical sadness, or that they would accept the paraphrase as capturing the point of their description. Usually when music is described as sad, the word "sad" is to be understood not as a term of musicological art but as preserving the usual sense in which it refers to the world of feeling, or to the exhibition of emotion.

To the extent that "the music is sad" pays heed to the usual, literal meaning of the word "sad," and to the extent that it seems essential, in characterizing the music, that this be acknowledged, I believe Budd is correct in regarding the use of such words as not paraphrasable in terms referring to (other) audible properties of the music or to technical devices (which may or may not be audible). This is not to deny a connection between music's expressiveness and such features or devices, but it is to deny the identity of the two. It is to deny that the former can be reduced to the latter without losing whatever it is that gives point to the use of the emotion terms. Very often, then, the use of such words is not eliminable and, therefore, not paraphrasable in terms having no literal reference to emotions.

Paraphrasability and Ineffability

Now, many of those who hold that "the music is sad" is metaphoric would agree with Budd's ineliminability claim, but they would oppose his denial that it is a condition for metaphoricity that all metaphors be paraphrasable. So they would not see their concession as undermining the view that "sad" operates as a metaphor in the given sentence; they would reject Budd's claim that, necessarily, metaphors are paraphrasable. Is Budd correct in holding paraphrasability as a condition for metaphoricity?

< 154 >

It might be argued thus: Some metaphors defy literal paraphrase without loss of sense. Literal language is sometimes a poor, crude instrument incapable of capturing, containing, and presenting important truths our experience reveals to us. Often the figurative use of language, rather than embellishing what might be stated plainly, aims to capture such truths; what cannot be uttered literally might be said, nevertheless, metaphorically. Metaphors present truths (indeed, important truths), and we are attracted to their use just because some of these truths are not literally expressible or, when expressed literally and accurately, are plainly banal. Metaphors that deal with such truths are not paraphrasable, because what they say lies beyond the realm of that which is literally statable. Now, the world with which music standardly deals in its expressiveness also defies literal description. Music expresses emotions with a specificity by comparison with which literal language is ham-fisted. For this reason, we frequently sense that music "says" more than we can adequately recount; music leaves us at a loss for words, or feeling that our literal descriptions are inadequate, gross approximations of what we find there. The only descriptions remotely adequate to an account of music must be metaphoric, because it is only metaphor that can deal with the kind of expressive truth that is music's common currency.

To reiterate, one might argue this: Often metaphor has a gestural character; it is way of indicating what lies beyond literal description. Music leaves us waving our hands in the air because it too deals with matters that escape the coarse mesh of literal language. Descriptions of music are pathetically inadequate when they are not metaphoric. The unparaphrasability of such descriptions, rather than calling into question their status as metaphors, reveals the limitations of literal language which resort to metaphor is an attempt to remedy.

I am on Budd's side on this issue, so the argument presented here, widely held though it is, is to be challenged. One might begin by questioning the idea of metaphoric (as opposed to literal) truth (see Davies 1984). Even if metaphors lead us to new understandings, it does not follow that they do so by *stating* something other than their literal meanings. If the notion of unstatable (but quasi-propositional) truth is rejected, the equation between a truth-presenting function of metaphor and of music loses its attraction. Rather than pursuing this line, however, one might deprive the view in question of its appeal by confronting the central claim according to which music is a source of ineffable knowledge in that it deals with a meaning lying beyond the remit of literal language. My aim in what follows is not to reject the idea of ineffability per se but to question the claim that music is important because its expressive character is ineffable. I hope thereby to

< 155 >

counter the view that music (or metaphor) importantly extends the scope of the knowable beyond the limits of literal statement. If the importance of music does not reside in its ineffability, the temptation to regard metaphor as providing the only possibility for an account in language of music's importance is undercut.

As noted, it is often said that musical expressiveness is ineffable, that literal language is inadequate to the description of music's expressiveness. Following Mendelssohn, the reason usually cited is that the emotions expressed in music are too specific to be captured by the clumsy categories imposed by words.[42] I find such claims about the inadequacy of language to be puzzling.[43] If the job of language is to provide categories and concepts in terms of which we can organize the buzzing confusion presented by perceptual and emotional experience into conceptually manageable packages, both for the sake of our own understanding and to make possible the public communication of that understanding, then language should not provide a one-to-one correspondence between concepts and the plenitude of perceptual discriminations of which we are capable.[44] The oddity consists in finding fault in the fact that language does not do a job that it is not designed to (and should not) perform.

William Kennick identifies the complaint that language is inadequate in lacking specificity when it comes to the naming of emotions as supposing "(1) that language should provide names for every distinguishable class of feelings; (2) that language should provide a name for every numerically distinct feeling; (3) that language should provide names which produce or evoke the feeling named, as well as naming the feeling; (4) that language should provide names which somehow contain or embody the feeling named" (1961, 319). He responds as follows:

If (1) is meant, then clearly there is no complaint; for either language al-

---

[42] See, for example, McAlpin 1925, Dewey 1934, Bennett 1936, Langer 1942 and 1953, Haydon 1948, Howes 1958, Cooke 1959, Ferguson 1960, Hepburn 1960/61, Carpenter 1966, Epperson 1967, McLaughlin 1970, Boretz 1970, Cavell 1977, Newcomb 1984, and Walton 1988.

[43] Others share my confusion. William Kennick says: "It is a curious sort of deficiency or inadequacy for which there is in theory no remedy. Suppose a man complained that there must be something wrong with his protractor because with it he could not draw a square circle. This complaint is unreasonable at best and at worst no complaint at all" (1961, 318). For a similar comment, directed against the views of Newcomb 1984, see Kivy 1989, 205–207.

[44] Perhaps this explains why writings on the phenomenology of music (such as Pike 1970) seem to say little that is interesting and why works on the metaphenomenology of music (for example Smith 1979) seem to build an impenetrable thicket. For discussion and examples of a phenomenological treatment of music, see Smith 1989.

< 156 >

ready provides names for every distinguishable class of feelings, or else we can readily invent such names. If (2) is meant, there is again no room for complaint. We do not complain because the English language, for example, does not contain the name of every child born of English-speaking parents. The kind of name that is in question in (2) is a proper name, and proper names are not part of a language. We could make them parts of the language, but to do so we should have to revise what we mean by a "language." If (3) is in question, there is again scarcely room for complaint. Names of feelings, although they may on occasion evoke the feeling they name, do not usually do so, and it would be a distinct inconvenience if they did. To complain that there must be something wrong with names of feelings because they do not evoke the feelings they name is like complaining that there is something wrong with the word "hot" because it does not produce a burning sensation in those who utter or read it. Finally, if (4) is what is meant, and I suspect that at the bottom it is, then the demand is self-contradictory. (1961, 319; see Hansen 1972 for other versions of (3) and (4))

At this point Kennick quotes Alice Ambrose as saying that, in terms of (4), the demand is that symbolism be abandoned for embodiment, so that understanding a statement about someone's experience would consist in *having* the experience. He continues: "This is not to deny that works of art serve purposes which language, ordinary or technical, does not serve. . . . But is to deny that there are meanings that cannot be said or communicated by means of language but can be said or communicated by works of art. Works of art may serve as vehicles of illumination and enlightenment, but they do not do so by saying the unsayable, communicating the incommunicable. In so far as they say anything at all—and there is no reason why they must do so—what works of art say can be said in words" (1961, 320).

Kennick's account of the reasons why someone might mistakenly hold language to be inadequate do not exhaust the possibilities. Budd (1989a and 1989b) offers further ones. He sees the indescribability claim as arising from the following: musical works that would be said to express the same emotion might differ in their value; the value of a musical work resides in its expressive power; therefore, the works in question cannot really be expressing the same emotion (since then they would have the same value); so the description of what is expressed must be inadequate; yet language does not allow for more detailed description; so the problem lies with language in that what music "says" is linguistically inexpressible. Budd rejects the crucial premise that sees all musical value as residing in expressiveness. If two works might

< 157 >

be valued for more than their expressiveness, or for something other than their expressiveness, they might express exactly the same emotion and yet differ in their aesthetic value. Budd also goes on to challenge the claim that language is inadequate as an instrument for capturing the precise nature or development of the emotions expressed by music. He comments: it is one thing to say that music expresses things for which there are at best highly general words and another to assert that music can express emotions or aspects of emotions for which there could be no fully adequate verbal formulation. And even if music alone could express nuances of emotion that are indescribable, where, Budd asks, would be the special value in that?

A further factor, mentioned neither by Kennick nor by Budd, seems also sometimes to come into play in claims for the ineffability of emotional experience. It is the view that, because of their privacy, emotions (whether in life or music) are less easily described than are "public" objects such as tables and chairs. If emotions are essentially inner, private phenomena, and if emotion terms take their meaning as labels attached to these phenomena, then, though I might be able to understand what *I* mean by such terms, having established their use through some private act of ostension, others will have difficulty understanding what the terms mean because they do not have (my) access to their denotata. In this view, talk of musical emotions is inherently vague and inadequate just because all talk of emotions displays this deficiency.

The most famous attack on the solipsistic implications of this pseudo-Cartesian view is that presented by Wittgenstein (1953). Often the emotions and feelings of others are quite apparent to us; for example, there might be no room for doubting that a screaming, injured person is in pain. There are many experiences we share; lots of us have hit our thumbs with hammers, for instance. Wittgenstein argues that the fact (if it is one) that others cannot have one's own experiences is no more indicative of the radical privacy of those experiences than is the fact that another cannot possess one's shadow grounds for regarding shadows as radically private objects. We share a public language in which experiences are named and described just because experiences must sometimes (if not always) display a public character. Their doing so is a condition, not only for our discussing the experiences of others, but for our comprehending and identifying (many of) our own experiences. Rather than a barrier to the communication of experience, language is one potent means by which experiences are clarified, conveyed, and expressed. Instead of being inadequate to the identification and description of experiences, language is chock-full of terms for experiences and their description. The temptation to regard discussion of emotions merely and inevi-

< 158 >

tably as metaphoric handwaving should be removed by the realization that literal language encompasses the world of emotion no less readily than the world of shoes and socks.

These points defend language against the charge that it is inadequate to the description of emotions and experiences. I have not argued that one can come to know such things *only* through description; we also acquire knowledge through direct, perceptual experience on many occasions. Some knowledge (for example, of how colors look) could be gained initially only via perception. The point, though, is this: these different routes—the propositional and the perceptual—both can lead to the same knowledge or understanding; that is, the knowledge afforded by experience is not exclusive of the knowledge provided through description. If a distinction is needed, it is one between the routes by which knowledge may be gained rather than between types of knowledge. I can know something of the way a person looks when you describe him as brown-eyed, dark-skinned, short, fat, and bald. Similarly, I can come to know from the description you base on your firsthand experience what it is like to be shot, or to give birth, or to be the first human to step on Mars.

Now, one does hear it said that a man cannot *really* know what it is like to have a baby, or that no amount of description can prepare one for the tension of combat, and so on. And the claim in such cases is, not that the description of the thing in question is often less complete than it might be, but that the knowledge to which firsthand experience of that thing gives rise could not be conveyed in its full richness by verbal description. The arguments just presented suggest that the claim can be exaggerated or misinterpreted, but they do not entail that such a claim is false or meaningless. Perceptual experience has a seamless plenitude that linguistic description does not retain. Though a given perceptual experience and a given description each might concern the same domain of knowledge, it is arguable that the knowledge conveyed by the description always lacks the textural detail of the knowledge acquired at first hand through perception. To that extent one might hold that direct experience can be a source of knowledge which, in its detail, is indescribable and, hence, ineffable; that is, one might stand by the ineffability claim, even if one does not couple it with the charge that language is inadequate to its task, or with the view that language deals with an entirely different domain of knowledge.

This is the view, apparently, of Diana Raffman (1988). She argues that our perceptual awareness of some musical aspects of sound is too "fine-grained" to be captured by our mental "schemas"; her examples are ones of subtle nuances of tone, attack, decay, phrasing, and timbre. According to her view,

< 159 >

some part of sensory-perceptual knowledge can be conveyed by description, but sensory-perceptual knowledge with a detail so fine that it falls through the conceptual net of our established schemas cannot be communicated, except ostensively, and in that way is ineffable.[45] It is part of her view both that much sensory-perceptual knowledge is verbally incommunicable and that this reveals no fault in language as such. She asks rhetorically: "If the raison d'être of schemas is to reduce information load: what point would there be to a schema whose 'grain' was as fine as that of perception?" (1988, 695).

We might wonder if the relevant experiences are ineffable in principle or only in fact.[46] If the latter is the case, we might coin neologisms (as do paint manufacturers for the colors and hues of the paints they sell) until we have mapped "quality space." We do not do this because the consequent gains in precision would be outweighed by other considerations: the language would be hard to learn, or cumbersome to wield, or as likely to confuse as to enlighten because of its detail. If, instead, these experiences are ineffable in principle, then there always will be discriminable differences our invented categories overlook. So, try as we might, a residue of perceptual experience would escape description or labeling.[47] If ineffability arises merely as a matter of fact, then the knowledge afforded by experience and by description might (ideally) coincide exactly. There would be nothing (ideally) a person might learn the one way that he could not learn the other, provided that he had prior experience of the referents of the "simple names" that were used. By contrast, if ineffability arises inevitably, then, despite the overlap between the two, the knowledge provided by experience would always in some respects exceed the knowledge that might be conveyed by description.

For my part, I am unconvinced by claims for principled, as opposed to factual, ineffability. Perhaps the argument between the alternatives is of little significance, however, given that, in the actual world, not everything that can be experienced at first hand can be described. For, so long as room exists

---

[45] In Raffman's view, the indescribable aspects of musical sounds are features of, and relevant to, discriminations between, not musical works themselves, but performances of works. She holds that a *work* can be known solely through description if one has acquired perceptual familiarity with the types mentioned in the description.

[46] So far as I can see, Raffman does not clearly commit herself to either view, see 1988, 697–698.

[47] Nowadays sounds sometimes are represented digitally as a series of os and 1s. If these representations are of a fidelity such that most people could not tell the difference between the sound of the original and the realization in sound of the representation, one might suspect that ineffability is a matter of fact rather than of principle. To reject such a conclusion, it would be necessary to argue that the realization of a digital representation is for most people discriminable from the sound of the original or, alternatively, that digital representations are such that they could not function as elements in a language.

< 160 >

for the notion of unstatable knowledge, there will be an inclination to suspect that there are important truths that cannot be stated. That is, there is a temptation to develop the view that we have ineffable, perceptual knowledge into the claim that there are ineffable truths that cannot be expressed in language and, further, that such truths are somehow more important or vital than those language can capture. To the extent that they present vital truths through our experience of them, artworks will be thought to have something important to "say" that cannot be put literally into words.[48]

This temptation should be resisted. Even if some kinds of perceptual knowledge provide access to truths that are literally inexpressible, there is no reason to think that such truths have a special importance. As Raffman emphasizes, the most mundane perceptual experiences lead to the acquisition of ineffable truths—for example, that the apple in front of me has a distinctive hue. Such facts are usually of no special importance. They do not comprise inexpressible knowledge of a type that anyone is likely to feel compelled or inspired to communicate. There is no reason at all to see a special significance in what is literally inexpressible, as if there must be a meaning to life, the universe, and everything lying just beyond our conceptual grasp and linguistic competence. The argument that here concedes the possibility of ineffable knowledge acquired through direct experience of music implies that what is known ineffably is a degree of detail and resolution in auditory impressions that exceeds the possibility of verbal description or specification, and not some new dimension of the eternal verities.

Moreover, we have already seen warnings in Chapter 1 of the dangers of extending the notion of nonassertible truth beyond that of fidelity, or "truth to life," to the idea that musical works "state" literally inexpressible truths. Even if we can gain inexpressible perceptual knowledge through hearing music, it does not follow that the music says anything about the subject of those truths. There may be no way of literally describing in all its detail the difference between the sound of an open-string harmonic and that of a stopped string, but this does not mean that a musical work that employs these different effects is always *about* the techniques employed in it.[49] Raff-

[48] For a sympathetic account of such a position, see Tilghman 1991, especially Chapter 3 on the early Wittgenstein, who held that ethics and aesthetics deal with what can be shown but not said, and that much of what is significant in human life belongs to their orbit. Tilghman rejects the view that the showable and the sayable are always mutually exclusive, though he does seem to believe that some important truths might be showable without being sayable.

[49] Danto (for instance 1981) has maintained that artworks are distinct from "mere real things" in that they "make statements" and are "about" their being artworks. I regard this as an extravagant, seductively attractive way of stressing that artworks can be identified and appreciated as such only where they are seen as embedded in an art-historical context. For an

< 161 >

man suspects that the "urge to verbalize" what we hear stems from the fact that the syntactic organization of music "tricks us, as it were, into expecting a musical semantics" that does not exist (1988, 705).

In the foregoing I have argued against the notion that the expressiveness of music and the importance we attach to this expressiveness, lies within and depends on the scope of music's ineffability. There is no more reason to accord to music's expressiveness a specially ineffable status than to do the same for color, though, as with color, some subtle aspects of our direct experience of music's expressive power may defy satisfactory description. Some nuances of experience, as given in the perception of music, are ineffable, but no more mysteriously so, or importantly so, than is the case with the most mundane kinds of perception. If we can talk of knowledge of the ineffable, the knowledge provided by music's ineffability does not have more claim to significance than does the knowledge provided by the ineffability of ordinary perceptual experience.

Over the previous few pages I have considered the view according to which music is ineffable in its expressiveness and, as such, can be described as expressive only in metaphoric terms that cannot be paraphrased because they deal with the indescribable. If some metaphors deal with the ineffable, Budd is wrong in insisting that paraphrasability (without loss of sense) is a necessary condition for metaphoricity. But I hope to have shown that, though musical expressiveness might have an ineffable aspect, there is no reason to suppose that music's ineffability is such as to render "the music is sad" unparaphrasable, nor is there reason to suppose that such importance as we might attach to music's expressive power resides in the ineffable character of what it expresses. If the descriptive content of "the music is sad" is lost in a paraphrase that eliminates emotion terms, this is not because "sad" is too vague a term for the expressive character of the music but because no other term truly describes the expressive quality displayed in the music. In that case, according to Budd's analysis, "the music is sad" cannot be metaphoric and must be a literally true description of the music.

How Could It Be True Literally That the Music Is Sad?

I can imagine a reader who insists that Budd's necessary condition of paraphrasability must be mistaken. He might reason thus: Basic intuition suggests that "the music is sad" *must* be metaphoric. "Sad," as used in "the

---

interesting attempt to apply a literal reading of Danto's position to the musical case, see Mark 1980 and 1981.

< 162 >

music is sad," trades on the word's usual meaning; it is not merely a homonym for the word that refers to human feelings. "The music is sad" filters, or otherwise maintains a connection, with the use of "sad" that makes reference to feelings. But the connection is not a literal one, since "the music is sad" seems to attribute a feeling to the music whereas we all know that music, being nonsentient, feels nothing. Taken literally, the attribution is false, yet "the music is sad" appears to convey some kind of truth about the music. So, "sad," as used in "the music is sad," displays the hallmarks of metaphoricity—a use that is patently nonliteral while trading on the term's literal meaning. If "the music is sad" fails Budd's requirement for metaphor—paraphrasability—then common sense recommends that the philosopher's theory, rather than the claim for the metaphoricity of "the music is sad," must be dropped.

Notwithstanding the wisdom of first intuitions, it might be possible to save Budd's view and to do so without pursuing the comparative merits of different theories of metaphor. There are several possibilities that allow for the literalness of "the music is sad." If any of these is plausible, Budd's position might be sustained. The possibilities are as follows: (i) "The music is sad" might be a way of asserting that the music symptomizes or exhibits in an identifiable way the mark of the composer's or performer's feelings of sadness (just as we might talk of the sadness in someone's tears or of the sadness apparent in the hushed voice of a mourner)[50] or (ii) "the music is sad" might attribute to the music the power sometimes to arouse sad feelings in a suitably qualified listener (just as we might call grass green due to its power sometimes to produce certain visual experiences); or (iii) "the music is sad" might literally attribute sadness to the music not as an occurrent emotion, but as an expressive appearance (just as we might describe a willow as cutting a sad figure). I discuss (i) and (ii) at length in Chapter 4 and develop (iii) in Chapter 5.

Both (i) and (ii) preserve a connection—causal or constitutive, rather than referential or denotative—between musical expression and a person's occurrent emotion. Given this, it is not initially implausible to see here a basis for the claim that the attribution of sadness to music might be literal. It is far less apparent that (iii) deals with literal, not metaphoric, predications for this reason: the primary, literal use of "sad" is in attributing an occurrent emotion to a person, but the use of "sad" mentioned under (iii) pays no

---

[50] For a variant on this approach, according to which the work literally expresses a mental state that can be attributed to a persona constructed by the interpreter as standing behind the work, see Vermazen 1986.

< 163 >

regard to any person's feelings. To make good the suggestion that (iii) might be offered in defending Budd's view from common sense, it is necessary to say a few words about the difference between secondary and metaphoric uses.

The use of terms such as "sad" in describing music as outlined under (iii), clearly is not those terms' primary use, if, as seems reasonable, the primary use concerns felt emotions. Not all nonprimary uses of words are metaphoric, though.[51] Dictionaries list many literal, secondary meanings for words, and we are as much masters of these subsidiary meanings as we are of primary meanings. For example, we talk without strain of the necks of bottles or the mouths of rivers. This use trades on the primary, biological reference, but the connection between the secondary and primary uses does not indicate the presence of metaphor in this case. The secondary meaning is listed in dictionaries and, more important, is subject to the conditions for consistent, widespread, interpersonal use that mark literal terms. The connection between the primary and secondary meanings might suggest that the secondary use began life as a metaphor; that is, it might indicate something about the history of the term's employment rather than about its present use.[52] The secondary use is established with the death of the metaphor (see Davies 1984). Secondary meanings are literal, not metaphoric; dead metaphors no more remain metaphors than false friends remain friends.[53] If

---

[51] See Tilghman 1984 for a useful and more detailed account of nonmetaphoric, secondary uses of terms in discussing art.

[52] It is in terms of their histories that one might distinguish secondary meanings from mere homonyms. Whereas the former extends or draws somehow on a term's primary meaning, the latter involves an alternative, unconnected meaning. Just as metaphors trade on the literal meaning of some of their terms, so too secondary meanings (unlike mere homonyms) take account of the term's primary meaning in that some aspect of that meaning is applied to a new context. This similarity is to be explained as a carryover from the origins of secondary meanings in metaphors. These metaphors have become so widely accepted and understood that they died, leaving a literal, secondary meaning as their residue. The potential for the new, public use might be so obvious, though, that the metaphor is stillborn, so that a secondary meaning is coined without a period of transition in which the term served as a live metaphor. Homonyms are taken into public use for another reason. They might be secondary in the frequency of their use or in their chronology, but they are not secondary in being derivative of, or otherwise connected to, the primary meaning.

[53] Dead metaphors can be revivified, but this does not show that they remain nonliteral throughout their lives; rather, it shows that any literal term might be given a metaphoric use. Sharpe holds that "the music is sad" is metaphoric but is "well on its way to becoming a dead metaphor," but he also believes that the meaningfulness of our predicating such properties or states to music depends on a continuing residue of metaphoric content. (1983a, 111–112). With this claim I disagree.

< 164 >

the metaphors are now dead, calling the use of the terms "metaphoric" adds a historical perspective but provides no analytical insight.

The claim made under (iii) comes then to this: Though the deployment of "sad" in "the music is sad" is not that word's primary, literal use, it does not follow that the use is metaphoric. Indeed, such terms have regular, interpersonal, and largely conventional application in describing music, so we might expect to be dealing with dead, not live, metaphors, that is, with literal, secondary meanings of the terms. So far as expressiveness is concerned, many so-called metaphors applied to music seem moribund. Equally Moalike in their lack of vivacity are many other of the allegedly metaphoric terms in which music is described—for example, where the texture or tone of notes is characterized as high or low, thin or thick, light or heavy, narrow or wide; or timbres are described as metallic, fruity, hard, or soft; or rhythms are called jagged, abrupt, square, spiky, or dumpy. When we call the rhythm dragging, the melody drooping, the timbre dark, the appoggiatura yearning, we seem to describe literal properties; we seem to describe qualities present in the sound of the work. As Thomas Clifton (1983) asks rhetorically, is it any more metaphoric to call Tamino's first aria in *The Magic Flute* "tonal" than "tender," when both are experienced as the way the music is?

There is obvious attraction in the view that music's being expressive is a matter of its symbolizing emotions: since music cannot literally be sad and given the acceptability of talk of musical sadness, there must be some connection between the sadness of music and the emotions felt by a person (or people); perhaps the most plausible connection to posit is a referential one in which the music functions as a (nonlinguistic, nonpictorial) symbol of the emotions it expresses. Equally, there is obvious difficulty in the view that music is a symbol: we do not understand or appreciate the music merely as a vehicle for reference; our phenomenal experience of music's expressiveness locates the feeling in the music, and it is just for this reason that expressiveness seems to be an artistically significant property.

In this chapter I have explored Langer's and Goodman's theories according to which artistic expressiveness involves a distinctive type of symbolism. Their views each aims to skirt the difficulty just outlined by stressing the opacity of the mode of symbolism involved in artistic expressiveness; the work invites employment as a symbol because it already contains what it might be used to symbolize. Since music cannot literally feel sad, Goodman holds that the exhibition of the expressive quality in the work is metaphoric, whereas Langer suggests that what is symbolized is the *form* of feeling rather than emotional experience as such.

< 165 >

These attempts to sidestep the most obvious of the inadequacies associated with theories regarding the artwork as deriving its significance from its functioning as a symbol create difficulties in their turn. Goodman can explain artistic expressiveness as symbolic in character only if he can distinguish literal from metaphoric possession/exemplification, and only if he can show the latter necessarily to presuppose a symbolic use. His theory seems to fail on both counts. Just what his "metaphoric exemplification" amounts to in musical expression is so obscure that the account is deprived of explanatory power. Meanwhile, Langer's own theory of the presentational symbol is no more illuminating. She implies that the incoherence of her view is evidence for its correctness when blaming the "inadequacies" of language for what are shortcomings in her own analysis. In dropping denotation/reference from her account of presentational symbolism, she seems to abandon talk of the symbolic function, but she offers no more than possession in its place. And, in discussing the subject of symbolization not as the expression of emotions but as the presentation of conceptions of emotions, she seems to eschew the kind of expressiveness we find so powerfully attractive in art. In brief, both theories fail to reconcile the opacity of musical expressiveness with an account of music as depending for its expressiveness on its being used as a special symbol. Expressiveness is retained, if at all, as a matter of possession, with the puzzle of how music might possess such features left unresolved; meanwhile, the emphasis falls on a special mode of symbolism the characterization of which for the musical case turns out to be far from perspicuous.

The discussion in these first three chapters suggests that the difficulty in discussing musical expressiveness does not lie in determining what type of symbolic connection is involved (linguistic, depictive, other) but in supposing that expressiveness is grounded in any symbolic relation. If we do not deem properties of music to be expressive because they stand to someone's feelings in a symbolic, referential relation, what other relation might be involved? In the following chapter I examine the possibility that the relevant relation is constitutive or causal.

< 166 >

FOUR

· · · ·

The Feelings of the Composer and the Listener

A theme common to the previous chapters is the idea that the mode of connection between music and its meaning is that of symbolization. The theories discussed differ on whether the mode of symbolism is systematized and, if so, whether the significance of the whole is generated from the combination of the parts in a way that recalls the symbol systems of language, of painting, or of neither. These various views were judged to be inadequate. Though it is natural to assume that music is meaningful as a symbol, or as a "sentential unit" within a symbol system, since these are paradigms of meaning, that assumption now appears to be mistaken. How does music secure its meaning if not as a symbol? In this chapter I consider two views that have in common both that they regard music's significance as residing mainly in its expressive power and that they account for its acquiring this significance in terms of the music's standing in a causal, rather than a symbolic, relation to the emotions it expresses.[1]

One might be led to such theories by several different considerations. Music is inanimate, yet it expresses emotions with a power and directness indicating that it cannot be regarded merely as a symbol of emotions (like

---

[1] Because these causal processes may be effective whether or not they are triggered intentionally, the theories considered here involve a shift from accounts of musical meaning as of the C, D, or E types toward the A and B types.

< 167 >

the word "sad"). The immediacy of the expressive character of music suggests that it deals with occurrent emotions rather than with labels for, names of, conceptions of, or thoughts about emotions. The emotions expressed in music must be the emotions of some person (since they are not felt by the music), but whose emotions are they? If the emotions expressed in music must have human owners, then the feelings are likely to be those of a character in the work, or the composer, or the performer, or the listener.

In a narrational or depictive artform, the artist might describe or picture a character who could be the "owner" of the emotions expressed in the work. A situation could be indicated in which a character in the work could be known to feel an emotion, or the character might be described or depicted as expressing an emotion, or we might be told (in the work's title, the words spoken, or whatever) that the character experiences some emotion. For example, a painter might depict a weeping woman cradling in her arms a dead man. Alternatively, the artist might describe, represent, or present material likely to be associated in the minds of the audience with the occurrence of some emotion. So, for example, the picture of the woman holding the dead man might be presented as a pietà. Moreover, the audience might respond emotionally to the characters described or depicted in such a work. I might admire Leonore's courage in Beethoven's *Fidelio*.

Now, the questions of how characters in artworks might "own" emotions, and of how the audience can respond emotionally to such characters, given that they are not believed to be actual, raise fascinating issues and difficulties. I pass these by, however, to concentrate on the case in which we attribute the emotion, feeling, or attitude not to a character in the work but to the work itself. As well as describing, depicting, and indicating by association the presence of emotion, works of art express within themselves emotions, feelings, and attitudes that cannot be attributed to any fictional (or actual) person described or represented within the work. An emotion or attitude may be expressed *toward* the propositional or representational content of the work. For example, the self-satisfied smugness of a pictured person may be depicted as contemptible. Furthermore, emotions may be expressed in works with neither propositional nor representational content nor any emotional associations. For example, the last movement of Beethoven's Symphony No. 7 is, simply, joyous. Indeed, pure music generally is regarded as the paradigm art for emotional expression. And expressiveness of this sort often calls forth from the audience an emotional response.

The two theories of musical expression discussed in this chapter aim to analyze the expressiveness belonging to the work rather than to a character in the work. The expression theory holds that this expressiveness is an ex-

< 168 >

pression of the emotions experienced by the composer (or the performer). By contrast, the arousal theory (also known as the evocation theory or, sometimes, as emotivism) claims that the emotions expressed in a musical work are those experienced by the listener. Some critics have attacked these theories for failing to explain all the kinds of expressiveness found in artworks, since they do not cover the feelings of a character described or depicted in the work.[2] This criticism is unfair, I think. Most expressionists (see, for example, Sircello 1972, especially chaps. 1–2) and arousalists recognize the distinction between the expressiveness of a work and of a character in it (and perhaps also a distinction between an emotional response to the one as opposed to the other). Though not unaware of the case in which a character is described or depicted as experiencing an emotion, these theorists aim to analyze the important and problematic case in which the emotion expressed in the work is attributed to the work. The expression theory identifies such emotions as the composer's, whereas the arousal theory identifies them as the listener's.

It is fair to say that, within philosophical aesthetics, neither theory is seen as totally respectable, but it is equally true that both views have always held widespread appeal. The attraction of these theories is not difficult to explain. We believe that the expressiveness of musical works occurs not by chance but by design, and that composers are responsible for the expressive powers of their works. Also, we know that musical composition can be an intensely involving experience revealing of the personality of the composer. We also appreciate that, as well as engaging the listener's intellect, music taps into his emotional life. The experience of listening to a musical work can be profoundly moving. Moreover, we regard the expressiveness of much music as integral, not incidental, to its character. A person who could analyze the structure of musical works and could provide a detailed technical description of the place and relations of every one of their notes, but could not correctly attribute expressive character to those works and showed no understanding of such a mode of description, would strike us not just as odd but also as having a flawed understanding of music. Such understanding as this person has would not count as evidence for her having an appreciation of music as such. Also, someone who could correctly attribute expressiveness to musical works, but who never felt inclined to respond emotionally to that expressiveness, would strike us as strange. Either the *attribution* would be odd, in the way that the correct use by blind people of color terms seems odd to sighted

---

[2] See Todd 1972 and Stecker 1983, but note that Stecker (1984) allows that no single theory can adequately explain expressiveness for all the arts.

< 169 >

people who do not have to infer or remember the correct use in a similar way, or the *lack of response* would be odd, in the way that it would be strange for an otherwise normal person to be indifferent to her own feelings and to the feelings of others. Finally, that we respond to music as we do is not independent of its being created by human agents. Just as we do not react to spoken utterances merely as vibrating air, we do not react to music merely as vibrating air. There is a sense of communion, even of communication, involved. Concerning this last point, the two theories considered in this chapter can often be seen to go together. It is because music is a vehicle for the communication of human feelings, often the composer's, that we respond to it as we do—or so it might be claimed. Both theories attempt to humanize music, to see it as the link connecting the emotions of the composer with those of her audience.

The Expression Theory

As I use it here, "expression theory" refers to a theory that explains art's expressiveness as arising from artists' expressing their concurrent emotions or feelings in the production of art.[3] The emotions read off from works of art are recognized and responded to as those of their creators: they are regarded as emotions felt by composers and given expression through the act of composition. In the crudest version of this view, one can read off a composer's feelings from his music just as one can read off a person's sadness from his tears. The audience's emotional response to the expressiveness of a musical work is a response to that work as expressing emotions felt by its composer at the time of creation. The emotions expressed in a musical work, rather than being consciously and coolly designed into it by its composer at a time of calm concentration, somehow are poured or discharged into the work during its creation.[4] Obviously, such an account accords with one common view of artistic inspiration (see Osborne 1977).

---

[3] The following discussion of the expression theory derives from Davies 1986. For an excellent account of the issues, see Robinson 1983b. The title "expression theory" has also been given to definitions of art as expressive (see Tolstoy 1962), to theories insisting that expressive properties, qualities, features, or powers can be predicated truly of works of art (see Sircello, 1965 and 1972), and to the view that artworks can cause emotional responses (see Elliott 1966/67).

[4] A variant of the expression theory might suggest that the emotions expressed in music are those of the performer rather than those of the composer—Kivy (1990b) attributes this view to Hanslick—or that the emotions of both are expressed. The idea that the two operate in tandem might explain how various performances can differ in the detail of their expressive character while preserving the emotional tone of the work as a whole: the composer gives the work its

< 170 >

The Feelings of the Composer and the Listener

In this version of the expression theory, composers express in their music emotions, feelings, moods, or attitudes rather than pure ideas, suppositions, or beliefs (though this is not to deny that emotions inevitably possess a cognitive dimension). The expression of emotion in art is thought not to be compared usefully to the expression of thought in words, although some of the theory's proponents might talk loosely of art as a language with which artists communicate with their audiences. An example:

> If, then, a composition should arise from a condition of joy, the composer may rightly be said to have expressed the condition out of which it arose. If the composer be in a state of joyousness when he composes, joy becomes his inevitable model and most assuredly induces his music. If it were otherwise, then would a composer write what he did not feel— surely a strange inversion of the character of creativeness. We rather hold that great music is only what a composer greatly feels; and it moves us because he himself is moved. True music, therefore, emanates from a condition of being, and is a direct expression of an inward state of soul. . . . A composer does not pick and choose his phrases. . . . Inspired music simply comes. . . . it issues from the fount of deepest life, and is borne along the tide of buoyant feeling. Though it may be approved of or corrected afterwards by the critical faculty, it is not argued out, but intuitively conceived. It is not the result of logical activity. It is an intuitive act of immediate seizure, not an act of deliberate judgment. . . . doubtless some "music-makers" have a superficial aptitude for writing without being profoundly moved; but it is exactly because the feeling impulses lack cogency, and emotional warmth has fled the heart, that so much unconvincing music is abroad. (McAlpin 1925, 436–437)

The crude version of the theory just outlined faces some obvious objections. It is not common for most composers to work creatively under the duress of emotion. Strong emotions would disrupt and distract them from the concentration and toil involved in composition. Besides, large-scale works might take months or years to complete. J. S. Bach's cantatas are not without their expressive qualities, but they were produced methodically and to regular order. The demands of his job dictated that Bach could not wait idly for an inspirational mood with the "right" emotional tone. Even those

---

general expressive character, but the performer shapes or highlights details on which expressive nuance depends. In the following discussion I leave aside the complications of considering the performer(s). The criticisms I consider can be applied as forcefully to the one thesis as to the other.

< 171 >

composers who do work under the influence of strong feelings do not necessarily convey those feelings to the music they write. For example, Stravinsky labored on his Symphony in C at the time of the death of his first wife and his mother. He writes:

> Three months later, March 2 1939, a hemorrhage ended my wife Catherine's fifty-year struggle with the same disease. . . . One of my infrequent absences [from the sanitarium to which he moved] was to attend the funeral of my mother, who died on June 7. For the third time in half a year I heard the Requiem service chanted for one of my own family, and for the third time walked through the fields to the cemetery of Saint-Geneviève-des-Bois, in Montlhéry, which is on the road to Orléans, and dropped a handful of dirt in an open grave. And once again I was able to go on only by composing, though no more than before do the parts of the Symphony written in these dark days represent an expression of my feelings of loss. The pastoral second movement was begun March 27, and completed July 19. (1972, 48)

Beethoven wrote the joyous last movement of his Piano Concerto No. 1 when racked with gastroenteritis. Even those composers who aim to pour their feelings into their music do not always succeed: composers of the second rank, such as Ernest Chausson and Henri Duparc, come to mind.[5]

The expression theory accepts what might be termed a "romantic" or a "Platonic" model of the creative process: the composer, gripped by emotion or inspiration, pours forth notes that carry the mark of the frenzy in which they had their genesis. The testimony of composers does not suggest, however, that this model is accurate. There is no uniformity in the creative process. The techniques involved in writing music (including expressive music) might be applied automatically, their use having been mastered in the past, or they might be applied with painstaking calculation. Mozart often worked in the former way, Beethoven often in the latter, and Berg sometimes in the one way and sometimes in the other. Schubert and Mozart aside, composition usually involves careful calculation, trial and error, and weeks or months of absorbingly hard work.[6] As a *general* account of the creative process, the expression theory is mistaken.

[5] For a discussion, see Hindemith 1953; for a reply to Hindemith, see Cooke 1959. Note that, though Cooke believes that composers do express their feelings, he does allow that expressiveness is inherent to the character of musical sounds, so I think Sharpe (1983a, 99–112) is mistaken in branding Cooke an expressionist.

[6] For a useful discussion of different creative approaches to composition, see Copland 1957, chap. 3.

< 172 >

The Feelings of the Composer and the Listener

Beyond such objections on empirical grounds, a main line of critique makes a conceptual point against the expression theory. The theory supposes that the expressiveness of a process is transmitted to the product having its origin in that process, that the expressiveness of an action is apparent in traces left by that action. Such suppositions are true neither in general nor in the particular case of a composer's writing a musical work. It is not the case that composers' feelings can be read off their artworks just as those feelings might be read off their tears; it is not the case that the expressiveness of works of art is appropriately to be seen as a direct and visible sign of the artists' feelings.[7]

Despite the obvious power of this objection, the expression theory has undoubted appeal. Some composers apparently felt emotional anguish as they worked (Mahler, for example), and their compositions seem to reflect this. Moreover, some listeners find in music's expressiveness the immediacy and power that one would associate with the direct expression of another's emotion. The experience of the last movement of Beethoven's Symphony No. 7 is more like an encounter with a person radiant with happiness than with a person who dispassionately says that she feels happy. And if anyone is responsible for the joyous character of the music, it is Beethoven, the composer. So, rather than abandoning the theory, one might attempt to resuscitate it by introducing refinements that avoid the difficulties identified so far. As a prelude to considering some ways it might be amended, I distinguish between different types of emotional expressiveness.

Primary, Secondary, and Tertiary Expressions of Emotion

Some emotions have characteristic forms of expression, which I here call *primary*. Sobbing, for example, is a primary expression of sadness and like emotional states. Primary expressions occur unintentionally and unreflectively. Indeed, these forms of expression may not be easy to mimic convinc-

---

[7] For versions of the objection, see Bouwsma 1950, Hospers 1954/55, Khatchadourian 1965, and Tormey 1971, chap. 4 and Appendix. I mention in passing a further criticism that seems to me to be unwarranted. This objection notes that, as it stands, the expression theory does not explain why artists' expressing their feelings in their art would be valued as the expressiveness of art is valued (see Todd 1972, especially 479). This objection is unfair in attacking the theory for not considering a matter that lies, anyway, beyond its immediate remit. The theory purports to explain what it is for art to be expressive, and there is no reason to expect that explanation to also make obvious why it is that we attach value to the expressiveness of art as we do. It is not difficult, anyway, to see how the theory might be developed to meet the objection; perhaps the creation of art is suited to the expression of important or highly specific feelings that are not easily described, or to other forms of communication.

< 173 >

ingly and, where it is known that they are deliberately adopted, they are usually seen to be merely pretended and not to be expressive of genuine emotions. Because they are not consciously contrived or adopted, these are forms of expression into which a person falls or to which he gives way. A sad person need not weep and need not always feel like weeping when he is sad, but *sometimes* he must feel like weeping when he is sad, and if he does not then weep it is because he controls the impulse to weep that goes with and is partly constitutive of sadness. The control and suppression of primary expressions of emotion may be intentional, although their occurrence or tendency to occur is not. Where a person's sadness is extreme, a sob may be wrung from him by the force of his feelings and in spite of his intention not to show his feelings (note the etymology of "express"). So primary expressions are not expressive because of their being intended as such. Rather, they are expressive in themselves of the emotions to which they stand as primary expressions.

Primary expressions of emotion might reasonably be characterized as "natural," but this would not be to deny that they are shaped by learning or conditioning. "Ouch" or "ow," uttered unthinkingly under circumstances in which the utterer had been caused sudden and unexpected pain, are primary expressions of that pain. But speakers of French under the same circumstances give primary expression to their pain by saying "ouf," and speakers of other languages use other vocables for the primary expression of sudden pain. Even the ways we smile or weep might be shaped subtly by cultural practices differing from group to group—that is, primary expressions are as likely to involve meaning B or C as meaning A.

Because they are not adopted intentionally and because they betray "inner" states, there are respects in which primary expressions of emotion are like symptoms (such as the spots of measles) or natural signs (for example, the smoke that indicates the presence of fire). In pursuing this comparison one might come to doubt that expressiveness is a notion happily applied to what I have called primary expressions. Spots signify or symptomize or betray the presence of measles, but they do not express measles. So, is it wrong to regard tears as expressing sadness? Some proponents of sophisticated versions of the expression theory argue that it is wrong, because they wish to move away from the idea that art is expressive as tears are, and in doing so they demote tears from their apparent status as expressions of feeling. These writers distinguish mere ventings from expressions of emotion and they dismiss what I have called primary expressions as mere ventings.[8]

---

[8] See Dewey 1934, chap. 4; Collingwood 1963, especially 60–61, and Ducasse 1964 and 1966. Hare (1972) gives a good summary of Ducasse's views. On Tormey's critique of Dewey,

< 174 >

The Feelings of the Composer and the Listener

To pursue the analogy with symptoms and natural signs as far as this conclusion seems absurd, though. Only philosophers (and only a few of them) would deny that tears are expressive of grief under the appropriate circumstances. As one way of holding back from the conclusion that tears no more express sadness than spots express measles, one might argue that tears are constitutive of sadness whereas symptoms and natural signs are merely causal concomitants.[9] I am not sure that I am convinced that the analogy fails in this way, or that it fails at all, but I agree that ventings can be expressions. Perhaps the point is this: whereas sometimes I can choose how my feelings are expressed, this is no more the case where the expressions are primary than when my spots signify that I have measles. But whereas *I* do not express my sadness by my tears (just as I do not express my measles by my spots), others can see my sadness expressed in my tears (just as they might see the measliness of my condition expressed in my spottiness). Even if my tears no more express sadness than my spots express measles, the expression (but not *my* expressing) of my sadness shows in my crying and, similarly, the expression of my measled condition can be seen in my spotting.

By the *secondary* expression of emotion I mean behavior that issues from the emotions felt, yet that could not be seen as expressive by someone who was not already aware of the agent's intentions or circumstances. Secondary expressions of emotion are usually intentional, though they need not be. They are distinguished from primary expressions in not being constitutive of the emotions to which they give expression. The connection between an emotion and its secondary expressions is contingent.

An example of a secondary expression of a person's emotion is that of a man's throwing himself into the activity of designing and building a house at a time of grieving for a dead wife and in response to that grief. Knowing his intentions and circumstances, one might describe the act of building the house as an expression of his grief—as his coming to terms with his grief, or his burying or turning his back on his grief, or his dissipating the force of his grief in action, or his creating a private memento of his loss, or his giving his grief time to subside.[10] These are, admittedly, attenuated uses of the notion of expression, but they have in common with the man's primary expressions

---

see Mitias 1992. Not all those who distinguish between venting and expressing are expressionists; see Tomas 1952, Alston 1965, and Benson 1967. For an alternative approach on the matter, see Vermazen 1986.

[9] See Wollheim 1964, 275–277 and 1966/67, 231–244, and Tormey 1971, 29–32, 47–50, and 98–102.

[10] If a person eats more when he feels sad, this might be an unintended secondary expression of his feelings. Obviously a tendency to eat is not constitutive of sadness, so one's eating would not be a primary expression of one's sadness. Someone familiar with one's character, habits, and circumstances might recognize in one's craving for éclairs an expression of grief.

< 175 >

of his grief that they are no less revealing of his feelings where the context of action is understood. Notice, however, that, whereas house-building and the house that results are expressions of grief to those who understand their motivation, we would not usually say either of the act of building or of the house that it is in itself expressive of grief. We would say that grief is expressed *through*, rather than *in*, them. This locution acknowledges the fact that the expressiveness of the man's actions depends on their being seen as resulting from certain intentions or circumstances.

Though the secondary expression of emotion is free expression in being largely unconstrained by conventions and rules, it is not so free that just any behavior might become a secondary expression of grief, say, merely as a result of the agent's intending that it be so. If the grieving man hit the high spots with a blonde on his knee intending that this be a secondary expression of his grief, we would not normally judge his actions to be such an expression. We would deny that his actions are at all expressive of grief and would be disinclined to accept the sincerity of his professed intention.

Tertiary expressions of emotion differ from secondary expressions in relying on the use of conventions and rituals. The conventions reveal the intentions of the agent as regards the expressiveness of her actions or their products. It is a condition for tertiary expressiveness that the use of the conventions be both intentional and sincere. So, if the grieving man built a mausoleum dedicated to the memory of his dead wife instead of a house, that mausoleum would be a tertiary expression of his grief if he were sincere about his feelings in expressing them this way. The building of mausoleums is a conventional expression of grief. Because of the conventional nature of tertiary expression, the man need not design and build the mausoleum. He may commission the design and its execution. If he takes an interest in neither, still the mausoleum expresses his grief. He cannot in the same way commission others to cry his tears (as a primary expression of his grief).[11] Nor, under most circumstances, can he commission others to give secondary expression to his emotions. Indifference is evidence of insincerity where a claim to secondary expression is concerned, but this need not be the case for tertiary expressions. The expressiveness is carried forward by the conventions for tertiary expressions in a way that obviously is not possible for secondary expressions.[12]

---

[11] He might employ professional mourners, though. Their tears are a tertiary, not a primary, expression of his grief.

[12] Whereas an assertion *that* one feels so-and-so reports, rather than expresses, one's emotion or feeling, tertiary expressions of emotions may be verbal—as when I express my contempt by saying "You miserable, sneaking worm!" or, more complicated, by the choice of terms with

< 176 >

Established conventions can be misused to present the appearance of an expression of grief where none is felt. Thus, a rich cynic who has loathed his wife and rejoices in her death might, as a private joke, commission a grand mausoleum dedicated to her memory. Because the established conventions can be used insincerely, they can be employed to lie, to stretch the truth, for ironic effect, and so on.

Back to the Expression Theory

How does the crude version of the expression theory categorize the expressiveness of art? In maintaining that the expressiveness of art stands to the composers' feelings as their tears stand to their felt sadness, the expression theory analyzes the expressiveness of art as primary. The position is attractive for several reasons. Emotions are expressed *in* primary expressions, whereas (usually) they are expressed only *through* secondary or tertiary expressions, and our experience of the expressiveness of art locates the feeling in it.[13] Moreover, the expressiveness of art moves its audience in a way that primary, but not secondary or tertiary, expressions of emotions do. Secondary and tertiary expressions of emotion are indirect, mediated, often formalized types of expression and, as such, they distance the audience from the emotions expressed through them. As a result, secondary and tertiary expressions of emotions seem not to call for an emotional response from others. By contrast, primary expressions of emotion confront others directly with the force of the person's feeling. Emotional indifference in the face of primary expressions of emotion is difficult to maintain and, anyway, not usually appropriate. Such indifference might rightly be seen as callous, for example. Now, in their manner of expression, musical works seem primary rather than secondary or tertiary. Compositions seem to present emotions immediately and directly to their audiences, and that expressiveness is often highly evocative of affective responses. Emotional indifference to music's expressiveness might properly be seen as evidence of a lack of appreciation and understanding.

Nevertheless, music seems clearly not to be a primary expression of anyone's emotion. The expressiveness of musical works is usually consciously contrived by their composers, which suggests that such works are secondary

---

which I develop a description of the emotion's object, or where my tone of voice reveals my attitude to the situation I report. On this point, see Benson (1967), who also talks of conventionalized expressions of emotions, using keening as an example.

[13] For a phenomenological account of this experience, see Casey 1971.

< 177 >

or tertiary as expressions of their creators' feelings. Even in those (comparatively rare) cases in which the composer writes an expressive work in an unreflective frenzy brought on by her feelings, still there are obvious grounds for hesitating to consider the composition a primary expression of her emotions. Primary expressions are partly constitutive of, not merely concomitant with, the emotions they express.[14] It is for this reason that children are taught the meaning of emotion words in connection with occurrences (or depictions, or descriptions) of their primary expressions. By contrast, the expressiveness of a musical work seems (at best) to be concomitant with the composer's feelings, even where the emotion expressed in the composition is the same as that felt by the composer. Unlike primary forms of expression, the expressiveness of the musical work would not be destroyed were we to learn that the composer had felt nothing during its creation, or that she had deliberately contrived the work's expressiveness. We could not teach the meaning of emotion terms to a child if our examples were all taken from instrumental music in which emotions are expressed (by contrast with representational paintings, or operas, or novels, in which persons are depicted or described as giving expression to their feelings).

A further respect in which the expressiveness of music differs importantly from the primary expression of emotion deserves comment. As the expression theory rightly observes, both the expressiveness of art and the primary expression of emotion are highly evocative of emotional responses. The expression theory fails, however, to note a crucial difference in the emotions evoked. The emotional response called forth by a primary expression of emotion (or by a representation of such) rarely *mirrors* the expressed emotion; rather, the response is suited to the character of the emotion expressed. Thus, sadness invites a compassionate response, wretchedness invites pity, anger invites fear, and so on. In contrast, the emotions expressed in instrumental music often call forth mirroring responses.[15] Sad music tends to evoke sadness; happy music tends to make people feel happy. We do not feel pity or compassion for Beethoven on hearing the sadness of the slow movement of his Symphony No. 3; rather, our own feelings echo the sadness we hear in the music. This suggests that we do not respond emotionally to art as we would to primary expressions of artists' feelings.

There is an obvious way of modifying the crude version of the expression

---

[14] The point is discussed at some length in Wollheim 1964, especially 275–277, and 1966/67, mainly 233–238, and 241–244; also see Tormey 1971, 29–32, and 47–50.

[15] See Hospers 1954/55, 337, Davies 1980 and 1983a, and Osborne 1983. Kivy, (1987, 1989, and 1990a) denies that sad music makes people feel sad, so he would reject the force of this objection to the expression theory. I debate the matter later in this chapter and in Chapter 6.

< 178 >

theory to meet the above objections: one might abandon the claim that musical expression is primary in favor of the view that the emotional character of the music is a secondary or tertiary expression of the composer's feeling. This departure from the crude version of the theory is likely to be accompanied by reminders that emotions cannot be *in* music (except metaphorically) and that "real" expression is to be contrasted with the mere venting of emotion (that is, with primary expression).

The attempt to refine the expression theory along these lines faces difficulties in its turn. The audience does not usually require knowledge of the artist's intentions, or of an extramusical expressive context, beyond that provided by the artwork before being able to appreciate the work's expressiveness. This implies that music, if it cannot be a primary one, is a tertiary rather than a secondary expression of its composer's feelings.[16] But if it is a tertiary expression, this fact is either independent of or irrelevant to the music's expressiveness.

Where the work undeniably is a tertiary expression of the composer's feelings, its being so is irrelevant to its artistic appreciation. A requiem for a dead person is a tertiary expression of the feelings of the person who commissioned or ordered it. The composer might "order" such a work from himself on a suitable occasion. Gabriel Fauré wrote his *Requiem* on his father's death and (since his sincerity is not in doubt) it is a tertiary expression of his grief. Fauré's *Requiem* might have been commissioned by another, though, and then it would have been a tertiary expression of that person's grief, not the composer's. Now, normally we regard as irrelevant to an appreciation of a work the feelings of the person who commissioned it.[17] There is no reason our attitude should be different where it is the composer himself who "orders" the work. Composers sometimes do give tertiary expression to their emotions in creating musical works, but this fact seems to explain neither how their music is expressive in itself nor why such an expression of the composer's emotion should be pertinent to the work's appreciation. Musical expression may be no less conventional than is the use of language

---

[16] Tormey (1971, 117–120) makes a similar point against the view that art may be analyzed as, in my terms, a secondary expression of artists' emotions, but he has little to say about the possibility of artworks' being what I call tertiary expressions of emotion. Sircello (1972, especially in chap. 2), recommends that art be seen as, in my terms, a tertiary, rather than a secondary, expression of emotions, moods, and attitudes.

[17] An obvious basis for this attitude is this: the work I commission might express my grief if the person I commission produces something recognizable as a requiem, even if that person is not sufficiently competent to imbue the requiem with a lachrymose flavor; that is, as a requiem the work might be a tertiary expression of its commissioner's grief, even if grief is not expressed in the work itself.

< 179 >

having communication as its aim. But the conventions of music, unlike those regulating communication, serve to reveal the contextual significance of elements, not to reveal the intentions that motivated their arrangement (whether or not such intentions might be inferred in the appreciation of the arrangement). There might, for example, be a convention such that anything made by a person wearing a pixie hat at my behest is a tertiary expression of my grief. Then, a composer who wears a pixie hat at my behest as she writes a piece allows for the tertiary expression of my grief. Similarly, a composer who wears a pixie hat in response to her own loss gives tertiary expression to her own feelings as she works. The resulting composition, then, is a tertiary expression of grief, but its being so seemingly has nothing to do with *its* character, or to an appreciation of it as the work it is. In such cases, the connection between my grief and the detail of the particular work that gives tertiary expression to my grief is arbitrary, so, where our concern focuses on the work rather than on me as its commissioner (or on the composer who writes in response to her own situation), its being a tertiary expression of grief is beside the point.[18]

The thrust of this argument might be parried as follows: tertiary expressions need not rely on *arbitrarily founded* conventions, for they might involve the appropriation of behaviors which, in other contexts, could count as primary expressions. Rather than commissioning a mausoleum, I might employ mourners to weep and keen, or I might say "I am grieved" not tonelessly but in a voice redolent with sadness. It might be argued, that is, that not all tertiary expressions reveal expressiveness by transparently directing attention beyond themselves. A tertiary expression might illustrate the emotion it expresses. A person might act out his (or another's) tears within a recognizable set of conventions for public presentations of emotion, thereby giving nonprimary expression to his (or another's) sadness. Rather than being arbitrary, such actions appropriate and structure the affective potential of behaviors which, in other contexts, are primarily expressive. Some tertiary expressions of emotion mimic in a conventionally circumscribed manner patterns which, elsewhere, would count as primary expressions. Even if

---

[18] Robinson argues (1983b) that, just as our interest in the expressive character of behavior presupposes that pretence is not the norm, so our interest in art as a human, communicative product presupposes that artworks typically express emotions felt by their artists. I sympathize with the point that we are attracted to artworks as of an artist, an oeuvre, a genre, a period, a culture, and so on. But I think an aesthetic interest in the expressiveness of artworks might presuppose not that the emotion was experienced by the artist but, instead, that that expressiveness reflects the world of human feeling as considered by the artist. My view, as outlined at the close of Chapter 5, is not far from Robinson's.

< 180 >

the music is a tertiary expression of the feelings of someone who stands in the background, the pursuit of tertiary expression through the simulation of primary expressions within the music might be thought to guarantee the intrinsic expressiveness of the music. The emotions presented by an actor do not express her feelings (let us assume), but as a tertiary expression of the playwright's feelings (assumed again) the appropriate emotion is presented in the vehicle for expression nonetheless. And it might be claimed that composers do the same. The music that gives tertiary expression to their feelings is chosen precisely for its containing behaviors appropriate to the primary expression of the feeling to be presented in the work.[19]

This response to the objection that music is not regarded merely as a vehicle behind which we can discern the composer's (or commissioner's) emotion maintains that the music might contain within it the emotion to which it gives tertiary expression. To that extent it more accurately matches the phenomenology of the experience of expressiveness in music than does the view that concentrates on the arbitrariness of tertiary expressions of emotions in music. It faces an obvious difficulty in its turn, though: it suggests that music is already as intimately connected to emotions as are an actor's tears, and that the expressive character inherent in music is *appropriated* by the composer in giving tertiary expression to her emotions. In doing so it assumes what it sets out to analyze—the expressiveness of music. Tears stand to sadness as among its primary expressions. That is why the expression of sadness might be simulated by crying and wailing. But music does not stand to any emotion as tears stand to sadness. So, even if music sometimes seems to play the role of a professional mourner in giving tertiary expression to the composer's feeling, it is necessary to do more than merely note our tendency to hear it in such terms. It is also necessary to explain *how* music could play that role. The crude theory held that music is a primary expression of the composer's feelings. The refined version of the theory holds that music might simulate the primary expression of an emotion that is not felt in fact. How, if it could not give primary expression to an occurrent emotion, to an emotion that is experienced rather than imagined, acted, or presented merely as an outward appearance, could music successfully simulate the primary expressions of emotion? In holding that the composer appropriates the ex-

---

[19] Here is a different way of putting the same point. The conventions allowing for tertiary expressions might be arbitrary in some cases, so that meaning D or E is involved, or they might regulate naturally significant elements, such as those which, in other contexts, give primary expressions to emotions, so that meaning B or C is involved. In the latter case, the character of the music is not expressively indifferent to the artist's act of tertiary expression, because that act deploys the potential for primary expression inherent in its elements.

< 181 >

pressive potential of musical elements to give tertiary expression to feelings that match the music's expressive character, this seemingly more sophisticated version of the expression theory must be appealing to, rather than analyzing and explaining, the expressive power of music.

The expression theory modified in this way fails. It preserves a connection between the music and the composer's feelings but holds that those feelings find tertiary, not primary, expression in the music. The price of this change to the theory is prohibitive. If the conventions of the relevant type of tertiary expression are arbitrary, the listener familiar with the composer's use of those conventions hears *through* the music that a feeling is expressed, but he does not hear that expression as something presented *in* the music with the force and immediacy of a primary expression. The tie to the composer's feeling is preserved, but in a way that makes the composer's (or commissioner's) act of expression of no artistic relevance. And if the conventions for the relevant type of tertiary expression feature elements which, in other contexts, would have primary expressive significance, then, though now it might be true both that the listener hears the emotion expressed *in* the music and that the music is a tertiary expression of the composer's feelings, one cannot explain the former fact fully by appeal to the latter. It is because such-and-such musical sounds express sadness that the composer employs them in giving tertiary expression to her sadness. In that case, though, one cannot explain how those particular musical sounds are sad by reference to their being a tertiary expression of the composer's feeling. The shift to regarding the composer's act of expression as tertiary rather than primary gives a more plausible account than did the earlier version of the theory of the relation between the composer's feelings and the character of the music. But that same change seems to demonstrate that, insofar as expression is heard *in* music, the expression theory provides no analysis of the basis of musical expressiveness, which was its original goal.

Is there another way of revising the expression theory without abandoning the claim that the music is a primary expression of the composer's feelings? Well, one might avoid the difficulties of matching the expressiveness of the musical work to the actual, occurrent emotions of composers by adopting a counterfactual strategy.[20] It might be argued, for example, that a musical work is sad if it sounds as if it were the product of a primary expression of sadness, or angry if it sounds as if it were the kind of thing a person would produce while in the grip of anger.

---

[20] See Barwell 1986. For another approach to the work as if it were the product of a persona imagined by the interpreter, see Vermazen 1986. Several authors give a central place, not to the

< 182 >

Now, in one way, this view is obviously right. It is equivalent to Carroll Pratt's aphorism: sad music sounds the way that sadness feels (or perhaps we should say it sounds the way a sad person should act). Notice, however, that this latest revision of the expression theory deprives it of content. Originally (it was alleged) we could explain the expressiveness of music by observing how it could be a primary expression of an occurrent emotion. If music *really* could stand to felt emotions as tears stand to felt sadness, the theory would have succeeded in explaining how music is expressive of emotion. Under the present view, however, the emphasis falls on the character of the music rather than on any occurrent emotion to which it (allegedly) relates as a primary expression. The theory testifies to the expressive character of the music, but it fails to explain, as the crude version of the expression theory set out to do, how music might be a bearer of emotional expressiveness by serving as a primary expression. Whereas the revisions of the theory dismissed earlier retain a connection between the music and the composer's expressing her occurrent emotions (in tertiary fashion), the current revision of the theory severs music's expressiveness from acts (whether of primary or tertiary importance) indicative of the occurrence of felt emotions. In doing so it emphasizes the expressive power of music but does not explain how music achieves that vitality. It emphasizes that the expression of emotion in music has an immediacy that recalls a person's primary (rather than tertiary) expressions of feeling, but it does not explain what it is about the music that makes it appropriate (not merely whimsical) to hear the music in such terms. Like the other rejected revisions of the theory, this one gives up on (or fails in) the attempt to analyze how music is expressive. It does not account for the ways we respond to and describe music's expressiveness; nor does it indicate why an appreciation of music's expressive character is such important evidence that a listener understands and appreciates the musical work.

Let me recapitulate the main points of the argument so far: The crude version of the expression theory is right in holding that music's expressiveness is aesthetically/artistically relevant to the work's appreciation where that expressiveness is perceptible within (not merely through) the work and is right also in maintaining that we react to music's expressiveness as if it has the compelling immediacy of a primary expression. It is correct in giving credit to the composer, who is responsible for the work's expressiveness if anyone is. Its failure lies in its attempt to marry these observations, in its attempt to explain their coherence as a result of the music's giving primary

---

artist, but to a fictional narrator or spectator and his feelings; see Walton 1979, Wollheim 1986 and 1987, Currie 1990.

< 183 >

expression to the composer's feelings. The move to a counterfactual account of the connection is no more plausible. To say that the music is experienced *as if* its expressiveness were the composer's primary expression of feeling does justice to the listener's experience of the immediacy and power of the music's expressiveness, but at the price of abandoning hope of explaining that expressiveness as depending on an occurrent feeling and on actions or movements transmitting that feeling. For the counterfactual account, the feeling is nonexistent, so the expressiveness cannot be explained by reference to it.

Of course, music can be used by composers to express their feelings, although evidence suggests that this is not common. Where it is so used, usually the composition must be understood as a secondary or a tertiary expression of its composer's feelings. Music that is expressive in this way need not be expressive in itself; a concern with music as a secondary or tertiary expression of feelings is a concern leading away from, rather than toward, the expressiveness *in* the work. Some revisions of the crude version of the theory explain how musical works express their artists' feelings, but they fail, either because they cannot justify the artistic relevance of the type of expression they discuss or because they presuppose that music displays the expressiveness in question. As a secondary or tertiary expression of someone's (actual) emotion or (actual) attitude, the expressiveness of the musical work is not (in any usual or obvious way) artistically important unless the elements of expression used by the artist (to the end of creating secondary or tertiary expressions of actual emotions or actual attitudes) already have expressive significance. What is artistically relevant is the expressive character present in the music, not the fact (if it *is* one, which usually it is not) that this expressive character has been created and employed because it matches a mood to which it gives secondary or tertiary expression.

The Arousal Theory

The view I call the arousal theory of musical expressiveness holds that a musical work's expressing an emotion consists in the work's evoking that emotion in the listener. The arousalist holds that music's sadness consists in its power to make the listener feel sad.[21] Music's expressiveness consists

[21] Kivy occasionally also describes as arousalist the view that people sometimes feel sad in response to sad music. Whereas arousalism entails that sad music is prone to make people feel sad, the belief that sad music might lead the listener to feel sadness need involve no commitment to arousalism. Arousalism offers an account of music's expressiveness. By contrast, a person might be agnostic about the proper analysis of what it is for music to be expressive, or might

< 184 >

solely in its power to move people. A musical work is sad just if it moves its listeners to sadness. Where E is an emotion, M is the music, and L is the listener, we get the following as a first approximation:

$$M \text{ is } E = M \text{ evokes } E \text{ in } L.$$

How might the arousal theory explain why it is the case, if the emotion expressed by the music is felt by the listener, that we attribute the emotion to the musical work? It might do so in terms of an analogy. Colored objects absorb some wavelengths of light and reflect others. They appear colored only to creatures with senses that record the reflected light as visual experiences (and have a need to make discriminations based on such experiences). In a world in which no such creatures existed, there would be a sense in which grass would not be green. Nevertheless, in this world, we attribute the color neither to the observers of grass nor to their perceptual experience of the color but to the grass. The observers have a perceptual experience *of* the greenness, but we do not normally attribute the color to the experience. If it makes sense, "What color is your perceptual experience?" is a question about the color the experience is an experience *of*. We attribute the color to the grass because perceptual experiences (or, at least, the discriminations based on them) have an interpersonal validity. Under "standard" conditions of observations, "normal" observers make the same or similar perceptual discriminations. Healthy grass looks green to most observers. If it does not, we are agreed on how to explain why; the observers may be red-green color-blind, the grass might be illuminated only by moonlight, and so on. Because the experience of color is widely shared in this way, that experience reveals more about the grass than about its observers, and it is therefore appropriate to attribute the greenness to the grass. By contrast, if the smell of linseed oil gives me hot flushes and makes me see flashing pink stars, we are not inclined to attribute the pinkness or the hotness or the starriness to the linseed oil—whereas, if this were the standard effect of its smell on people, we might do so. So, it can be argued, though the experience of the emotions expressed belongs to the listener, the expressiveness is correctly attributed to the music as a dispositional property because responses to music have an interpersonal validity as do experiential responses to the colors of objects.[22]

---

subscribe to some thesis other than the arousal theory, while believing that listeners sometimes respond to sad music by feeling sad.

[22] This is the view of Speck (1988). He thinks that those who would object to the arousalists' predicating the emotion of the music might also be committed to challenging the projection of dispositional properties, such as warmness, onto things in general.

< 185 >

It might be thought that the experience of music is culture-bound as the perception of color is not. It might be argued, that is, that the analogy with color perception is not sufficiently strong to explain why the expressiveness is attributed to the music. Several (complementary) lines of reply to this point can be adopted. (i) One might accept that the recognition of expressive properties in music lacks the universality of color judgments but argue that the analogy remains sustainable. Even if judgments about musical expressiveness are not intercultural, within a given musical culture a high degree of interpersonality is found in judgments of music's expressive properties. The expressiveness is to be predicated of the music, not the listener, though the judgment expressed thereby is to be relativized to the culture in which it is made. (ii) Or one might argue that, at heart, musical expressiveness has a natural, cross-cultural foundation, even if the musical conventions of various cultures build on that foundation in different ways, so that more is involved in the appreciation of musical expression than a crude, uneducated reaction to a musical stimulus. In Chapter 1 I suggested that musical intervals might be naturally ordered with respect to their tensions, whereas their expressive function within a work could depend on conventions affecting the number and frequency of intervals in use. In this view, there is cross-cultural agreement among suitably qualified listeners (those familiar with the relevant styles and their conventions); the appearance of wide, cross-cultural disagreement arises only because members of the one culture usually lack experience with the musical conventions governing the music of the other. (iii) Alternatively, one might accept that the expressiveness of music is culture-determined but argue that judgments of color are no less culture-determined. If the greenness is to be attributed to the grass, notwithstanding the relativity to culture such a judgment presupposes, then the expressiveness can be attributed to the music; that is, the analogy holds strongly. In pursuing this line one might point out that not all cultures divide the visible spectrum into seven colors. The Welsh language, I have been told, includes only four color terms, and the Eskimos not only have many words for snow but also make distinctions between shades and hues of white which other cultures do not. If these facts are consistent with the dispositional analysis of color attributions, then the analogy is not affected by cultural-based differences between the musics of various peoples.

This discussion of the analogy between color attributions to objects and expressive attributions to musical works points to an aspect of the arousal theory I have yet to outline. Just as there is a principle or process explaining the commonality of the response to various objects' colors—a story about the absorption and reflection of light and of the effects of light on the optic

< 186 >

nerve—so too there should be underlying principles and processes through which music gains the power to affect the listener's emotional state. If the listener is caused by the music to experience emotions that are then attributed to it, the music must possess properties that do this causing, and these properties must be describable and enumerable without reference to the listener's response. To take a deliberately crude example, it must be the case that the listener is caused to feel sad, say, by the music's minor key, slow tempo, discordant appoggiaturas, or whatever.[23] There must be musical properties, describable in musical terms, conferring on the work its power to affect the listener. In principle there must be rules or laws governing what kinds of properties produce what kinds of affective responses, though in practice we might not be able to abstract such rules. Our difficulty arises not because the laws do not exist but rather because they are so context-dependent and because their contexts are so complex, rich, and heterogeneous that there is no simple way of encapsulating in a manageable, comprehensible formula the process of their working. Accordingly, the previous definition should be amended to read:

M is E = M evokes E in L in virtue of its possessing properties *a, b, c* (properties that might be specified in musically technical terms without reference to E).

This amendment improves on the earlier definition in several ways. First, it stresses that the relevant response must arise from an experience of certain types of features in the musical work. In this way it can deal with cases in which the music becomes merely the occasion for a response—for example, that in which a father is saddened by a work because it was his dead son's favorite, though normally the piece would be described as happy. This person's response depends not on the musical detail of the work but on its association with the mourned-for son. Second, the definition now allows that the experience is cognitively founded and culturally shaped in that the experience of *a, b,* and *c* should involve thoughts about the particular musical work, knowledge of wider musical considerations, such as style, and a sensitivity to the history of musical practice. If *a* is a return to the tonic key from that of the mediant minor, *b* is a recapitulation, and so on, then the response is to the music's expressiveness only if the musical factors are brought, whether transparently or opaquely, under appropriate descriptions.

---

[23] The work of Leonard Meyer and Deryck Cooke might be seen as revealing some of the musical features on which music's expressiveness supervenes.

< 187 >

As I have sketched it, the connection between the relevant features of the music and the listener's emotional response is a direct, unmediated one. This is the preferred view among arousalists, I think. But some, such as John Nolt (1981) and Harold Fiske (1990, 128–129), hold what might be termed an "associationist" version of arousalism. On this conception, the music triggers memories and associations which, in their turn, bring to mind or cause feelings that are projected onto the music. The aforementioned mourning father arrives at his response by a process of association, but, since in this case the musical work does not express sadness, it would be inappropriate for him to project his response onto the work. On the grounds that his associations are too personal, the father's case is to be distinguished from that in which the association leads to an emotion, or to the thought of an emotion, that can be attributed to the musical work. The associations that are to count presumably are very widely shared across the culture. In this way the associationist might hope to avoid the objection raised by Pratt against what he calls the "empathy theory": "Rakes and Strumpets would hear wanton wiles in the music of the B-minor Mass, and prudes might fail to detect a trace of romance in the sounds of the Liebestod" (1952, 14).

But even if the associationist's interpolation of several psychological steps between the musical features and the listener's response does not necessarily lead to subjectivism, that stretching of the chain tying the music to the response generates other difficulties. Stanley Speck (1988) is an arousalist who rejects the associationist's theory. He notes that musical expression has a vividness, immediacy, and potency that counts against the view that there is mere association between musical movement and the arousal of affect. Associationism is also criticized by others who would reject arousalist theories in general. Victor Zuckerkandl says: "There is no musical experience without emotion, that is to say, there is no way of grasping a musical context, the motion of tones, otherwise than by partaking in it, by inwardly moving with it—and such inward motion we experience as emotion. But the inward motion of the man is one thing, the motion of the tones is quite another; and the latter is the cause of the former, not the other way around" (1959, 245).[24]

I mentioned that the improved definition allows weight to the cognitive and cultural nature of the understanding that causes the listener's affective response. Most arousalists hold that the response revealing of the affective power of music is evoked only if the listener attends to the course of the

---

[24] Cooke (1959) is another who rejects associationist or projectionist accounts of music's expressiveness; for more recent and sophisticated critiques, see Kivy 1980, Osborne 1983, and Allen 1990.

< 188 >

music. This condition is important, for resort to it can explain many cases in which music expressive of some emotion fails to arouse that emotion in the listener. If the listener is distracted from the music or fails for another reason to focus on the music, the listener's lack of a response, or inappropriate response, does not count against the arousalist's theory. Even where the listener's concentration on the music is unbroken, factors present in the situation might inhibit or overpower the response the music is inclined to evoke. For example, feeling low, I might attempt to cheer myself by playing happy music, such as the third movement of J. S. Bach's *Brandenburg* Concerto No. 2. The attempt might fail, though I concentrate on the music, for, so entrenched is my sadness that it cannot be budged. Just as another person might fail to cheer me out of my low mood with his clowning antics and happy face, so might I fail to drive the blues away when I expose myself to cheering music. Because music's power to evoke a response might always be defeated, and because the expressiveness of music is a matter of its possessing that power whether or not that power triumphs over all competing factors, it is appropriate to modify the proposed definition yet further. According to the arousalist:

M is E = M tends to evoke E in L, given that L attends to the music in the absence of factors that inhibit or interfere with L's emotional response to M.

This leads to a modal definition:[25]

M is E = M would evoke E in an L attending to the music in the appropriate manner unless the tendency for M to evoke E in L were thwarted or perverted by [a list of inhibiting or interfering factors].

A fully developed version of the theory would spell out, so far as is possible, the types of factors that might alter, mitigate, or prevent the propensity of the music to arouse the emotion it expresses. Some of these factors would apply generally; for instance, a quite different kind of music blaring from the neighbor's speakers would block most people's response. Other of the factors would apply to specific cases; for example, that the music being played not only was the favorite work of one's dead son but also that the son was killed by the obsession that led him to play it non-stop on the comb-and-tissue.

Objectors to the arousal theory seek to find counterexamples in which

[25] Nolt (1981) is one who stresses the advantages of a modal formulation of the theory.

< 189 >

there is a mismatch between what the work expresses and what the listener feels. Defenders of the theory attempt to explain away such counterexamples, either by arguing that the response is to something other than the music or by identifying interfering or inhibiting factors that have perverted the listener's tendency to respond in a way revealing the music's expressiveness. We have already seen instances of these lines of thought. The father saddened by the happy music his dead son liked is responding neither to the music nor to thoughts about the music but to thoughts of his loss occasioned by the music. And, even where the music is the object of attention, the listener's prevailing mood might overpower the countervailing emotion the music tends to promote.

Sometimes we react to musical works without its being the case that the character of the response can be attributed to the musical work in question. For example, I might be amazed by a musical work that does not express amazement; the intricacy of the contrapuntal writing might be intriguing. And sometimes the listener's response is an affective one, though the work is not expressive, or expresses a feeling different from that experienced by the listener. For instance, in a work that aims to be happy I might be saddened by the poverty of the musical ideas and the crudity of their treatment. In both these types of case the response depends on attention to the work, it is a response to musical features, and no interfering or inhibiting factors seem to be in play.

The arousalist might agree that such cases would count against her theory if they stand. She replies by arguing that, despite appearances to the contrary, the response is not a response evoked by the musical work as such. Either the listener's attention lies elsewhere or some external factor blocks the music's tendency to arouse the appropriate response; for both the proposed counterexamples, it might be suggested that I respond to the composer's skill, or the absence of skill, rather than to the music as such. Nolt (1981) adopts this strategy in arguing for the arousal theory (as applying to the arts in general). He discusses a case in which a pile of newspapers causes annoyance in being presented in a gallery as an artwork. He suggests that the response could not be a response to the pile of newspapers, since the responder would pass by an exactly similar pile of newspapers in the street without feeling annoyance. If the response of annoyance is a response to something other than the pile of newspapers, then it cannot be used as a counterexample to the arousalist's analysis of the expressive character of an artwork that is a pile of newspapers. Robert Stecker (1983) correctly counters this argument by pointing out that the pile of newspapers in the street would not annoy only because it would not be brought under the relevant description: pile of newspapers

< 190 >

presented qua artwork. The responder would be just as annoyed by the newspapers in the street if he believed that pile was being presented as an artwork. That the person would not respond with annoyance to the newspapers in the street does not show, therefore, that the response in the gallery is a response to something other than the pile of newspapers (brought under the relevant description). So, the objection stands.

Nolt's way of dealing with cases of this type strikes me as quite implausible, for the counterexamples in question are ones in which the listener attends in the appropriate fashion to the music; they also are ones in which no interfering factors seem to come into play. Nolt maintains that the response is not a response to the music as such; if it were so, we would attribute the aroused emotion to the music. But if the circumstances of listening assumed in the examples are not optimal, then what circumstances could be? If all responses are attributable to the music just so long as they are aroused by it, then either the music expresses the annoyance it generates or the annoyance is not evoked by the music. Nolt opts for the second alternative, but under the conditions described this choice seems as unattractive as the first.

A much better way of dealing with the counterexamples is to accept the examples but deny that they reflect adversely on the arousal theory. Though the arousalist holds that music is always expressive in virtue of its tending to evoke an emotional response, this position does not entail that all emotional responses to music are responses justifying attributions of expressiveness to the music. The music might tend to evoke responses, including affective responses, having no bearing on its expressive character. The arousalist holds that it is a necessary condition of a musical work's expressing an emotion or mood X that the music tends to arouse X in a listener who attends to the work; she need not hold that it is a sufficient condition for the music's expressing X that it tends to evoke X in an attentive listener.

Now though, if the music tends to arouse X, Y, and Z while it expresses only X, what is it that distinguishes the arousal of X from the evocation of Y and Z as regards the correct identification of the work's expressiveness? I consider two answers to this question, rejecting the first for the second.

The counterexamples described above are ones in which the listener responds to an aspect of the music (the intricacy of the contrapuntal writing, or, in the other example, to the poverty of the ideas), but not to its expressiveness as such. Perhaps we should distinguish among aroused responses those that are evoked by the work's expressiveness from those evoked by some other aspect of the music. This appears to be the line recommended by Peter Mew when he writes, "An emotion can properly be ascribed to a piece of music by a given listener if and only if, when that listener is fully attending

< 191 >

to the music, the music causes him to feel that emotion *by or in directly expressing it*" (1985a, 33, emphasis added). Now, this strategy faces two obvious difficulties. The first is this: it is not difficult to change the example, so that it is the expressiveness to which one responds by feeling something else; I might be repulsed by the banality of the music's expression of sadness or bored by the predictability of the theme's expressive character. The second difficulty with this strategy is that it appears to lead to circularity: one cannot analyze musical expressiveness as music's power to evoke a response of a particular *type* if one can identify that type only as the response that is a response to the expressiveness of the music.

Justine Kingsbury (1991) generously suggests that it may be an infelicity of phrasing that intimates that Mew holds this second, circular view. His point, she thinks, is this: An emotion can properly be ascribed to a piece of music by a given listener if and only if, when the listener is fully attending to the music, the music causes him to feel that emotion objectlessly. If the music is the intentional object of the response, then the response is a response to the music, but the character of the response is not attributable to the music. If, on the other hand, the music is not the intentional object of the response, but the response is a response to the music (that is, the response does not have something else as its intentional object), then the response is attributable to the music. If I am sad *about* the music (for example, about the poverty of its ideas), then my response does not reveal the music's expressive character. But if the music makes me feel sad (though I don't feel sad about the music or about anything else)—that is, if the music is the cause and the perceptual object of my response, but not its emotional object—then the sadness I feel is attributable to the musical work.

Kingsbury points out that, if the *Eroica* makes me feel sad about the transitoriness of human happiness, then, by this account, sadness is not ascribable to the music. Because she believes that Mew wishes to allow cases of this type as revealing the music's expressive character, she considers how the type might be accommodated. She suggests that, whereas the emotion evoked by attention to the music initially is objectless, that emotion can be predicated of the music, even if the listener subsequently brings an appropriate intentional object (such as the transitoriness of human happiness) to mind. In other words, though the emotion's intentional object is suggested by the expressive character of the initial response (rather than emerging from the unconscious, or being there at the outset), the expressive character of the initial response is attributable to the music. So, in the end, what distinguishes various affective responses to the music is not whether those responses take

< 192 >

intentional objects but whether the affective response *initially* lacks an intentional object.

According to this latest revision, the arousal theory holds that music expresses those emotions that it tends to arouse as "objectless" responses; these responses are caused by the music and take the music as their perceptual object, but neither the music nor anything else is the intentional object of the response (a response that does take the music, or some part of it, as its intentional object is not a response indicating the music's expressive character). Now, if the response central to the arousal theory is not a possible response, the theory can be rejected out of hand. If sad music *never* makes people feel (objectlessly) sad, the arousal theory is bound to fail. Some commentators have offered arguments designed to show that this is the case.

No musical work can really make people feel (objectless) sadness, it is argued, for these reasons: (i) If one did, that would give the listener a reason for avoiding that work in the future, whereas we do not avoid listening to sad music. Sadness, and hence anything giving rise to it, is to be dodged where possible. We need not listen to musical works. That we do so is a sure indication that it is not sadness sad music leads us to feel. (ii) Emotions like sadness necessarily take intentional objects. As the arousalist describes the response, either it is objectless or it takes something other than the music as its object. In the latter case, the response is not a response *to* the music. In the former case, the response cannot be one of sadness. (iii) Emotions often have characteristic behavioral expressions; the listener's response to music lacks the behavioral expressions appropriate to sadness. Normally when we feel sad our response is identified as sadness in part because of what it is a response to and in part because of the way it is expressed in behavior. If the arousal theory were right, the listener's response would be identifiable in the absence of both these factors, but such an identification is not possible under those circumstances.

The most vigorous defense of these arguments is by Peter Kivy (1980, 1987, and 1989). Others outline one or more of these points before attempting a reply.[26] But not everyone dissatisfied with these arguments is an arousalist; not everyone who believes that sad music sometimes makes listeners feel sad also believes that the nature of musical expressiveness is to be analyzed in terms of this tendency—instead of holding that music is sad because it causes sadness, one might think that it is because the music ex-

---

[26] For example, see Hepburn 1960/61, Hospers 1964, Davies 1980, 1990, and 1991c, Levinson 1982, Callen 1982a and 1983, Mew 1985a, Speck 1988; and Radford 1989, 1991a, and 1991b.

< 193 >

presses sadness that it affects the listener. Because these arguments bear not only on the arousal theory but also on other accounts of the response to music's expressiveness, I consider them in detail in Chapter 6. In brief, I do not find the claims to be decisive, so I do not accept them as refuting the arousal theory. Though I do not believe that the arousal theory provides a successful analysis of musical expressiveness, I do agree with the arousalist that, sometimes, sad music makes people feel sad and happy music tends to make people feel happy.

How might one challenge the arousal theory while accepting that sad music sometimes moves listeners to sadness? As I pointed out before, one does so by finding cases in which we wish to say that the music expresses sadness though it does not, for example, move the listener to sadness despite the listener's careful attention to the music in the absence of conditions that might inhibit or block her response. It could be that the listener feels nothing, or that she responds to the music without mirroring the emotion the music expresses. In the latter case, the listener has a response taking the music, or some part of it, as its emotional object, whereas the objectless response predicted by the arousal theory is absent.

Nolt (1981) identifies and attempts to counter a case of the latter type, one in which we find a sickly sweet violin piece to be cloying or a play to be overly sentimental. Such works (or performances) are not sad but ludicrous, he says, so it is no objection to the arousalist's theory to note that they do not evoke sad responses. The obvious difficulty with Nolt's reply is that the work's being ludicrous is consistent with its also being sad. The two properties are not exclusive of each other. So Nolt cannot explain the failure of a mirroring response merely by arguing that the work is ludicrous. In this case, it is because the expression of sadness is somehow inept that we find the work ludicrous.

I mentioned the more appropriate line for an arousalist to take previously: she must argue that, despite the listener's attention to the work, the listener's objectless response is blocked or inhibited. Kingsbury (1991) indicates how an arousalist might employ such an argument: It could be that the piece sounds ludicrous because the expressive conventions to which it conforms are those of another age; changes in style, fashion, and taste distance us from the work, so that it is very unlikely that its sadness will move us to feelings of sadness. Such a work once would have tended to evoke sadness, even if now it never does. Because it takes its identity in part from both its temporal location and the conventions of the genre in which it is to be located, the sadness belongs still (and always) to the work, even if the work is now a source of mirth.

< 194 >

This line of reply might work if it suits the facts, but it is highly doubtful that considerations of this sort always apply. Simply, there are many cases in which the listener attends to the work, is fully acquainted with the conventions of the work's style, identifies the style and genre correctly, approaches the work when he is not jaded, or preoccupied, or tired, or distracted, but nevertheless in which the listener fails to feel the same emotion as that all experts, including himself, hear expressed in the work in question.

It has been pointed out that something might possess a dispositional property though that property is never activated (see Callen 1982a). A glass might be fragile without ever breaking. Indeed, a fragile glass might be almost impossible to break—where it has been set in a solid block of plastic, for instance. These facts can provide no consolation for the arousalist, however. A musical work could have a tendency to arouse objectless sadness in the listener but never do so because the work is never performed, for instance. But where the conditions are such that the disposition should be realized if it holds, then if it is not manifested the piece does not possess the dispositional property. If the glass never breaks when dropped onto a hard surface, it is not fragile. And the relevant conditions are met for the musical case by the listener who attends to the work, is familiar with its style, starts from an affectively neutral condition, and so on. According to Kivy (1983), when the appropriate conditions are met music never evokes the response described by the arousalists. By contrast, I believe that sometimes it does so. The point, though, is that the arousalist talks of the *tendency* to produce a response to allow for the case in which the response fails under suboptimal conditions. Where the conditions are ideal, the response described by the arousalist should occur. Kivy thinks it never occurs then, whereas I think it sometimes does not occur then. Neither view can be congenial to the arousal theory.

Cases of a mismatch between the listener's response (if any) and the quality of expressiveness the music is agreed to exhibit are too common to be ignored (Allen 1990) and prove fatal, I think, for the arousal theory. Sometimes the mismatch can be explained away; sometimes the conditions prevent the music from "doing its thing." One cannot simply assume, however, that there *must* be some unidentified blocking or inhibiting factor wherever the response is absent or has the "wrong" form; one cannot do so without rendering the arousal theory unfalsifiable in a way that calls into question its credentials as an attempt to describe the way the world truly is. There is no reason, I think, to suppose that inhibiting or blocking factors can be invoked to explain the frequency with which a mismatch between the work's expressiveness and the listener's response arises.

< 195 >

Before closing this discussion, I review a recent attempt to recast the arousal theory to avoid the problem of mismatched responses. Derek Matravers (1991) presents a view that distinguishes the arousal theory from emotivism and favors the former.[27] Whereas the emotivist takes the work to evoke the emotions attributed to it, an arousalist, Matravers says, might hold that the work expresses the emotions that are attributed to it just in case it arouses different feelings of a kind appropriate to a response to the expression of the relevant emotion. So, for example, music is sad not because it leads listeners to feel sad (emotivism) but because it leads listeners to feel pity (arousalism, in his view), pity being a standard response to sadness.[28] A picture expresses sadness if its content, and the manner in which that content is presented, calls from the engaged viewer a response of pity. Matravers extends his theory to the nonrepresentational arts. Emotions have cognitive, physiological, and phenomenal components. Where the work presents no content, then the audience's response lacks the cognitive component—the audience is not sad *about* the work or its (nonexistent) content. Nevertheless, a musical work might arouse the physiological and phenomenal aspects of pity—a feeling of pity that is not an instance of pity about the work—and in doing so, it is properly to be described as expressing sadness. Matravers explains why music expresses sadness, but not shame or embarrassment and the like, by noting that, in the absence of the cognitive element, there is no characteristic response to another's shame or embarrassment.

Matravers allows that an expressive work need not arouse a response; this would occur, for example, when the listener distances herself from engagement with the work to understand or observe how it achieves its expressive effects. He compares criticism in the arts with wine tasting: rather than drinking freely, the critic sips the experience before turning to the bucket.

This view, if it works, avoids some of the objections raised earlier. In particular, it dodges those objections that deny the listener feels the same emotion as that expressed in the music. But it does not avoid all the problems that face its cousin. If there are works that are properly described as sad but do not typically arouse a response (whether echoing or reactive), the theory is in trouble. Matravers deals with non-responses by allowing for the possibility of an intellectually detached interest in the artwork. This seems to establish an unacceptably schizophrenic division between the approach

---

[27] The demarcation is invented by Matravers; so far as I can see, there is no warrant for it in the literature or elsewhere.

[28] Anticipations of this view can be found. For example, Coker (1972) holds that music expresses anger just in case the music makes the listener want to flee.

< 196 >

aimed at understanding the work and that engaged with the work at an affective level. Matravers implies that the critic is to be compared to a doctor who recognizes the sadness of a situation but who maintains a detached attitude to be able to carry out her job, but we might deny the aptness of the analogy. In effect, Matravers regards thoughtful attention to the work as an inhibitory factor rather than as a condition for the appropriateness of the response, and that view is unconvincing.

If it works, Matravers's theory faces such difficulties—but does it work? I doubt it. (i) I doubt that there is a regular association between sadness and pity that would allow one to move naturally from the presence of the one to the idea of the other. Your sadness might be the object of my pity on some occasions, but it might equally be the object of my anger on others (for example, where I see your feeling as unwarranted self-indulgence), or of my disappointment (for instance, where I see your feeling as a giving way to the neurosis I hoped your psychoanalyst had cured), or of my cruel triumph (for example, because I aimed to make you suffer), or of my indifference. Also, my pity might take your sadness as its object sometimes, but it might equally take your happiness as its object (for instance, where I believe that your happiness is a sign of your living in a fool's paradise that is soon to be shattered), or it might equally take your low intellect, ugliness, poverty, and so on as its object, even where you seem content with your lot. Pity can take many objects other than another's sadness, and another's sadness can be the object of many feelings other than pity. So, even if music does lead listeners to feel pity, it is not obviously natural to attribute sadness to it. (ii) Anyway, I doubt that pity can lack an emotional object. Matravers conceives of listeners feeling pity without their pitying the music or anything else. This is possible, he thinks, because pity has a distinctive physiology or phenomenology that can be recognized as that of pity even where the cognitive content and intentionality of the experience are absent. But I do not believe the idea of objectless pity to be more coherent than that of objectless envy, shame, or embarrassment.[29] (iii) Besides, I doubt that listeners do feel pity in response to pure music, so I doubt that they attribute sadness to the music on the strength of their feeling pity. One might pity a character in an opera—Rosina in *The Marriage of Figaro*, say. One might pity a performer for having fluffed some notes, or for having to play for so long, or whatever. One might pity the composer, perhaps, if one thinks that she must have been a tortured soul to have written such music. But, simply, listeners who respond to Tchaikovsky's Symphony No. 6, for example, do not identify their feelings as ones

---

[29] Issues raised here are pursued in greater detail in the following two chapters.

< 197 >

of (objectless) pity. I surmise, then, that Matravers's innovation faces more difficulties than it solves.[30]

Where emotions or attitudes expressed in music cannot be attributed to some person depicted in the work (such as to a character in an opera), the expression theory attributes them to the composer who, after all, is responsible if anyone is for the appearance of expressiveness in her works. A crude version of the expression theory rightly acknowledges that we respond to the expressiveness of art as if it were a presentation of primary expressions of emotion, and it correctly notes both that it is just such expressions that are artistically/aesthetically important features of musical works and that music's possessing such features stands in need of explanation. This version of the expression theory founders, however, because it mistakenly sees art as a primary expression of artists' feelings. It assumes wrongly that all *appearances* of primary expressions of emotion must *be* primary expressions of occurrent emotion if they are not to be deprived totally of expressive character. This involves a misconstrual of the relation between artistic expression and the expression of actual emotions in behavior. Alternatively, in revised form, the expression theory wrongly supposes that there is artistic/aesthetic relevance in artists' giving secondary or tertiary expressions to their feelings in their creative acts. The expression theory is not wrong in holding that composers feel emotions that (sometimes, at least) they intend to express in their music, and it is not wrong in holding that such intentions may be realized successfully, but it is mistaken in maintaining that the expressiveness of pure music can be explained and analyzed as composers' expressing their feelings.

The arousal theory, in contrast, describes the emotions expressed in music as those experienced by, or likely to be experienced by, listeners who attend closely to the work. This theory is right to attach importance to the power of music to move the listener, and right also to consider the listener's affective reaction as often revealing the character of the music provoking the response. A person who never responded emotionally to music, although inclined to attribute expressiveness to music, would strike us as a very cold and odd fish indeed, and we might wonder whether this person really could appreciate and understand what she hears, even if she could provide technical descriptions of what happens in the work. But the emotions expressed in musical works and the feelings experienced by listeners to those works seem not to be connected with a regularity suggesting that the former can be ex-

---

[30] For further criticisms, see Ridley 1993.

< 198 >

plained in terms of the occurrence of the latter. Sometimes we are inclined to attribute an expressive character to a work where, despite the absence of interfering or inhibiting factors, we are not liable to respond by feeling the corresponding emotion. The arousal theory is not wrong, I think, in holding that listeners are often led to feel emotions that mirror those expressed in musical works, but it is in error in assuming that musical expressiveness can be explained and analyzed as music's power to evoke such responses.

The arousal theory has undergone something of a revival in recent years.[31] Nevertheless, it is not an inherently attractive theory. In general we believe that we respond to expressive music because it is expressive—that we can justify our affective responses by reference to the character of music. According to the arousal theory, music's expressiveness just is its power to produce an affective response. In equating the two, the theory denies to us the possibility of *justifying* the response by reference to the expressive character of the work. At best, we could justify the response by describing the music in technical terms—that is, by pointing to the purely musical elements that are (said to be) evocative of emotional responses—not by reference to the expressive character of the music. The arousal theory reverses the order of things, as it were. Instead of allowing that sad music makes us feel sad because it expresses sadness, the theory maintains that sad music expresses sadness because it makes us feel sad (if it does).

Both the expression theory and the arousal theory seem to assume that all expressions of emotion (if they are not merely descriptions or symbols referring to feelings) must be expressions of occurrent emotions. Accordingly, these theories set out to locate an "owner" of the feelings expressed in pure music. The expression theory turns to the composer, whereas the arousal theory turns to the listener. The arguments I have offered here suggest, however, that we locate expressiveness in the music itself; the possibility of expressiveness in music seems to inhere ultimately in qualities of sound, and to that extent it is independent of composers' and listeners' feelings. It is because music can express sadness that composers sometimes write such music in expressing their sadness; it is because music can express sadness that it sometimes leads us to feel sadness as listeners. The music itself is the owner of the emotion it expresses. But, in that case, the emotions it expresses are unfelt. How could that be?

---

[31] Contemporary versions of the theory are sophisticated and qualified. Kivy (1983) identifies Callen (1982a) as an arousalist, and Ridley (1986) attributes the view to Mew (1985a and 1985b); Nolt (1981) and Speck (1988) are explicit in their commitment to the position.

< 199 >

F I V E
· · · ·

*The Expression of
Emotion in Music*

The conclusions for which I have argued in previous chapters are negative ones. I have suggested that music is not usefully to be compared to a natural language with respect to its meaning. Neither does music comprise a special, nondiscursive symbol system aiming at denotation. Music does not have depictive content as representational paintings do. The emotions heard in music cannot be explained as those felt and vented by composers, even if sometimes composers do express their occurrent emotions in the act of composition. Neither does the expressiveness of music consist in its power to move the listener, even if listeners are sometimes moved by music. These theories locate the significance of music as falling beyond the boundaries of the musical work—as something referred to, or denoted, or symbolized, or depicted, or vented, or aroused.

In this chapter I consider a different view: the theory that locates the significance of music as internal to the work, as residing in intrinsic properties. I argue, in particular, that the emotions expressed in music are properties of the work. On the face of it, the project I have set myself lacks plausibility. Emotions are felt and necessarily involve thoughts (for example, about the character of their emotional objects, to use Kenny's 1969 terms), but music is nonsentient, it feels and thinks nothing. Emotions are often expressed in behavior, but music is not an agent and, hence, is incapable of action. Even if music has a dynamic character resembling that of human action, at best

< 201 >

music can present movement, not behavior. Music just does not seem the sort of thing that could possess emotional properties.

Considerations such as these have led to two responses. (i) Accepting as incontrovertible the evidence of our experience of music's expressiveness, it might be suggested that the emotions expressed in music are of a distinctive type, in that they are not felt, lack emotional objects, and are not expressed through action. In this view, the emotions expressed in music are sui generis. To the extent that such emotions are atypical and defeat analysis in ordinary terms, they are mysterious. If one believes that there is more of importance between heaven and earth than can be described by science or analyzed by philosophy, that mystery can be seen as something to be celebrated, not lamented. (ii) Accepting as incontrovertible the argument suggesting that music is incapable of containing emotion, it might be suggested—and has been by Eduard Hanslick—that emotions are not expressed in music. To the extent that music is beautiful and significant, its beauty and significance is purely formal, since music cannot directly embody the world of human experience. Moreover, if music invites understanding and appreciation, a concern with emotions has no part to play in (indeed, is a hindrance to) the enjoyment of music.

I begin this chapter by arguing that each of these viewpoints is unsatisfactory. Their inadequacies should make clearer the form a theory must take if it is to be successful in explaining how music might possess expressive properties.

The Emotions Expressed in Music Are Sui Generis

Several writers hold that the emotions found in music are of a distinctive kind.[1] The claim is introduced not only to answer the charge that emotions in music lack features (intentionality, experienced feeling tone, expression in action) characteristic of ordinary emotions but also, perhaps, to indicate why the words naming emotions seem inadequate, sometimes, when applied to music. The following is typical: "Musical feelings have their own character: they are not the feelings we know and roughly name in our experience outside of music, and they do not lead in themselves to ideas or concepts of other feelings. Thus music may be an emotional experience, and still not represent emotional contexts belonging to other areas of life, for the emotions it formulates are not identical with those accompanying extra-musical

[1] For example, Lippman 1953, Laszlo 1967, and Stevenson 1958a. Osborne 1982 comes close to this view.

< 202 >

experience, nor does the one kind necessarily remind us of the other" (Lippman 1953, 569).

The problem with this approach is that it quickly becomes impaled on one or other of the horns of a dilemma.[2] In denying any connection between musical and "real" emotions the theory seems to explain away, rather than to explain, musical expressiveness. If there is no connection between musical sadness, say, and the sadness people experience, then "sad" is a homonym and there is no more connection between the two kinds of sadness than there is between river banks and savings banks. The musical quality in question might as easily have been called "blerkness" as "sadness." But why would we find blerkness in music so moving, or a source of interest and value? To sever the connection between emotions in art and emotions in life is to make mysterious the power of artistic expressiveness to involve and affect us as it does. Now, if one dodges this first horn of the dilemma by allowing that, despite their differences, there is a connection between emotions expressed in music and "real" emotions, one comes to face the second horn. Since the connection is not philosophically obvious or self-explanatory, an analysis of its character is in order. One must question why, in view of the differences, we are inclined to recognize a humanly expressive aspect in musical themes and the like. The claim that musical emotions are sui generis is offered, however, as a way of denying the need for, and of predicting the failure of, any such analysis.

Hanslick: Emotions Are Not Expressed in Music

The best critical account of Hanslick's views of which I am aware is Malcolm Budd's (1980 and 1985a).[3] I rely on his arguments in the following.

Hanslick argues for both a positive and a negative conclusion. The former is that music aims at the creation of beautiful forms of sound, the beauty being in the formal content and not in external connections. Negatively, Hanslick tries to establish the conclusion that instrumental music cannot express definite emotions. What is the relation between these theses? Does the positive view, when coupled with the negative thesis, exclude altogether the possibility of expressiveness in pure music? Clearly Budd believes so, as

---

[2] As noted in Hospers 1954/55, especially 326–327, Scruton 1974, especially 38–43, and 1983, Davies 1980 and 1986, Shiner 1982, and Matravers 1991.

[3] For other useful commentaries, see Harrell 1964, Payzant 1986, Kivy 1988b and 1990b, and Higgins 1991. For discussion of differences between Geoffrey Payzant's and Gustav Cohen's translations, see Payzant 1981 and 1986, Epperson 1987, Levinson 1987a, and Kivy 1988b. For useful background to Hanslick's famous work, see Payzant 1989.

< 203 >

do Joan Hoaglund (1980) and Peter Kivy (1990b), but the point has been debated. Geoffrey Payzant (1986, Translator's Preface) takes Hanslick to deny that expressiveness is music's defining purpose rather than to deny that emotions can be expressed in music. Both Robert Hall (1967) and Joan Stambaugh (1989) think that Hanslick regards music as expressive. Hall (1967), Kivy (1990b), and Wayne Bowman (1991) point to the prevalence of descriptions of music as expressive in Hanslick's writings as a music critic. Hall, like Payzant, interprets this as evidence that Hanslick takes instrumental music to be capable of emotional expression; Hanslick is concerned only to deny that aesthetically relevant expression depends on associations or information external to the work and its materials. By contrast, Kivy denies that Hanslick understands or develops the view according to which expressiveness might be a property directly attributable to musical materials; that is, in arguing against the expression theory, arousalism, and the idea of musical representation, Hanslick (mistakenly, in Kivy's view) takes himself to have covered all the possibilities and hence to have proved that emotions are not expressed in music. I am inclined to concur with Kivy.[4]

Hanslick supports his negative conclusion with three theses: (i) Instrumental music cannot represent definite emotions; (ii) descriptions of pure music employing terms for emotions can always be eliminated in favor of other descriptions using other (figurative) terms; and (iii) the aim of instrumental music is not the evocation of an emotional response. I discussed (ii) in Chapter 3 when considering the view that descriptions of music as expressive are metaphoric. There I agreed with Budd that Hanslick does not, and could not, substantiate (ii); Hanslick fails to show that "the music is sad" can be replaced without loss of sense by descriptions not mentioning emotions. The issues raised by (iii) were foreshadowed in Chapter 4 and are taken up again in Chapter 6. Here I concentrate on (i), the main line of Hanslick's negative argument, but before doing so I consider a set of subsidiary views presented in the elaboration of Hanslick's positive thesis.

The Subsidiary Argument: Hanslick on Texts

As I have indicated, Hanslick's concern lies primarily with pure, instrumental music. Seemingly he believes that, if opera, song, and the like are "representational" or expressive, they are so in virtue of the contribution

---

[4] It may be that there is an inconsistency between Hanslick's philosophical position and his critical practice, or it may be that Hanslick justifies his style of criticism merely as a useful substitute for purely musical descriptions; see Bowman 1991.

< 204 >

made to the whole by the words, or the dramatic action, or whatever (such a thesis recalls the discussion of hybrid artforms in Chapter 2). A widely held stance is that music needs word to have specific meaning or expressive character.[5] Hanslick's position differs from this common view mainly in insisting that, in the absence of words or dramatic context, music is not capable of expressiveness (because it is not then capable of expressive definiteness, and expressive definiteness is a necessary condition for expressiveness simpliciter). If emotions are incapable of expression in symphonies, sonatas, and the like, then, Hanslick suggests, the contribution of music within artistic hybrids, such as opera, could not be an expressive one.

Hanslick believes that music can possess beauty and is to be appreciated when it does. Because he does not believe music to be expressive of emotions, he does not see musical beauty as depending on such expressiveness. And because he sees expressiveness (in hybrids to which music contributes) as depending on nonmusical features, he tries to establish the independence of musical beauty from textual significance in such artforms as song. Sometimes he adopts a counterfactual approach, trying to show that, if music were capable of expression, musical beauty would not depend on its expressiveness. At other times he considers the place of music in hybrids (especially those in which music is very important, such as song), aiming to show that the musical beauty of the work does not rely on the expressive capacity of the text set.

The first argument presented by Hanslick for the conclusion that musical beauty does not depend on expressiveness is this: some beautiful music expresses no definite emotion; so, even if music were capable of expressiveness, this would be irrelevant to its beauty. Budd offers the obvious rejoinder that the argument is a non sequitur. At best it shows that the expression of emotion is not a necessary condition for, or ingredient in, musical beauty. Hanslick's stronger claim, that expressiveness never could contribute to musical beauty as one of its elements, is unproved.

The next argument in the set discusses the nature of song. Hanslick notes that changes in the music of a song can destroy its beauty without altering the accuracy of the representation of the feeling. As Budd notes, Hanslick here assumes what is at issue: that "the representation of feeling" resides exclusively in the text. It is true, as Hanslick claims, that contrasting musical settings of the same words might differ in their musical beauty. It does not follow from this, however, that expression does not occur in music. Neither

---

[5] Typical are McMullin 1947, Brown 1948, Lippman 1953, 1966, and 1977, Davison 1954, Cazden 1955, and Howes 1958.

< 205 >

does it follow that, were such expression possible, it could make no contribution to the beauty of the work.

This argument has a complement. Hanslick notes that composers, of whom Handel is an example, sometimes set texts with very different expressive imports to the same music (sometimes the music appears not only with different words but in a different work.) Hanslick sees this practice as pointing to the independence of music and expression. But Kivy (1990b) denies this and believes that such plausibility as the argument appears to possess depends on Hanslick's choice of excessively vague examples, or on his being overly specific about the emotional import of the texts in question. Kivy notes that there is no problem in holding that the same vigorous music can be used to set one text dealing with passionate anger and another illustrating passionate love, provided that the music is passionate in character and does not contain further expressive elements. Moreover, it is not true that just any music might be used appropriately with just any text. Pizzaro's rage music in Beethoven's *Fidelio* would not be at all suitable in mood for the love duet between Leonore and Florestan. So the practice, where it occurs, does not show that music is expressively neutral, as Hanslick claims.

The last in this set of Hanslick's arguments also concerns the relation between texts and music. Hanslick asserts that vocal music becomes the less beautiful the more accurately it represents a definite feeling. The more closely the music imitates speech, the more accurately it represents feeling, he says. He points out that recitative is that form of music most closely resembling speech, yet recitative is less musically beautiful than most music. (Had he been writing now, Hanslick might have taken "rap" as his example.)

It is important to recall the intellectual background against which this view is presented. One of the more common arguments for musical expressiveness emphasizes a connection between our hearing expressiveness in music and our hearing expressiveness in utterance, or nonmusical vocalization. Kivy (1980) discusses the views of Francis Hutcheson, Thomas Reid, and Arthur Schopenhauer, all of whom see this resemblance as central to the expressive character of music. Such a thesis remains popular. Kivy himself stresses the resemblance between music and the voice as important in explaining music's expressiveness, and others have made this resemblance crucial.[6] As I read it, Hanslick is offering a reductio of such a position. If expressiveness relies on a resemblance between inflections of the voice and music, the type of music that most clearly imitates the voice should be the

---

[6] See Rieser 1942, Adorno 1973, Scruton 1974 and 1983, Lippman 1977, and Hoaglund 1980. Brown (1948) and Coker (1983) allow a qualified importance to the voice.

< 206 >

most expressive.[7] The music which, by this criterion, is the most expressive is recitative, yet recitative is widely regarded as low in musical beauty. So musical beauty cannot depend on expressiveness, given this theory of musical expressiveness.

Now, a defender of the resemblance between music and the voice as explaining our experience of expressiveness in music might reject Hanslick's assumption that such a resemblance depends primarily on the musical imitation of the inflections and rhythms of speech: recitative is closer to the voice than other kinds of music only if "the voice" is equated with the speaking voice. It seems to me, though, that this strategy might be counterproductive. Music *can* resemble the inflections and rhythms of speech and, when it does so, is normally regarded as comparatively inexpressive. Now, if *this* resemblance is discounted, it is not clear what remains to ground the expressiveness shared by our experiences of music and of human vocalizations. Music is experienced as no less expressive than is the voice, but the possibility of explaining that common experience as resting on some deeper resemblance between expressiveness in the two cases may be lost. To say that music resembles the voice in its expressiveness, then, is to testify to the phenomenal character of the experience, but it is not to explain the foundation of music's expressiveness as depending on similarities between musical tones and vocable elements.

In response, it might be suggested that the expressiveness of music rests on a resemblance not with the speaking voice but with wordless howls, groans, and the like. Such vocal "expressions" have inflections that might be imitated by music, though these inflections are not those of measured speech, which are the structures mostly imitated in recitatives. Recitative is inexpressive because it does not, after all, resemble the kinds of utterances that are expressive of emotion. The resemblance grounding musical expressiveness is, to take an eighteenth-century musical commonplace, that between the interval of a falling minor third and the lover's sigh. Krzysztof Penderecki's *Threnody for the Victims of Hiroshima* is harrowing in its expressive quality because it so closely resembles a prolonged, wordless scream of agony, wrung simultaneously from countless throats.

If this is the line to be taken, it faces obvious difficulties. The expressiveness of howls and groans standardly depends on our taking them to be (or

[7] Note, though, that not all those who emphasize music's similarity with the voice regard resemblances in inflection as important. Schopenhauer, for example, does not. See Rowell 1988 for the idea from India that music is like both the voice and breath in that it resonates with the soul.

< 207 >

knowingly entertaining the thought that they are) voiced ventings of felt emotions. In music, similar sounds do not stand to occurrent emotions in like manner: the listener does not believe (and neither does she standardly make believe, I think) that the music is an inarticulate cry betraying a person's felt emotion. So the analogy with the voice might always be questioned (I pursue this question further later). Besides, musical analogues of groans, belches, and wordless cries are not nearly so common in music as is expressiveness itself.

Hanslick makes a further point about the relation between music and words: there can be a mismatch between the expressive character of a text and the kind of music to which it is set. Hanslick asserts that the music of the famous aria sung by Orfeo on losing Euridice in Christoph Gluck's *Orfeo ed Euridice* is better suited to a text expressing joy. Kivy (1988b) notes that Hanslick complains that Gluck's music does not match the expressive quality of the text. Hanslick might have said that the dynamics of the music do not match the dynamics of the emotions expressed in the text (though the claim would have been false), but this is not what he says. The mismatch he identifies must be one between the expressiveness of the text and of the music. But then Hanslick is unfaithful to his main, negative thesis in that he assumes here that music does possess an expressive character.[8]

Perhaps Hanslick might be saved from this accusation if he were read as claiming that, given the conventions mistakenly thought to generate musical expressiveness, Gluck's treatment should be inappropriate to the text. Alternatively, perhaps Hanslick should be read here as having adopted his counterfactual mode of discussion.[9] Hanslick might be allowing, for the sake of the argument, that the music is expressive, and also accepting that the aria is beautiful, while trying to show that its beauty does not depend on its expressiveness because there is a mismatch between the conventionally expressive character attributed to such music and the emotional tone of the

---

[8] Hanslick's discussion of Gluck's music parallels his remarks about Handel's reusing musical ideas in setting different texts. To be consistent, he should conclude from his observations on Orfeo's aria not that the music fails to match the mood described in the text but that quite different music would have been no less (and no more) suitable to the text.

[9] Hanslick's consideration of Gluck's music (1957, 32–34; 1986, 16–18) comes a few pages before the explicit introduction of the counterfactual approach. According to the Cohen translation, Hanslick says: "The beautiful in music would not depend on the accurate representation of feelings even if such a representation were possible. Let us, for argument's sake, assume the possibility and examine it from a practical point of view" (1957, 38–39). The Payzant translation has Hanslick writing this: "Even if it were possible for feelings to be represented by music, the degree of beauty in the music would not correspond to the degree of exactitude with which the music represented them. Let us for the moment, however, suppose that it is possible and consider the practical consequences" (1986, 21).

< 208 >

text. More likely, though, Kivy is right in observing a lack of rigor in Hanslick's argument, which, after all, was produced partly as a polemic against a school of criticism that regarded talk of the composer's or listener's emotions as paramount in musical criticism (see Payzant 1981).

Hanslick's Main Negative Argument

Those of Hanslick's arguments considered so far are not impressive, but the defense of the primary, negative thesis—that music cannot express definite emotions—is much stronger. Hanslick tries to establish his conclusion by arguing (i) that music cannot represent thoughts, and (ii) that definite feelings involve or contain thoughts (by which they may be individuated). Perhaps he would have accepted that emotions necessarily possess some feeling tone, but clearly he regards the cognitive aspects of emotions (beliefs and desires targeted on the emotion's object, for example) as no less necessary.

Someone who holds that emotions are "visceral perturbations," that different types of emotions are distinguished by the sort of perturbation experienced, and that the causal context, emotional object, desires, and behaviors that go with emotions are merely contingent ancillaries would readily diagnose an error in Hanslick's argument. It will seem to this person that Hanslick emphasizes the cognitive at the expense of the affective and, in doing so, misunderstands the nature of emotions. He might conclude that Hanslick's argument entirely misses its target, since music might express emotions by imitating such visceral perturbations, whether or not it can present the thoughts that are merely emotions' accompaniments.[10] Nowadays, though, the philosopher is likely to be far less quick to dismiss Hanslick's line, for, following Wittgenstein and others (such as Kenny 1969 and Wilson 1972), it is widely accepted that, in the typical cases, the cognitive and behavioral aspects of emotions are a part of their essential nature. In fact, Hanslick's view of the emotions is philosophically prescient, and this explains, I believe, the continuing relevance of his main negative argument.

In considering (i)—that music cannot represent thoughts—Hanslick quickly moves to discussing resemblance; he assumes that, since music cannot represent as do words, it must do so by imitation, if at all. He readily concedes that music has a dynamic character and, in this, resembles human behavior, but he notes that many different emotions, and many things that are not emotions, possess the same dynamics in common. So, even if music can imitate the dynamics of the experiential aspect of emotions, or of the

---

[10] So reason Pratt (1931), Langer (1942), and their ilk, such as Sherburne (1966).

< 209 >

behavior that expresses emotions, it cannot specifically represent those movements or patterns as the dynamics of emotions.[11]

Many of those who write on this subject concede to Hanslick part (i) of his argument: thoughts (especially those involved in locating and characterizing the object of an emotion) are not expressed or signified in purely instrumental music.[12] One philosopher does challenge this premise, however: Jerrold Levinson (1990a, chap. 14) argues that certain musical progressions might have the power to regularly call to mind in culturally backgrounded people certain thoughts, thoughts appropriate to the emotions in question. He goes further: music might "hook into" whatever is distinctive about an emotion, so that it "resonates" with some distinctive aspect of that emotion, without its also signifying that aspect or the emotion. In this way it might bring an emotion to mind without directly referring to, or denoting, or signifying that emotion.

I find the first of Levinson's points to be reasonable. At the close of Chapter 1 I listed several ways in which music might take on meaning—for example, by quoting themes with established associations with cultural contexts or with words. I do not believe that composers' use of such strategies is aesthetically irrelevant to the appreciation of their music, so I agree with Levinson that, sometimes, music quite properly can be understood to express some thoughts. But I doubt that this phenomenon is a marked feature of all music we would regard as expressive. Levinson's observation suggests that Hanslick's claim should be qualified somewhat, but it does not undercut the force of Hanslick's argument.

Levinson's second point—that music might resonate with an emotion—is rather obscure, I think. What could he have in mind here? Perhaps something like this: sonata form commonly involves an alternation of contrasting themes and tonalities and frequently displays the character of a struggle or conflict, without (of course) signifying who or what struggles with whom or what, or why; perhaps, then, it is appropriate that we hear some sonata-form movements in terms of struggle, though no particular instance of nonmusical

---

[11] Scruton (1983), Stecker (1984), and Levinson (1990a, chap. 14) agree that Hanslick denies the possibility of musical representation. Kivy (1984, 144) is more careful in observing that neither Hanslick nor Gurney deny that music could be representational. He quotes Hanslick (1957, 36) as saying that music can imitate objective phenomena only, and never the specific feelings they arouse, but he regards this remark as a slip on Hanslick's part, a departure from the formalism that holds: "It is impossible to form any but a musical conception, and it can be comprehended and enjoyed only in and for itself" (1957, 50). Whether or not Hanslick thought that musical representation is possible—cuckoo calls, perhaps—it is clear enough that he denies that emotions may be represented in music.

[12] See, for example, Budd 1985a, Kivy 1987 and 1990a, Putman 1987, and Walton 1988.

< 210 >

conflict is signified in the music; see Kendall Walton 1988 and 1990. That Levinson might develop his second point in this manner is suggested by his use of the following argument: *Specific* objects attach only to *particular* instances of an emotion; the *class* of an emotion's instances does not take an emotional object. Now, music cannot supply a specific object, but it might indicate the intentional aspect of the emotion; the music might seem to be *about* something. Even though one must imagine that the emotion expressed in a musical work takes a particular object, there is no need for the object itself to be given in the music. Music deals with types of emotion, not particular instances, so it need convey only the impression of its being object-directed, not the particularity of any specific object (similarly, a painting might show someone looking at a particular thing but not the particular thing looked at). Music might convey the idea that what is wanted may come about (thereby revealing the expressed feeling as hope) without indicating what is wanted. Besides, we can think of an emotion without thinking of all its distinctive features. Music might bring hope to mind, for example, without also invoking every element of an experience of hope.

Levinson's suggestion comes to this: the emotions expressed in music are not particular in the sense of taking particular objects; the sadness of a musical work is not like the particular sadness of hearing of the death of a friend, for example. If music can convey a sense of "aboutness," or of purposiveness, it displays the intentionality that characterizes emotions, even if it does not signify definite thoughts picking out a particular object for the emotion expressed. And, if music can convey thoughts characterizing the *formal* object[13] of an emotion, it can express an emotion of the general type, even if it does not signify the particular emotional object of the given emotion in its musical presentation. If music can convey the impression of being about some unspecified but eagerly anticipated event, and if it has the appropriate noncognitive profile, then it can convey sufficient cognitive content to reveal the emotion expressed as one of hope.

This suggestion of Levinson's is ingenious, though I am skeptical of its ultimate success. I agree that musical movement and structure are experienced as teleological (an issue I discuss further later), in that musical movement seems not merely to be random but to aim at goals; for example, the arrival of the tonic key or tone marks a return and point of repose; usually

---

[13] The formal object being the description under which the objects of an emotion must be believed, or be knowingly imagined, to fall in being objects of that given emotion. The formal object of envy must include, for example, the description of the thing envied as not belonging to the person who experiences the envy. As a possible illustration of the formal object of sadness, I use "something that is viewed as both unfortunate and regrettable."

< 211 >

the work comes to a close and does not merely come to a halt. I also agree that, in consequence, music displays a kind of purposiveness and coherence. But Levinson's argument works only if this experience of musical purposiveness brings to mind, if not a particular emotional object, then the type of propositional content that characterizes the formal object of an emotion; for example, that the purposiveness of a given work concerns some unspecified but eagerly anticipated event, so that hope is expressed in the music. I am doubtful that instrumental music conveys propositional content, even at this level of generality.

In the discussion to which I have referred, Levinson does not argue that all expressive music signifies or, through resonance, leads us to think of the formal object of the emotion expressed. Rather, his aim is to show that this might happen sometimes and that, in this manner, emotions individuable only via the description under which we bring their emotional objects (that is, only by their formal objects) might sometimes be expressed in music. (Emotions of the type in question usually are thought to include hope, envy, and pride.) In this conclusion Levinson may be correct. Nonetheless, I believe that if he is correct the possibility arises only in works that already display expressive complexity—that is, in contexts where at least some emotions are expressed without its being the case that their formal objects are signified. If I am right, the possibility for which he argues depends in turn on music's expressing emotions in the way Hanslick denies to be possible. Levinson's exceptional cases presuppose (I believe) a more general possibility for expressiveness in music, and Hanslick's argument aims to deny that more general possibility. Accordingly, Levinson's argument could be fully convincing only if premise (ii) of Hanslick's argument could be shown to be false, as Levinson himself clearly appreciates.

Part (i) of Hanslick's argument looks secure. If allegedly expressive music does not convey ideas, as language does, and does not represent or symbolize thoughts and scenes, as pictures or conventional symbols do, then the emotions allegedly expressed in music lack propositional content. If premise (ii) is also true—if emotions are individuated in terms of their propositional content—then Hanslick's conclusion is supported: music cannot express definite emotions. To show this is to be only a short step from showing that emotions are not expressed at all in music. Or, to come closer to Hanslick's own positive conclusion, if music is expressive, what it expresses is purely musical beauty.[14]

---

[14] Howes (1958) points out that beauty is not an emotion as such. He means this as an objection to Hanslick, but I doubt that Hanslick would dispute the point.

< 212 >

Except for Levinson, those who would dispute Hanslick's conclusion are inclined to reject (ii), rather than (i). They concede, if only for the sake of the argument, that music cannot represent thoughts, but they deny that all emotions are to be individuated by reference to their propositional content; in particular, not all emotions are individuated via their formal objects. Hanslick's claim in (ii) is vulnerable to at least three approaches: (a) It is deniable that all emotions, or like states, are object-directed. Emotions that are identifiable despite their not taking emotional objects obviously are not individuated solely in terms of the character of their emotional object. (b) Some emotions might be individuable by the feeling tone, or pattern of feeling tone, that is partly constitutive of their nature. (c) Some emotions might be individuable in terms of the behaviors that typically give expression to them. I consider these possibilities in turn. The fate of Hanslick's argument rests finally on one's evaluation of these counters to the crucial part (ii) of his argument, so I investigate them in some detail.

(a) Not all emotions, or like states, are directed at emotional objects.

Many writers on this topic deny that instances of objectless emotions (or of emotions not intimately connected to their emotional objects) are exceptional in ordinary cases.[15] Sometimes one feels sad without its being the case that there is anything about which one feels sad. Now, if one can have an emotion and know what it is without knowing what its object is, or if one can experience an emotional mood that does not take an object and know

---

[15] For example, Sharpe 1975, Budd 1980 and 1985a, Kivy 1980, 1989, and 1990a, Callen 1982a and 1983, Putman 1987, Levinson 1990a, and Matravers 1991. The same point is made in many general discussions of the emotions; for instance Moravcsik 1982, Robinson 1983a, and Lamb 1987. Both Kivy (1990a) and Putman (1987) refer to Moravcsik 1982 in their discussions. By contrast, Scruton (1987) appears to hold that all emotions take objects, and Best (1985) maintains that the vast majority do so. Mew (1985a) takes an intermediate line while developing his version of an arousal theory of musical expression: though typical emotions always take objects, those aroused by music are exceptional in that they do not, or need not do so. Care must be taken over terminology here. One might be tempted to draw distinctions between emotions proper, feelings, and moods. Such a distinction is implicit in Day 1969, where hope is discussed. In Day's view it is a necessary condition for something's being an emotion that it involve characteristic sensations and physical symptoms. He distinguishes hope (which lacks these characteristics, he says) from emotions proper. For a contrary view, see Lamb 1987, where it is suggested that moods are objectless *instances* of emotions, not distinct types. Now, if "emotion" is treated as a generic term, one will hold that not all emotions take, or are individuated in terms of, their emotional objects. If "emotion" is treated as a specific term, one might continue to hold that all emotions take emotional objects, while allowing that other like states, such as moods, do not. For my part, I regard it as appropriate that "emotion" be used in the wider sense.

< 213 >

what it is, then it cannot be the case that one's emotion is individuated by reference to the character of its emotional object. Such cases falsify Hanslick's (ii).[16] Even if some emotions are individuated by reference to their emotional objects' satisfying the formal object of the given emotion, not all are. Budd makes the point with characteristic exactitude:

> If there are feelings or emotions that do not include a thought, they will be untouched by Hanslick's argument against the possibility of the representation in music of definite feelings, since the argument turns essentially upon the consideration that music cannot represent a thought. Hanslick presents cheerfulness as a definite feeling that cannot be represented in music. But cheerfulness seems rather to be either a quality of character or a mood, which in either case consists in being in good spirit, and which does not include a specific thought. Hence, Hanslick's argument cannot be used to establish the impossibility of its musical representation. And this holds good for any similar quality of mood or character. (1985a, 24–25)[17]

As the second part of the quotation reveals, the charge is not merely that part (ii) of Hanslick's argument is narrow in its scope but also that it is narrower than Hanslick appreciates. It is apparent in the examples he discusses that Hanslick means not only to deny that music could express hope and the like but also that he means to deny that it could express happiness or sadness. These latter cases might be objectless moods, though, so his argument fails to apply to them as he believes it to do.

Are there any kinds of emotion for which Hanslick's argument holds good? Are there any kinds of emotion that must be individuated in terms of their cognitive content? It is common to accept that there are. These are of the type Julius Moravcsik (1982) calls "Platonic attitudes." If I feel jealousy, it must be the case that I am jealous of some person, creature, or thing I believe (rightly or wrongly) to attract the attention of the object of my desires, thereby excluding attention to me more than I would like; if I feel hope, it must be the case that there is some state of affairs I believe to be happier than the present one and to which I look forward. The cognitive content (that is, the formal objects) of such emotions, which are often called "higher," is essential to their being the emotions or feelings they are. More-

---

[16] As observed in Budd 1985a, Putman 1987, Kivy 1990a, and Levinson 1990a.

[17] The view that music expresses objectless moods is recommended in Osborne 1982, Sharpe 1982, and Radford 1991a.

< 214 >

over, it is usually also claimed that such states lack distinctive behavioral expressions. There may be no phenomenal difference to distinguish hope from a general feeling of well-being, or even from anticipated dread, and there may be nothing in behavior to distinguish a nervous person from one anxious to go to the toilet. Such emotions or feelings cannot be individuated except by reference to the thoughts they involve.

Budd (1985a), Daniel Putman (1987), and Kivy (1990a) accept that, for feelings or emotions of this kind, Hanslick's argument succeeds. Platonic attitudes are not susceptible to expression in music because music does not represent the thoughts without which such emotions or feelings could find expression.[18] Each of these writers rejects the general conclusion of Hanslick's argument because each thinks that some emotions or moods might be expressed in music, but each also accepts that Hanslick's argument is successful in showing that such feelings as shame, pride, dignity, hope, and piety cannot be expressed in music.

Levinson (1990a), as we have seen, is not willing to give up the fight so readily. Apart from holding that music might sometimes convey definite thoughts, or might resonate in a way that calls to mind relevant thoughts, he also argues that the "higher" emotions might have distinctive characteristics other than their cognitive content; each might have a distinctive profile even when the cognitive aspects are put aside. Perhaps music could connect with these other aspects, he suggests, and its doing so might be sufficient for expressive success. And, even if the cognitive aspects are the only distinctive feature of the emotion in question, music might be able to convey enough of those aspects—sufficient of the idea of intentionality and of other elements of the emotion's cognitive profile—to secure its successful expression. It need not be necessary for music to convey the rich complexity of context that characterizes a specific instance of such an emotion, indicates Levinson, since the music presents only a token of the general type.

Levinson pursues his argument from a conviction born of his own experience. He believes that the second statement of the second subject in the exposition of Mendelssohn's *Hebrides* Overture is expressive of hope,[19] one of the "higher" emotions. We get here, he suggests, a hopeful counterreaction to the dark mood that prevailed formerly. There is some relation to an inner

[18] Price (1992) holds that the Platonic attitudes are as easily disengaged from their objects and relevant beliefs as are anxiety or fear, and he insists that they do have typical bearings (such as a proud bearing and lofty look). He does not believe that the Platonic attitudes are expressed in music, but his grounds for this are not the usual ones.

[19] Tovey (1972, 93) describes the theme as possessing a serene tone in the recapitulation. Bennett suggests that both hope and anxiety are "the very character of music" (1936, 115).

< 215 >

feeling characteristic of hope, a bodily bearing or stance appropriate to hope, some conceptual contents perhaps definitive of hope, and perhaps a general impression of aboutness. These features are sufficient to justify the claim that hope, rather than something else, or nothing, is expressed.

In a similar vein, Kivy (1990a) allows that music can be pompous. No doubt he does so because he accepts that some music is properly to be experienced as displaying this character. Less charitable than Levinson, he describes the case as one in which "the exception proves the rule." Pomposity is associated with a fairly "gross" behavioral pattern—it struts and postures—despite its being a Platonic attitude. Music may embody the feeling of pomposity because strutting and posturing might be captured in musical gesture and tone. Kivy goes on to deny that music could express the related feeling of pride, presumably because pride does not have a gross behavioral pattern that might be recognized independently of the cognitive context, even where the context requires no more than a token of the general type of the feeling. The same point might be made about, say, envy. I doubt that anyone would hold that pure instrumental music could "hook into" sufficient features of envy that it might be musically expressed.

I find Levinson's position and Kivy's less generous concession congenial. It might indeed be the case that not all the "higher" emotions are equally "high." For at least some of the Platonic attitudes, it could be that the dynamics of their progression, or of the behaviors by which they are expressed, are distinctive enough that music might, along with the use of conventions that standardly can be relied on to call certain types of thoughts to mind, provide a context for their successful expression. To that extent I also agree with Levinson that Hanslick's argument does not succeed in showing that the "higher" emotions are never capable of musical expression. Nevertheless, I think these arguments erode, rather than demolish, Hanslick's line of thought. I would continue to maintain, with Kivy, that the "higher" emotions are not susceptible to musical expression for the most part.

Now, those who would argue against part (ii) of Hanslick's view while accepting its part (i) must demonstrate that emotions can be individuated by reference to features other than their cognitive content or, like Levinson, argue that features additional to their cognitive content might contribute to their identification. If the arguments offered here for (a) are convincing, this must be possible in some cases; if there are emotions or feelings that do not take objects, or that can be individuated without reference to the character of their emotional objects, then such identifications must be possible. I now consider the two most likely candidates, those mentioned in (b) and (c): that

< 216 >

emotions might be individuable via their sensational features or by reference to the behaviors through which they are expressed.

(b) Some emotions might be individuable in terms of the feeling tone, or pattern of feeling tone, that is partly constitutive of their nature.

Hanslick specifically denies the possibility envisaged. He concedes that music has a dynamic character that might mirror the fluctuations of tension and release accompanying some given episode of occurrent emotion, but he suggests that such echoing is insufficient to establish signification or expression. Quite different emotions might share the same dynamic form; for example, instances both of sadness and of happiness might well up and subside in the same fashion. Moreover, many processes that are not emotional display similar dynamic patterns, yet we do not thereby wish to claim that music expresses or signifies these processes.[20]

Budd (1985a) replies to this argument as follows: if emotions are stripped of their propositional content, then a feeling tone might remain, and music might represent the pattern of this feeling tone, if not emotions as such. In Budd's view, emotions, stripped of context, propositional attitudes, and behavior, might leave as their residues feeling tones of two basic types, the pleasant and the unpleasant. If music could represent changes in feeling tone, then it could perhaps stand in a symbolic relation to an important element of the emotions. He tentatively suggests that consonance and dissonance might be regarded as musical analogues of pain and pleasure, since the move from the one to the other might be experienced as a move from discomfort to satisfaction.

Budd's argument surely is too weak to establish that music is expressive of emotion, as I think he realizes. Since music is nonsentient, it could not experience feeling tones, so, to establish the basis for musical expression by reference to sensations, it is necessary to argue that music represents, rather than possesses, such things. Hanslick would deny that it could do so, and that claim looks reasonable. Distinctive of pleasure and pain, as feeling

---

[20] The view that emotions have characteristic feeling tones is denied by Osborne (1982 and 1983). Among those who hold that there might be such things are Ferguson (1960), Mew (1985a), Levinson (1990a, 334), and Goldman (1992). Matravers (1991), as noted in the previous chapter, thinks that emotions such as pity might be individuable solely in terms of their physiological and phenomenal elements. For a fuller discussion in a wider context, see Lyons 1977; Lyons holds that a very few members of the set of sensations (for example, those that go with the activation of the tear duct) that accompany some emotions could be characteristic, if not unique. Also see Stocker 1983.

< 217 >

tones, is the way they *feel*, not a dynamic pattern they display. The fluctuation of such feeling tones might generate patterns of tension and release, and patterns of tension and release might also be experienced as occurring in music—for example, where a discord is resolved to a concord—but, without assuming what one is supposed to be analyzing, it is difficult to see how an inference from the musical pattern of tension and release to a pattern generated by a fluctuation in feeling tones could be licensed. And one might go further: even if such an inference could be justified, which I doubt, a yet more implausible inference would be needed to move beyond mere feeling tones (which, after all, are only sensations of vague pleasure and pain) to emotions proper.

A similar point can be made against Walton (1988), who concedes that music might be confined to imitating the dynamics of emotion but denies that it follows from this that musical expression is so vague as to be empty, since music can imitate those dynamics in great detail. If this were accepted, Walton's point would count against the claim that the resemblance between music and emotions is no more striking than that between music and other dynamic processes. As it stands, though, it does not meet what I take to be Hanslick's major challenge. Music might exemplify (not merely resemble) complex dynamic patterns, but it does not and could not exemplify those patterns as patterns *of feeling*. Such gestalts, divorced from propositional attitudes and unconnected with feelings, are not indicative or expressive of felt emotion, so no degree of resemblance between the dynamics of such behavior and the movement of music could establish that emotions are expressed in music.

Those who respond to Hanslick are not unaware of this point. Walton (1988 and 1990) claims that make-believe bridges the gap between dynamic similarities and the expression of an embodied emotion.[21] Levinson (1990a, chap. 14) claims that music may "hook into" ideas, so that similarities in the dynamic character of music and of the emotions might be supplemented in a way that licenses a move from talk of musical patterns to talk of the patterns of emotions. Putman (1987) implies that mere iconographic similarity between the forms of feelings and musical structures justifies our attributing emotional expression to music. In doing so he cites Kivy 1980 with approval.[22]

[21] For comment on Walton 1988, see Budd 1989a.

[22] I am not confident that he grasps Kivy's position, which I take to be more concerned with similarities between behavioral expressions of emotion and the dynamic character of music than between behavioral expressions of emotion and their sensational patterns. Putman's view strikes me as more closely aligned with that of Susanne Langer. Hall (1967) claims to recognize

< 218 >

The Expression of Emotion in Music

So far as (b), the claim that emotions have distinctive feeling tones, is concerned, I am inclined to side with Hanslick. Like him, I doubt that particular emotions usually display characteristic orderings of sensation. I suspect that often there is a pattern to the way emotions succeed each other, but not that emotional types have a distinctive sensational structure. Moreover, whatever the degree of similarity, I agree that, where music does not succeed in intimating thoughts, the inference from a pattern to what it is a pattern of is a wild one.

(c) At least some emotions might be individuable in terms of the behaviors that typically give expression to them.[23] This suggestion, along with its consequence that music might be able to create designs of movement resembling such behaviors, seems more promising. To grant this, though, is to be far from being committed to the view that music expresses emotions through such resemblances, for the type of objection that makes (b) problematic also applies in this case. Such behaviors standardly give expression to emotion only if they stand in an appropriate relation to relevant experiences of sentient beings. So Hanslick might argue this way: whatever similarities hold between the dynamics of music and the dynamics of the behavioral expressions of emotions, such similarities would legitimate the move from talk of movement to talk of the expression of emotion only if the dynamic patterns of music stand in a similar relation to occurrent emotions—and they do not so stand (later in this chapter I argue that this argument can be challenged).

The final conclusion to draw from this examination of Hanslick's views perhaps is this: It may be that some emotions, moods, or feelings do not take objects and do not involve beliefs or make-beliefs about such objects. Equally, it may be true in unusual cases that music brings to mind the kind of thoughts that characterize emotions. But, in the end, the cases under discussion are ones in which an emotion is expressed only if it is felt.[24] So the

---

an affinity between Hanslick's view and Langer's, but I take this to show that he misunderstands Hanslick's position. He supposes that Hanslick believes that musical materials have expressive power and, since Hanslick acknowledges that music might share with the emotions their dynamic character, he takes Hanslick to be claiming that music operates as an iconic symbol of the forms of feeling. Epperson (1967) similarly claims that Hanslick's view is compatible with a Langerian account.

[23] Skeptical that emotions have characteristic behavioral patterns is Osborne (1982 and 1983); also see Sircello 1972 and Kivy 1980, chap. 12. Kivy makes the point that the relevant expressive behavior need be neither necessary nor sufficient for an occurrence of the emotion.

[24] The point is discussed by Roberts (1988), who regards feelings as paradigmatic but not as necessary for some emotions. Lyons (1977) argues that all occurrent emotions involve feelings, even if they are not reducible to feelings. Others, such as Currie (1990), accept this view.

< 219 >

musical expression of emotion, on the model presupposed in the previous discussion, requires that the music stand in a suitable relation to an occurrence of feeling. Since no one seriously maintains that music itself can experience emotion, the arguments offered here are relevant only if there is some way of forging a link between what happens in the music and a sentient being's having, or make-believedly having, the appropriate feelings. The replies—(a), (b) and (c)—addressed to Hanslick's argument suggest that different emotions or moods might lack one or other of the features Hanslick regards as necessary for emotion. Some might lack emotional objects; others might be identifiable solely from the pattern of feeling tone involved; yet others might be identified from a collation of features lacking the concrete detail and definitiveness of ordinary emotional contexts. No matter how far such arguments are taken, however, they run against the fact that emotions or moods are experiences of sentient beings, whatever other elements might be absent from these experiences sometimes. So these considerations count for expressiveness in music only if one can establish a connection between occurrent emotions and musical events, whereas Hanslick's argument is concerned ultimately with the denial of the aesthetic relevance of any such connection.

Those who would develop their replies to Hanslick in the context of theories of the types discussed in previous chapters have a ready reply to this point. The "owner" of the emotions expressed in music is the composer, according to the expression theory; or the listener, according to the arousal theory; or, rather, the music symbolizes an occurrence of feeling, or the general form of feelings, according to the view that sees music as a kind of symbol; or music describes, rather than experiences, emotion, according to the view that music is like a natural language; or music depicts its subjects as pictures do. As the discussion in the previous chapters should make clear, I find such replies to be unsatisfactory. In each of these views, the music is an expression of something external to it: the emotion expressed is not directly attributable to the music itself. To remain true to the theme of this chapter, which considers the idea that the expressiveness is a property internal to the musical work, another reply is required. And the thrust of Hanslick's argument makes clear the difficulties confronting that reply. While one retains the view that the emotions expressed in music are occurrent emotions, one must make good not only the claim that music imitates, resembles, or signifies some aspect of the expression of felt emotion but also the thesis that, because of this resemblance, imitation, or signification, one can move with ease from talk of such similarities to talk of expression as the expression of an occurrent emotion. Like Hanslick, I think that such a move is likely to be

< 220 >

impossible to justify. If one wishes to claim that the expressive character of music is a property belonging to the work itself, as Levinson and Putman do, for example, it is not directly to the point to argue that occurrent emotions need not take objects, or involve thoughts, given that it remains patent that music is not the type of thing that could feel the emotions to which it gives expression.

Equally unjustified, I have indicated, is the "solution" that dismisses such difficulties as merely symptomatic of the special character of musical expressiveness, as revealing that the expression of emotion in music is sui generis in that, in the musical case, one happens to be dealing with emotions that are not directly experienced, whether in fact or in make-believe, by anyone.

From these considerations, Hanslick would have us arrive at the conclusion that music is incapable of expressing emotion. The moral I draw from the discussion so far in this chapter is, instead, this: if music expresses emotion, the emotions in question cannot be ones that, necessarily, are sensationally experienced. The lesson to be learned from Hanslick is that the emotions expressed in music are not of the kind that depend on thoughts and, crucially, not of the kind that need be felt. This is to be married to the idea culled from the earlier rejection of the view that the emotions expressed in music are sui generis in being unfelt and objectless; namely, that the account of musical expressiveness is plausible only if the relevant sort of expressiveness is familiar from mundane, nonmusical contexts. Only if we are comfortably acquainted with unfelt, objectless emotions in ordinary contexts is it plausible to argue that (similar) emotions are expressed in music.

Emotion Characteristics in Appearances

In their primary use, the words naming emotions, feelings, and moods refer to experiences. This is not to say that emotions are radically private, purely mental states or events. As I have suggested previously, the kinds of causal contexts in which they occur and the kinds of behaviors to which they give rise are public matters that are partly constitutive of, not merely incidental accompaniments to, their nature. Equally, the thoughts, beliefs, and desires that also are constitutive of emotions necessarily have public expressions. To emphasize that emotions are experienced is to draw attention to facts such as these: On particular occasions, a person may experience an emotion without showing this, though it could not be the case for any emotion that it was never displayed in a public fashion. Sometimes, a person may pretend to experience an emotion without experiencing that emotion. Though we can be fooled by such pretense, we could not always be fooled

< 221 >

and, thereby, be incapable of distinguishing genuine expressions of emotions from feigned ones. Generally speaking, a person's sincere report of his emotional condition decisively identifies the emotion he feels, unless self-deception is possible; the person who experiences an emotion very often is in a better position to identify its character than is an onlooker. This is not solely because he has better access to his own sensations, but because he has better access to his own beliefs and desires as well. If there is no question of self-deception or of insincerity, a person's apparent misuse of emotion terms more likely indicates that he does not grasp their meaning than that he misidentifies his own condition. On the other hand, a person's report of his emotional state should not always be accepted uncritically, especially if he cannot explain how the context, or his behavior, is appropriate to the emotions he claims to feel. Sometimes a person might have to infer the nature of his own feelings, and that inference could be mistaken; more often, though, their nature is apparent to him without reflection.

Other uses of emotion terms do not involve reference to occurrent experiences but retain an obvious and direct connection to their primary use. I might describe a person as sad, meaning not that she feels sad now but that she is the kind of person who, more often than others, is disposed toward that feeling. In this case I make a prediction about the frequency of her feelings, without attributing an occurrent feeling to her. Or I might describe a person as sad as a result of entertaining without belief the thought that she feels sad; that is, I might talk of the sadness I make believe she is feeling, without believing that she now feels as I say.

These uses of emotion words have no application to music. Music is nonsentient; it does not experience emotions; it lacks the thoughts, attitudes, and desires that are characteristic of emotional experiences and that contribute to their being the emotions they are. Moreover, though it is not inappropriate to imagine that a person could be feeling an emotion she is not now experiencing, there is no point to entertaining thoughts about what music might be feeling.[25]

The uses of emotion words listed here are not their only ones, however. In the following I concentrate on a different, secondary use that is familiar to us. This employment pays no regard to experience; it concerns, instead, what I call "emotion characteristics in appearances."[26] The character of a person's

---

[25] There might be a point to imagining what the composer or the performer was feeling, but if this is appropriate it is so because we are already aware of an expressive character in the music.

[26] In developing this argument, I rely on points made in Davies 1980.

< 222 >

appearance, bearing, face, or voice sometimes is described by using emotion terms. We might say "He is a sad-looking person" or "He cuts a sad figure." In such cases we do not mean that the person feels sad; neither do we mean that he frequently feels sad, or that we make believe that he feels sad. The reference is not to any emotion, in fact, but to the look of him.

Several aspects of this use distinguish it from that in which we refer to feelings or experiences. Emotion characteristics in appearances are necessarily publicly displayed, whereas occurrent emotions need not be displayed. They are worn "on the outside" without being "experienced on the inside." A person who changes or suppresses whatever made her appear to be sad-looking ceases to be sad-looking, ceases to have a sad appearance; by contrast, a person can change or suppress the expressions of their occurrent emotion without ceasing to feel that emotion. A person is sad-looking even where her appearance is adopted for the sake of pretense, whereas it is not true that a person feels sad if she pretends to be sad without feeling that way. A person who contrives a sad look may attempt to deceive us into believing that he feels sad (or into thinking that he is a naturally sad-looking person) and, as a result, we might make false predictions about his future behavior (or future deportment). By this ruse he may mislead us about his feelings (or his natural comportment), but he could not deceive us in the same way about the emotion characteristic worn by his appearance. The person who wears a sad look is as liable to be mistaken about the emotion characteristic displayed in her appearance as is anyone else (if not more so), whereas a person is less liable to be mistaken about the emotions she feels than is an onlooker.

Of course, there is an intimate connection between occurrent sadness and sad-lookingness. Frequently a person is sad-looking because he feels sad. Then his sad-lookingness betrays or expresses his feeling. As I use the terms, a concern with emotion characteristics in appearances is not a concern with the connection between appearances and feelings, should such a feeling happen to exist. Emotion characteristics are attributed to the appearances people present and not, as is true of emotions, to the people themselves. It is faces and the like that are sad-looking. Faces do not feel emotions and do not think thoughts; they are nonsentient. Emotion characteristics in appearances do not, like felt emotions, take emotional objects or involve beliefs, desires, or attitudes. To say that someone displays the emotion characteristic of sadness in his appearance is not to say that he feels sadness or that there is anything about which he feels sad; it is not to attribute to him a feeling of sadness at all. As I employ the terms, "emotion characteristics in appearances" are used without reference to the person's feelings, or proneness to feelings, or to feelings counterfactually imagined of him. Normally it is clear

< 223 >

from the context whether we are referring to a person's feeling or merely to the look of him. If this is not clear, one can sensibly ask for clarification.

My point is that emotion words have a common, licit use that does not involve even implicit reference to the occurrence of feelings. Although "He is a sad-looking person" may be used to refer to a person's (present or predicted) feelings, I distinguish the no-reference-to-feeling use as a distinct one. It is in this latter case that emotion words refer to emotion characteristics in appearances. The distinction invoked does not depend on a difference in verbal forms; for example, between "He looks sad" and "He is a sad-looking person." These forms of verbal expression may lend themselves equally to the two uses I have distinguished. Where there is implicit or explicit reference to a person's feelings, "sad" does not refer to an emotion characteristic in appearance as I intend that notion.[27]

The criteria for a sadness characteristic are given solely in appearances. It makes no difference whether the appearance is consciously adopted or worn naturally. Strictly speaking, a person can pretend to be sad-looking or be sincere in being sad-looking only in respect of what he actually feels. Many notions on which our ordinary discussions of emotions center—sincerity, pretence, the nonexpression of felt emotions—rely on this distinction between expressions of felt emotions and emotion characteristics in appearance.

The use of emotion words in attributing emotion characteristics to appearances is secondary on the use of such terms in referring to occurrent emotions. It is not difficult to see why the meanings of emotion terms have been extended to this secondary use. The behavior giving one's appearance its emotion characteristic is the same as the behavior which, in other contexts, expresses or betrays the corresponding felt emotion. To be a sad-looking person is to look as if one feels sad. It is the behavior that characteristically and naturally expresses felt emotions which, in other contexts, generates the corresponding emotion characteristic in an appearance. For this reason, it is understandable that the same words are employed with the same sense in the two uses, though their referents differ in these uses.

The necessarily public character of the behavior revealing emotion characteristics in appearances, the fact that this behavior neither is motivated by

---

[27] Kivy makes a point about the grammatical form of reports of musical expressiveness. He claims that music does not express sadness but instead is an expression of sadness; see 1980, 12–14, where he cites Tormey 1971. In his view, if something *expresses* sadness, it stands in the appropriate relation to occurrent sadness, whereas it can be *an expression of* sadness without expressing an occurrent emotion. As I have indicated, I doubt that any particular form of words standardly captures the distinction so neatly.

< 224 >

nor is expressive of the beliefs, attitudes, and desires that are tied to felt emotions, and the further point that such behavior is not "expressed" or squeezed from the person by the power of their feelings all have important implications for developing an account of emotion characteristics in appearances.

(1) Some behavior that might indicate a felt emotion could not give rise to a corresponding emotion characteristic in an appearance. Much of the behavior that expresses an emotion can be seen to be expressive in that it reveals the emotional object of the emotion, the desires felt toward that object, and other propositional attitudes relevant to the context in which the emotion arises. Emotion characteristics in appearances do not cause such behaviors because they do not involve such thoughts and desires. Rather, they are revealed in those actions which, to put it crudely, are directly expressive of the feeling component, rather than the thought component, of felt emotions. To see movement as flight (to or from) is to recognize a relation between the action and its object. Where there is no such object, there is movement, but not flight as such. By contrast, radiant smiles can be seen as expressive of happiness in the absence of evidence about the object of the smiling person's happiness. Those behaviors showing emotion characteristics in appearances must be of the latter type rather than the former; they must be the kinds of behaviors that can be recognized in another as possessing expressive import in the absence of a knowledge of that other's propositional attitudes and their objects, since such propositional attitudes do not occur in, or are irrelevant to assessing, the emotion characteristic in appearances. These kinds of actions were described in Chapter 4 as "primary" expressions of emotion.

(2) Not all actions that might give expression to an occurrent emotion are equally likely to occur in the corresponding emotion characteristic in appearance. A person who continually weeps without cause and without feeling sad displays the sadness characteristic in his appearance, but usually sad-looking people frown, say, rather than continually weep. Of the behaviors giving primary expression to felt emotions, those most likely to feature in the corresponding emotion characteristic in appearance are ones a face, voice, gait, or deportment might fall into without intentional pretense or genuine feeling. Though a person might intentionally contrive an emotion characteristic in her appearance, more commonly such appearances are not consciously adopted. Usually such appearances are not forced on one by the tension of feelings, since they often occur where feeling is absent.

(3) It is not obvious that all emotions have natural, primary expressions of the kind discussed here. Earlier I talked of the "higher" emotions, of Pla-

< 225 >

tonic attitudes, such as hope, embarrassment, puzzlement, annoyance, and envy. I suspect that such feelings or emotions lack natural, primary expressions. The behavior through which they are expressed is behavior of a kind that points to the beliefs, desires, and objects which, in these cases, are so central to their nature. I doubt, then, that any behavior can be seen to be expressive of such states except insofar as it reveals the person's having thoughts of the appropriate kind. To say that a person looks envious is always to refer, I think, to how they feel, or are prone to feel, or could be feeling, and is not to refer to an emotion characteristic paying no regard to feelings. Because I think that the "higher" emotions do not possess characteristic behavioral expressions inextricably bound to the propositional attitudes that mark them as the emotions they are, I also do not believe that these "higher" emotions have corresponding emotion characteristics in appearance.

Other emotions have typical behavioral expressions that retain their expressive character to an observer who knows nothing of the emotional object, beliefs, desires, and context of the person experiencing them. I take sadness and happiness to be examples of these emotions. Moreover, moods must also have recognizable expressions of the type in question, both because moods might be objectless and because, in such cases, it is sometimes possible to identify another's mood. Emotion characteristics in appearance correspond to happy and sad emotions or moods.

(4) General sadness and happiness can come in many particular forms. Grief, despondency, depression, dejection, gloom, moping, broken-heartedness—all are species of sadness. Joy, elation, delight, high spirits—all are species of happiness. I suspect that what distinguishes the species within these genera is the nature of their formal objects or, sometimes, their lack of an object. The members of each set share similar primary expressions. Now, if one describes a person as looking grief-stricken, this is often a remark about his feelings, or his hypothesized feelings. But it might be clear from the context that it is a grief characteristic in his appearance that is being discussed (though I think this would be an unusual use of "grief"). Given, in that case, no concern with his feelings, with death or loss, and so forth, one would not say anything different if one were to describe the appearance as gloom-laden, or simply as sad-looking. Because the expression, deportment, or whatever giving rise to the one appearance is no different from that producing the others, these attributions would have the same content. Grief is different from gloom, but there need be no disagreement between descriptions of an appearance as displaying the emotion characteristic of gloom and of grief. The uses would be metonymic, with each taking a species to stand

< 226 >

for the genus. Similarly, a joyous appearance might equally be described as happy-looking.

There is obvious disagreement, however, if a given experience is described both as sad-looking and as happy-looking. The behaviors appropriate to the one appearance are not appropriate to the other, and the attribution is to be justified by reference to those behaviors.

A final point: the appearances that display emotion characteristics are not always human appearances. To return to examples I used first in the 1970s, Basset hounds and Saint Bernards are sad-looking dogs. Presumably they do not feel sad more often than any other breed of dog. The sadness lies in their appearance and not in their feelings.

Dogs have their own, doggy ways of showing their feelings. Happy dogs wag their tails, try to lick their owners' faces, and so on; sad dogs tuck their tails between their legs, hang their heads, howl, and so forth. Though some people claim that dogs are capable of pretense with respect to their feelings, we generally seem to think that doggy behaviors almost always *express* the doggy feelings they display; that is, our interest in appearances of doggy sadness is an interest in that appearance as revealing what is felt and not a concern with a doggy emotion characteristic in appearance. If we were to take dogs to act or look as they do when expressing doggy feelings on occasions when they do not feel those feelings, we would attribute doggy emotion characteristics to their appearances based on the similarity between the behaviors. But we do not do so; we are inclined to take *appearances* of doggy feelings as always tied closely to expressions of doggy feelings.

The emotion characteristics we attribute to the appearances of dogs are not those of doggy, but of human, emotions. The relevant resemblance is between the facial features or comportment of the dog and the looks of sad people; in these cases we find a similarity with human, rather than with doggy, behaviors or physiognomy. Of course, that this usage rests on a perceived resemblance with human expressions of feeling, and not doggy ones, emphasizes the complete absence of reference to felt emotions; we do not for a moment think the dog is human, or that dogs express their feelings through actions that imitate ours.

The appearances of inanimate or nonsentient things are also sometimes seen as presenting emotion characteristics. Weeping willows may be sad-looking, but not happy-looking, because their shapes are seen as resembling those of people who are downcast and burdened with sadness. Cars, viewed from the front, might be seen to bear some resemblance to the human face, with the headlights as the eyes, and so on. Depending on the disposition and shape of the grill, for instance, some cars are sad-looking while others are

< 227 >

happy-looking (and many have expressionless faces). Where sadness is attributed to willows, cars, and the like, there can be no doubt that it is emotion characteristics that are involved, for there is no question of these trees and machines feeling the emotions presented in their appearances.

Resemblance is a symmetrical relation, as noted in Chapter 2, but we are much more inclined to find faces in the appearances of cars than to find cars in the appearances of faces. The reasons for this are clear enough. Given the importance in general to us of other people and of a concern with their feelings, we are motivated to see faces or human characteristics where we can, but we are not similarly motivated to see willows and cars where we can. This is not to say that we set out deliberately to look for resemblances to humans, though we may do so. Rather, we find such resemblances sometimes forced to our attention. The disposition to find human appearances wherever possible seems inherent to our mode of experiencing the world rather than a point of view we might adopt solely at will.

The Expression of Emotion in Music

The reader will have correctly anticipated that I intend to claim that the expressiveness of music consists in its presenting emotion characteristics in its appearance. Such a view meets the conditions for a minimally adequate account drawn from the earlier discussion. While acknowledging that talk of musical sadness, say, involves a secondary, derivative use of the word "sad," I have argued that this secondary use is one of a familiar kind. It is a use established in ordinary, nonmusical contexts in which we attribute emotion characteristics to the appearances of people, or nonhuman animals, or inanimate objects. To that extent, the expressiveness attributed to music is not mysteriously confined to the musical case. Moreover, the view I advocate avoids the difficulties raised by Hanslick's objections. Emotion characteristics in appearance are attributed without regard to the feelings or thoughts of that to which they are predicated. These expressive appearances are not emotions that are felt, take objects, involve desires or beliefs—they are not occurrent emotions at all. They are emergent properties of the things to which they are attributed. These properties are public in character and are grounded in public features. The sadness of music is a property of the sounds of the musical work. The sadness is presented in the musical work. There need be no describing, or representing, or symbolizing, or other kinds of denoting that connect the musical expressiveness to occurrent emotions, for the expressive character of the music resides within its own nature.

Earlier I suggested that voices might display emotion characteristics (with-

< 228 >

out giving expression to felt emotions). This would be a matter of cadence, intonation, phrasing, timbre, tone, and tessitura—that is, of features of sound. Since music is an art of sound, it might be thought that music presents emotion characteristics by resembling some features displayed in the vocal expression of occurrent emotions. Such a view finds support in Kivy 1980, and no doubt there is some truth to it, yet I think that not much musical expressiveness relies on this similarity.[28] To my ears, the likeness between music and the voice is slight. Equally, I find little resemblance between music and the human face, though faces are prime presenters not only of expressions of felt emotion but also of emotion characteristics.[29] I believe that the expressiveness of music depends mainly on a resemblance we perceive between the dynamic character of music and human movement, gait, bearing, or carriage.[30]

Motion is heard in music, and that motion presents emotion characteristics much as do the movements giving a person her bearing or gait. With that said, one might let the argument stand. But I believe that there are features of musical movement that help draw attention to the relevant similarities, so a discussion of the nature of movement in music is called for. My claim is that musical movement invites attention to expressiveness because, like human action and behavior (and unlike random process), it displays order and purposiveness. Musical movement is invested with humanity not merely because music is created and performed by humans but because it provides a sense of unity and purpose. We recognize in the progress of music a logic such that what follows arises naturally from, without being determined by, what preceded; in this, musical movement is more akin to human action than to random movement or to the fully determined movements of a nonhuman mechanism. This feature of music, as I have said, arises from the character of musical materials themselves, not solely from the recognition that human hands shape those materials.

Movement in Music

Frequently in the preceding pages I have mentioned the motion of music. That music is experienced as spatial and as involving motion is widely ac-

[28] Perhaps the relation is closer than I have allowed in the case of tone languages—that is, languages in which pitch has a direct semantic function—such as are found in China and Africa.

[29] Hospers (1954/55) draws the analogy between an expressive face and music's expressiveness, as do Scruton (1974) and Evans (1990), but others such as Hoaglund (1980) comment that the gap between the two is too large for the analogy to bridge.

[30] This view is shared by Meidner (1985), who says that resemblance to the demeanor of the body is important, the voice less relevant, the face irrelevant.

< 229 >

knowledged.[31] Hanslick sees the phenomenon as central to music's nature.[32] Many who think that music expresses emotion tend to locate the basis of its expressive power in its dynamic character.[33] Several writers attempt a more or less detailed account of the basis of our experience of motion in music.[34] For the most part, the accounts are phenomenological and it is hard to see how it could be otherwise. Since the idea of musical movement is so prominent in the literature, particularly in analyzing the nature of musical expressiveness, I review the topic here.

In the paradigm (nonmusical) case, movement involves the passage of an individual through space and time. It presupposes (i) the existence of an individual with an identity that persists through time and is independent of its location, (ii) a set of coordinates relative to which the location of the individual can be measured—that is, motion is relational; and (iii) changes in the location of the individual (or its parts) at different times. For example, the earth moves in its orbit about the sun.

The recognition of motion requires the ability to identify an individual that alters its location (in relation to the relevant coordinates) through time. Sounds and musical themes can be individuals of the appropriate sort and, accordingly, can be heard to be in motion. The brass band plays the overture from Bizet's *Carmen* as it marches by; the theme moves along with the musicians. A similar movement might occur as a result of the spatial disposition of a stationary orchestra; the theme moves from the audience's left to the right of the stage as it is passed from the violins to the cellos. (This kind of musical movement is employed most famously in the compositions written by Andrea and Giovanni Gabrieli for San Marco in Venice.) If we allow these claims about musical movement, however, we still have not captured the phenomenon discussions of musical movement attempt to describe.

Usually it is claimed that music unfolds within and through aural space. Aural space is not to be confused with real space; it has no location relative to the equator, for instance. Crucial to the experience of aural space is the

---

[31] Music is described in such terms in Dräger 1952, Lippman 1953 and 1977, Dickinson 1957, Stambaugh 1964, Scruton 1974 and 1983, Newell 1978, Alperson 1980, Orlov 1981, Ingarden 1986, and Gärdenfors 1988.

[32] Whereas Smith (1979) advocates the elimination of visual metaphors—those concerning light and space—from discussion of music on the grounds that music is audial rather than visual. But he seems to have nothing to put in their place.

[33] See Pratt 1931, Dewey 1934, Langer 1942, Haydon 1948, Cooke 1959, Ferguson 1960, Epperson 1967, Hansen 1971, Coker 1972 and 1983, Davies 1980, Kivy 1980, Meidner 1985, Walton 1988 and 1990, and Putman 1989.

[34] See especially Zuckerkandl 1956 and 1959; also Pratt 1931, Albersheim 1960, Pike 1970, McDermott 1972, Robert P. Morgan 1980, Clifton 1983, and Rowell 1983.

< 230 >

recognition that notes at different, determinative pitches are high or low with respect to each other. Basic here is the fact that, at the interval of an octave, a note is identified as of a type that previously appeared in one "place" and now reappears higher or lower in the pitch continuum.[35] People singing in parallel octaves (as occurs generally when men and women sing a melody together) sometimes claim to be singing in unison. In the sense that they sing the same note types, if not at the same pitches, they are not totally mistaken. I suppose that, if we did not experience octaves as recurring instances of the same individual, which instances are to be distinguished in terms of the individual's location in aural space, we would not be inclined to hear relations between notes at other intervals in spatial terms. Coordinates are established within aural space by the way we hear and individuate pitches.

Is the experience of pitch as spatial transcultural? Henry Orlov doubts this. He sees such ways of hearing (merely) as confined to some musical cultures the members of which must be taught the skill: "Suffice it to mention the most important dimension of Western music that is described in terms of high and low tones is equally alien to little children in the West and to the Africans, who, as Alan Merriam witnesses, found his question about high and low tones 'silly,' preferring to speak instead of 'weak' and 'strong' or 'small' and 'big' sounds" (1981, 136). I find that Merriam is by no means as definite on the point as Orlov claims. It is, he says, the Flathead (Amerindians) who rejected as silly questions not about the connection between pitch and space but about the connection between pitch and color (1964, 94). On pitch Merriam says this:

> Among the Bashi . . . , reference is commonly made to what we call a "high" tone as a "small" or "weak" tone, and to what we call a "low" tone as a "big" or "strong" tone, and Tracey . . . reports a similar usage for the Chopi. Walter Ivens notes for the Lau of the Solomon Islands that: "In singing, a low note is called *bulu* (black), and a high note *kwao* (white). These names are taken from charcoal marks made on a plank to

---

[35] Victor Zuckerkandl calls this "the miracle of the octave" (1956, 102, 322). The most striking demonstration of our tendency to equate notes at the octave is provided by an experience of the "paradox" (described in Shephard 1964) of a constantly ascending scale that goes nowhere, an aural equivalent of M. C. Escher's ever-ascending staircase. The generation of the "paradox" relies on our unthinkingly shifting attention from a note to its octave. Perhaps the phenomenon is not confined to humans; Lerdahl and Jackendoff record that animals trained to respond to a note of a given pitch react more to the octave than to other intervals if a wrong note is played (1983, 290).

< 231 >

indicate the tune: the heavy down-strokes being 'black,' and light up-strokes 'white.'" . . . Among the Basongye . . . high tones are "small" (*lupela*), and low tones are "big" (*lukata*). (1964, 96–97)[36]

The claim that the use of spatial terms in connection with the experience of music is arbitrarily cultural would be stronger, I suggest, if cultures were less consistent than they seem to be in the synaesthetic equations they use. Zuckerkandl (1959) notes that the ancient Greeks used "sharp" and "heavy" for pitch as well as high and low (we of European culture also use "sharp" and "flat" as pitch qualifiers). He does not doubt that musical perception generally is spatial, despite some cultural differences in terminology (1959, 14–15). Pratt (1931, 47) quotes the psychologist Carl Stumpf as saying that "high" and "low," or similar terms, are applied to pitch in all languages and he rejects the view that this can be explained merely as involving arbitrary associations.[37] High/low, small/big, thin/fat are spatial terms. That music is heard in spatial terms would appear to be more or less universal.

Music is heard and described in spatial terms. What of movement within this space? Notes are heard not as isolated individuals but as elements in themes, chords, and the like. These higher units of organization involve motion that unfolds through time. There is movement (stepwise, not gliding) between the notes that constitute the theme. Rhythm, meter, and tempo generate the pace of this movement. The experience is not merely one of succession, but of connection.

If melody, rhythm, meter, and tempo generate the experience of motion across the surface of sound, simultaneity of sounds (harmony, polyphony, counterpoint) provides the dimension of depth or volume. Also important here is texture, which is as likely to be a matter of instrumentation as of voice-spacing and the number of notes per unit time. An orchestral unison has a depth and power a solo violin could not achieve. Register also seems relevant to musical depth. A trombone has more weight (inertia) of tone than a flute when the two play the same note at the same volume. Loudness or softness also can contribute a spatial effect, as can the character of the attack and decay of the note.[38]

[36] As Kathy Higgins has pointed out to me, Feld (1988, 87–89) observes that the Kaluli of the Bosavi rainforest describe sounds as "insides," "underneaths," "reflections," "flow," and "hardness"; in the forest there is "lift-up-over sounding."

[37] Against this, Maconie (1990) maintains that Western music is discussed in spatial terms only because, and since, it has a notation. Like Burton (1992), I am unconvinced by this idea. Hanfling (1992, 69) writes that "high" and "low," as applied to notes, are reversed in some languages, though he cites no evidence for the claim.

[38] Some of these effects are discussed in Dräger 1952.

< 232 >

The Expression of Emotion in Music

Our experience of movement in music no doubt depends to some extent on our associating the movements of the performer with the sound of the music. As Olga Meidner says, "every performer uses his muscles and to some extent can be seen to do so. Thus even for listeners music is consciously associated with actual movement as well as evoking pre-conscious empathic and kinaesthetic perceptual impressions of movement" (1985, 351). Often the association seems far from arbitrary, in that qualities of the performer's gestures transfer directly to the sound of the tones she plays. An aggressive down-bow at the heel of the bow wrenches the string of a violin into motion and the resulting note sounds as if it is beaten rather than caressed into existence. Where notes are produced by blowing, striking, or scraping, the manner in which the instrument is approached directly affects audible properties of the tone played, such as its entry and decay. Levinson (1990a, chap. 16) offers many such examples; a keyboard glissando has the insouciance of the gesture involved in the action (a flick or turn of the wrist) that produces it.

But just as musical movement is heard as depending sometimes on the actions involved in performance, so too our descriptions of human actions depend sometimes on the movement we hear in music. We say of the pianist's hand that it moves *up* the keyboard to reach the higher notes, but no part of the keyboard is higher than another. Similarly, in moving *up* the fingerboard to reach the higher notes, the cellist's fingers move nearer to the ground; we locate the performer's body in such cases in aural space rather than in real space. Donald Callen (1985) refers to our moving to music, not merely as an epiphenomenon caused by "resonance," but as important in "modelling" the movement of the music, thereby leading to an affective response that better reveals the expressive character of the work. Callen's talk of "modelling" is indirectly important in reminding us that movement in music is not merely a matter of crude imitation or association; rather, we hear in music patterns of tension and release, and these resemble in their structure kinaesthetic aspects of movement as well as the teleological character that marks human action.[39]

It should comes as no surprise, then, that we call the sections of symphonies, suites, and the like "movements." And that the general terms for loudness and softness are "volume" or "dynamics." And that music is described constantly in terms primarily used to denote space, movement, and action:

[39] Minimalist composers such as Steve Reich and Philip Glass sometimes set up mesmerizingly static patterns in their music. Such pieces rely for their effects on the listener's awareness of the dynamic potential of music; they are written *against the background* of musical teleology.

< 233 >

abandoned, waltzing, singing, rushing, hesitant, vivacious, distant, multi-layered, turgid, transparent, shallow, fast, slow, dragging.

Musical movement in aural space differs from the paradigm of movement introduced earlier in two respects (only the first of which usually attracts attention): (i) Nothing goes from place to place. The theme contains movement but does not itself move; the notes of the theme do not move, although movement is heard between them.[40] Following from this, (ii) there is no independently identifiable individual that moves.[41] As a way of acknowledging this departure from the paradigm case, musical space and movement are described as "ideal" (by Edmund Gurney) or "virtual" (in Langer 1942 and 1953), or "metaphorical" (in Pratt 1931). Sometimes it is suggested that musical time is "virtual," "aesthetic," or "subjective," as opposed to "real."[42]

The discrepancy between musical movement and the paradigm of space/time movement has been seen both as grounds for questioning the claim that music moves and for celebrating music's special, mysterious powers. Budd (1983 and 1985a) takes the former position in his criticisms of Pratt and Scruton. He regards talk of musical motion as an eliminable metaphor with no explanatory power.[43] Zuckerkandl adopts the latter stance. He makes much of the fact that pitch changes can be shown on an oscilloscope though no changes in spatial location are revealed thereby. He concludes that music presents the pure, unmediated essence of motion—"the most real motion"—in that it is not concerned with individuals locatable within the space-time coordinates predominating in the scientific sphere (1956, 138–139). It seems to me that he exaggerates. No essentially relational properties are revealed unequivocally on any piece of scientific apparatus designed to record at different times changes in intrinsic properties. No special power or virtue accrues to music from the fact that the nature of musical motion is not apparent in a printout from an oscilloscope.

One might deal with the apparent discrepancy between musical movement

---

[40] Roger Scruton says: "We may find ourselves at a loss for an answer [to the question 'What is this line that moves?']: for, literally speaking, nothing *does* move. There is one note, and then another; movement, however, demands *one* thing, which passes from place to place" (1979, 81). Wilkinson (1992) also stresses this point.

[41] Meidner (1985) offers an analogous case: the flashing lights warning of fog on motorways are perceived as a pair that jumps up and down, though no pair of lights moves.

[42] See Langer 1942 and 1953, Zuckerkandl 1956 and 1959, Stambaugh 1964, Newell 1978, and Ingarden 1986. For criticism of Langer's claims in this regard, see Alperson 1980.

[43] As I see it, he is not so much concerned to reject this type of metaphoric description as to deny that it can explain musical expressiveness, since, in his view, the "explanation" replaces one mystery with another.

< 234 >

and the paradigm in two ways. One might reject the differences as more apparent than real, arguing that musical space is heard as wedded to actual space and that the same physiological mechanisms operate in either case. This is the line favored by Pratt (1931, 48–54), who suggests that notes of different pitches are heard as coming from different (real) spatial locations. These claims are criticized by Budd (1983 and 1985a), and rightly so in my view.[44] Alternatively, one might question the dominance and exclusive authenticity of the paradigm. This second course is the one I prefer. If many familiar kinds of movement do not involve change in location, the musical examples cease to be distinctive or puzzling and talk of motion, to the extent that it is ordinary, will involve moribund, rather than lively, metaphor in such cases; that is, musical motion will be neither unusual nor mysterious (as Budd fears and Zuckerkandl hopes).

Time itself is frequently described in spatial terms: there is the flow of time; there is the passage of time; time unfolds; things happen in due course. Sometimes alterations other than straightforwardly spatial ones are described as involving movement. For example, a river is in constant motion, though it does not move from place to place unless it shifts its banks. By contrast, the erosion of a mountain through time is not likely to be described as involving the motion of the mountain. What distinguishes the mountain from the river? The answer, I think, is that rivers, as opposed to mountains, are conceived of as processes. The river does not move but is constituted by the motion of the water it contains. In the case of a river, of course, something—droplets of water—does move from place to place. Not all processes are constituted by elements that have a location in space, however. There may be political moves toward war in the Middle East; the Dow Jones Index responds by dropping; as a result, the government lurches to the right; this causes my spirits to plunge; the peace movement attains new standing. In these cases, no identifiable individual changes its location in space and nothing moves from place to place. These all are cases of temporal process. They differ from the river in that neither they nor their constitutive elements exist in space.

I suggest that music is an art of temporal process.[45] A theme is constituted by movement in the way that the progress of the Dow Jones Index is. The progress of the Dow Jones Index can be graphed, but the coordinates against

---

[44] Also see Meidner 1985. This is not to deny a connection between hearing music and some aspects of "ordinary" spatial perception; for a useful discussion, see Lippman 1963.

[45] Mention of music as process, though perhaps the intended use differs from mine, is to be found in Hegel according to Dräger 1952, Stambaugh 1964, and Lissa 1968.

< 235 >

which that movement is recorded are not in real space (even if the graphic representation is; compare this graphic representation with musical notation). The Dow Jones Index can be set against the New Zealand's Barclay's Index over the same period; many temporal processes are multistranded (compare this with harmony and polyphony). The use of terms of position and movement concerning music is perhaps secondary, but this does not entail that such terms operate as live metaphors. The same secondary use is common outside the musical context, as I have indicated, and talk of one note's being higher than another is no more metaphoric, I think, than is talk of a rise in the Dow Jones Index. Musical movement differs from the paradigm (spatial displacement) introduced above because the movement is that of a process in time, not because musical movement is aberrant or distinctive. In musical cases, one can deny the appropriateness of such characterizations, or deny the objectivity of the phenomenon experienced, only by calling into question very widespread, mundane descriptions and experiences of nonmusical phenomena. Moreover, the description of music in such terms does not seem eliminable; I doubt that one can discuss tonality, or the closure at the end of a Beethoven symphony, say, without invoking notions of space or movement.

One feature of much musical movement has yet to be mentioned: Typically, the movement is not heard as random; it is not like the dots and dashes on the screen of a TV tuned off the station. Usually musical movement is heard as teleological, as organized around a target that exercises a "gravitational pull" on other notes. In tonal music, the target is the tonic. The tonic is heard as a point of repose. Notes other than the tonic are heard as drawn toward it, with the strength of the attraction depending on the place of the note in the scale, on its "distance" from the tonic. For example, in the major scale, melodically the leading note is the most strongly drawn to the tonic. Chords are comparatively tense or relaxed (discordant or concordant) in relation to the tonic chord; discords strain for resolution. As a result, the course of music, its motion, corresponds to an experience of increasing or diminishing tension, push and pull, pulse and decay, with closure achieved at the arrival of the final tonic. Music not only is experienced as involving motion relative to a framework of musical space, it is experienced as involving motion relative to a particular, pitched note (and its octaves, and a triadic chord with the tonic as its fundamental), and the progress of that motion is experienced as possessing a pattern of tension and relaxation. Tonality cannot be described without invoking spatial terminology.

Most writers on the topic emphasize the importance of tonality in giving musical motion its teleological character. Some (such as Cooke 1959) believe

< 236 >

that the major scale has an objective validity through its relation to the harmonic series of overtones.[46] This view implies that people from different musical cultures and backgrounds should be no less adept at hearing (experiencing/feeling) the pattern of tensions generated within any work in the major key as are initiates to the style. To the extent that musical expressiveness depends on such patterns, people from different musical cultures and backgrounds should be as skilled as initiates at identifying the expressive character of the work. Difficult though it is to interpret the evidence, these suggestions seem not to be true.

Other writers challenge the idea that the harmonic series gives special, natural status to any musical modality.[47] The just-intonation scale differs in some respects from the natural series of overtones (the seventh harmonic is flatter than its equivalent in the scale, for example). Further, the scales used in the West have been much affected by temperament, and many different systems of temperament have been applied to them (see Lawrence 1987). Finally, within the scale, any note might become the tonic within a modal system. So the claimed correspondence between the major key and the natural series of harmonics can easily be called into question. Moreover, the major scale (widespread though it may be) is far from universal. Although the sameness of notes at the octave might be recognized cross-culturally, the way the octave is divided (musical scales) varies from place to place and time to time. The Indonesian *slendro* scale, for instance, differs markedly from the major scale.

That all scales suppose the sameness of octaves and that most include a perfect fifth or fourth is evidence, perhaps, that there is some natural, universal basis for scalar organization. Equally, though, differences between scales and their modal treatments indicate a strong cultural element in the use of musical materials. Within any culture, the immediate experience of the tonality/modality of a piece, and consequently of the patterns of tension and release in connection with musical movement, depends on the listener's familiarity with the musical style in question. The expressive character of the piece is unlikely to be identified or experienced correctly by someone not conversant with the practice of the musical culture (or the style of the musical subculture) within which the piece finds it home. The point can be taken further: many musical factors other than tonality affect musical movement,

---

[46] Note that complementary arguments claim to show notions of consonance and dissonance—that is, the relative tension of chords—to be universal. For a critique, see Cazden 1962.

[47] See, for example, Farnsworth 1948, Walker 1960, Lerdahl and Jackendoff 1983, Serafine 1989, and Maconie 1990.

< 237 >

as was noted earlier. One could not reasonably expect a person from a culture in which music is monodic or antiphonal to appreciate and understand polyphonic music. And one could not reasonably expect a person who belongs to a culture in which tonality and harmony perform important structural roles to recognize the cadential function served by gongs or drums in Javanese gamelan or Japanese Kabuki, for example.[48]

In the terminology introduced in Chapter 1, an appreciation of musical movement involves the recognition of meaning B or C rather than of meaning A; if there is a natural element in scalar organization across the globe, it is one hedged about and transformed by arbitrarily cultural conventions. This is consistent with the view that all musical cultures recognize (in their own music) the possibility of teleological movement. It is also consistent with the view that judgments about the teleology of musical movement are intersubjective, and not purely personal (private), even if they are neither universal nor independent of a familiarity with the musical conventions governing musical practices.

The discussion of the teleology of musical movement as a function of tonality/modality has led to questions about the character of atonal music. One might expect music that avoids tonality (as twelve-tone composition is often conceived as doing) to be experienced as generating random movement.[49] If music takes its meaning from its structural integrity and expressive nature, and if these depend on the teleological character of musical movement, then atonal music might be thought to lack sense.[50] Even if one does not agree with this conditional, if one sees musical movement as depending on tonality/modality one will accept that movement is typically confined to music featuring clear tonal centers. The following qualification is typical: "Musical tones (at least in diatonic music) have perceptible dynamic qualities" (Hansen 1971, 79).

There is a basis, I think, for concerns of the kind mentioned here—some contemporary works seem to go nowhere and, once started, have no reason for ending when they do—but it is not obvious why whole schools, as opposed to particular works, should be condemned on this score (that is, this

---

[48] I have mentioned differences in the musical styles of cultures, but other relativities might also make the expressive character of music from an unfamiliar society opaque. For example, it may be that different cultures do not always associate the same emotions with the same degrees of tension, or it may be that expressions of emotion play roles, or occupy places, other than those with which we are familiar.

[49] For example, Lissa (1965) denies that there is a continuous flow of sound in pointillist twelve-tone works.

[50] Cooke (1959) and Albersheim (1960 and 1964) claim that movement in twelve-tone music is random and that "random" equates musically with "meaningless" or "pointless."

< 238 >

could be due to factors other than departure from tonality). The question is this: are there ways of organizing musical materials, other than traditionally tonal ones, that might be used to create musical structures that can be perceived to be coherent? The works of contemporary Western composers (as well as much non-Western music) suggests that there are. Twelve-tone technique is consistent, in fact, with near-tonal writing and has been used in this manner by Schönberg (see Cone 1960 and 1967), Berg, and Stravinsky. Even if one abandons the major scale, it is possible to create tonal centers (no less transient than those in Wagner's music, for example) with motivically structured tone rows, as Anton Webern does. There are many ways other than restricting the number of available chromatic pitches to draw more attention to some notes than others, to establish nodal points of relative repose. Means other than scalar ones can create patterns of tension and release. Rhythm, instrumentation, dynamics, and register all have their part to play in shaping the progress of a musical work. Several writers suggest that the directionality of musical movement is not automatically abandoned when traditional (Western) tonal approaches are rejected.[51]

My overall theory, then, is this: In the first and basic case, music is expressive by presenting not instances of emotions but emotion characteristics in appearances. Our experience of musical works and, in particular, of motion in music is like our experience of the kinds of behavior which, in human beings, gives rise to emotion characteristics in appearances. The analogy resides in the manner in which these things are experienced rather than being based on some inference attempting to establish a symbolic relation between particular parts of the music and particular bits of human behavior. Emotions are heard in music as belonging to it, just as appearances of emotions are present in the bearing, gait, or deportment of our fellow humans and other creatures. The range of emotions music is heard as presenting in this manner is restricted, as is also true for human appearances, to those emotions or moods having characteristic behavioral expressions: music presents the outward features of sadness or happiness in general.

This theory has several advantages over those considered previously. It allows that expressiveness is a property of music that is always publicly evidenced and directly manifested. It does not rely on a connection between musical expressiveness and someone's occurrent emotions, emotional object, physiological condition, or cognitive state. It involves an attribution of expressiveness that has a familiar use in nonmusical contexts. More than

[51] See Ferguson 1960, Lissa 1965, Pike 1970, and Robert P. Morgan 1980, but note that the latter also acknowledges that there is a "shallowness" in much recent music.

< 239 >

this, the theory accords quite neatly with our experience of musical expressiveness, since I take that experience to be one finding the expressiveness in the work and regarding that expressiveness usually as rather general in character.

Of course, many have argued that music is expressive because it is experienced as similar to human behavior and comportment.[52] Typically though, such views hold that this resemblance grounds an inference to someone's felt emotion or felt mood, or to some abstract notion of an occurrent emotion. The position for which I have argued is distinguished by its explanation of how expressiveness resides in the appearance presented in the music, without any connection to occurrent emotions. In this view, emotion is immediately, not mediately, presented in music, just as it is in the sad-lookingness of the basset hound.

Kivy's Version of the Theory

The account of musical expressiveness just outlined derives, as I noted, from Davies 1980. Also in 1980, Peter Kivy's prize-winning *The Corded Shell* was published. In that Kivy argues for a position on the expression of emotion in music like the one I have presented. I review the main points of his version here.

Hearing the expressiveness of music is like seeing the expression of sadness in a Saint Bernard's face.

> Thus, what we see as, and say is, *expressive of* φ is parasitic on what we see as, and say is, *expressing* φ; and to see X as expressive of φ, or to say X is expressive of φ, is to see X as appropriate to expressing φ, or to say that it is appropriate to such expression. It is in this way that the expressiveness of music is like the expressiveness of the Saint Bernard's face.
> . . . We see sadness in the Saint Bernard's face in that we see the face as appropriate to the expression of sadness. And we see it as appropriate to the expression of sadness because we see it as a face, and see its features as structurally similar to the features of our own faces when we express our own sadness. (Kivy 1980, 50–51)

We hear the expressiveness of music as a result of recognizing a resemblance between it and aspects of human (or doggy) behavior, bearing, voice, and

---

[52] For example, see Brown 1948, Coker 1972, Swanwick 1974, Sharpe 1975, and Stecker 1984.

< 240 >

physiognomy. Music also resembles other things or processes, but that resemblance is not forced to our attention. A connection is made between music and appearances of emotion, but not between music and other things it might resemble, because we are psychologically disposed to make the connection (and to give it a "direction") only in the former case. "It is a hard psychological fact that we tend to 'animate' what we perceive. Tie a piece of cloth around the handle of a wooden spoon and a child will accept it as a doll; more to the point, *you* will see it as a human figure." Just as we are inclined to animate what we see, so too are we inclined to animate what we hear (Kivy 1980, 50, 60–62).

We justify our attribution to music of emotive predicates as we would justify the claim that the Saint Bernard's appearance is expressive of sadness—by pointing to features of the music, or of the Saint Bernard's appearance, corresponding to the behaviors, physiognomies, or demeanor through which felt emotions are expressed; that is, the criteria for musical expressiveness are parasitic on the public criteria for human expression (Kivy 1980, 67–68). Kivy appreciates the need to argue that occurrent emotions have characteristic forms of behavioral expression and does so in his Chapter 12. Because there are objective criteria that provide the basis for our attributing emotions to people, and because the grounds for our attributing an expressive character to appearances (without regard to feelings) derive directly from these criteria, the expression of emotions in music is no less public or objective than is the case with other attributions of emotion.

Kivy acknowledges that not all types of musical expressiveness are covered by this, the "contour" model. He cites chromaticism and the interval of the minor third as expressive of sadness, but as not expressive in virtue of resembling human expressive behavior. Accordingly, he allows for a second, "conventional" type of musical expressiveness, for an expressiveness established within the musical tradition by the close association between certain musical practices and expressive contexts (1980, chap. 8). Elements that have become conventional in their expressiveness often may have derived their expressiveness originally from their contributing to expressive contours; this might have been the case with the interval of the minor third, which once was experienced as discordant, and hence as "restless," but is no longer heard as a discord because of changes in musical syntax. Alternatively, regular associations with words might have been involved in imparting an expressive character to some musical devices, a character they have come to retain through their entrenchment within the musical tradition. Expressive properties that are conventional in this way are no less objectively expressive than

< 241 >

are the "natural" expressions presented by musical contours that resemble expressive behaviors (1980, 134).

Kivy shows due care in distinguishing expression by contour from expression by convention. To the extent that behavior expressive of emotions might be conventional, the "natural" expressiveness presented by music in its contour is also conventional; that is, the contour model of musical expression may be no less conventionalized than is the convention model. The difference between the two, as Kivy sees it, lies in the source of the relevant conventions. The conventions pertinent to understanding musically expressive contours are ones established in extramusical contexts, whereas those relevant to understanding musical expression by convention are forged within the musical sphere (1980, chap. 8).

In fact, I suspect that Kivy operates with a more complex and sophisticated view than he explicitly acknowledges. As becomes clear in his Chapter 9, he allows implicitly for a further dimension of conventionality as affecting expressive contour in music. A person might fail to recognize the expressiveness of musical contour because she does not know the conventions governing the behavioral expression of emotion in a culture. But she might also fail to recognize the contour for what it is because she lacks familiarity with the musical conventions of the style or genre. Kivy implies (rightly in my view) that expressive contour is structured (to some extent at least) by musical conventions (governing style and the like), so that expressive contours are not necessarily apparent for what they are to someone not at home with the type of music in question.[53]

Now, I think that Kivy is correct to emphasize that the "natural" expressiveness of musical contour is an expressiveness that operates for us in a way structured by contexts provided by conventions that may be musical, extramusical, or both. Though I have argued above that music is expressive as a result of presenting emotion characteristics in appearances, I should at this stage acknowledge the extent to which naturally expressive elements are taken up within traditions of musical practice and style (such as those involved in tonality, modality, polyphony, or harmonic writing) that are highly conventionalized. That is to say, I regard musical expressiveness when conveyed through the appearance of emotion characteristics as belonging not to meaning A, as outlined in Chapter 1, but to meaning B or perhaps to mean-

---

[53] This interpretation is at odds with Kivy's maintaining that conventions for expressiveness by contour are established only in extramusical contexts. Kivy is mistaken, I think, in seeing the distinction between the two kinds of expressiveness as depending solely on the source of the relevant conventions.

< 242 >

ing C. I follow Kivy's lead also in accepting that expressiveness might be introduced into music by means of meaning D, examples of which were given in Chapter 1, rather than through the presentation of emotion characteristics in appearance. I write more of these matters in what follows.

Conventions and Cultural Relativity

I have suggested that music is expressive in that it is experienced as presenting the kinds of behavioral features producing emotion characteristics in appearances, and that in other contexts such behaviors give primary expression to the corresponding felt emotions. At first sight this implies that musical expressiveness is natural, a case of meaning A. Now, if such a view entails that the recognition of musical expressiveness is a cross-cultural phenomenon—that music really is a universal "language of the emotions"—it would be subject to the objection that the musics of different cultures are expressively opaque from one to the other. For that matter, it might be thought that my account also entails that emotion characteristics in human appearances are recognizable from culture to culture, and this view might also be challenged. I reply to these points as a way of developing the theory so far recommended.

I could claim that the behaviors generating emotion characteristics in appearances differ from culture to culture and time to time, in which case they might better be seen as involving meaning B or meaning C (or, on a radically relativist view, meaning D or meaning E) than meaning A. That such behaviors are frequently fallen into, rather than contrived, need be no bar to such a line, since many culturally acquired patterns of behavior soon become unthinkingly habitual. Nevertheless, I am inclined to take a different tack because I think that the behaviors in question are grounded in our common humanity rather than in arbitrary cultural differences; that is, I believe that Chinese sad-lookingness is much the same as French sad-lookingness.[54] Whether members of different cultures are equally inclined to attribute sad-lookingness to Saint Bernards and to willow trees might be another matter, however. The kinds of attitudes one has to, and the beliefs one holds about, animals and nature might inhibit such a tendency. So far as I know, the peoples of all cultures are inclined to attribute expressive properties to their music (including, where they have it, to instrumental music).

[54] The claim is, of course, an empirical one. For support, see Ekman, Sorensen and Friesen 1969. I am not sure whether Kivy also holds this view. He does note that an Australian aborigine cannot be expected to see expression in a sketch by Rembrandt of a face. As Kivy sees it, this is

< 243 >

Because I hold that expressive behaviors owe as much to our common humanity as to our various cultures and that music is expressive in being experienced as like human action, I think that there is a common expressive element found in the musics of different cultures. I know of no culture that consistently expresses sadness with jaunty, fast, sprightly music, nor of any that expresses happiness with slow, dragging music. To take one example, Westerners formerly unacquainted with Javanese music are very unlikely to take the gamelan music that accompanies the weeping of puppet characters in *wayang kulit* for happy music, or to mistake battle pieces for funeral music.[55]

Though the expressive character of some unfamiliar kinds of music might be accessible in the way I have just claimed, it remains true that it is not always so. There are many cases in which aficionados recognize the expressive character of a musical work but in which people from other cultures would be at a loss to find or to identify that expressiveness. Japanese Noh and Kabuki involve music of this kind, I think. How is this to be explained? As I indicated in Chapter 1, meaning A can be incorporated within, and structured by, conventionalized practices generating meaning B or meaning C. Someone unfamiliar with the relevant conventions, and the subsequent transformation of meaning A, is unlikely to appreciate the significance of the natural elements taken into use. Music is a highly sophisticated, complex art in all its manifestations, and the conventions structuring musical works and practices vary considerably from culture to culture and time to time. Even if music builds on a natural foundation in its expressiveness, that expressiveness is apparent only to a listener familiar with the conventions revealing how that foundation has been built on. I offer some crude illustrations.

The emotion characteristics presented in music depend on its dynamic character—for example, on patterns of tension and release. What it is that generates a dynamic character varies considerably with the conventions governing the use of musical materials in different places and periods. In Western music after the twelfth century, the production of musical movement depends on the use of polyphony and harmony set in a tonal or modal context. A person at home only with monodic music would be in no position to

---

not because the aborigine fails to read the expressive conventions, but because, to begin with, he fails to read the pictorial ones (1980, 91).

[55] For a discussion of basic, cross-cultural structures in musical perception, see Serafine 1988 and 1989. And note that the cultural context in which music plays an expressive function needs to be treated with some care. In some cultures, for example, death might be an occasion for public celebration rather than for private grief. A person not realizing this might be surprised to find raucous, seemingly joyous music played at funerals.

< 244 >

perceive the dynamism of contrapuntal music or could easily be mistaken about its character. Similarly, a person familiar only with music in which the most tense interval is a major third is bound to be utterly distracted by much of the music of Stravinsky. Even if some intervals are naturally more tense or concordant than others, one can get a sense of the fluctuation of tension and release within a musical work only if one can feel the stability of the points of repose, and that requires an awareness of the range of intervals that might be used within the style and the relations that might hold between them. A person who cannot hear a modulation from one tonic to another can have no sense of the tonal organization of the music in question or of the contribution made to the structure of the work by the use of contrasting tonal centers. To someone raised on the major scale, almost all the intervals of the Javanese *slendro* scale sound so horribly out of tune on first hearing that no sense can be made of the different relationships holding between them. To such a person, a shift from the mode (or *patet*) of *manyura* to *nem* does not sound like a modulation at all. And, for such a person, unused from Western music to the cadential function of long-lasting, gong-punctuated structures, the colotomic pattern is likely to be missed altogether, even if the sound of gong *agung* is unmistakable. Similarly, a Javanese musician is bound to be nonplussed in considering the significance of the relation established between clapsticks, the didjeridu's fundamental, the didjeridu's first harmonic, the point of voice entry, and the point of voice exit in traditional Australian aboriginal music.

Even if the expressiveness of music is grounded in elements the experience of which may have an extracultural significance, so refined is musical practice that one can organize the musical sounds one hears only in the light of knowledge of arbitrary and quite various conventions governing the use of the basic elements of music—timbre, pitch, harmony, tempo, rhythm. In our own cultures, we imbibe this knowledge, just as we absorb a working knowledge of our native tongues, along with our mothers' milk. The conventions become transparent to us, so familiar are we with them, so that nothing could seem more natural, say, than to follow a dominant seventh with a tonic chord, though one might not know these technical names. Arbitrary conventions and natural meanings mix and mingle so that, in practice, there is no separating the one from the other, unless one self-consciously adopts the task.

If expressiveness gives music meaning, then the meaning involved is meaning of type B or C rather than of type A. It is a meaning hedged about with and transformed by mutable, arbitrary conventions. Where things are structured in such an obvious way by conventions, there is no easy way to distin-

< 245 >

guish elements appropriated for their natural significance from coincidental similarities—just as one cannot tell, merely by listening to a foreign language, whether something that sounds like "slither" has an onomatopoeic meaning or not. Music's expressiveness might be rooted in resemblances between the ways we experience musical movement and human behaviors presenting emotion characteristics in appearances, but one can be sure about the expressive character of any musical work only if one is familiar with the musical conventions that structure the musical practice or style in question.

That the expressive character of the music of cultures other than those we know might be opaque to us does not count against the theory developed here. Rather, it emphasizes that musical expressiveness, considered as a kind of meaning, is best to be regarded as of type B or C rather than of type D or E. The expressiveness of music is not always established by arbitrary association or symbolic construction, but, for all that, the natural element appropriated in the creation of musical expressiveness is controlled and structured by the conventions governing its context, so that not all music wears its expressive character on its sleeve.[56]

Disagreement in Responses

One objection raised to Kivy's contour version of the theory of musical expressiveness suggests that there is not the high level of intersubjective

---

[56] Though Kivy would reject my talk of meaning in connection with music, his explanation of the expressive opacity of the musics of different cultures is very like that I have offered; see 1980, chap. 9. He says this: "Thus, in calling expressiveness by contour 'natural,' we only mean to say that its 'conventional' aspect is relative to a wider set of conventions than merely the specific conventions of musical expressiveness, not that it is natural in the sense of perceptible to some hypothetical 'naive' listener, free of everything but the requisite biological equipment for hearing. There is no such expressiveness in music, whether or not there is anywhere else" (1980, 85). Kivy emphasizes, as I have done, that to hear music qua music (that is, qua art), not merely as sound, is to hear it in terms of the conventions applying to it. In listening to the music of another culture, we are liable to hear it through the conventions of the music of our own culture, and thereby to misunderstand it and to miss its expressive character. Kivy contrasts the monophonic nature of much Indian music with the harmonic/polyphonic style of Western music in making the point. He also rejects the possibility of our testing his theory against the responses of listeners from different cultures to natural sounds. He does so because he believes, rightly in my view, that we appreciate natural sounds aesthetically only by approaching them as if they were musical, which is to hear them via the musical conventions in which we are versed. People from different musical cultures hear natural sounds differently. Just as there can be no musically naive response to musical works qua music, equally there can be no naive aesthetic response to natural sounds. Kivy, personally, hears the call of a local bird in terms of the first four notes of the subject of one of J. S. Bach's Eight Little Fugues for Organ (1980, 92). For my part, I hear the opening of one of the songs of the European blackbird (*Turdus merula*) as recalling the first five notes of the last movement of Beethoven's Violin Concerto.

< 246 >

agreement about musical expressiveness the theory presupposes.[57] Anthony Newcomb (1984) sees considerable disagreement in descriptions of music's expressiveness not because he hears music as inexpressive but because he regards its expressiveness as ineffable, as not easily captured by language. Accounts of a given work's expressiveness differ because each listener must grope for descriptive terms when none are entirely appropriate, so it is not surprising that different listeners settle on different descriptions, all of which are inadequate to the case in hand. I have already argued against the ineffability thesis in Chapter 3. I suggest here that, if expressiveness is to be a property of musical works, there must be high agreement among qualified listeners about what these properties are. If such is the case, Newcomb does not fully appreciate the force and nature of the objection he raises, for his own position—that music is ineffably expressive—is called into question if disagreement is as widespread as he thinks it is.

Psychologists use Rorschach blots as a diagnostic tool. Their subjects report on what they see, or think of, in observing these symmetrical inkblots. Because there is no particular thing these blots signify, the response elicited reveals something of the observer's character and psychological predilections. The technique would not work, or work so well, if one were to use an unambiguously representational painting, say, because then the report would likely concern what the painting represents. This would tell us about the painting rather than about its observer. The response to the Rorschach blot is useful to the psychologist because people differ in their responses, and this is encouraged by the fact that the inkblots do not have a character that constrains or inhibits the response. A "normal" response is not normal because it is especially appropriate to the particular inkblot, or even because it is the same as that given by other respondents; it is so because it does not reveal a psychology that is statistically unusual, such as an obsession with shrimp.

Observers might report their experiences in the face of a given object of perception. Whether those responses tell us something about the nature of the perceptual object or about the respondents depends importantly on the level of agreement in those responses. This remains true even in those cases in which the properties have a relational component in that they depend on the background, skill, or capacities of the observers. Only creatures with perceptors sensitive to certain bands of light, and with appropriate interests in certain kinds of perceptual discriminations, could perceive colors, but we attribute the greenness to the grass, rather than to the perceptual experience

[57] See Taruskin 1982, Newcomb 1984, and Neubauer 1986.

< 247 >

of the observer, because of the high level of agreement about this color property among different observers under roughly standard conditions. In the absence of a coincidence in responses, we take those responses as revealing something about the observers, not something about the thing observed.

To argue that the expressiveness is a property of the musical work is not to deny that it is a complex property with a relational component. Just as the greenness of grass is apparent only to creatures with perceptors of a certain sort and with concerns that depend on their making color discriminations, so the expressiveness of music is apparent only to someone who brings to the experience of the music a certain (cultural) background and interest. But to argue that the expressiveness is a property of the musical work *must be* to deny that there is complete diversity in identifications of music's expressive character. It would be appropriate to attribute the expressiveness to the music, as opposed to the listener, only if there were sufficient agreement among suitably qualified listeners to establish interpersonal standards for correct and incorrect responses. If there were no such agreement, talk of expressiveness would reveal, not the nature of the musical work, but rather the idiosyncratic psychology of each listener. Such talk would be not descriptive but symptomatic. With this in mind, I think that Kivy is right to defend the claim that there is interpersonal agreement about the expressive character of musical works, and I believe that Newcomb is too sanguine in assuming that he can continue to maintain that musical works are expressive while denying that there is significant agreement among listeners as to the nature of that expressiveness.

In fact, the charge that listeners do not agree about such matters counts, not only against a theory such as Kivy and I have espoused, but also against any of the theories of musical expressiveness discussed previously. To hold that music symbolizes or otherwise denotes emotions, or that it represents them, or that it can be heard as a direct expression of the composer's feelings, or that its expressiveness consists in its power to move the listener, is to hold a view about *musical* expressiveness (as a complex, relational property) only if one supposes that there is a degree of agreement about what it is that music expresses. To suppose that expressiveness is properly to be predicated of musical works, as these theories do, is to be committed to holding that there is significant agreement about the truth of such attributions. Each of these theories takes as given that expressiveness is attributed to musical works and attempts to elucidate the truth conditions for such attributions. The conflict between the theories I have been considering concerns the analysis of that predicative use, concerns the truth makers for such attributions. So, to suggest that there is no interpersonal agreement about the expressive character

< 248 >

of musical works is to challenge a supposition common to these theories and thereby is to reject as mistaken the enterprise of analysis in which they engage. Hanslick, for one, recognizes this. He appeals to the "disagreement thesis" to deny that music can express emotion.

Kivy's (1990b) rejection of Hanslick's disagreement thesis is blunt (also see Kivy 1980, in which Gurney as well as Hanslick is identified as an advocate). Simply, Kivy asserts, it is false to say that people do not agree in characterizing the expressiveness of musical works. Kivy's confidence is born as much of his grasp of the conceptual point as of his examination of other listeners. Pratt (1931) also gives short shrift to Hanslick's claims, but, as a psychologist, he sees the issue as simply empirical. Pratt (1952) cites an experiment in which there is greater than 90 percent agreement about the expressive character of certain musical passages when subjects are invited to match a list of adjectives to those passages. Swanwick (1973) also records a significant level of agreement, and Evans (1990, 62) regards the high level of agreement as widely overlooked.

A skeptic might reject the force of the conceptual point and challenge the empirical evidence; after all, the argument will come to be one about the interpretation and significance of *degrees* of nonconformity among listeners' responses to, and descriptions of, music. It might be noted that the many experiments conducted by psychologists in the hope of understanding how we listen to music are notoriously difficult to interpret. Often the subject is forced to choose between alternatives specified by the experimenter, so the range of responses is restricted. Often no attempt is made to distinguish between responses the subject would recognize as personal and those intended to characterize an objective property of the music. Frequently, subjects are invited to respond to types of music with which they are not well acquainted (see Swanwick 1973).

Still, it is undeniable that there is some variety, for any work, in the accounts different listeners might offer of its expressive character. How is this to be explained (or explained away)? Four points are relevant, initially, to an attempt to dismiss such disagreements as merely apparent: (i) Not all listeners are properly qualified (by being acquainted with the conventions applying to the given category of music). The reports of unqualified listeners can be discounted as unlikely to reflect an understanding and appreciation of the music in question.[58] (ii) Reports based on private associations are to

---

[58] This also is stressed by Kivy (1980, 147). Just what the qualifications are is a question hotly debated; I address that question in Chapter 7. In brief, I think the qualified listener must be at home with the style or idiom of the work; perhaps also with other works of the genre, the

< 249 >

be discounted. If now I am delighted by the slow movement of Beethoven's Symphony No. 3 because I happened to be listening to it when, in the past, I received news of my lottery win, then my delight is not to be counted as a response to the music as such. Put another way, the variety of response labeled by Kivy as "they are playing our song" is to be dismissed, since responses of this type result from private associations that such music calls to mind rather than from attention to features of the music. The listener must attend to the music as such and must offer her description as an account of the music's character. (iii) Different performances of a given work might not emphasize the same features. Klemperer's and Toscanini's interpretations of Beethoven differ markedly (Davies 1987). To the extent that the expressive character of a work may be affected by the performers' interpretation, it can be necessary to discount descriptions of a given work where those descriptions are concerned with factors influenced mainly by the particular interpretation of a given performance. Only descriptions characterizing the work, as opposed to features distinctive to a particular interpretation, are at issue; or, alternatively, only descriptions of a single interpretation are to be compared. (iv) Some judgments that seem to be about the music should properly be understood, instead, as observations about its composer.[59]

If these points are granted as restricting the range of responses to be considered, it is still likely that a variety of responses will be recorded by different listeners describing the same work. The debate now concerns the level of specificity at which agreement is to be sought. Those who hold that musical works express emotions with great precision would be inclined to regard as incompatible descriptions of the same work as both sad and gloomy. This difference would be seen as marking a significant disagreement. In contrast, those who hold that musical works express only broad categories of emotion, such as sadness or happiness, would regard these two reports as evidencing high agreement, since sadness and gloom belong together in the same genus. If music, in being expressive, should be heard as drawing with a broad brush, then it is plausible to find very little disagreement in judgments about the general expressive character of musical works. Differences in the choice of words, as between "sad" and "gloomy," might be dismissed then as cosmetic. Few qualified listeners would describe the overture to Mo-

---

composer, the period, and the culture. Such matters are well-described in Levinson 1990b and 1992b.

[59] For example, to describe a work as original might be to say more about the composer's skill and timing than about the work as such; see Kivy 1990a, 178–179. For a rejection of this thesis and of the view of the ontology of the musical work it presupposes, see Levinson 1980 and 1990a, chap. 10. For a general discussion of the issues, see Davies 1991a.

< 250 >

zart's *Marriage of Figaro* as expressive of sadness; though these listeners might choose to describe the overture with different emotion terms, they would be terms denoting feelings or emotions belonging in the "happy," not the "sad," category.

Kivy (1989) conducts his debate with Newcomb in the manner just indicated. Newcomb (1984) sees no virtue in one-word descriptions of music. Kivy replies that this is like objecting that Tarski's theory of truth is trivial because he talks only about the sentence "Snow is white." Kivy denies that he believes that "sad" is the limit of the expressive description a qualified listener might offer of the slow movement of Beethoven's *Eroica*; there also are elements of the funereal and the consoling to be heard. But he attacks Newcomb's view that music expresses subtle expressive properties (SEPs) and the conclusion drawn by Newcomb from this: that Kivy's theory is inadequate because it cannot countenance such expressive properties. Kivy defends his position, which accommodates both gross expressive properties (GEPs), such as sadness and happiness, and moderate expressive properties (MEPs), such as that of being funereal or consoling, but excludes SEPs from the realm of musical expression.[60] His informed philosophical opinions when combined with his musical intuitions lead him to the conclusion that SEPs are not expressed by music and, hence, that his theory is not the weaker for excluding them. Kivy develops an ad hominem argument: Newcomb's counterexamples are ones in which words or dramatic content, as in opera, allow for the expression of rather specific feelings. Kivy accepts that, where words are added to music, what otherwise would be GEPs or MEPs are transformed into SEPs, but he denies that this shows his account of the expressive possibilities of pure music to be mistaken.

---

[60] A MEP is usually a more specific or complexly qualified version of a GEP. By contrast, a SEP is likely to be a particular instance of an emotion, tied in its individuality to the context of the person experiencing it, the detail of its particular object, and so on. Newcomb's SEPs are ineffable in instrumental music because we have no direct access to what makes them the distinctive individuals they are; we have no idea, for example, of the emotional object of the feeling expressed in the music. Newcomb thinks, that is, that the emotions expressed in music are no less specific than are actual instances of object-directed emotions, though the music indicates no particular object or context. It is the possibility of SEPs of this type in instrumental music that Kivy rejects as incoherent. In my opinion he is right to do so. Note: One would err in equating Platonic attitudes, which are more intimately linked to specific emotional objects than are some other emotions, with SEPs on these grounds. Platonic attitudes might be GEPs, MEPs, or SEPs. If instrumental music might sometimes express Platonic attitudes, as Levinson argues (1990a, chap. 14), it expresses them as GEPs or MEPs but not as SEPs. It is clear from his account that the hope Levinson hears expressed in Mendelssohn's *Hebrides* Overture is not a particular instance of hope taking a particular object. As he describes it, hope is expressed as a GEP or MEP.

< 251 >

The relevance of this debate to the present context should be plain enough. Newcomb denies that there is intersubjective agreement among listeners as to the expressive properties of musical works because he takes instrumental music to be expressive of SEPs, that is, of fine-grained species of emotions. At this level of description, listeners' accounts of the expressiveness of musical works do not agree. Kivy pursues his argument against Newcomb by arguing that, when one appreciates that music expresses only GEPs or MEPs, the disagreement claimed by Newcomb is by no means evident.[61] He says that language is no less suited to the description of music's expressiveness than it is adequate to the description of mundane emotions in ordinary contexts. Thus he rejects the ineffability thesis (or the implications drawn from it), both as a claim about music, in particular, and about emotions, in general.

Scruton's Version of the Theory

A theory outwardly similar to mine and Kivy's has been offered by Scruton.[62] I am in sympathy with Scruton's account, but I have reservations about its formulation. Scruton appears, at first, to jettison the idea that music has an identifiable expressive character and to concentrate instead on the idea that music is expressive tout court. He claims that music is expressive without expressing any particular emotion at all. There is expression without there being expression of emotions (or of anything else). The verb "to express" is used intransitively in connection with music. This use also occurs in other contexts; we might describe a face or gesture as expressive without taking it to express anything in particular. Where such intransitive expression is involved, the problems that go with characterizing musical emotions do not arise because no emotions are expressed.

Against Scruton, Neubauer (1986) notes that the *Oxford English Dictionary* does not recognize an intransitive use of the verb "to express." Philosophical issues are rarely to be settled by reference to dictionaries, but one might expect that, if the use identified by Scruton is a common one, it would be recorded as such. An adverbial form is noted in dictionaries. Something can be done expressively, and in such a case it might not be to the point to ask what is expressed, because the adverbial use draws attention to the

---

[61] Kivy (1980, 47–48) indicates that he is not too much bothered by the difference between one critic's describing a work as expressive of "noble grief" and another's describing it as expressive of "abject sorrow."

[62] See Scruton 1974, especially 78–83, as well as 1980b and 1983. For a discussion, see Sharpe 1975.

< 252 >

flamboyant style of the action rather than to the feeling or thought given expression. Similarly, one might describe something as expressive without indicating what is expressed. But that we might focus on the style of expression does not entail that there can be expression in the absence of something's being expressed. In describing a face, say, as expressive, one is saying that it clearly or strongly reveals or betrays feelings, moods, or attitudes. One is noting something about the face's potential or character, a something that presupposes the possibility of a transitive use of the verb "to express." The attribution is not of a feelingless, thoughtless expression but of the *manner* in which feelings, moods, or attitudes usually are expressed by the face in question. To say that a musical work is expressive is not to say that, while the expression remains, like the Cheshire cat's smile, emotions are absent from it. Rather, it is to say that the expression (with its identifiable character) is a significant feature of the work. One might then have many (innocuous) reasons for not being specific in one's account of the character of that expressiveness and one might have reason to stress the style or manner of expression, but this does not mean one cannot talk about what is expressed.

As Scruton develops his view (1980b and 1983), he acknowledges this point. He aims, he says, not so much to deny that we can indicate the way music is expressive but to deny that, in being expressive, the music is expressive by virtue of standing to an occurrent emotion as expressing it. He suggests that, while using "express" in the intransitive sense, one could go on to identify what is expressed as, say, "sadness" without thereby implying that someone feels or felt the sadness given expression in the music. Scruton notes that a face might be sad-looking without expressing a sadness that is felt, and he takes this as revealing a close connection between the transitive and intransitive notions of expression.

This development of his view involves a shift of ground, I think. As first introduced, the intransitive view of expression rules as illegitimate the question "what is expressed?" Now though, it appears that the intransitive use allows for the recognition of an expressive character in music, such as sadness, but rules as illegitimate our taking that character to be the expression of a felt sadness. The first story of intransitiveness is not fully convincing, as I have suggested. The second seems redundant. There is no virtue in describing the second view as one about an intransitive type of expression, since it allows that the music presents an identifiable expressive character.

The detail of Scruton's theory brings it nearer to the one I have defended. He claims that there is an irreducible analogy between our hearing or seeing an expressive character (paying no heed to felt emotions) in voices or human

< 253 >

gesture and our hearing expressiveness in music.[63] His is an advance on the sui generis theory of musical expressiveness, which he criticizes, in that he allows that musical expressiveness depends ultimately on the similarity between our experience of musical expressiveness and our experiencing the human voice or gesture as possessing an expressive character. But, with his insistence on the irreducibility of the analogy experienced between the two, he stops short of explaining how music might invite this regard.[64]

By contrast with Scruton, I have tried to draw out the analogy between our experience of music and of human behavior that presents emotion characteristics in its appearance, both in the discussion of emotion characteristics in appearances and in the account of musical movement. Perhaps Scruton would accept my efforts while maintaining that, in the last analysis, there remains an unbridgeable gap between our experience of musical expressiveness and our recognition of expressiveness in human faces and gestures. He stresses (1983) that, whereas faces are naturally seen as bearing an expressive character because they (also) express felt emotions, music (and willow trees) cannot stand in the same relation to felt emotions. He implies that it is for this reason that the analogy between the two always falls short. I take up that issue now.

Is the Favored Theory an Improvement on the Sui Generis One?

Earlier I criticized the view that sees musical expressiveness as sui generis on the grounds that it answers the question "Why do we hear expressiveness in music, when music feels nothing, lacks beliefs, and so on?" by saying "We just do. Funny world, folks." It might be thought that the theory I have outlined is open to a similar objection. I have claimed that we hear expressiveness in music because we experience music as presenting emotion characteristics in appearances, just as we see emotion characteristics in the behaviors of people. To the extent that I have implied the irreducible similarity of these kinds of experiences, it might be thought that the theory fails

---

[63] Urmson (1973) anticipates this view but, wrongly in my view, claims to be analyzing musical depiction, not expression.

[64] Scruton is criticized on this score by Budd (1985a, 144–148 and 1985b); also see Mew 1985a. I would level a similar complaint against Shiner (1982), Best (1985), and Evans (1990). David Best stresses that we no more take artworks merely for physical objects than we take people merely for physical bodies (1985, 109–110). I agree, but I think our reaction to artworks stands in need of discussion, whereas Best says, "All we can say is that such a response is immediate, primitive, natural" (1985, 180). Evans emphasizes that judgments of expressiveness are learned and refined rather than primitive, but he denies that such judgments are subject to truth or appropriateness conditions.

< 254 >

finally to be convincing. Someone might always hear the lowness, slowness, thick texture, minor key, and discordant appoggiaturas of a musical work yet fail to hear the sadness of the work. If I reason with such a person, I will suggest to him that he hear these musical features as like the human behaviors that generate emotion characteristics. But he might always agree with me that the music possesses the features to which I draw his attention while, nevertheless, he fails to hear the music as expressive. To the extent that the justification of attributions of expressiveness to music falls short of entailment in this way, it might be thought that the account I have defended fares no better than the sui generis theory that was rejected.

Benjamin Tilghman (1984, particularly 175–178), raises such an objection to Kivy's view. According to Tilghman, the experience of art as expressive is irreducibly like the experience of human expressions (of occurrent emotions); that is, artistic expressiveness is not grounded in any similarities between human physiognomy and the "physiognomy" of art. An analysis such as Kivy recommends leaves the philosophical problem untouched, he says, because the similarity must be described by the very language the resemblance is supposed to underwrite. In describing the music as expressive one describes it not merely as moving but as acting. The attempt to ground the analogy appears convincing only if one assumes in the description of the music what is at issue; namely, that the music is an agent and, as such, a potential bearer of expressiveness.

Despite these criticisms, however, I am not sure that the theory defended by Tilghman is far from the one he attacks. It may be true, ultimately, that the experience of expressiveness is grounded in irreducible experiences of similarity between, for example, spatial and musical movement, or musical movement and intentional human action. For all that, though, there is philosophically interesting territory to be explored between the experience of artistic expressiveness and the irreducible experiences of similarity in which, finally, it is rooted. And it is just that territory with which the theories presented by Kivy and myself are concerned. Tilghman himself (1984, 184) allows that, to take an analogous case, the experience of seeing a duck in the duck-rabbit figure is not irreducible as is the experience of seeing a dot in the picture as the duck's eye. Here he allows that there could be a point to an analytical approach to the phenomenon, even if at some stage one comes to irreducible givens.[65]

---

[65] I find something odd in Tilghman's complaint that Kivy leaves the philosophical problem untouched when Tilghman's professed aim is to show that there is no such problem (see 1984, 169).

< 255 >

Now, as I have described it, musical expressiveness is an aspect (or an emergent property, or a supervenient property) depending for its character on the structure of musical movement. In pursuing Tilghman's objection, we need to consider the case of the person who is deaf to music's expressiveness but whose hearing is not defective. He hears the musical movement but does not experience it as analogous to human behavior and denies any expressive character to the music (while accepting that, were it to correspond to behavior of the appropriate sort, the musical movement would be expressive of an emotion characteristic in its appearance). This person does not dispute the evidence to which I refer in arguing that the music is sad, say, but he fails to experience the music as I do, as sad. If there is no further analogical evidence I can adduce, then all the grounds by which I support my judgment that the music is expressive fall short of convincing my interlocutor.

A first point: There is no way of ruling out the possibility of aspect-blindness. Someone might have perfect vision and yet fail to see the duck-aspect of Jastrow's duck-rabbit figure. Given that expressiveness is an aspect of music, grounded in first-order musical properties, neither is there a way of ruling out the possibility that someone might be incapable of hearing expressiveness in music while he hears the movement others describe as having an expressive character. It does not follow from this that there is an inherent inadequacy in the kind of evidence one offers for one's judgment as to the expressive character of the music. The failure, if there is one, lies in the blindness shown by the other.[66]

Kivy (1980, 148) is inclined to deal with the case of the expression-deaf person by denying its possibility. Or, rather, he suggests that the person who fails to hear expressiveness in the music should be equally deaf and blind to the expressiveness revealed in the voices, actions, or appearances of people. Someone who could recognize the resemblance between the music and human behavior, but who could not hear the expressiveness, would strike us as a person who did not understand the meaning of emotion terms. Expressiveness is a seamless web, Kivy holds, in that there would be no grounds for believing that a person could recognize it in the appearance of a Saint Bernard, for example, if he could not also recognize it in music.

As I understand the point, it might be put this way: one could not teach a child the meaning of a word such as "sad" by dealing solely with cases of sadness in music; one could not teach the primary meaning of a word

---

[66] Though one might teach the expression-deaf person correct uses of expressive predicates regarding music, the basis for her usage differs from the norm. She must remember or infer the presence of the relevant property, whereas this is heard ordinarily.

< 256 >

through consideration of cases to which the word applies only in a secondary use. Such is the relation between the primary and secondary use, though, that a mastery of the primary use brings the secondary use with it as a bonus, so to speak. For that reason, one criterion of someone's having mastered the primary use is his ability to go on to employ the secondary use once he becomes aware of its possibility. The person who cannot hear the expressiveness of music is, therefore, not someone who has failed merely to master the secondary use; he is someone who, in this failure, might be judged not to have grasped the primary use either.

There is a different way of developing the argument. Moravcsik (1982) suggests that some judgments presuppose that the matter judged is approached from a particular "emotional" stance.[67] For example, one can assess something to be futile only if one is in a certain mood or emotional state of purpose-seeking and searching. Applying this view to judgments concerning music's expressiveness, we can note that a certain stance to music is presupposed—namely, the animating tendency described by Kivy. For a person who does not adopt that stance, musical movement is not heard as like human action and expressiveness is not heard in the music. That viewpoint is one applying not just to the musical case but to the general context in which one deals with fellow humans. Without it, the actions of others appear merely as movements and one takes others to be automata rather than agents. The person who is blind to the expressiveness of music is someone incapable of approaching music from the animating perspective. But now, that suggests that the same person is also incapable of taking the same stance with respect to human beings or to the products of human intentional action, such as utterances, for the tendency should operate in either case. Given these considerations, the counterexample posed by deafness to music's expressive properties may not be as philosophically coherent as first appears.

The possibility (if there is one) of aspect-deafness concerning music's expressiveness illustrates this: reason-giving always ends, as anyone faced with a child's repeated "why"s appreciates; there is always a point at which reasons of the required type come to a halt, so that one can say no more than "That is the way it is for us." So it is for the theory I have offered above. I can give no further reasons why we should experience music as like the behavior that in people generates emotion characteristics in appearances;

---

[67] For other relevant discussion of the centrality of desires or "concerns" to the identity of one's emotions or feelings, see Robinson 1983a, Stocker 1983 and 1987, Gordon 1986, and Roberts 1988.

< 257 >

beyond the fact that this seems the way music is experienced, I can give no reason that would satisfy the person deaf or blind to experiences of that kind.

That all arguments come to an end somewhere, however, does not mean that a philosophical argument can end wherever the proponent might please with some statement of (allegedly brute) fact. I claim to have taken the argument well beyond the point at which the sui generis position finds its foundation; I regard the question "How might music express emotions it does not feel, that take no emotional objects, and so on?" to require an answer. In the theory developed here I have tried to show that the question as posed can be met by arguing that music is expressive of the emotional character of appearances that are not felt and are not object-directed. A philosophically satisfactory solution to the problem posed by music's expressiveness will find bedrock somewhere, I allow, but for my preference not at a point leaving as its residue a philosophically intractable mystery. The sui generis account of music's expressiveness gives up in a manner that acknowledges and celebrates the mystery without resolving it, whereas the theory I have presented offers an answer, I believe.

Kivy's Evolutionary Story

As I said earlier, reasons of a given kind must run out somewhere. I hope they do so at a point at which our common intuitions are rooted, so that disagreement might be brought to an end. Sometimes, if not all issues are settled, it might be possible to appeal to a different order of reasons, when considerations of the first sort expire, as a way of continuing the debate. In effect, Kivy shifts the ground of the argument in this fashion. Rather than appealing solely to the sort of reasons that might be seen as justifying an experience of music's expressing this or that emotion, he appeals to evolution to explain why we might hear expressiveness in music. Rather than pursuing the argument about what in music is standardly to be experienced as analogous to what kind of human behaviors, Kivy turns to providing an explanation of a different order: he considers why we might be disposed by evolution to hear musical movement as irreducibly similar to human behaviors. (One might see this as the way to continue the debate against an expression-deaf person who is unconvinced by the weight of testimony that she differs from the norm.) Now, I am not sure that the theory for which I have argued depends for its endorsement on one's accepting the success of this shift to a different arena of debate, but I outline Kivy's argument for its undoubted, if speculative, interest.

In the account of expressiveness in music developed in *The Corded Shell*,

< 258 >

Kivy appeals to the notion of resemblance, treated as a conceptual primitive, and couples this with the idea that a psychological principle leads us to pick out some resemblances above others and to give a direction to the relation of resemblance. This has led to the charge that Kivy fails in his account to clarify the notion of musical expressiveness.[68] Kivy acknowledges that his notion of resemblance was "rather pallid" and now (1989, 172–175; 1990a, 2–10) attempts to give it color by offering a more detailed, though conjectural, account of the psychological mechanisms that motivate us to animate the experience afforded by music. He suggests that we are "hard-wired" to animate our perceptual experiences because of evolutionary advantages that come from doing so. In the case of vision, we are likely, for example, to take a stick for a snake, because this is safer than being indifferent to things that look like snakes. We are inclined, that is, "to perceptually, as it were, shoot first and ask questions afterwards" (Kivy 1989, 173). The same psychological mechanism operates for hearing, but this sense modality has no built-in "startle mechanism." We are not inclined to mistake the music's expressiveness for an instance of real expressiveness, as we mistake sticks for snakes. "In the sense of hearing, [the psychological mechanism] seems, at least in the musical cases, to take the form of a subliminal 'animation' process—a kind of 'living background noise' that, in turn, causes us to hear (among other things) expressive properties in music and, no doubt, other sounds. . . . [It is] a subliminal vestige of a startle mechanism that once was as vivid and conscious as its visual counterpart is at present" (1989, 174–175). The asymmetry between the senses is explained mainly by reference to the dominating importance of sight. Though sounds do not demand interpretation so insistently as do visual patterns, there remains a compulsion to make sounds linguistically meaningful—to hear sound as human utterance.

It seems to me that Kivy labors hard to little effect in distinguishing the visual from the auditory as he does. Even if it is true that, for our species, sight tends to dominate, I think that we are no less liable to take the sound of one thing for the sound of another than to take the sight of one thing for the sight of another. We are as likely to take a strange click in the dark for the cocking of a gun as to take a stick for a snake. If this does not happen in the musical case, it is because we are secure in our beliefs about the context and source of the sound. But in the same way, we do not normally mistake a portrait for the person depicted in it. These observations do not count against Kivy's claim that we animate our perceptual experiences but rather against his connecting this tendency directly to the possibility of perceptual

---

[68] See Budd 1981 and 1991 and Hanfling 1992; also Tilghman 1984.

< 259 >

error. Knowing that we are looking at a painting, and not a person, nevertheless we animate what we see. For example, we say that the person pictured is looking to her left, though we know perfectly well that paint pigment cannot see.

Perhaps Kivy takes the line he does because he fears that, if the tendency to animate our perceptual experience is not tied to the possibility of perceptual mistakes, it can no longer be justified as producing evolutionary advantages. If so, I believe he may be mistaken. Often it is the case, I think, that a "mechanism" with an evolutionary function best serves that function when we possess it as not linked directly to the ends it serves. Curiosity, tempered by good sense, is a means to ends with evolutionary advantages for us (to knowledge of things that might help our survival, for example), but curiosity functions for us as an end in its own right. We are curious about all sorts of things a knowledge of which may have no survival value. Curiosity might have survival value in general, but for particular cases the exercise of curiosity might have no direct connection with promoting our survival as individuals, or as a species. There is an obvious reason why, as an evolutionary strategy, it might be better to foster curiosity for its own sake than to tie it to the pursuit of direct payoffs for the individual or the species: we cannot easily anticipate which bits of knowledge will later prove useful.

I suspect that it is possible to extend the point made above to cover our tendency to animate our perceptual experiences. In general terms, there is an evolutionary advantage to our acting this way—not just to avoid the dangers posed by snakes but because we are social species which, to survive and cooperate, must presuppose that it is dealing with like beings, not automata. But the "mechanism" operates, in particular cases, independently of its evolutionary target. We are inclined to animate our perceptual experiences not only where we believe that it is appropriate to do so but also under some circumstances where we do not believe this to be the case. One such circumstance is provided by the contemplation of artworks—by novels and paintings no less than music. In these cases, as Kivy astutely observes, it is bound to be important to us that we recognize the works as the product of human efforts and, hence, as invested with human significance, even if we are not at all inclined to mistake paintings for people or musical phrases for linguistic utterances.

Some Differences between Kivy's Account and Mine

I have suggested that Kivy and I present versions of the same basic theory. Our positions are not identical, though. Here I mention three differences: (i) Kivy sometimes implies (wrongly I think) that music expresses emotions

< 260 >

rather than presenting emotion characteristics in its aural appearance; (ii) Kivy is less inclined than am I to allow that Platonic attitudes might be expressed in music; (iii) I believe Kivy to be mistaken in denying that music never is about the emotions expressed in it. There also is a marked difference between our views on the character of the listener's response to music's expressiveness, but that is a matter I pursue at length in the following chapter.

First, Kivy represents his conclusion as follows: "We have some idea . . . of just what emotions music can be expressive of: they are not the Platonic attitudes but the garden-variety emotions in their nonspecific form" (1990a, 181). Music cannot express those emotions or feelings, such as hope, that necessarily are cognitive and lack distinctive behavioral expressions, but it can express garden-variety emotions, which (as Kivy presents them) are occurrent emotions that take objects. Music does not express particular, token instances of such emotions but rather the template or type of such an emotion.

The quotation suggests that Kivy takes music to express a special variety of felt, object-directed emotions, for the garden-variety emotions *are* felt, object-directed, and tied to beliefs, desires, and other cognitive states. If this is his view, his theory differs, after all, from the one I promote. As I hear it, music does not express emotions, not even in a "nonspecific" form. Instead, it presents emotion characteristics in appearances. Such appearances do not express occurrent emotions; the face of the Saint Bernard looks sad, but it does not express garden-variety sadness. Emotion characteristics in appearances are not garden-variety emotions as Kivy describes them, but they are related to garden-variety emotions in that the behaviors producing the former are like the behaviors giving natural or primary expression to the latter in other contexts.[69]

Of course, not too much weight should be put on a single, brief passage. But I would not draw attention to it were it merely an infelicitous slip of the pen. Kivy writes often as if it is some kind of ordinary emotion that is expressed in music, not an expressive appearance that is presented, so it is easy for the reader to become confused about the character of Kivy's thesis and its consequences.[70]

---

[69] Note that Kivy argues (1980, chap. 12) that occurrent emotions have characteristic behavioral expressions, but he does not develop, as I tried to do, an account of the relationship between such behaviors and those generating emotion characteristics in appearances. Kivy does emphasize, however, that the expressive character of appearances is parasitic on behavior expressive of felt emotions.

[70] Price (1981 and 1992) makes the point against Kivy that the animation of music is not possible because music is so unlike the human body that it would be nonsensical to imagine of music that it is living and in sorrow. Such imagining would be on a par with imagining the square root of two to be red. Obviously Price here takes Kivy to be claiming that the emotion

< 261 >

The aforementioned quotation points to a further difference between Kivy's position and my own. Kivy denies that music expresses the Platonic attitudes—hope, envy, admiration, and the like. As noted earlier in this chapter, he concedes (1990a) that music might express pomposity but regards this as the exception proving the rule. For my part, I am inclined to be less dogmatic on this matter. I agree with Kivy that the standard case of musical expression is one in which the appearances of emotion are apparent in patterns of musical movement, and that the emotion characteristics that are recognizable solely from such public displays are limited in their number mainly to the sadness and happiness types. The point of current disagreement concerns the possibility of sophistications on this basic mode of expression. Kivy denies that the Platonic attitudes could be presented musically, while I am less sure of this.

I have commented:

> It is arguable that, *as feelings*, emotions have natural progressions; for example, from slightly hysterical gaiety to fearful apprehension, to shock, to horror, to gathering resolution, to confrontation with sorrow, to acceptance, to resignation, to serenity. Such progressions might be used by the composer to articulate in his music emotions other than those that can be worn by appearances without regard to feelings. Thus, by judiciously ordering the emotion-characteristics presented in an extended musical work the composer can express in his music those emotional states not susceptible to presentation in mere appearances. These emotional states belong naturally within the progression of emotions whose characteristic appearances are given in the music. In this way hope, for example, may be expressed in music, although hope cannot be presented as the emotion-characteristic in an appearance. Thus the range of emotions that can be expressed in music, that music can be said "to be," goes beyond the range of emotion-characteristics that can be worn by appearances. Nevertheless, the expression of such emotional states as hope in a musical work depends directly upon and is controlled by the emotion-characteristics in sound presented in the musical work. Before hope can be expressed in a musical work that work must have sufficient length and expressive complexity to permit the emotions presented in its "appearance" to form a progression in which hope occurs naturally. (Davies 1980, 78)

---

is present in the music, not merely as the expressive character of its appearance, but as an experience. Such a reading is mistaken, I believe, but Kivy's presentation sometimes invites it.

< 262 >

It may be, I suggest, that there are predictable progressions of emotional states or feelings, established naturally or by convention. Just as music might present the characteristic of an emotion in its aural appearance, so too it might present the appearance of a pattern of feelings through the order of its expressive development. If the outline of the pattern is sufficiently distinctive and complex, it may be that it is appropriate to "fill in" missing elements. For example, if hope belongs within the expressive pattern developed in the music, hope should be heard as indicated in the music. Two further points: (i) As mentioned previously, I think that Platonic attitudes such as envy could not be presented in instrumental music. In part this is because I doubt that there is any distinctive pattern of emotions in which envy is a natural element. The argument I have offered, if it works, is not to be generalized as admitting the musical expression of all Platonic attitudes. (ii) Earlier I noted that several writers claim that emotions have a dynamic pattern in their sensational aspect, and that music might generate a similar dynamic pattern. I doubt that this is the case usually. I wonder, though, if these writers might not be more concerned, if unwittingly, with relations between successive emotional states rather than with patterns internal to any particular emotion. If they are, I see their arguments as having some force.

Levinson agrees with the thrust of my view, but he says this: "Davies is unduly pessimistic in denying that there are subtle behavioral/figural/postural manifestations that might characterize one who is hopeful, particularly at peak moments." Levinson would not restrict the range of relevant contextual features to matters of natural progression, since "there are other means by which a passage's relation to other passages, to the piece as a whole, or even to passages outside the piece might bring its specific character into relief or (more accurately) invest it with that character" (1990a, 357). I remain pessimistic, as Levinson does not, that hope has a characteristic mode of behavioral expression.[71] But I am inclined to agree with Levinson's second point. In Chapter 1 I noted types of meaning D that operate in music, including instrumental music. For example, through quotation of or allusion to a melody, an instrumental work might import the textual, dramatic, or other associations of that tune. Such cases are not commonplace but, where they do occur, a context rich in cognitive content might be created within such a work. Music's symbolic potential might be used to load a work with materials that embed its expressive content in a matrix that invests that expressive content with more subtlety, definition, and cross-relation than otherwise

---

[71] Also see Day (1969), who denies that hope involves characteristic sensations or physical symptoms.

< 263 >

would be the case. One way music might plug into (to use Levinson's termi-nology) the kinds of contexts in which hope finds expression is through the marriage of such meaning D as it permits and the meaning B it presents expressively; or, to use Kivy's terms, it might be in this manner that music's "gross expressive properties" are transformed into "medium expressive properties."

Kivy is adamant in denying that music can express hope, but there are remarks of his suggesting he could, if he chose, concede the possibility of such expression. He allows (1980, 103–108) that a text can particularize the expressiveness of a work (not merely that of a character depicted in the work). Later he also allows that purely instrumental works might (properly) bring words to the listener's mind: "Because the musical audiences of Bux-tehude, or Pachelbel, or J. S. Bach connected particular chorale melodies with particular texts—not just consciously but internally, in their blood and bones—the composers could rely on the introduction of these melodies into their music, even without the words, to produce an expressive effect beyond merely what the musical contour and non-textual conventions might pro-vide" (1980, 134–135). It seems to me that these two points concede all that Levinson might want when he claims that music sometimes can hook into matters providing a sufficiently rich cognitive context for the expression of Platonic attitudes. Of course, Kivy could always deny that this happens in the particular case discussed by Levinson, Mendelssohn's *Hebrides* Over-ture, but he might be open to a charge of inconsistency were he to deny the general possibility for which Levinson argues.

A third difference between Kivy's views and mine comes to this: Kivy has always been passionate in denying that music is *about* anything; he rejects the view that it *refers* to emotions or *means* anything (for example, 1980, 117–118; 1990a, 193–195). It is not difficult to see why he would hold this view if he thinks that music is expressive in presenting emotion character-istics in its "physiognomy." The behavior productive of emotion characteris-tics in human appearances is like the behavior giving primary (rather than secondary or tertiary) expression to an emotion. Primary modes of expres-sion might be taught, rather than being instinctual, and might be convention-alized to a degree (as allowed in Chapter 4), but we would regard them as possessing meaning of type A rather than of type C, D, or E. Similarly, the corresponding behavior that creates an appearance with an emotion charac-teristic is usually fallen into, not consciously contrived. Reference, or deno-tative meaning, must be intentionally achieved. So it seems to follow that, usually, nothing is meant by an emotion characteristic in an appearance. As Kivy reminds us, the sadness of a Saint Bernard's appearance does not mean

< 264 >

anything, does not involve reference to sadness. Now, if music is expressive as is the Saint Bernard's appearance, it should also follow that, in being sad, say, music is not about the sadness it presents.

Such reasoning has an initial plausibility but strikes me as mistaken. Music does not merely present emotion; it "comments," or may "comment," on the emotions so expressed. I suggested in Chapter 1 how this might be the case. Meaning A might be appropriated, thereby becoming meaning B or meaning C, depending on the way it operates. Meaning B and meaning C involve intentional use and are referential. For instance, the spots of acne have meaning A, but if I were so unkind as to present a spotty-faced student to the class as an example of the acned condition, the student's spots would refer the class to the spots of acne through my use of them (Davies 1990). Similarly, Saint Bernards do not mean anything by their appearance, but a sculptor who chooses to make a statue of a dog may intend that expressive appearance to refer to the emotion it presents. And even if she does not, the work might have an unintended referential character, just as a painting might have an unintended representational character (see Chapter 2).

Musical works are shaped with certain effects in mind. Composers more often than not are successful in their intentions; mostly they make their works to have the properties those works display. Were this not so, we would not be interested in musical works (as distinct from natural or other sounds), and we would not be interested in those works as the creations of their composers, as we are. Composers are rarely indifferent to the expressive character of the materials they shape. Even if the composer does not manufacture the expressive potential of the materials she uses, she does put that expressive potential to work. Her choice of sounds with one expressive potential rather than another suggests that it is not inappropriate that we find significance in the appropriations that occur. Music can be used to refer to the emotions and should be sometimes understood as doing so.[72]

Now, though Kivy allows that expressiveness is used deliberately by composers on some occasions, he denies that this is common: "The composer more than likely had no intention of representing expressive behavior, nor, for that matter, need he even have intended his music to be expressive at all" (1980, 64). "Thus, in spite of the fact that there are *some* cases in which composers intended, I believe, to write expressive music by writing music representative of expressive behavior, I advance the view here that expressive music only *resembles* expressive behavior. For in most cases it no more *represents* it than the face of the Saint Bernard represents a sad countenance"

---

[72] The point is made also in Higgins 1991.

< 265 >

(1980, 66). "Because music *can* be sad and joyful, tranquil and quiet, it can represent or be about sadness and joy, tranquility and quietude; but it *is* so only in certain circumstances" (1990a, 194). Though Kivy allows this— "And because a piece of music can be melancholy and then joyful, it can be interpreted as representing a melancholy and then joyful human experience or a melancholy followed by a joyful event" (1990a, 198)—he goes on to explain that music is about the emotions only when the composer explicitly indicates the intention that this be so by her choice of title or whatever.

I find these remarks to be misleading. Kivy writes as if music can be about the emotions only if it can *represent* them and changes the argument from the issue of expression to that of representation. When he considers the composer's role, Kivy shifts immediately to rejecting the idea that music is primarily representational. I agree that it rarely is the case that composers try to represent in their instrumental music behavior expressive of emotion, but I regard that as quite a different matter from their trying to express an emotion in the music, which is something they do often. There is all the world of difference between a work's being expressive and its being representational, and the issue is not one about composers' intentions with respect to the latter but regarding the former. A work might be expressive without this having been intended or considered by its composer, but I very much doubt that this is the normal state of affairs. Indeed, to the extent that expressiveness in music is conventionalized, it is hard to believe that, in employing the relevant conventions, composers are unaware of the expressive effects so generated, even if the production of those effects is not uppermost in their minds. "Aboutness" involves something like reference; for expressive music, this aboutness is often secured by the composer's deliberate appropriation and use of sounds with an expressive character, not by the depiction of an incidence or expression of occurrent emotion; that is, aboutness might come from the deployment of expressive properties independently of the pursuit (or otherwise) of depiction.

Newcomb (1984) has complained that Kivy's theory underplays the importance of the composer's role, and we can see why he might think so. Kivy (1989) replies as follows: even if we are hard-wired to perceive the paint used by Reynolds in painting the *Blue Boy* as blue, he was not hard-wired to choose that color of paint. He continues:

> Mozart chose materials [for the last movement of his final symphony], some of which we are hard-wired to perceive as triumphant (given, always, that we perceive music, or any other art, in a network of conventions). All artists make use of what they know about how people

< 266 >

perceive in order to get their desired effects; and some of those ways people perceive are hard-wired. There is no more reason to think that, on my account of musical expressiveness, the composer's freedom to make music expressive of what *he or she* intends is curtailed than to think that (as I believe) some aspects of representational seeing are hard-wired implies undue constraints on the painter's freedom to represent what he or she wills. But, obviously, *all* artists are limited in what they can do by the genetic endowment of human beings: what we can or cannot hear, or see, or comprehend. (1989, 179)[73]

This response meets the thrust of Newcomb's objection and indicates Kivy's awareness of some of the issues I have raised, but it does open the door to the idea Kivy is so keen to reject elsewhere, that music can be used to refer to the emotions it expresses. It is not unreasonable for us to take Reynolds's *Blue Boy* to be about its represented subject. Why, on Kivy's argument, would it not also be reasonable to take Mozart's music to be about the triumph presented there, even if Mozart's music must be understood as involving much more than this?

Musical Expressiveness and the Value of Music

Kivy's approach to the issue of musical "aboutness" has far-reaching consequences. It makes it difficult for him to explain the human appeal of music and the value we place on it, I believe. In the following I argue that these difficulties do not flow from the general theory of music's expressiveness to which we both subscribe but, rather, from aspects peculiar to Kivy's own version of it.

Earlier I claimed as a virtue of my account of music's expressiveness that it locates the expressive character in the sound of the musical work itself, so that expressiveness belongs to the music and is experienced by the listener no less immediately than are the work's other audible properties. It is surprising, then, to find criticisms such as the following:

We hear the feeling directly in the music and we experience it in the music as immediately as we experience our own feelings and moods in ourselves; we do not infer it from the structure of the music as we infer

---

[73] Note that this is offered by Kivy as a defense of the view in *The Corded Shell*. It does seem to me that here he departs from, rather than elaborates on, his earlier position. Compare the present quotation with those given earlier (265–266) from Kivy 1980, 64 and 66.

< 267 >

sadness from a sad-looking face or emotion from an emotional gesture or utterance. Our direct experience of feeling in song and still more in instrumental music is characteristically different from our knowledge of other people's feelings from their emotional utterances. A rather better analogy would perhaps be the way we perceive the expressive aura that attaches to some natural objects—the dolefulness of the weeping willow, the tranquility of an Essex countryside, or the harsh melancholy of a foghorn. (Osborne 1982, 23; also see 1983)

Person A who wants to express to person B by touch a certain disposition toward B or some third entity would not normally perform an action designed to exemplify the "appearance" of an emotion. (Indeed, the term "appearance" seems to be a category mistake here.) The disposition and the emotion are one. . . . In both actual and created situations, without the disposition the emotion is hollow, an intellectual exercise. And without the disposition the emotion cannot be adequately communicated. . . . Musical experience does not rely on the use of inferences and the need for conceptual clarification. Rather, being touched by music is a reminder of dispositions we already share with other human beings. (Putman 1985, 62–63)

In contrast to purely visual works of art, even those depicting human characters in extreme emotional states, music has an emotive vividness and immediacy that seems traceable only to the peculiar emotive impact of sound. If this impact descends from an imitation of human expressive features, then it would seem to follow that the expressed emotion will be equally (if not more) vivid and immediate where it can be recognized directly in the faces and gestures of depicted characters. This simply is not the case. (Speck 1988, 44)

Needless to say, I reject these criticisms. In some instances they misrepresent the theory. I have suggested that the experience of hearing the sadness in the music is no less like seeing the sadness in a weeping willow than it is like seeing the sadness in a face, so Osborne draws a false distinction in preferring the former analogy to the latter. The cases are different only if one takes a concern with the sad expression of a face to be an interest in the face as always symptomizing inner feelings, and I have argued that is not, in the first instance, how one approaches musical expressiveness.[74] I agree with

[74] Even then, I reject the notion that we always must *infer* the feelings of others from their appearances. If the relevant behaviors and appearances can be constitutive of feelings, then

< 268 >

Putman that music's expressiveness "is a reminder of dispositions we already share with other human beings," but I see the relevant dispositions as those leading us equally to find expressiveness (without regard to occurrent emotions) in the appearances worn by faces, basset hounds, willow trees, and the like.[75] And I believe that Putman is wrong in holding that one would not attempt to express one's own feelings by appropriating the expressiveness inherent in an appearance. I might deliberately put on a face to show how I feel, or I might point to a mask of tragedy in response to an enquiry about my mood. As I argued in the previous chapter, if it is their feelings composers wish to communicate in their works, they might do so only by recourse to such means. If they do so, an inference might be required by the listener—an inference from the expressive character of the music to the fact of its intentional use in an act of communication. But, in my view, no inference is required from the music's dynamic character to its expressive content. Against Speck's statement, I say that the analogy between the expressiveness of music and human behaviors lies in the way the two are experienced rather than in crude imitation (according to which a tremolo is the fluttering heart, a descending arpeggio is a falling tear, and so on). Besides, provided that one takes care to distinguish the expressive character of a painting from its depiction of instances of emotions, it is arguable that paintings have no less expressive immediacy than does music. Just what is the "peculiar emotive impact of sound" such that it makes music more directly expressive than the visual?

Underlying the worries presented by the authors quoted is a concern with this important issue: we value music for its expressiveness. We are involved with, and moved by, the expressiveness of music. It draws us into the emotional weave of human life; we experience it as a communication from the composer or performer. As Budd frequently points out (1981, 1985a, 1989a, 1989b), any plausible theory of music's expressiveness should make clear why we value expressiveness in music as we do. It is not plain how the analysis of musical expressiveness I prefer could do so, however.[76] That theory describes music as expressive in presenting the appearances of emotions. What could be the value in mere presentations not directly connected to the human world of occurrent feeling? Willow trees present expressive aspects, but we do not value them for doing so. Why should the musical case be

---

feelings might be apprehended *in* them, not merely deduced as lying *behind* them. Meidner (1985) also makes the point.

[75] At least one reader seems to take the point; see Allen 1990.

[76] The point is also made in Callen 1982a and 1983, Tilghman 1984, Putman 1985, and Higgins 1991.

< 269 >

different? Moreover, in some instances we value the expressiveness of music for the sublimity of the emotions expressed. But the theory under consideration restricts the range of emotions instrumental music might be expressive of, and so it cannot allow for such cases.[77] In the following I consider the connection between musical expressiveness and value. I hope to show that my own view fares better in meeting the objection raised here than does Kivy's. Some of the considerations relevant to this discussion are also taken up in Chapter 6.

First, some ground-clearing observations. There are many reasons why we might take an interest in music and many points of view from which it might be evaluated. Very important among the evaluations we make are those concerned with the artistic value of the work, with the value it has as a musical piece treated as such. Even where our concern with music is motivated by a concern to approach works as artistic individuals, we can often find or make time to listen to many pieces, and our evaluations take that into account, aiming to identify many works worth attending to in a variety of contexts. The judgments we reach should have interpersonal validity in that they should point to those works which, for the given genre and context of listening, will be found rewarding by suitably qualified listeners. Though an aesthetic interest in artworks typically involves a concern with their individuality, benefits also arise from an interest in art in general, benefits without which we would not value art as we do.[78] We value music for things other than its expressiveness. For example, we might admire the technical skill, structural integrity, economy, and resourcefulness with which a fugal subject is treated by J. S. Bach. In some such cases, the music would not be described as expressive or, if it is expressive, its expressiveness might be incidental and relatively unimportant in our assessment of the work.[79] Sometimes we might regard the style or species of expression as disvaluable in a work. The piece might be judged to be overblown and bathetic, without there being any indication that the composer failed in the task she set herself.[80] And there are cases (in dramatic works) in which the expressiveness gained might be deemed a fault for its inappropriateness in the given context.[81] Finally, there is the obvious point that different works that express

[77] This issue is raised in Osborne 1982 and Speck 1988; also see Levinson 1992b.

[78] For a fuller discussion of these issues, see Davies 1987 and Levinson 1992b; also see Davies 1991b, chap. 3.

[79] Kivy (1987) observes that Georg Telemann wrote yards of sad music and clearly implies that no value accrues to the works in question from their expressiveness.

[80] I would be tempted to pass such a judgment on Bruckner's Symphony No. 4, for instance.

[81] Kivy (1980, 71–73) condemns Barbarina's aria in *The Marriage of Figaro* on these grounds.

< 270 >

the same emotion and seem equally successful in doing so need not be evaluated as of equal merit. Together these considerations suggest to me that the achievement of expressiveness is neither a necessary nor a sufficient condition for musical value.

It remains true, however, that in some cases we value works in part for their expressiveness, or for the composer's expressive achievement. Why do we do so? Four considerations that I do not regard as exclusive or unrelated might be offered in explanation of the phenomenon: The expression of emotions in music (i) conveys knowledge of the natures of emotions (either by reflecting or, more directly, by arousing them), (ii) has a therapeutic effect (by quieting the spirits, relieving tensions, or purging us of strong emotions by arousing a response), (iii) joins us with others, thereby providing a sense of community, and (iv) gives pleasure in their contemplation. To the extent that knowledge, relief, communication, and pleasure are valued, music also will be valued for providing such experiences.

As noted, the theory of musical expressiveness I support seems ill-equipped to justify the value of music's expressiveness in such terms. Where is the value in our knowing what the appearance of emotion (without regard to feeling) sounds like in musical terms? Why would we be aroused to respond to the mere appearance of an emotion if that musical countenance does not express a felt emotion? Why would we feel a communion with others as a result of seeing such an appearance, given that the look of Saint Bernards gives us no special sense of community with them? Why would we take pleasure in observing an expressive cast without regard to feeling, when we take no such pleasure in the expressive character of willow trees? One answer to these questions notes that music is powerfully evocative of emotional responses. The mirroring feelings awakened in the listener are uncluttered by the motives, desires, and the need to act that are their usual accompaniments. The listener is able to reflect on his feeling as he could not normally do and, thereby, he may come to a new understanding of it. The power of music often resides in the way it works on our feelings rather than in its effect on our thoughts (Davies 1980, 86).[82]

The expressiveness of music can be powerfully moving. It moves us not only to admire the composer's achievement but also, sometimes, to feel the emotions it expresses. Expressive "appearances" are highly evocative, even where one does not believe that they relate to someone's occurrent emotion.

---

[82] Also see Levinson 1981 and 1982, Callen 1982a, and Putman 1987. Goldman (1992) suggests that the expressiveness of musical passages is more important in revealing to us the nature of the musical work than of the world.

< 271 >

We value these experiences for the knowledge of the emotions they provide, for the therapeutic value (if there is such) they provide, and because we take pleasure in being stimulated to feeling. Moreover, though we do not take the music to be a primary expression of the composer's feelings, there are occasions on which we might reasonably take it to be a tertiary expression of emotions she has experienced. As a result we feel contact with the emotional life of another. And even if we do not take the music's expressiveness as indirectly related to the composer's occurrent emotions, we very often take the music to connect in a wider sense to the composer's experience of affective life in general. We regard the expressive character of music as a matter of design (even if the composer appropriates naturally expressive elements rather than creating such elements ex nihilio). Accordingly, we hear in the music not merely a presentation of expressive appearances but also a type of reference, or ostension, effected through the composer's deliberate use of her materials. In the majority of works (in which the expressive character of the music seems to be more than accidental or incidental), we hear the music's expressiveness as a central element in an act of communication. Though expressive appearances are not backed by occurrent emotions, the intimacy of their relation to occurrent emotions, coupled with their deliberate use and shaping by the composer, entitles us to recognize and appreciate a connection between music and the wider affective context that is the milieu for human interaction. We approach music not as a natural object but as a human product imbued with a significance derived from the life and experiences of its creator (and its performers). Music, unlike willow trees and Saint Bernards, is redolent of the intentional context in which it is created and performed, and this, quite properly, affects the way we are inclined to experience its expressive aspects. Those aspects are enriched and emboldened. They become for us not merely accidental (but, nevertheless, provocative) resemblances, as is the case with the looks of willow trees and Saint Bernards, but resemblances invested with the power of the human intellect and experience.

Limitations inherent in the medium of pure sound and in the kinds of expressive character that might be presented solely in appearances restrict what might be conveyed by the composer; where it comes to the sublime, what is sublime, in my view, is the nature of the expressive achievement rather than the subtlety or originality of the feelings captured in the music. I do not accept, that is, that music deals in emotions with which we are not familiar in more mundane contexts. Neither do I accept that instrumental music deals frequently with such feelings as hope, anger, or envy. But I do hold that, because it operates through appearances and evokes emotions

< 272 >

under circumstances differing significantly from those in which such emotions normally arise, composers can have much more to "say" about emotions than those emotions have to "say" about themselves under standard conditions, despite the limitations within which composers operate.

Kivy is inclined to reject these sentiments and, for that reason, has more difficulty in explaining why we attach to the expressiveness of music the value we do. Two aspects of his version of the theory lead him to this stance: (i) As we have seen, in holding that expression by contour is natural, he tends to discount the role of the composer in the expressive process, as if the composer's intentional use of expressive contours adds little to the significance of expression within the work. So, it is not open to Kivy to see the value of music's expressiveness as residing in an act of communication. The Saint Bernard communicates nothing by its sad look and, according to Kivy, music likewise is not about and does not mean anything by the emotions of which it is expressive. On this point I am in fundamental disagreement with Kivy. In my view, the composer's use of the expressive potential of her materials makes all the difference between the attitude we should adopt to Saint Bernards' expressive appearances and the attitude we should adopt to the expression of emotion in music. (ii) Kivy asserts that music never arouses the emotions of which it is expressive and, accordingly, does not acknowledge that it has a value in providing us with a context in which such emotions might be experienced, purged, and examined. His denial of this view is founded on questions that seem to have considerable power: Why would anyone value being made to feel sad? How could a response be characterized as one of sadness if one does not believe that there is anything in the music to feel sad about? Why, if they feel sad, do audiences remain at concerts and act as if they are enjoying the experience of listening to the music? I believe such question might be answered and address them in the following chapter.[83]

What resources remain to Kivy in explaining the value of music's expressiveness? He does allow that the expressive character of music (the contour through which it is expressive) is parasitic on expressions of felt emotions in the sense that those same contours, when presented in behavior and backed by felt emotions, are expressive of occurrent emotions. So he can accept that a degree of inference from the one to the other is possible. He does allow that, rarely, composers intend to represent the emotions heard in their music. So he can admit that expressiveness is sometimes a form of communication.

---

[83] Osborne (1982) and Higgins (1991) see my version of the theory as having the advantage over Kivy's in that it allows that music evokes the kinds of responses Kivy wishes to deny.

< 273 >

And he does accept that we often find the composer's expressive achievement moving, even if we are never moved to feel the emotions of which the music is expressive, so he can allow, to some extent, that the value of music resides in the manner in which it works on our emotions. Undoubtedly these points go some distance toward meeting the objections under consideration as they apply to his own account—but I doubt that they go far enough to meet the full force of those criticisms.

The explanation of musical value to which Kivy subscribes is set out in *The Corded Shell* in Chapter 11. There he applies Sircello's (1975) theory of aesthetic/artistic beauty, concluding that musical expressiveness is valuable both where it is not a defect and is possessed to a degree that is unusual. One might always dispute Sircello's theory and some of the detail of Kivy's application of it to the musical case, but these are not issues I pursue here. I would, however, draw attention to this point: In Kivy's version of it, the account finds no place for a connection of intimacy between the world of human feeling and the value we attach to musical expression. Kivy never suggests that the value of music depends on its bonding the composer and listener, or on its engaging with the affective side of human existence. It is no wonder, I think, that Kivy's theory has been regarded as open to the charge that it cannot explain the importance we attach to music's expressive powers. But, as I see it, the problem lies not so much with the theory of music's expressiveness (to which both Kivy and I subscribe) as to implications Kivy draws (wrongly, in my view) from it.

So far I have accepted that the value of musical expressiveness resides in the value of things to which the experience of it might lead: knowledge, cathartic release, a sense of community and involvement with others and with human affective life in general, pleasure. It might be thought, however, that I err in allowing such matters to ground the value of music's expressiveness, for to do so is to treat the value of music as instrumental rather than as intrinsic and individual to the work in which it occurs.[84]

I agree that, given an interest in musical works as music, we value musical works individually and treat them as ends in themselves. The value they have as individuals of a type (as individual concertos, symphonies, and the like) resides, I believe, in the enjoyment that goes with appreciating and understanding them as the individuals they are.[85] To understand a particular work

---

[84] I think this is Budd's view; see 1989a and 1989b. He makes the point that different works expressing the same emotion would be intersubstitutable as means to such ends, but this is not how we treat them.

[85] The pleasure involved is one bound up with and inseparable from the nature of its object, so such pleasure is not an end to which the music merely is an independently specifiable means;

< 274 >

is not always to find it pleasing, because one might find it to be mediocre or worse, but the approach seeking to understand musical works is the approach leading to the deepest appreciation of their nature, and, in general, the more appreciation the more enjoyment.[86] To agree with Budd on such points is not, however, to accept that we do not also value music in general for the knowledge and others things it conveys. We do not treat individual works merely as means to such long-term goals; rather, we treat them as ends in themselves. Nevertheless, our interest in musical expressiveness does have such long-term effects, effects that themselves have value, and it is arguable that we would not regard music in general as worthy of interest, or as more worthy than a passion for tiddlywinks, were this not so (Davies 1987).

Part of the difficulty that arises in explaining the value of musical expressiveness lies in framing the question. If not all musical expressiveness is aesthetically/artistically valuable, the question is naturally to be construed as one about the worth of particular instances of musical expressiveness. At that level, the answer is not so difficult. The expressiveness is valuable because it contributes (though in a way not easily or appropriately separated from the contribution of structural and other elements with which it is integrated) to the value of the work. If this reply is not accepted as of the kind sought, then the question becomes one about the value of the work in question rather than of the expressiveness within it. And now, if the grounds for evaluating works of the given kind are disputed, the question changes yet again to this: but why is an interest in music to be valued? The philosophical question about the value of musical expressiveness turns, finally, to a discussion of the value of music in general. The point, of course, is not to reject the value of music and the importance that music has for so many people but to provide a philosophical foundation explaining these things. Now, though, when the question is set on the wider stage, it seems to become intractably difficult, for so deeply embedded is music in the lives of so many people that the question becomes one about the meaning of life itself.

A few people are entirely indifferent to music of all kinds. If music were suddenly to disappear, they would notice its absence but would regard the world as basically unchanged. But for a majority of people music is an important, not an incidental, feature of life and the world. Music accompanies weddings, comings of age, and deaths; it goes with shopping, eating, and

---

see Schaper 1983, Davies 1987, and Levinson 1992b. So, I think Taruskin (1982) is wrong to criticize Kivy for discussing pleasure rather than value as such, for the two are intimately related.

[86] Here I concur with Kivy 1990a, 115–118.

< 275 >

jogging. Members of this majority often choose *to listen* to one or another kind of music, not merely *to hear* the music surrounding them. Such people might not perform, but they sing, hum, and whistle; they find melodies catchy, and so on. Music warms their world. In an important sense, the world would not be for them the same place were music absent from it. And for a further, significant minority, music is yet more than an important element in the fabric of life; it is integrated into their personal being and becomes a part of what gives meaning and identity to their lives. Without music, the members of this group would no longer be the same individuals, for music shapes their conceptions of themselves no less importantly than do their relations to family, friends, lovers, and work. Listening to or performing music is for such a person a mode of existence and self-realization.

In the last analysis, the value of music lies in its potential to contribute to the manner in which the individual finds meaning in life and in which the culture at large defines its place in history and the world. Music in general has this potential because it engages with fundamental human concerns and practices, even if its contribution is indirect and not geared to practical, particular concerns. Music possesses its import not solely by virtue of its expressive power, but its expressiveness is one of the more important aspects of this engagement, given the central importance to us of the affective dimension in life. Music in general could not serve as a source of knowledge, psychological therapy, human communication, and community were it not expressive, and sometimes striking in its expressiveness.

Kivy takes on the wider issue, that of the importance of music in human life, when he attempts to argue, not only that music is valuable and important, but that it may be so profoundly (1990a, chap. 10). To be profound, music must (i) be about (ii) a profound subject (iii) treated in an exemplary way or in some way adequate to that subject matter. As his model for profound music, he takes the style of contrapuntal writing exemplified in J. S. Bach's chorale prelude on "Wenn wir in höchsten Nöten sind." Because Kivy denies that instrumental music is about anything—and denies in particular that is about the emotions it expresses—he suggests that the first condition is met only by recognizing that, by revealing the possibilities of musical sound itself, music is about those very possibilities.[87] The second condition seems to be met because music is of abiding interest and importance to many people. The third condition is satisfied by great instrumental works. Nevertheless, Kivy acknowledges the failure of his analysis. Many things are of abiding interest without involving profound subjects and, since "the possi-

---

[87] A discussion of musical meaning on a similar wavelength can be found in Raffman 1991.

< 276 >

bilities of musical materials" is not a profound subject matter touching the moral heart of human life, instrumental music fails the crucial second condition.

I sympathize with Kivy in his struggles with a topic of such difficulty. But I cannot refrain from observing, yet again, that Kivy's formalist tendencies, as revealed both in his choice of example and in his denial of the possibility of musical "aboutness," generate many of the difficulties his view of musical value acknowledges without being able to answer. Levinson suggests that the following should not be dismissed in a consideration of musical profundity: "1) It explores the emotional or psychic realm in a more insightful or eye-opening way than most music; 2) it epitomizes or alludes to more interesting or complex extra-musical modes of growth and development than most music, and gives us a vicarious experience of such modes; 3) strikes us as touching, in some fashion or other, on the most fundamental and pressing features of human existence" (1992a, 59).[88]

In this chapter I have argued that expressiveness can be an objective property of musical works, though, obviously, the emotions expressed are not felt by the music. Music presents emotion characteristics. Just as a willow can be sad-looking, or a person's face happy-looking, music can present an expressive appearance in its sound (without regard to anyone's felt emotions). This is because we experience the dynamic character of music as like the actions of a person; movement is heard in music, and that movement is heard as purposive and as rationally organized. Within musical styles, these natural propensities for expressiveness are structured and refined by musical conventions, so that the expressiveness of a work might be apparent only to someone familiar with the conventions of the relevant style.

Music might be experienced as expressive without its having been designed by its composer to present the expressive character it wears. Usually, though, the composer contrives and controls the expressiveness of the music. This is why music can properly be understood as referring to, or being about, the world of human feelings.

---

[88] For further comment on Kivy's analysis of musical profundity, see Sharpe 1991, White 1992, and McAdoo 1992.

< 277 >

SIX

· · ·

The Response to Music's Expressiveness

In Chapter 4 I considered the listener's response to the musical work in terms of the arousal theory. That theory attaches special importance to the response in which, say, sad music makes the listener feel sad; it holds that music is sad because it arouses sadness in the listener. I foreshadowed in this earlier discussion problems posed by the claim that sad music evokes sadness in the listener. In this chapter I reply to some of those difficulties. I do so not because I wish to defend the arousal theory of musical expression but because I believe that such "mirroring" responses to music's expressiveness are possible and fairly common. On the account defended in the previous chapter, music possesses its expressive character independently of its arousing emotions reflecting that character. Nevertheless, I believe that sad music might lead some listeners to feel sad, even if music's expressiveness is not to be explained by its power to awaken that response. To defend this view, it is necessary that I consider the objections raised previously.

The Problematic Cases

While attending or listening to opera, ballet, or song, a person might respond to the events that are depicted or narrated. He might be amused at a performance of *The Marriage of Figaro* by the count's discovery of Cherubino in Susanna's room, he might pity Rosina's suffering and admire her

< 279 >

dignity. The description of such responses—that is, of responses to fictions—is not without its difficulties, but here I am not concerned primarily with responses of this type. Neither am I interested in responses to the performance as such, or to the composer's life and character. A person might be horrified by notes fluffed by the horn players, or exhilarated by the unusually fast tempo, or disappointed by the banality of the interpretation. She may be moved by thoughts of the composer provoked by the music. On hearing Mendelssohn's *Elijah* she might be saddened that the promise of Overture for *A Midsummer Night's Dream* was never to be realized by the mature composer.

The following discussion does not concern responses to fictions, or to the performance, or to the composer's life but instead to the character of the musical work itself. But again, not all such responses interest me, for many are philosophically unproblematic. In this category fall the following: a person might be surprised by an unexpected chord on first hearing a work; or he may be delighted and awed by Bach's ingenuity and technical mastery in writing the cancrizan and mirror fugues found in *The Art of Fugue*; or he admires the felicity and skill with which Mozart reconciles the demands of fugal writing with the tonal and melodic structure of sonata form in the last movement of his Symphony No. 41, K. 551; or he dislikes the banality and sentimentality of a work; or, simply, a person might be moved to tears by the beauty of a musical piece.

As I say, my concern does not lie with such responses, though they are reactions to the character of the musical work itself. There is nothing philosophically puzzling about such cases. Those that have an emotional character neatly fit the model sketched in previous chapters: Emotions typically take objects that are believed to answer to a description in terms of which the response is appropriate. Usually a person is sad *about* something and, usually, the object of her emotion is believed by her to be unfortunate and regrettable (to adopt terms used by Kenny 1969, "that which is unfortunate and regrettable" is the *formal* object of sadness). Also, emotions typically involve desires and dispositions which, other things being equal, issue in actions that depend on the character of the emotion experienced. If I feel fear I am disposed to flee and desire to escape; if I feel pity I want to comfort the object of my compassion; if I feel sad I am inclined to weep or to look unhappy. Further, emotions usually involve some physiological response. Finally, emotions arise within identifiable types of causal circumstances. The death of a friend would be expected to cause grief rather than happiness, for instance. Now, in the examples mentioned in the preceding paragraph, the music is a proper object of the response and the response generates appro-

< 280 >

priate actions. The person encourages others to listen to Bach's fugues, praises the fugues, listens to them more often than she listens to the banal and sentimental work, smiles, perhaps, while listening, and the like.

By now the reader will have inferred that my concern lies with cases that are problematic in that the music seems not to be their "proper" object and in which the behavior that marks the response seems not to be appropriate to its alleged character. Of special prominence among the problematic instances are some in which a person claims to be moved to an emotion "mirroring" the expressive tenor of the music. In the discussion that follows I focus on "pure" or "absolute" works—symphonies, string quartets, and other instrumental pieces—for it is in the context of reactions to such works that the problem is at its clearest and most acute.

To take an example much favored in the literature, Beethoven's Symphony No. 3 (*Eroica*) is not normally regarded as something unfortunate and regrettable and hence is not an appropriate object of a listener's response of sadness. Yet people sometimes claim that the work's slow movement makes them feel sad. These people listen to the work when they are under no duty or compulsion to do so, they do not attempt to prevent performances of it from continuing, and they show no signs of deep emotional distress while listening to its slow movement. They encourage their friends to listen to this music and themselves seek it out rather than avoid it. The problem posed by such examples can be stated more abstractly: There are many cases in which musical works express some emotion and the listener (claims to) mirror this emotion in her own response to the given work. The listener is moved (or claims to be moved) to feel sadness at the sadness expressed in the music or to experience happiness at the happiness expressed in the music. In these cases the music seemingly is not the proper object of the response, though it is its cause.

Cognitivism

One way of dealing with the problem posed by such cases is by explaining it away. It might be said that listeners are mistaken in holding that sad music makes them feel sad or that happy music makes them feel happy. These listeners mistake the character of their response (they feel something other than they say), or they mistake the object of their response (they respond not to the music but to something else). It might be argued, accordingly, that all emotional responses to music are of the unproblematic, object-directed kind

< 281 >

discussed earlier. This view, which I call cognitivism, is held by Peter Kivy.[1] He maintains that, unless they are pathological, responses to music must be of the "garden variety"; they must be unproblematic in being object-directed. We respond emotionally to music with admiration and the like, he allows. Sometimes we respond to the expressive character of music and, where expressiveness is central to a work's character, Kivy recognizes that we must react to this in understanding the work. But, he stresses, we are not moved by sad music to sadness, unless the banality of the music's sadness, or its inappropriateness, or the ineptitude of the composer is a proper object for a sad response.[2] Kivy denies (1987 and 1989) that he is moved to sadness by the sadness of sad music and he claims that, without undue leading, those who claim to feel sad will often retract when they are questioned about their responses.[3]

Some cognitivists deny validity or reality to any emotional responses occasioned by music; they describe the aesthetically proper response as an intellectual, not an emotional, one. For example, Frank Howes notes: ". . . In healthy people at a concert introspection shows that it is not specific emotions that are produced even by Strauss' erotics or Tchaikovsky's melancholics, or Beethoven's heroics. . . . His [the listener's] pleasure, his enlightenment about anger, is his recognition of it and heightened understanding of it. Our pleasure then is a recognition of the truth of the emotions portrayed, not an emotional vibration in sympathy with them. It is in fact a

---

[1] See Kivy 1980, 1987, 1989, and 1990a. Note that, in a piece too recent to be discussed here, Kivy (1993) has revised his position.

[2] Sharpe (1982) agrees. Kivy makes clearer in 1990a than elsewhere that the emotional response may be a response to the music's expressiveness, not just to its formal or representational character, but he plainly holds that such responses, to be acceptable, must take the expressive achievement as their emotional object. The appropriate response is admiration, surprise, disappointment—not sadness, unless the expressive effort is so dismal as to call for sadness. Price (1992) is mistaken in claiming that Kivy holds (i) that the music could not be both the cause and the emotional object of an aesthetically appropriate response, and (ii) that music cannot cause ordinary (garden variety) emotions in the listener.

[3] Matravers (1991) is another who denies that mirroring responses are generated in the musical context, despite listeners' assertions to the contrary. He holds that sad music, like sad people, arouses in the engaged listener feelings of pity (rather than of sadness). Indeed, in his view, we know that the music expresses sadness just because we are aware that it arouses feelings of pity in us. Now, as I indicated in Chapter 4, this position strikes me as simply false. I do not believe that listeners recognize in themselves feelings of pity for the work, thereby coming to attribute sadness to the music. Further, if the account of music's expressiveness I have defended is correct, such a response would verge on the irrational. If music presents an expressive appearance without regard to occurrent feelings, then there is no ground for a pitying response. If one does not believe that Saint Bernards feel sad, though their faces wear a sad-looking expression, one has no reason to pity them. (But, as Kivy maintains, one might have reason to admire the skill of a sculptor who could capture the sad-lookingness of a Saint Bernard's expression.)

< 282 >

form of knowledge. What gives it a deceptive appearance of emotion is its sensuous quality" (1958, 36–37). The most famous statement of a cognitivist position, Eduard Hanslick's, presents a similar position. Apparently he would banish all emotional responses in favor of dispassionate cognition. He wanted, in particular, to purge from the practice of music criticism idle and meaningless talk of emotion. The critic should focus on the music rather than on emotions provoked by personal associations triggered by the music.[4] To talk of such feelings is to direct attention away from the musical work. (The only difference Hanslick would admit between the person who said he felt sad because a tune was his dead son's favorite and the person who said he was moved by the sadness he heard in the music would be that the former is more honest, or less self-deluded, than the latter.) The critic should discuss neither expressiveness nor emotional reactions but musical beauty.

Kivy is not a cognitivist of this stamp. He does not draw an exclusive division between the affective and the intellectual, as Howes does. Kivy (1990b) criticizes Hanslick for not recognizing the critical relevance of musically based emotions—that is, of emotions for which the music could properly be (judged and believed to be) the emotional object. Kivy allows that listeners may be intensely moved by the music they hear. He denies not that they are moved but that they are moved to feel emotions that echo the expressive character of the music. That Kivy does not renounce to the listener the propriety of an intensely moving emotional response is presented by him as a major advantage of his type of cognitivism over Hanslick's.

Kivy's version of cognitivism is not a new one in its outline. Carroll Pratt asserts: "The music may be joyful. It may be sad. But in neither case does he, the listener, experience joy or sadness. He likes the music. He admires the skill of the performers and the genius of the composer. But he himself is not bowed down with grief nor lifted up with joy" (1952, 7; also see 1954). Elsie Payne (1961; also see 1973) offers empirical evidence, elicited in psychological experiments, for a similar view. She quotes one person questioned: "The biggest reactions to music—shivers down the spine, weeping, etc., when they are experienced, are a response to sheer beauty, rather than any emotion the composer is trying to express" (1961, 43). Like Hanslick (1957 and 1986), both Payne and Pratt allow that a small minority of listeners appear to be moved to sadness by sad music, but they clearly regard such people as exceptional and their "visceral" responses as aberrant. As Pratt concedes, "a few people do undoubtedly soak in some sort of emotional

---

[4] Hanslick's own works of criticism reveal him to be a person who was much moved by the "tonally moving forms" of music. Some find an inconsistency here; for example, Kivy (1990b).

< 283 >

bath while listening to the heart-rending measures of Tchaikovsky" (1954, 291). A theorist such as Kivy could not accept that these seeming counterexamples to cognitivism are exceptional in the sense of being statistically uncommon; he must argue that the alleged counterexamples can be explained away or else dismiss them as pathological. Kivy marshals several arguments, reviewed later, in the attempt to do so.

At first glance Kivy's approach faces an obvious problem: it runs against the undeniable tendency that people sometimes display to describe their responses as mirroring the music's expressive character. There is always the worry, when a philosopher's theory leads him to insist that most people do not understand their own feelings, motives, and beliefs, that the problem resides with the theory. Why should we revise our ordinary descriptions of our responses to suit some philosopher's view? The question is not rhetorical (though students would usually take it that way). We might do so when we recognize that the philosopher's account accords nicely with some of our deep-seated intuitions. We should always be prepared to revise our thinking after conceptual analysis when that analysis appears to be well-founded and coheres with many of our most basic intuitions. Allowing this, though, where it is not self-evident that the philosopher's theory is better based than are some of our current beliefs, the onus of proof surely falls on the philosopher to demonstrate the attractiveness of her view. Kivy's theory does not strike me as obvious in its correctness, so I see the burden of proof as falling on his shoulders. Instead of taking up the challenge, however, he shrugs it off.

Kivy refuses to accept that the onus of proof falls more heavily on himself than on his opponents. He notes (1989) that, though he must deny that some listeners are correct in the account they offer of their experiences, his opponents must claim in turn that he, Kivy, is mistaken when he denies being moved to sadness by sad music. Neither approach can claim the privilege that goes with its meshing directly with agreed, deep-rooted intuitions, since both theories must insist that one or other listener is mistaken in the characterization of her own reaction.

I do not find this argument convincing. Someone who subscribes to the arousal theory discussed in Chapter 4, according to which music expresses sadness (merely) in virtue of arousing the emotion, would have to claim that Kivy is mistaken when he denies being made to feel sad by music he correctly describes as sad (if there is no evidence of factors that might interfere with such a response).[5] Kivy's point does count against an arousalist. But some-

---

[5] I wonder: would one's holding a philosophical view on the matter count as an "interfering factor"?

< 284 >

one, such as myself, who rejects the arousal theory and takes the sadness to be an objective property of the musical work might allow that it is common for a mirroring response to occur without also holding that it must do so. I can accept that Kivy is never moved to sadness by sad music, so it is not true of all his opponents that they must judge listeners of his persuasion to be mistaken about the nature of their responses (Davies 1991c). In *Sound Sentiment* (1989), Kivy constantly conflates arousal theory with the view that mirroring responses to music's expressiveness occur. The belief that mirroring responses are common does not commit one, however, to the arousal theory's account of expressiveness in music. The arousalist offers an analysis of what it is for music to be *expressive*, whereas the "mirrorist" claims that music's expressiveness (whatever its basis) often leads to a response of a distinctive kind. Not everyone who believes that such responses occur also believes that the arousal theory is correct in its analysis of the nature of musical expressiveness. I do not. Indeed, I have argued (1980) that "mirrorism" is compatible with an analysis of musical expressiveness like Kivy's own. Even if all arousalists are "mirrorists," not all "mirrorists" are arousalists, and Kivy's point does not count against "mirrorists" who reject the arousal theory. Kivy cannot redistribute the burden of proof so easily as he says.

Perhaps Kivy overlooks the possibility of other commitments because he finds arousalism everywhere. He may be correct in supposing that arousalism is rife, but he is ungenerous in his use (1989) of the following ad hominem argument. According to Kivy, most people, including his philosophical opponents, believe that they must choose between two possibilities: (i) that music does not move us at all, and (ii) that music moves us to feel the emotions it expresses. They opt for (ii), if only because they know (i) to be false. The attraction of (ii) should be removed, however, by the recognition of a third possibility, the one Kivy advocates: (iii) music moves us by its beauty, felicity, and so forth; that is, sad music moves us, but not to sadness. Now, Kivy may be correct in believing that some people do not notice the third option, and that those people would think twice about describing their response as one of sadness when they were made aware of it; but he is wrong, surely, to imply that those who defend (ii) do so only because they are blind to the possibility of (iii). I can find no evidence that Colin Radford (1989) or Jerrold Levinson (1982) (two of the philosophers against whom he employs his ad hominem argument) favor (ii) because they regard (i) and (ii) as the only alternatives. Radford (1991a) denies being an arousalist; he shares with Kivy the view that expressiveness is a property of the music independent of the music's power to affect the listener emotionally. Levinson explicitly

< 285 >

acknowledges the possibility of type (iii) responses and denies being an arousalist, while holding that type (ii) responses occur (see 1990a, 334, for instance).[6]

The onus of proof does fall on Kivy, I believe. Fortunately, he has discussed the topic in detail, combining a vigorous attack against arousalism with a defense of the assertion that only the pathologically inclined are saddened by the sadness of music. Before I explore his arguments, I explain why I find his own account unattractive. As noted already, Kivy's cognitivism flies in the face of the testimony offered by some listeners about the character of their emotional response to music. This is no small matter, but there is another issue that concerns me more. Kivy's view of the listener's feelings does not clearly allow us to say that we respond to the sadness of sad music as such. In his theory, a person responds to the beauty of the music (or alternatively, to its failure in this respect). If she reacts to the music's expressiveness, she responds with admiration or disappointment to the way this expressiveness is realized.[7] However, so far as I can see, there is no room in this account for the claim that the listener responds directly to the fact that the music expresses, say, sadness rather than happiness, or to the quality of the sadness expressed. Kivy's theory allows that *how* the sadness is expressed affects the listener's response—she reacts to the felicity or otherwise of the expressive achievement—but the theory makes no allowance for the idea that *what* is expressed shapes the response. Kivy's theory explains why I am moved to delight or repulsion by the manner of the music's being expressive, and to that extent it gives a central place to the importance of music's expressiveness as motivating the listener's response. At the same time, though, the theory permits no distinction between an aesthetically proper response to a sad work and to a happy piece, given that the aesthetic achievement is as thorough in the one case as in the other. I am uncomfortable about the way *sadness* drops out of the account here, so that it is "pathologically" abnormal both to respond with sadness to the sadness of music and to regard the expressive character of the music as relevant to one's own reaction. It is as if

---

[6] In Davies 1980, where I defended the "mirrorist" view against objections such as those in Kivy 1989, I stress that type (iii) as well as type (ii) responses occur.

[7] Whether the response also involves admiration of the performer's or composer's skill depends, I suppose, on the extent to which one takes the performer or composer to be especially responsible for what comes off in the music. Kivy often writes as if it is (solely) the natural possibilities of sound combinations that are exciting or boring, happy or sad, but I do not suppose that he means to dismiss as irrelevant the contribution made by the performer or composer to the result.

< 286 >

Mahler's Symphony No. 8 and Symphony No. 9 should leave one feeling the same way.

Replies to Cognitivism

Someone who would defend the claim that sad music can lead people to feel sad, without its being the case that the sadness of the music is believed to be unfortunate and regrettable, might take one of two tacks. A first approach argues that, contrary to appearances, the music is a proper object of such a response. Those who take this line frequently argue that the imagination, rather than belief, ties the response to the music. As it were, both the music and the imagination contribute something that shapes the response, and the response is properly described as a response to the music because what is properly imagined is controlled and directed by the nature of the music. An alternative line recommends that non-object-directed responses are not so aberrant as cognitivists would have one think. The emotional response to music might not be object-directed in the standard fashion, but, so the argument goes, this does not mark it as pathological. In this section I discuss these strategies in turn and the criticisms they attract. I agree with cognitivist criticisms of the first approach but defend the second.

Music Is an Appropriate Emotional Object for the Response

Leonard B. Meyer (especially 1956, but also see 1973 and 1989) is one who believes that he can characterize the response to the expressive character of musical works on the model applying to emotional reactions in general. According to Meyer (1956), "affect" occurs when a tendency of the organism to think or act in a certain way is arrested or inhibited. The relation between the blocking of desire and affect is that of stimulus to response. The affective response to a stimulus is not conditioned or otherwise learned; it is a natural reflex. The affective response is a pattern reaction that operates or tends to operate, when activated, in an automatic way. The stimulated affect is, at first, a "feeling tone"; it is not yet a *particular* emotion. Feeling tone is, as it were, pure emotion unadulterated by thought or cognition; it is the raw stuff from which all emotions are molded. The feeling tone is differentiated into *an* emotion (sadness rather than anger, say) as a result of cognitive processes. These involve the choice and characterization of the object of the emotion, no doubt in accordance with the particular tendency whose blocking provided the stimulus. Emotions are differentiated ac-

< 287 >

cording to their formal objects. The feeling tone is differentiated into a given emotion when an object is brought under a relevant description.

Turning to aesthetic responses, Meyer holds that music is eminently suited to the stimulation of affect. At any moment within a piece only a limited number of continuations, some of which are more likely than others, are available to the composer. The range of the continuations and their individual likelihoods are governed by a work's style and genre. (Virtually the whole of Meyer's work is given over to a consideration of the ways stylistic considerations bear on the range of continuations available and their individual likelihoods.) A listener who is acquainted with the style of the work makes predictions, consciously or otherwise, about the way the work will be continued. If these expectations are contradicted or delayed in their fulfillment, affect is stimulated. By deviating from the listener's expectations the music denies or "blocks" their realization and evokes a feeling tone in the listener. The listener need not attempt to differentiate this feeling tone. Where he does not, he may be inclined to talk of "musical emotions" that cannot adequately be described in words. But for Meyer the possibility of the listener's differentiating the feeling tone is a real one. How is this to be done, given the absence of a putative emotional object for such a feeling tone?[8]

I interpret Meyer's position as follows: There are, within any culture, groups of emotions having a common pattern of behavioral expression. For example, the dynamics of the behavioral expressions of sadness, grief, disappointment, and regret are similar and can be distinguished from the behavioral expressions of joy, happiness, and enthusiasm. Music can be heard as imitating the dynamics of behavior. As listeners we hear these dynamics and imagine that the music is through them expressive of, say, sadness. In so doing we (imaginatively) make the music the emotional object in terms of which our feeling tone can be differentiated. We might with equal appropriateness imagine that a given work is expressive in itself of grief, disappointment, or regret (because of the dynamic similarity between the music and the behavioral expressions of sadness, grief, and the like) and respond accordingly, but, since such musical movement is unlike the behavioral expressions of happiness, joy, enthusiasm, we could not appropriately imagine that the same work is expressive of happiness. If we respond to such a work as if it were happy, our response reveals our lack of understanding of the music.

---

[8] The answer to this question is presented in the final chapter of Meyer 1956. In fairness to Meyer, note that the issue is peripheral to his main theme, which is the attempt to analyze the way the listener's expectations arise from considerations of musical style.

< 288 >

So, although the music becomes the emotional object of our emotion as a result of an act of the imagination, the exercise of the imagination here is restricted and controlled purely by musical features, by the dynamic movement of the music. The music provides a rein on the imagination. There is a need for a similarity between the dynamic pattern of the characteristic behavioral expression of the emotion we imagine into the music and the movement of the music. Where there is such we can justify what we imagine the music to express and, also, our own emotional response to that expression. Any single musical work tolerates and supports a wide range of emotional responses, since it may be imagined appropriately to be expressive in itself of several emotions, but it cannot be imagined correctly to express just any emotion.

Meyer's views are vulnerable to many criticisms: his "syntactic" approach to music overemphasizes the status of the unpredictable at the expense of the structural significance of similarity; he adopts a crude, stimulus-response model of the emotions and regards them as primarily physiological while underplaying their intensional character; he draws a sharp line between the emotional and the cognitive, regarding the two as exclusive.[9] But the relevant criticism, so far as cognitivism is concerned, must be this: Even if the imagination is controlled indirectly by musical patterns of tension and release, in Meyer's view the listener's response is "differentiated" as a given emotion by reference to things lying beyond the boundaries of the musical work, to things not deriving their nature from the character of the music. At best, there is a resemblance between the dynamic character of the music and the emotions to which it leads our thoughts. Beyond that, there is nothing licensing an inference from the musical context to the emotional one. Either the contribution of the imagination to the experience (as described by Meyer) is aesthetically/artistically gratuitous in going beyond what is required for appreciation of the music's character, or it is aesthetically/artistically unhelpful in leading the listener away from the work, thereby distracting rather than assisting her in the attempt to appreciate the work.

The cognitivist's objection—that, when people respond with sadness to sad music, the music is merely the occasion and not the object of the response—is developed most famously by Hanslick. He holds that, where the music is not the emotional object of the response, as is true when sad music (allegedly) makes the listener feel sad, the response is to thoughts, memories, or associations prompted by the music, not to the music itself. Hanslick con-

[9] For discussions, see Taylor 1974, Budd 1985a, Tormey 1988, Hansen 1989, and Higgins 1991.

< 289 >

tinues: Music leads us to think of things, to remember past scenes or events, or to entertain the actuality of imagined scenes or events. It does not achieve this result by representing these things as pictures might; rather, it calls such scenes or ideas to mind by being associated with them or by sharing some (dynamic) similarity with them. For example, a dramatic musical passage may lead us to think of a thunderstorm. The scenes and events we think of, not the music itself, provide the emotional object of our response. In this way we make our experienced emotion "manifest" to ourselves. The music sets the train of thought in motion (and therefore is the "ultimate cause" of the emotional response), but it is the thoughts to which the music leads, not the music itself, that supply the emotional object of the response (its "proximate cause"). The thoughts initiated by the music are not controlled by the music. The character of the music is not essentially relevant to the nature of the thoughts we have or, therefore, to the emotion we feel. The response is not "aesthetical." When we say "The music is sad," normally all we mean is that the music makes us think of things that lead us to feel sad. Indeed, if Kivy (1990b) is right, Hanslick goes yet further in holding that the response is aroused only if the listener is already disposed by his emotional condition to respond as he does: so, music might make a person feel sad (only) if he were already depressed; that is, not only does the nature of the response not depend directly on the detail of the musical work, but also the initiation of the response does not lie with the music.

Hanslick's view of the listener's response assumes that a concern with musical expressiveness takes attention away from the music rather than toward it; that when we are interested in musical expressiveness our minds are crowded with memories or imagined scenes, that we are in a kind of reverie; that there can be no such thing as an emotional response to musical expressiveness which is revealing of understanding and appreciation of the work as such; that we cannot distinguish between the music's effect on our emotions and its own expressive character. As generalizations, these claims seem false; even if, sometimes, some responses are merely associative, as Hanslick describes, it is not obvious that all instances of sadness elicited by sad music are of the variety he despises. As Budd (1980 and 1985a) notes, whereas Hanslick rightly rejects the relevance of responses merely occasioned by the music, he does not show that emotional responses are never aesthetically relevant, or never required, or unimportant.

Hanslick holds that, because music does not feel emotions, and because it cannot represent or otherwise symbolize feelings, emotions are incapable of being expressed in music. For this reason he thinks that thoughts of emotions prompted by music cannot be of aesthetic/artistic relevance, because the

< 290 >

train of such thoughts must fall beyond the control of the development of musical materials within the work. Meyer's approach is vulnerable to this attack because it treats the music as a trigger that activates the listener's feeling in an automatic fashion, leaving associations brought from outside the musical context to give that response its emotional individuality. Now, one might do better than Meyer in avoiding Hanslick's line of objection if one could argue that the listener's response not only is initiated by the music but also depends on attention to the course of the music for its elaboration and articulation. Where such a theory emphasizes the role of the imagination, that role is not one of free association but of thoughts (entertained without belief) prompted directly by the music and responsive to all its subtle nuances.

One who argues in this manner is Donald Callen (1982a, 1983, and 1985). He is inclined to agree (especially 1982b) with Kivy's account of the nature of musical expressiveness, but he does not see that account as going far enough (also see Higgins 1991). Music does not merely possess sorrowful qualities, like the face of a Saint Bernard; it has a dynamic vitality that justifies our thinking of it as emotionally alive, as presenting the emotional life of an agent. Musical expressiveness has purposiveness and coherence that invests it with humanity and makes it seem like a communication. We experience music as fictionally expressing (but not representing) emotions; we experience it as an organic, living whole. So it is that it calls from us human involvement and response, engagement with the music, as no static image of feeling would.

According to Callen, our experience of music involves the imagination (since we do not believe the music to be an actual agent with feelings), but the imagination is directed and controlled by the musical context (1983, 77–80). It is, anyway, natural for us to vivify the music. Music encourages the listener to move in a way that resonates with its own dynamic character. The way we move affects our feelings (as well as vice versa); the movements we make, and their affective content, model for us the expressive character we hear (in a stylized form) in the music. When now the imagination contributes to the process we have a sympathetic identification not solely of expressive quality but of (fictional) human feeling in the music. The point of bringing to the music a model of human expressive behavior is to understand the music; to the extent that many important aesthetic qualities are expressive ones, such an approach not only is proper but is perhaps essential to the fullest appreciation of the music. Though Callen (1982a) is not entirely opposed to the suggestion that his theory turns all music into program music (dealing not with definite thoughts, events, and objects but with emotions

< 291 >

and their progression), he stresses that the focus falls on the appeal to images and ideas, rather than on the invention of programmatic thoughts, as part of the process of coming to understand the music.

I wish to distinguish two aspects of Callen's account. The first involves the claim that, to appreciate music fully, one must hear its expressive character (if it is expressive), and doing so is not a matter of observing in a detached fashion a given aesthetic property but one of being involved with the work and no less liable to respond to its expressiveness than one would be to react to a person's emotion. One way of putting the point might be this: we do not associate music with human movement because it happens to be playing while people dance; rather, people dance to music because it invites motion from them. The association between music, specifically rhythm, and movement, including movement expressive of emotion, is not arbitrary (for discussion, see Keil 1966). Only if it were so would going from one to the other lead the listener away from the music. Instead, the connection is natural, though stylized and conventionalized to some extent, so that his making the association leads him toward—indeed, may be essential for—an understanding of the music. This natural connection is founded on similarities revealed to the imagination, the workings of which lead him to approach and appreciate music not as pure sound but as human utterance.

Now, on this reading, I find little to disagree with in Callen's position. But I note that it would be an exaggeration to regard such a view as going far beyond the account of expressiveness in music offered by Kivy. Kivy emphasizes that we tend to animate the inanimate and that our doing so is a crucial aspect of our hearing expressiveness in music. The reading given here of Callen's position makes a similar point and provides some suggestions about the psychological processes that might underpin the process. Callen implies that Kivy's account would leave us with a stilted, wooden, inactive expressiveness in music, but I doubt that such a view correctly represents Kivy's view. Kivy stresses, as I also have done, that the expressiveness of music is intimately tied to its dynamic character, and that music presents not so much an appearance of the human face as one of human deportment, gait, or action. Kivy perhaps is less inclined than Callen to place weight on the fact that music is to be appreciated as embedded in the human context of creation and performance, but there is nothing inherent to his theory preventing its accommodating that point.

If Callen differs from Kivy, he does so most obviously in emphasizing the place of the imagination in the experience of music. Is he right to do so? I doubt this, for reasons set out in Chapter 2 in the discussion of Kendall Walton's similar views. Hearing the sadness in the music does not require

< 292 >

the use of the imagination *as imaging*; nor does it require one's actively entertaining the thought of the music's expressing an occurrent emotion. If recognition of music's expressiveness requires imagination, it does so in the way veridical perception often does: hearing the sadness in the music takes the same kind of imagination as is involved in seeing from the petrol gauge that the car is low on gas, or in realizing that Cousin Mabel, whose closest friend is married to an Australian, might be offended by jokes about antipodeans.[10]

Much of the undoubted appeal of Callen's arguments depends, I believe, on its inviting the reading presented here. There is much to indicate that Callen hopes to say more, however, so I offer a second reading (which might be seen as augmenting the first). This second reading gives a central place to the imagination as involving imaging, and generally to the experience of music as depending on its being treated as fictionally presenting an agent's feelings. Sometimes when Callen discusses the imagination he clearly has in mind the case in which one pictures scenes one does not take to be actual, or where one explicitly entertains some idea one takes to be false in reality. He seems to regard this imagining to be central in explaining the listener's affective involvement in the music; that is, he assimilates the approach to music with that to fictions in general. Though we do not believe music to be an agent capable of feeling anything, it is no less real or moving for us than is Anna Karenina in Tolstoy's novel or Macbeth in Shakespeare's tragedy. If there is a difficulty in explaining why we respond to music as we do, the problem is the general one of explaining why we react to fictions despite our believing them to be fictions (see Callen 1982a, 390)—and that problem can be removed, where the object is known to be presented fictionally, by showing how the imagination might take over from belief the role of locating the emotion's object.

We respond emotionally to fictions. We pity Anna Karenina her plight, for instance. Such responses are problematic in that the beliefs normally required for a response of pity are absent. The reader of Tolstoy's novel does not believe that Anna Karenina exists, so he does not believe that there is a person, such as is described, to be pitied.[11] Now, the subject of emotional

[10] The criticism is also raised (against Scruton 1974) by David Best. He concludes, "My point is that imagination may be equally necessary to understand and respond to certain people and situations in life" (1985, 178).

[11] Note that it need not be the fictionality of the character, so much as the non-current factual nature of the situation of the character, that creates the problem (see Currie 1990). Though de Gaulle was a real person and aspects of that real person's life feature in the fictional work *The Day of the Jackal*, one can feel concern for the fate of the de Gaulle in the fiction while knowing that the real de Gaulle was not assassinated. The point can be taken further. Film of concentration camp victims can be intensely moving, though we know that the victims are no longer in

< 293 >

responses to fictional characters and situations is a topic that has attracted much attention, and I am not in a position here to review all the arguments and considerations that have been canvassed. The relevant point is this: some philosophers argue that, for fictions, the imagination can supplant the role of belief in securing the object of the emotional response.[12] They appeal not to the sense of imagination in which it involves false belief but to the sense in which one knowingly entertains the reality of what is narrated or pictured in the fiction; they make use of the notion of make-believe. Where the response is to an artwork that is a piece of fiction, and where its narrated or pictured contents constrain the imagination (so that one entertains the actuality of the scenes and events depicted or narrated and does so in accordance with the conventions appropriate to the work's genre), the response is aesthetically/artistically appropriate.

Literature, theater, film, painting, and the like supply a content (semantic or representational) on which one can exercise one's make-believe without departing, as it were, from the boundaries of the work. This content shapes, controls, and directs the audience's imagination. This is anticipated by the artist and expected of the audience. The activation of make-believe is frequently involuntary (in the sense that often it is difficult to consistently view the action of a film as the posturing of mere actors) and the role played by the imagination is not (or should not be) especially creative or individualistic. To the extent that the imagination is in the control of the work, the response remains a response to the work, not the result of a private fantasy. Accordingly, one can justify the emotional response to a narrational/representational work much as one would justify a response founded on belief. One argues, for example, that the hero's grief is self-indulgent, and hence that it is proper that one feels contempt rather than compassion for him. Representational/fictional artworks might call forth as many emotions as there are types of situations calling for such responses in real life.

Now, suppose that some version of this theory solves the problem of the response to a fiction by showing how such an affective response might take (what is known to be) a fiction as its emotional object by making believe in its actuality. Then we can assume that responses to the characters of operas, songs, and ballet also might be founded on the imagination rather than on belief. Is Callen correct in suggesting that the imagination might play a simi-

---

the situation depicted. In this case one does believe that the filmed scenes took place, but one does not have the belief that would appear to be required for the response—that the scene depicted is more or less current.

[12] See, for example, Scruton 1974, Walton 1978 and 1990, and Currie 1990.

< 294 >

lar role in justifying as aesthetically/artistically appropriate a sad response to the sadness of a work of pure music? I deny this.

It is appropriate to respond imaginatively to a literary or pictorial work so long as the imagination is prompted and controlled by the work's contents, but if pure music offers no such content the exercise of the imagination is unrestricted by such works, even if the imagination is responsive to some features of the course of musical events (see Davies 1983a).[13] A person makes no mistake in treating representational music (if there is any such) as depictive, but she would err if she took all musical works to be representational (or narrational), because she would seek to find in such works properties they do not possess. Alternatively, if she thinks that she can justify her response as a response to the work and its properties by treating all musical works *as if* they were representational, thereby attributing counterfactual properties to them, she makes a different mistake. Counterfactual properties are not possessed by the work in some strange way; they are not possessed by the work at all. So a response to such properties is a response to some phantom work, and not to the actual work. We are *capable* of listening to pure music as if it presents a content to which we can apply our imaginations, but the exercise of this capacity with respect to pure music is not consistent with the claim to be concerned with the work's appreciation. Where the imagination is not constrained by the work's contents, the response initiated through make-believe is personal and probably idiosyncratic; there is agreement in responses only by chance and only at the most general level of shared associations. In these cases the music is merely the occasion for the response—its initiating cause, as Hanslick says, rather than its object. Moreover, since the exercise of the imagination is invited neither by music of the kind in question nor by the conventions generating the properties of such works, the "programmatic" approach to pure music is aesthetically gratuitous. As Kivy (1989) puts it, the response is not "musically proper."[14]

[13] If it takes imagination to hear notes grouped as a theme, or a theme as quizzical, or a relation between themes—which, anyway, I am inclined to doubt—then the imagination required is not of the make-believing variety. The theme comprises the notes; that is not something the listener should make believe.

[14] Kivy (1983 and 1989) dismisses Callen as an arousalist who (like Meyer) sees no problem in giving the imagination free rein. This view is ungenerous, not only because Callen's position invites the first, as well as the second, of the readings I have offered, but also because Callen clearly recognizes that the theory relies for its plausibility on the idea that the exercise of the imagination is no more free in the musical case than it is when the work to be appreciated is a play, painting, or novel. Kivy implies that Callen does not understand what needs to be argued, whereas I believe instead that Callen happens to be mistaken in the truth of one of his premises. There is more justice in the similar campaign mounted by Kivy (1980, 31–33) against the views

< 295 >

This is not to deny that, where it is prompted into action, the imagination secures the object of one's response. Rather, the point is that, since what is make-believed lies beyond the control and content of the work, the object of one's response is not the work as such, so there is no reason to regard the response as relevant to, or revealing, an appreciation of the piece as an artwork. One's imagination (or memory) might interfere with the experience despite one's best efforts to attend to the work—for example, where the oboe leads one to wonder about the musicality of ducks, or where one cannot hear a tune without also recalling the words of the toothpaste advertisement in which it was used. Music can suggest mental images to the listener, as no doubt occurred when someone decided to draw dinosaurs in animating (in the Disney film *Fantasia*) Stravinsky's *Rite of Spring*. And music undeniably has great associative power: a wisp of melody might bring with it a cascade of powerfully poignant memories.

The point, as I say, is this: Where it comes into play, either by choice or unexpectedly, the imagination (as make-believe) might pick out the object of one's response as readily as does belief in other contexts. Where what one imagines is governed by the content of a work of fiction, that content is the emotional object of the response and the response may be artistically/ aesthetically appropriate, revealing one's understanding and appreciation of the work. But where pure music is involved, either one does not need to make-believe anything to respond to the work's contents (in which case make-believe does not after all take up the slack created by the absence of beliefs appropriate to sad responses and the like) or make-believe supplies an emotional object for one's response but does so by going so far beyond the work's contents that there is no reason to regard the *music* as the emotional object of the response. The imagination (in the form of make-believe) supplies an emotional object for one's response to pure music only at the expense of guaranteeing that it is not the musical work as such to which one responds. For pure music, make-believe can no more locate an object for the listener's response in the musical work than belief can.

There is a second point to be made against the theory that assimilates the response to music's expressiveness with the case in which one responds imaginatively to a fiction (see Davies 1980; Osborne 1982). *Usually* when one responds emotionally to another's (real or fictional) expression of emotion, one does so by feeling something different from the emotion to which one is responding. If another is sad, then I am likely to feel pity or compas-

---

of Charles Avison and, again (1990a), against Mew 1985a. Also see Sharpe 1983b for an interesting discussion of ways the response elicited by an artwork might be "deviant."

< 296 >

sion; if another is angry, I might feel fear. Of course, where two people respond to the same emotional object, they are likely to respond in the same way provided that they subscribe to the same beliefs or make-beliefs; my sibling and I might both be saddened by our uncle's death. Sometimes another's response (with its own object) could be the emotional object of a similar response from me (that is, because the different objects of our responses are brought under the same formal object); you are angry because you think you are cheated; I am angry with your being angry because you promised yesterday to try to control your vile temper. But, as noted above, in the case in which the emotional object of my response is another's response (whether real or fictional), then typically I do not have the reason that person has to respond to what is the object of their response. You are upset because you have cut your finger; I am compassionate because you are upset.

Now, what is distinctive to the case of the response to the expressiveness of the musical work (in the problematic case I am considering) is that it is alleged to take on the emotional character of the musical expression. Sad music (it is said) makes one feel sad; happy music makes one feel happy. This is a type of expressive contagion differing from the standard case. This response is not like that in which I feel compassion for another's sadness (of course, I do not believe that the music feels sad, so there is no object apposite to a compassionate response from me). Neither is it like the example in which I respond to your anger by feeling angry because of your broken promise. Nor is it a reaction like that in which the sad music makes me feel sad because it betrays the composer's early promise. In the case in question, it is said to be the sad character of the music that calls forth my sad response, but it does not call forth my response as would something I believe, or make believe, to be the formal object of sadness. The mirroring response to music's expressiveness typically differs from the emotional response that has as its object another's emotional state in that the character of the latter response is usually distinct from the emotion that is its emotional object.[15]

---

[15] Gregory Currie (1990) argues that literary works of fiction are to be taken to have fictional narrators (who may be distinct from the narrator as written into the work, should it have one) and that the response appropriate to what is expressed in a fictional work involves feeling what the fictional narrator feels. Suppose Currie is correct in this. One could not then use his argument to show that fiction invites a mirroring response. The reader does not respond to the fictional narrator's response by mirroring it. Rather, both the narrator and the reader respond to the story and that is why their responses should agree. The two responses differ in this respect only: whereas it is fictionally true of the fictional narrator that he has the response, the reader's response is founded on make-belief. The two responses should match in their character if the reader has the proper understanding of the events narrated, which is the understanding the fictional narrator has. I conclude, therefore, that Currie's views cannot be adapted to the present

< 297 >

It is difficult to see how any argument, such as Callen's, that attempts to justify the rationality of the emotional response to music by assimilating that case to the one in which one responds (with imagination supplanting the role of belief) to a fictional situation could do the necessary job. The disanalogies between the two types of cases are significant. Musical works of the kind under consideration do not present a content on which the imagination might be (or needs to be) exercised. Either the relevantly expressive properties can be appreciated without make-believe or the use of make-believe in building around them a web of fiction leads one away from the work because one's "building" is not controlled in its detail by features of the work. This is not to deny that there are problems about the rationality of emotional responses to fictions, but it is to point out that special and more acute problems arise in justifying the response to pure music. So one cannot comfort oneself with the thought that identical problems arise in connection with literature, and one cannot support an argument for the rationality of emotional responses to pure music as one might do (or try to do) for emotional responses to literature. Moreover, whereas the response to a fictional character's feelings parallels the reaction we might have to an actual person's feelings, in that the response differs from what the other feels (because it has an emotional object—namely, the other's feeling—differing from the emotional object of the other's response, which is some aspect of her situation), in the case of music one's response echoes the expressive character of the work (and one does not take the expressive character of the work to be an occurrent emotion with an emotional object).

Earlier I suggested that an extension of Callen's view, a second reading, would find him suggesting that the imagination could and should play the role in music appreciation that it takes in the appreciation of fiction. I hope to have shown that this more adventurous approach is unwarranted, even if it is the one intended by Callen. The problem posed by the apparently emotional-objectless, mirroring response to music's expressiveness is not solved by the suggestion that the imagination supplies an emotional object for the response. I doubt that one can justify the aesthetic/artistic appropriateness

---

issue, for the correspondence between responses he considers is not of the mirroring variety. Both Levinson (1982) and Walton (1990) have suggested that the listener echoes the expressive character of the music in her response as a result of imagining (or by finding herself imagining) that the feeling expressed in the music is her own. This suggestion raises as many problems as it solves, I think: the issue then might become, just how is such identification possible? and what is the point of one's making it?

< 298 >

of make-believe as securing the response to an emotional object for the musical case as one might in characterizing the reaction to a fiction.

Objectless Responses

So far I have agreed with Kivy's line. If the emotional response of the listener requires an object, and if that object must lie beyond the boundaries of the musical work (since an appropriate one is not presented within the work), such a response is not a response to the music's expressiveness. I also agree that there may be occasions on which a listener misdescribes his response in equating its musical cause with its object, so I accept in addition that some alleged counterexamples to Kivy's theory might be dismissed as involving such an error. But I doubt that these allowances dispatch the problem. An important possibility remains to be considered: that the response does not take the musical expressiveness as its emotional object not because it has another object but because the response lacks an emotional object. Kivy dismisses this possibility on the grounds that objectless responses are not of the garden variety. That point is one I reject eventually, but first I consider two unsatisfying accounts of objectless emotional responses to music's expressiveness.

In the previous chapter I considered the view that the emotions expressed in music are sui generis—that such emotions are distinctive in being unfelt, nonintensional, and so forth. I rejected this position for its failure to address the philosophical puzzle posed by music's expressiveness. Only someone dedicated to seeing virtue in intractable mystery could find such a view appealing. I noted that the account in question severs all connections between musical and ordinary emotions, making impossible an explanation of the appropriateness of our using emotion words, as opposed to our coining neologisms, to name the musical qualities in question. Now, someone who argues that the emotional response to music's expressiveness similarly is of a distinct, noncomparable variety would receive related objections.[16] According to this implausible position, the response to music's expressiveness just is distinct from all other types of emotions in lacking an emotional object, in not leading to the appropriate desires and actions, and so on. Adopting Kivy's strategy, we might ask: what reason is there to believe such

---

[16] Pratt (1931) attacks Ducasse (1966 [1929]) for holding this view. A contemporary version of the thesis can be found in Mew 1985a. Mew holds that responses to music are distinctive in not requiring an object, and he suggests that the listener imaginatively might supply an object for the response but need not do so. Radford (1991a) claims that Kivy treats the response as sui generis, but I find no evidence in Kivy's views for this assertion.

< 299 >

responses belong in the same "garden" as emotions? I agree with Kivy's challenge; unless one can explain the connectedness between such responses and standard cases of emotional experiences, then no plausible theory is on offer.

A second approach might characterize objectless emotions thus: Emotions necessarily involve physiological processes and states. Perhaps music triggers a primeval emotional response, bypassing the usual cognitive and causal context for emotions to plug directly into the emotional centers of the brain. It evokes emotions as pure physiological responses, initially uncluttered by thoughts believed or imagined. The first part of Meyer's theory, as outlined earlier, is an example of such a view. According to Meyer, affect occurs when an expected event is defeated or delayed. Meyer's theory concentrates on an account of the purely musical processes that give rise to expectations and of the regularity with which composers set out to thwart or, more often, delay the realization of those expectations in novel ways.[17]

Accept for the moment that there is a physiological basis to emotions and that music can elicit equivalent physiological reactions. Presumably what one experiences are sensations and their physiological accompaniments (faster pulse, tightening of the diaphragm, exhalation, and relief). Because of their intensional content, their social context, and their significance, emotions are far richer than are sensations of this sort. So, unless one favors a crude stimulus-response account of emotions, this theory fails to deliver a satisfactory analysis of the emotional response to music. Even if it is a necessary condition that emotions involve physiological processes and states, and sensations attendant on these, the existence of such sensations is not a sufficient condition for the presence of an emotion. Even if emotions are not purely cognitive states but must be accompanied by and connected with physiological conditions and changes, it is not so that emotions are purely physiological. At best, then, this theory provides some account of the feeling tone of the experience, but it fails to explain why the experience is of an emotion.

For Meyer, music gives rise in the first instance to "undifferentiated affect"; he implies that emotions cannot be individuated by the feeling tone that is partly constitutive of them. Kivy (1989) is inclined to agree that no emotions have a distinctive feeling tone. By contrast, Budd (1985a) and Currie (1990) suggest that the feeling tones of emotions fall roughly into two phenomenally distinct categories—the pleasant and the unpleasant. Suppose we accept this more liberal view. In doing so we might also allow that sadness and happiness can sometimes be individuated solely in terms of their feeling

---

[17] Coker (1972) is another who presents a physiological account of the response.

< 300 >

tones.[18] I do not concede, though, that in generating pleasant or unpleasant sensations music leads the listener to feel objectless happiness or sadness. I allow only that, if there is a response independently identifiable as emotional, it might (sometimes) be individuated as belonging to one of two broad types based on the sensations experienced. Where there is no more than a physiological reaction, the experience might be one of warm fuzzies or cold chills, but it is not one of emotion as such (even if all emotions involve some such sensations). Many causes produce physiological reactions without also giving rise to emotional responses.

In the previous few pages I have rejected two approaches aiming to establish as reasonable the idea that emotional responses to music's expressiveness might be objectless. Now I present an account of such responses which, it seems to me, is defensible.[19] I start from the assumption that at least some people some of the time are correct in characterizing their reaction to musical sadness as one of sadness. This response, rather than being pathological, can be revealing of aesthetic/artistic appreciation, I maintain. I allow that the musical expressiveness is the perceptual object and cause of this response, but not its emotional object, because the musical expressiveness is neither believed nor imagined to answer to the appropriate formal-object description.

Kivy (1989) constantly insists that the response to music must be of the garden variety. There are at least two things he seems to mean by this. The first is that the response to music, unless it is to be intractably mysterious, should be importantly similar to responses occurring in other contexts.[20] This is a claim I endorse. The second is that the response must take the music as instancing the appropriate formal object. This is the claim disputed. The issue is one about the number of "varieties" found in the "garden" of emotions. Kivy writes as if there is only one (the object-directed emotion characterized in Kenny 1969) and styles his account accordingly. To challenge Kivy's view I argue that objectless responses, far from being aberrant, are familiar and common. Such responses might be distinguishable from emotions proper, but more as another species of the same genus than as something radically distinct from emotions. Kivy's "garden" contains more varieties of response types than he countenances. The second step in the

---

[18] Levinson (1982 and 1990a, chap. 14) seems to take the argument further, suggesting that a range of emotions might be individuated solely by their feeling tones. I doubt this.

[19] I first outlined the following view in Davies 1980 and 1983a; a similar account is offered in Radford 1989 and 1991a.

[20] McAdoo (1992) is mistaken in taking Kivy's rejection of "associationism" for a denial of a connection between music's expressive properties and the world of human feeling.

< 301 >

reply to Kivy's line is to argue that the response to music is comparable to objectless reactions of the garden variety.

I start by considering Radford's views since Kivy discusses them. Radford (1989) suggests some possible candidates for objectless but perfectly ordinary emotions. The weather in Britain is depressing, but, even if it makes people depressed, it is not what they are depressed about; they might be depressed about nothing. Yellow is a cheerful color and its presence in a person's environment might cheer her, might "color" her mood. Kivy (1989) attacks the first of these examples. He accepts that the British weather does depress people (by being cold and damp), but he notes that to say the weather is depressing is merely to report its effects and not to attribute to it an expressive character. We do not say of the weather that it is depressed, as we might say of a musical work that it is sad. So the example is not one in which one responds to an *expressive* character displayed in the cause of one's reaction. In this way the analogy with the musical case is challenged, for Radford is trying to explain how music's sadness might lead to a response of sadness.

Radford (1991a) complains that Kivy mistreats the example. Radford says that the weather can be depressing without affecting one directly, through its coldness, dampness, or whatever. Perhaps this is so, but the point leaves Kivy's main criticism untouched: we do not regard the weather as expressing depression or respond to it because it is depressed, so there is no basis here for arguing that the sadness of music leads the listener to feel sad.

But if Kivy can deal with Radford's first example, the second—that yellow is a cheerful color which, as such, cheers those surrounded by it—presents problems for his view. These he ignores in failing to discuss the case. Note that Kivy cannot dismiss this example as he does the first, for, whereas he denies that depressing weather expresses sadness or depression, he accepts explicitly that canary yellow is a cheerful color: he holds (1990a, 183) that an interior decorator cannot choose canary yellow for a room without also choosing a cheerful color. To deal with this case, he must allow that yellow is a cheerful color while denying that it cheers those who live in yellow rooms. Radford (1991a) finds that claim implausible, as I do myself.

One point perhaps to be derived from Radford's discussion is this: Moods and feelings often seem to lack any emotional object. I can be depressed without there being anything about which I am depressed. Perhaps, for that very reason, we might distinguish moods from emotions proper. Be that as it may, moods belong in the same "garden" as emotions, I think; so, we find in the "garden" emotional-objectless responses. Radford (1991a) claims to be a "moodist" about musical expressiveness. But the response to music is not like an objectless mood, for the former involves close attention to the

< 302 >

music and is a reaction to that close attention, whereas the latter is objectless not only in lacking an emotional object but also in lacking a specific cause and focus. If I am depressed by the state of my bank balance, then my depression has an emotional object as well as a specific cause. By contrast, the case in question is one in which I find myself feeling depressed without there being any particular thing about which I am depressed. A cognitivist of Kivy's stamp might exploit the disanalogy between the cases. If the response to music is to be admitted to the "garden" by virtue of its resembling some other reaction we accept as ordinary, then the resemblance should be closer than that between objectless moods and sad responses to sad music.

A nearer case to the musical one, a case in which the emotional response depends on the expressive character of its cause, is the following. Moods seem often to be contagious; we can catch a mood as well as respond to one. The company of sad people can be depressing (whether or not their sadness is also the emotional object of a response such as sympathy or compassion). This might be explained as depending on empathy. A sensitivity to the emotional tone of a situation is likely to be a desirable attribute in human beings and is likely to be one that plays its role even where the situation does not call directly for an emotion-directed response (such as sympathy), or plays its role as something additional to the object-directed response it awakens. The case described here comes closer to the musical one in that it is the expressive character of the situation that affects one's reaction. Though more proximate, there remain crucial respects in which the two cases differ. That the company of sad people makes me feel depressed or generally sad is a reason, other things being equal, for my avoiding their company. There is no corresponding desire to avoid sad musical works. Moreover, the sad people *feel* sad, and that might be thought to be relevant to the mood I come to feel. In the musical case, by contrast, I do not believe (nor do I knowingly entertain the thought) that the music's sadness is a sadness felt by anyone.

In the previous chapter I claimed that music is expressive in presenting the appearances of emotions without regard to feelings. Such a view is consistent with Kivy's physiognomic theory of musical expressiveness, so I take it that he could have no objection to my assuming in what follows the truth of such an analysis of expressiveness in music. Now, to find a case closer to the musical one than those considered so far, we might ask if the expressive character of *appearances* might affect us as do the moods or emotions of others.

Tragedy and comedy are commonly represented by two masks, one with a sad expression and the other with a happy one. A person surrounding herself with masks of the tragic type (or working in a factory in which they are made, say) might find the atmosphere depressing and catch the sad

< 303 >

mood; a person surrounding herself with masks of the comic type might be inclined to feel more cheerful than otherwise would be the case. Now, since the person does not believe that the masks express emotions that are felt, there is no reason any emotional response is called for. Nevertheless, not only do we find the moods felt by others to be contagious, we sometimes also find expressive appearances similarly affecting. The person would explain her responses as depending on, and as echoing, the expressive character of the masks (though she would not thereby show the masks to be the emotional object, in Kenny's use of the term, of the response). If one wished to feel happy one might do so by surrounding oneself with happy-looking people. That one need not believe that the happy-looking people feel happy before their appearance can have a mildly cheering effect on one, and that no belief that they felt happy would have this effect on one if they never showed their happiness, indicates that emotional responses of this kind are made to emotion characteristics in appearances rather than to felt emotions as such (Davies 1980). In a view, such as Kivy's, according to which music wears an expressive physiognomy (without thereby betraying a felt emotion), if one could explain one's sadness as arising from an environment in which one were surrounded by sad-looking masks, so too could one justify a sad reaction to sad music.[21]

Where one catches the sad mood expressed in masks, the expressive appearance of those masks is the perceptual object of the response but not its emotional object. Such a response could not be justified as most emotions are—by showing that its object is properly to be seen under the relevant description—since one does not believe or knowingly imagine that the masks satisfy the formal-object description that would mark the response as a sad one. Is the response mysterious or aberrant, though? No less mysterious or aberrant, I would suggest, than is the recognition of expressiveness in music on Kivy's own account. In his view we have a tendency to animate the inanimate and thereby to see it as possessing expressive features. This tendency is nonrational, but Kivy is content to offer an explanation of the phenomenon as resulting from evolutionary processes having functional value (1989, 172–175). Why could one not extend that argument to allow for the type of response just described? Given the importance to us of the feelings of others, and given the intimate association between feelings or moods and their characteristic appearances and expressions, it might be natural for us not only to animate the inanimate in the way Kivy suggests but also to have our own

---

[21] One writer who finds this characterization of the listener's response more congenial than Kivy's is Higgins (1991).

< 304 >

feelings animated in their turn by that process. If Kivy's post hoc explanation (1989, 166–167) of musical expressiveness is acceptable, then why would a similar explanation not account for the mirroring response to the expressiveness (see Davies 1991c; Radford 1991b)?

One could not justify such a response as one would justify an emotional-object-directed response—by arguing that the expressive physiognomy instances the formal object of one's feeling. This does not mean, however, that no justification is available. If one were saddened by expressive appearances of happiness, and if one could offer no reason to support the belief that such appearances instantiate the formal object of sadness, then one's response would be mysterious and aberrant; to use Kivy's term, it would be pathological. But the same is not obviously true of a response echoing the expressive appearance that is its perceptual object. That response has an appropriateness that nonmirroring, objectless responses do not. In justification, one argues that the response's perceptual object possesses the expressive appearance reflected in one's own reaction. Emotion characteristics in appearances do not demand a response from us in quite the way our beliefs that others are gripped by felt emotions do, but to the extent that they do invite a response it is the mirroring response, and not another, that is called for.

Radford (1975) describes responses to fictions as "irrational." He denies (1991a and 1991b) that the response to music is similarly irrational, since we are not sad *about* or *for* the music as we are for Anna Karenina, but he does hold, nevertheless, that such responses lack justification. I agree that they cannot be justified in the standard way—by reference to beliefs (or thoughts knowingly entertained) about an emotional object—but I do believe that they might be justified to a degree. Not just any objectless reaction to an emotion characteristic in appearance can be appropriate. A description of the perceptual object of the response as having the expressive character echoed in one's feeling provides an explanation of the nature of one's response.

The view for which I am arguing here provides an answer for another of the problems raised by Kivy—that concert audiences do not act as if they feel sad in listening to sad music.[22] In the standard case of object-directed emotions, one's beliefs not only anchor the emotion to its intentional object, they motivate the desires that dispose one to action. If I feel sad because I believe the situation to be unfortunate and regrettable, I will try if I can to

---

[22] Radford might disagree; he claims (1991a) that happy, popular music does elicit from the listener behavior indicative of happy-feelingness—smiles, dancing, and the like.

< 305 >

alter the situation so that it is no longer unfortunate and regrettable. In the case of a mirroring response to an emotion characteristic in an appearance, many beliefs relevant to motivating action are absent. Since I do not believe (or knowingly imagine) the situation to be unfortunate and regrettable, I do not want to alter it as I would were my response emotional-object-directed; if I am at a musical concert, I have no reason to act to prevent the concert from continuing, for instance.

Kivy also notes that people do not betray feelings of sadness in their behavior at concerts: they do not look unhappy, or as if they are fighting back tears. These are typical behavioral features of felt sadness, and one would expect them to be evident if sad music leads some people to feel sadness. In his view, people can be moved by music even to tears, but they are moved by the beauty of the music or its performance, and it is evident in aspects of their behavior—fervent applause, recommendations that others listen to the work—that the tears they shed are not those of sadness. Now, one might be tempted to question the inference Kivy draws from his observations of those around him at concerts. In our society, people often attempt to suppress or control the outward manifestations of their feelings in public, and this tendency might be amplified in the special social context of a concert in which one is surrounded by others trying to listen in silence to the performance (Kingsbury 1991). There are conventions allowing for the expression of strong emotions at concerts at particular moments (such as at the end of the piece), but they deal with expressions of approval. Such conventions may be violated, as in the riot of disapproval that greeted the first performance of *The Rite of Spring*, but they are powerful constraints for all that. This line against Kivy strikes me as unappealing, though. Like Kivy, I doubt that most listeners feel emotions strong enough to require suppression; whereas he concludes that they do not feel sadness, I draw the moral that the sadness they feel is not of a type or strength that often would drive them to irrepressible crying.

In the previous chapter I noted that emotion characteristics in appearances are rather limited in type (sadness and happiness rather than hope or pride) and that, within these types, only some of the repertoires of behaviors that might give expression to the corresponding felt emotion are relevant. The appearances are those into which one might thoughtlessly fall rather than those to which one would give way in the grip of strong feeling. Sad-lookingness without regard to sad-feelingness is displayed not by constant crying but by a downcast demeanor. Emotion characteristics in appearances lack the power of the more dramatic forms of behavioral expressions of felt emotions. With this in mind, it can be seen, I think, why emotional responses

< 306 >

to emotion characteristics in appearances have a comparative mildness of vivacity. Sad-lookingness might lead, in others, to sad-feelingness, but their sad feelings are not of the desperate variety that wrings tears from them. The response is like a perceptual-object-directed mood. Not only does the response lack many beliefs which, standardly, would lead to action, it also lacks the beliefs that give intensity to those feelings. The point made here is not one about "aesthetic" responses as such but a more general one about responses in any situation to emotion characteristics in appearances. Such appearances work on our feelings, I believe, but they do so in a context guaranteeing that our feelings lack the intensional elements on which their strength commonly depends.

Why Would We Listen to Music If It Makes Us Feel Sad?

My account, if it works, solves one problem with which I started: it deals with the claim that the music is not a candidate for the emotional object of the listener's response by arguing that, while this is true, this does not show that the response is not one of the garden variety, even if it is not of the variety most often found in the "garden." And I have attempted also to deal with the charge that people do not display the behavior typically associated with sadness in responding to music. Another of the problems with which I commenced remains, however. If it is sadness that sad music makes people feel, why would they bother to listen to sad music? To put what I take to be a related point: why would one value being made to feel sad?

The Dilemma Posed by the Sad Response

It seems that one is trapped on the horns of a dilemma. If we enjoy the sadness that we claim to feel, then it is not plainly sadness that we are talking of, because sadness is not an enjoyable experience. On the other hand, if the sadness is unpleasant, we would not seek out, as we do, artworks leading us to feel sad. Kivy dodges the dilemma by arguing that expressively successful sad music does not make people feel sad, though it moves them to admiration and the like. Someone who wishes to claim that music can lead us to feel sad must confront the dilemma.

How might one argue that the sadness evoked by music is, if not pleasant, then less unpleasant than ordinary, emotional-object-directed sadness? It is common to reply that the "negative" response to music is not a full-blown instance of the emotion and, to the extent that it is not full-blown, is not so

< 307 >

unpleasant as usually would be the case.[23] Such responses lack "life implications" (Davies 1980); they do not involve, for example, the desires or the need to act which normally would be their accompaniments. Much of the unpleasantness attaching to such emotions might usually reside in the actions to which they lead. Levinson (1982) goes so far as to suggest that their absence might make it possible for us to savor the unpleasant character of our responses (also see Putman 1987); Radford (1991a) describes music as an "especially inviting" way to experience the somber, indeed tragic aspects of life. A traditional view of aesthetic experience regards it as "distanced," and this distancing is identified as a feature arising from the lack of life implications in the responses aroused. Marcia Eaton (1982) identifies another element in aesthetic experience—that of control—as ameliorating negative aspects of emotional responses to artworks (also see Mew 1985a and Goldman 1992). In responding to artworks we are usually in command of our situation, and that provides a security counteracting the unpleasant aspects of our experiences. In ordinary contexts, where so often we lack control of the events with which we are faced, we cannot calm our emotions in the same way. Among the eight reasons offered by Levinson (1982) for our acceptance of negative emotions are three appealing to the element of control provided by our imaginative involvement in the work: (i) We can imagine the musical expression as that of an anonymous agent and, in doing so, can follow its course and final resolution. This gives us a sense of mastery over, or accommodation with, powerful emotions. (ii) Or we can imagine that the emotions expressed in the music are our own and thereby come to a sense of our possessing the power to express and control emotions. (iii) Or we can imagine that the emotions expressed in the music are the composer's and thereby achieve a feeling of communion with the emotions of another.[24]

The detail of these claims deserves critical comment. As Eaton notes, distance might transform an unpleasant experience into a pleasurable one—for example, a fire might seem beautiful rather than terrifying—but it cannot explain away the unpleasantness of a sad response to an artwork, except by showing that the response is not one of sadness at all. But Eaton's own theory, appealing to the notion of control, also looks suspect. As the reader of

---

[23] For example, Levinson (1990a, 333) agrees with Kivy that the emotional response is not one of *real* sadness; he sees the issue as one about whether something *like* real sadness is experienced.

[24] In these cases, Levinson appears to be talking about our apprehension of the music's expressiveness rather than our own feelings. He does note, however, that there is a problem not only about the negativity of our own response but also in explaining why we should be interested in expressions of negative emotions. These three suggestions seem to be offered as an answer to that second problem rather than to the first.

< 308 >

a novel or member of an audience at a concert, one does not control the course of the artwork. A person's mastery of the situation amounts to the possibility that he might always put down the book or walk out of the concert. If he continues to read or listen, though, it seems he does not exercise control of a type that could mute the force of a sad response. The response he feels might not be under his control. Moreover, Eaton's view faces a further problem in seeming to entail the false idea that a person's experience of art would be the more enjoyable if he *could* always suppress the inclination toward negative responses (see Iseminger 1983). Finally, Levinson's appeal to self-empowerment through imaginative engagement with the musical work might be queried also. Kivy (1989) finds Levinson's approach "fantastic." If we indulge in such imaginings then we are not concentrating on the music (as we should). Levinson (1982) anticipates this objection and replies: the problem of negative reactions is posed as much by nonaesthetic as by aesthetically proper responses. He also questions whether such imaginings are, anyway, aesthetically improper, since the imagination is directed by the work's character. Levinson does not, however, anticipate this objection raised by Kivy (1989): in the cases described by Levinson, the satisfaction comes from the negative emotion's being vanquished during the work and from the sense of power going with that; yet, says Kivy, we do not experience a surge of satisfaction or relief when the work attains its happy conclusion. Thus, our experience of responding to music does not fit the model proposed by Levinson. To this I add: not every sad piece ends happily. The problem of explaining why we are interested in works such as Tchaikovsky's Symphony No. 6 or Berg's *Wozzeck* remains.

Despite these reservations about the arguments directed at the first horn of the dilemma, the observation that responses to artworks lack life implications is successful to some extent in showing, if not that the sadness of the response is pleasant, that the sadness is less drastic or dire in its unpleasantness than often is the case for sadness experienced in nonaesthetic situations. Success of this sort must be partial, however. The artistic context of appreciation might strip the emotional response of some of its aspects—desires and the need to act on them, the vitality of the feeling tone of the experience, and so on—but it cannot remove altogether the unpleasantness that is in part constitutive of negative emotions. If the baby is not to be thrown out with the bath water, the emotional experience cannot be characterized as a pleasant one, though it might be argued that its unpleasantness is muted by features of the aesthetic context in which the response occurs.

A standard approach to the second horn of the dilemma—why would we bother with artworks if they make us feel sad?—involves arguing that there

< 309 >

are benefits to be gained from tolerating negative emotional responses to artworks, and that these benefits outweigh or compensate for that unpleasantness. A first version of the line might be put this way: artworks are a source of knowledge and deep enjoyment, so, if they happen also to make us feel sad sometimes, that is a price we might pay willingly for the sake of other values. The obvious difficulty with this version is that it treats the emotional response as incidental, in that the work's value is not described as depending on its expressive character. It implies that the work would be better for its not leading us to feel sad, since the benefits as described do not depend on our feeling sad. Moreover, given the number of worthwhile artworks, the view also implies that we might always pursue the benefits of an interest in art while conscientiously avoiding those works that might make us feel sad. For such reasons this reply to the dilemma's second horn is feeble.

A stronger counter would concede that the value that leads us to seek out artworks making us feel sad depends to some extent on their affecting us in that way, despite the unpleasantness of the response. In Aristotle's view, negative responses to artworks have value through their cathartic effects; they purge our emotions. On the face of it, this view is not attractive. It implies that the value of experiencing such emotions is the relief we feel when the work comes to an end. No doubt the torturer's victim feels enormous, wonderful relief when the torture is ended, but one would hardly regard that as a reason for undergoing torture for its therapeutic consequences. Even if the negative emotions experienced in connection with artworks are muted in their character, it remains unclear why one would seek them out for the sake of catharsis. The answer to criticisms of this sort no doubt depends on the elaboration of the notion of catharsis, so that it is shown to involve more than mere relief from suffering. It may be, for example, that catharsis provides a knowledge not obtainable in any other way. Or it may be that dispositions of a kind that are only rarely exhibited need the outlet art offers. Because such responses arise in a context in which belief and the desires and need to act depending on belief are absent, it is possible to take a reflective attitude toward one's response and thereby to come to a better understanding than otherwise of the general nature of the emotions involved (again, appeal is made here to the lack of life implications in the experience). Moreover, the knowledge acquired might have a special significance when gained at first hand; it might have a heuristic value not conveyed by merely "propositional" knowledge. Levinson (1982) suggests that negative emotional responses to artworks reassure us of our emotional sensitivity and humanity (also see Callen 1982a). Another practical value of such knowledge, perhaps,

< 310 >

is that it builds character, or makes us better able to handle emotions in a mature way in other contexts.

Kivy (1989) is skeptical of arguments such as these. He doubts, and I agree, that there is much evidence to suggest that those who interest themselves in artworks expressive of sadness, and who claim to respond to such works by feeling sad, have a deeper understanding of emotions than do others, or that they are better able to cope with life's tragedies as a result of their experiences. Accepting (for the sake of argument) that some people are moved to sadness by sad music, Kivy allows that such experiences might be tolerated for the sake of other benefits, or for the sake of benefits depending in practice on the production of the unpleasant experience itself, but he holds that, though such claims are not thoroughly implausible, they fail to answer the problem adequately. His point, I take it, is one about degrees of plausibility. At best, such arguments explain why one might *resign* oneself to such experiences. That account is inadequate to the phenomenon in question, because people show no more reluctance in the face of tragic than of other good artworks. Indeed, they avidly seek out all artworks, including tragic ones. One might resign oneself to going to the dentist, but few people adopt to that experience the attitude commonly taken to artworks, which, after all, are not usually forced on one by others or by the circumstances of life. Just as the considerations offered against the first horn of the dilemma remove some of its edge without disposing of it, so the arguments offered against its second horn, to the extent that they work, are finally unconvincing.

Yet again, I find much to agree with in Kivy's discussion, but a crucial reply to worries such as his remains to be considered. Once more, it addresses the second horn of the dilemma. It does so, however, in a manner differing from the approaches already indicated, in that it calls into question the formulation of the problem.

Understanding Art

I suggest in this section that one should ask not "Why do people concern themselves with music that makes them feel sad?" but instead "Why do people concern themselves with music?" Part of the puzzle, I suggest, arises from too narrow a focus.

The problem posed by negative responses to artworks frequently seems to be presented as one concerning our interest in a subset of artworks. Radford says, "If there is a problem about sad music making people sad, because why then should they want to listen to it, there is no corresponding problem

< 311 >

about why people would and would want to listen to happy music" (1991a, 249). But there is a problem, as I see it, concerning happy music, though I admit the difficulty is less obvious. Much happy music is trite and boring. That a musical work expresses happiness is not, just like that, a good reason for wanting to listen to it, and if a person is addicted to such music their commitment might be no less puzzling than is that of the person who willingly listens to sad music. To see the puzzle as arising only in connection with a subset of artworks is to misconceive the problem and to do so in a way making it difficult to answer.

Whereas there are many motivations for an interest in music, to be interested in music "aesthetically," "for its own sake," is to aim at understanding a work, such as Beethoven's Symphony No. 5, for the piece it is. Those of us who have this concern have it because we derive pleasure from music in understanding it. Not every work affords pleasure when it is understood, though. To the contrary, it is just because some works are appreciated that they are avoided, for they are revealed to be overblown, lifeless, and mechanical in their predictability, or whatever. My point is a general one: much music presents a content such that the deeper one's understanding, the more enjoyable is the experience, and we value as great those works providing such enjoyment.

Now, if it is true that (many) people concern themselves with music for the sake of the enjoyment that comes with understanding it, and if it is also true that works dealing with "negative" emotions are no less worth understanding than those dealing with "positive" feelings, the listener should be as interested in the one kind of work as the other. And in either case, if the listener aims at understanding and appreciating the music, and if the emotional response is an aspect of the understanding she gains, then it is to be welcomed. If one desires comprehension, and if a response of sadness can indicate an appreciation of the nature of the given situation, just because it is appropriate to that situation, then the response, despite being negative, allows the satisfaction that goes with understanding. The response is not merely a by-product of the process of understanding; it is not merely a pleasant bonus or an irritant to be accepted with resignation. The response is not an incidental accompaniment but rather something integral to the understanding achieved. It is not something with which one puts up for the sake of understanding; it is an element of that understanding. If negative responses are no less an aspect of artistic appreciation than are positive responses, and if the concern lies with artistic understanding rather than, say, emotional titillation, and if understanding requires effort and commitment whatever emotions might arise in connection with it, then the question to be

< 312 >

asked cannot narrow the focus to the negative emotions without losing touch with the wider context in which the explanation should be sought. Many people engage with music for the enjoyment of understanding and appreciating it, or at least in anticipation of its meriting these in an enjoyable way. Understanding sometimes leads to responses, some of which are pleasant and some of which are unpleasant. The enjoyment of appreciating art is not reducible to the enjoyment of responding to it with pleasant emotions, no more than it is inhibited by a negative emotional response; the enjoyment of understanding is no less consistent with the one response than the other.

We pursue artworks that are liable to give rise to negative emotional responses no less avidly than those likely to produce positive emotional responses because what motivates our interest is a concern with locating those artworks that merit understanding and these are as likely to be works causing negative as causing positive responses. The works to avoid are those that are unlikely to repay the effort of appreciation—works that are clichéd, banal, boring. Some works might generate pleasant reactions to their expressive character, others unpleasant ones, but the latter works are neither more nor less to be avoided than the former if one is motivated to seek the pleasure that goes with understanding rather than mere titillation.

Personally, I avoid many films and books depicting gore and violence. Equally, though, there are books and films I avoid no less assiduously because I believe them to be happy in a trite, overly sentimental fashion. Also, there are books and films I seek out though I know in advance that they are gory or violent. The issue for me in these cases is neither that of whether negative emotions are dealt with nor that of whether the work might make me feel sad or depressed; it is, instead, whether I predict that the work presents a content worth appreciating and understanding. The distinction rests on my anticipated judgment of the work's artistic merits. If it strikes me as worth the effort, I accept that what I understand, through its very comprehension, might generate experiences that are not in themselves enjoyable. My attitude is not one of resignation, because I do want to understand works that richly reward the effort involved.[25]

Some individuals are not much interested in any art, and many of those who are interested in some kind of art are not much interested in all forms of art. But to love music from the late eighteenth century, say, is to be inter-

---

[25] I am not always so high-minded; sometimes I choose mindless entertainment over the artistically demanding (I have nothing against the pursuit of titillation as such). When I do, I prefer those entertainments that I expect to amuse me or make me feel happy over those I expect to make me sad. In the case of art, I doubt that its powerful attraction can be explained merely as a mindless pursuit of emotional frissons.

< 313 >

ested in understanding all such music if it rewards the effort required. For some (good) artworks, negative emotions come with the understanding we seek. These are not enjoyable emotions, but they are, for some people at least, an inevitable aspect of the understanding and appreciation they seek from art. The response would not be better for lacking this aspect because the response would, for the works and people concerned, not then be an understanding, appreciative one.

The view for which I have been arguing bears affinities with that presented by Nelson Goodman (1968, 248–251), though the brevity of Goodman's observations on the topic makes difficult their interpretation. Goodman rejects as unacceptable any crude distinction between the emotional and the cognitive; emotions centrally involve propositional attitudes, usually beliefs, and are not reducible to raw feels. Accordingly, an emotional response can provide evidence of a person's understanding (of a situation, and so forth) no less clearly than would their descriptions. Negative responses to artworks—for example, the horror and revulsion we feel at Macbeth's murder of Duncan—are no less indicative of understanding than is a dispassionate account of the work. "In aesthetic experience, emotion positive or negative is a mode of sensitivity to a work. The problem of tragedy and the paradox of ugliness evaporates" (Goodman 1968, 250).[26]

Levinson (1982) acknowledges Goodman's argument but thinks that it falls short of explaining why one should take the trouble to ascertain the properties of works that lead to negative emotions. But I think that Levinson does not give due weight here to Goodman's point that negative responses are no more problematic than positive ones, since both kinds of responses arise equally from an understanding engagement with the work. Goodman appears to reject, as I have, the approach that frames the problem as one arising peculiarly with respect to an interest taken in only some artworks, those liable to arouse negative responses. I read him as suggesting that the problem really is to be understood as one about why people concern themselves with art at all.

In his brief discussion of negative emotions, Goodman seems to have in mind responses occasioned by narrational or representational works rather than by pure music. In such works there is a content providing in an obvious way, via imaginative involvement, for emotional responses showing appre-

---

[26] Also suggestive is the idea that the enjoyment of sad and repulsive themes in art can be explained by appeal to considerations of a generality that might explain a concern with art in general: "What we are enjoying is the artist's delight in his power to match these themes . . . what he can do with all the traditional and conventional means at his command" (Saw 1962, 242).

< 314 >

ciation. It is less plain, perhaps, how mirroring responses to the expressiveness of pure musical works (as described previously) might evidence such an understanding. I have argued that, to the extent that such responses are founded on a recognition of the expressive character of the musical work, they provide evidence at one level of understanding and appreciation of the music's character. But someone who believed that such music really is to be understood only by the person who has a grasp of the technical means by which structure and expressiveness are generated in the given case might doubt that the level of understanding demonstrated by such responses is adequate to a proper appreciation of music.

To make good the arguments offered earlier in this section, I must reply to this doubt. I do so in the following chapter, in which I turn more directly to the discussion of what it is to understand music. One comment, though, is appropriate at this stage. As I have described it, the mirroring response to the expressive character of a musical work tends to be reflexive and less thought-founded than is a standardly object-directed response. To that extent, the mirroring response is rather primitive in its character. It might be doubted that such a response could always be a response of understanding, since the rich complexity of musical works suggests that any merely reflexive response lacks the sophistication on which the comprehension of musical works might be thought to depend.

A first point, by way of reply, is that the mirroring response, as I sketched it, does not involve the intensional character of the standardly object-directed response, but it is not without a cognitive component. It rests on the recognition of the expressive character of the music, and nothing I have said suggests that character is apparent to the thoughtless listener or to the person who hears music without listening to it. As allowed in the previous chapter, even if there is a natural element to the expressive character of much music, that natural element is often elaborately structured by conventions shaped through history and is not readily available to listeners lacking practical knowledge of the relevant musical style acquired through exposure to works in it. A second point: Musical works often present a sequence of expressive elements; the appreciation of those works depends, not merely on a listener's mechanically mirroring that sequence of emotions, but on the recognition of the pattern of temporal connections established. A frenziedly happy section might serve to heighten the overall mood of sadness, for example, so a listener who felt alternately happy and sad would not necessarily appreciate the dramatic and structural significance of the composer's use of her expressive materials (Davies 1980). Even if the mirroring response is the first to be

< 315 >

prompted, the listener can and should reflect on its appropriateness in the wider context.

Life and Suffering

I have argued that the issue is not so much why we concern ourselves with a subset of artworks that lead us to feel sad as why we take pleasure in understanding art that might involve a negative response to some of the properties of the given work. Someone might take the point but claim that it shifts, rather than answers, the problem with which we began. My earlier answer to the problem was that art is enjoyable through the understanding of it. Now, though, the problem is revived in this form: why should we find *that* enjoyable? Why do we enjoy understanding art, given that sometimes an aspect of that understanding can be unpleasant; and, more generally, given that an appreciation of art can require hard work and practice; and, finally, given that the understanding often does not serve obvious, practical goals? The answer to such a grand question lies beyond the scope both of my subject and my powers, but I cannot resist pursuing it a short distance.

Many people watch or listen to the daily news broadcasts (and do so knowing that much of the news will be depressing). Why? Presumably because they would rather know what is happening than not; they would rather know the worst than live in blissful ignorance. Much of what is reported in the news deals with events that do not touch one directly—accidents on freeways in foreign countries and the like—but one attends to the news despite this obvious fact. We are interested in understanding the actions of people and the complex products of human society not always for the sake of the benefits flowing to us from doing so, though there may be many such, but because such things have an abiding interest. Given the importance of information, it is not surprising that curiosity has considerable motivating power. Curiosity motivates us, I believe, even when it is not regarded as a means to some particular end. We are curious on occasions when no obvious, immediate, practical value derives from the trait.

Our interest in art, I have suggested elsewhere (1991b, 57–62), is a spin-off, activated by curiosity. We are a creature concerned (up to a point) with understanding and appreciation for their own sakes, in the sense that not all the things that concern us are tied directly to specifiable, practical goals. An interest in art in general may have many practical consequences of value (as a source of knowledge, heightened moral sensibility, character development, and so on), and perhaps the arts would not be regarded as a good thing were this not so, but to be interested in art usually is to be interested in works

< 316 >

approached not for the sake of their typicality but of their individuality. We are capable of finding enjoyment in attempting to comprehend such works in their particularity; to the extent that the identity of such works is relative to context, an interest in their individuality involves a concern with the piece as of a genre, of an oeuvre, of a style, of a school, of an artistic period.

In reply to the question "Why do we enjoy art (and the news for that matter) if the experience sometimes is constituted in part by features leading, through our grasp of their character, to negative responses?" I have said, "We are just like that." One way of elaborating that answer would be by explaining why we find interest in human action and the complex products of human agency. In turn, this would involve an account of human nature and psychology in terms of evolutionary theory, the demands of social life, and whatever else might be relevant. Rather than taking that course, I settle for emphasizing how much and how often we are "just like that." If the puzzle is one about the meaning of life (not just about the importance of both art and the broadcast news), I might hope to be excused from answering it.

Loss, deprivation, suffering, pain, struggle, and discomfort—all are part of life. Sometimes these things are avoidable; sensible navigators on the ocean of existence give rocky outcrops a wide berth. But also, such things are, as it were, inherent to the medium of life rather than merely a part of its content that one might try to skirt. They come unavoidably with life itself, so the living of a life includes one's dealing with such things as an inescapable part of existence.[27] In this world, to choose life is also to choose loss, pain, and the like. And we do choose life, even at an age when we know what that choice includes.[28] Suffering and discomfort are by no means always worse than death or unconsciousness. Sometimes they are preferable to sensory deprivation, or to being ignored, as is apparent from the behavior of children who, if they cannot attract attention to themselves in any other way, do so by being naughty, even knowing that their actions will lead to penalties.

Negative emotions and feelings are not unavoidably a part of life merely as the price of admission, as an unpleasant extra tolerated so long as it does not prevent our participation in the games that give us pleasure. They are

[27] So it is that prudence, courage, fortitude, stalwartness, endurance, and commitment are numbered among the moral virtues (or are the stuff from which virtuous actions might be forged) and their opposites are counted as vices. If the world yielded without resistance to our every whim and desire, the virtues as we understand them could have no social significance, for there would be no occasion for the exhibition of the qualities of character they involve.

[28] The evidence of attempted suicides suggests (for those who do not have the wit to recognize the point from their own experience) that pain, loneliness, grief, humiliation, and the like can be so acute that death is to be preferred to life. But suicide is far from the most common form of death overall.

< 317 >

more intimately elements in the activities giving our lives meaning and importance than this view suggests. Some of the projects providing the greatest fulfillment demand fearful risks and known costs. Yet people commit themselves cheerfully to intellectually and physically demanding professions, to intense personal relationships, to birthing and raising children, and so on—and they do so not entirely in ignorance of what the future holds in store. Often the hard work, pain, anxiety, and stress are so much a part of the project that it would no longer be the same project were their possibility removed. One expects to bring up children, not angels, so one expects all the difficulties and disappointments, as well as all the rewards, that go with trying to teach slowly maturing human beings how to become adults who might respect themselves and deserve the respect and affection of others. There is no gain without pain, as they say. The deepest satisfactions sometimes depend not just on what was gained but on how hard it was to attain.

These observations cannot be dismissed as covering merely the serious side of life. People race in cars at speed, crawl through mud and water in narrow tunnels in the bowels of the earth, wrestle with the intellectual problems posed by chess, crosswords, and the like, throw themselves off bridges with bits of elastic tied to their ankles, attempt time and again to improve their ability to hit a small ball into a slightly larger hole a quarter of a mile away, and so on, and so forth. They do such things not always for money, or esteem, or fame, or glory, or because they have a duty to engage in such activities, or for the sake of their health and character development (though they may be mindful of such matters sometimes) but also, and mainly, out of love of the activity. These activities are engaged in for fun! Many involve unpleasantness in one way or another, if only as hard work directed to no obvious payout beyond what is found in the activity itself.

In some cases the unpleasant aspects might be regarded as mere inconveniences that must be tolerated, but in others the unpleasant side of the activity is integral to it—integral not in the sense that, masochistically, the unpleasantness is to be enjoyed for its own sake but, rather, in the sense that the activity found enjoyable would no longer be what it is if that unpleasantness (or the risk of it) were absent. For example, the danger faced by the mountaineer is not tolerated merely for the sake of the view from the top; if it were, the person would opt for a safe helicopter ride if she had the choice. The dedicated mountaineer's enjoyment is taken in the activity of climbing mountains. Now, to ask if climbing would be the more enjoyable if the climb were always without danger is to ask a strange question. Climbing on mountains is inherently dangerous, so it is not clear how to make sense of the question. And to ask if climbing would be more enjoyable for the person if

< 318 >

she were always without fear is also to ask a far from straightforward question. If the enjoyment derived from climbing comes from meeting the demands of the activity, then the climber must display the requisite skills, and these include a proper assessment of the dangers posed by the mountain and, in view of this, the adoption of methods making the climb as safe as it can be, given the route, and so on. It is far from clear how someone could recognize the danger for what it is while never feeling fear, though the person might display the courage or nerve required to overcome that fear calmly. The fear comes from understanding the conditions of climbing, and it is that very same understanding that provides point to enjoying the exercise of the skills required in climbing (one among many of which is that of controlling one's own anxieties). The climber takes pleasure in mountaineering—in its challenge and so forth—and, if the activity were to be such that it might be climbing-in-a-context-in-which-fear-could-not-naturally-arise, then it would no longer be the climbing she enjoys; climbing of that kind just is not mountaineering, it might be said. To understand why the mountaineer take on a scary activity is to understand how she can find enjoyment in a complex activity including among its elements the possibility of ever-present fear.

Why do people climb mountains for fun? For the same sort of reason they take an interest in the appreciation of music, or marry, or work at carpentry as a hobby. Because they choose the enjoyment that comes with taking charge of their own lives, even if that means taking on the negative as well as the positive constituents making life what it is. One's own life is what one does, and what happens to one, and what one makes of what happens to one, in the time between one's birth and death. A person who rehearsed too hard or waited too long for the right moment would find, not that he was prepared for life, but that the life he had lived was the life that consisted in preparing for something else, not the life he took himself to be preparing for. And a person who tried always to shun confrontation with pain and suffering would miss out on everything normally judged to make life worth living, while condemning himself to the sadness of realizing that the wait was in vain. At least some of the pleasure life can give comes from one's attempting with a degree of success to deal with one's situation and circumstances—controlling what can be controlled, accepting with grace and equanimity the unavoidable. If the appreciation of art is especially important in this process, it is so not because it is a training or a substitute for life (as sometimes is held) but because it is a celebration of the ways people engage with each other and the world in giving significance to their existence.

< 319 >

In this chapter I have addressed the question of the listener's emotional response to music, especially to its expressiveness. Kivy denies that sad music moves people to mirroring emotions on the grounds that such responses are not of the garden variety in that they lack emotional objects, are not clearly expressed in behavior, and make mysterious the interest taken in music expressive of sadness. Whereas I agree with Kivy that many arguments offered in justification of such responses are unsuccessful (for example, that we tolerate negative responses to music for the sake of the knowledge of the emotions we thereby gain) or inappropriate (for example, that the imagination takes over the role of belief in securing an emotional object for such responses), I believe a coherent account of such reactions can be given. They are no less common in nonaesthetic than in musical contexts, I suggest; they are of a familiar kind. Moreover, even if such responses are not to be justified as are the object-directed variety, mirroring responses are not irrational.

< 320 >

SEVEN

· · · · ·

Musical Understanding

Not all the effects caused by music depend on the listener's understanding it as music. It is said that music soothes the breast of the savage beast. In any event, "classical" music (loosely described) in the milking parlor leads cows to give more milk. This increased yield does not show that cows understand music. It does not even show that cows enjoy music as music. At best it indicates that cows like the noise made by music (of a particular kind). Before the listener can understand (or misunderstand) music, he must be able to hear its noise as the sound of music. In this chapter I begin by considering what is involved in hearing music as music and, more particularly, what is involved in hearing specific instances of music as the bits they are. I start with this topic because, if music is the object of understanding, the ability to pick out such an object is a prerequisite for its comprehension.

The Sound of Music and the Noise It Makes

According to Peter Kivy (1986 and 1990a), music does not affect us as drugs do. A drug produces its effects without one's being aware of how it does so, or even without one's knowing one has been exposed to the drug. By contrast, a person responds to a musical work as such only if she attends to the music in the appropriate way. To be enjoyed and appreciated, music should be listened to, not merely heard.[1] Music is unlike a drug in that it is

---

[1] Price (1992) mistakes Kivy's position in holding that Kivy denies that the cause of one's response can be its perceptual object.

< 321 >

created to be understood by its "consumer," and the effects it has on us as music depend on our attempting to understand it.

The difference between the ways drugs and music have their effects is perhaps not so stark as Kivy suggests. On the one hand, the user's beliefs can play a part in securing the effects of a drug-taking episode. This is why, in trials of new drugs, the subjects are not told whether they have been given the drug under test or a placebo. Marijuana might have stronger effects when the user is passing a joint among giggling friends than when she is alone. And, on the other hand, music might trigger some responses simply by being heard. For example, it might affect in a predictable manner the heartbeat or the rate of respiration; it might trigger muscular twitches. Nevertheless, despite such qualifications, Kivy's generalization stands: many drugs produce most of their effects irrespective of the user's cognitive engagement in the process by which they work, whereas music invites, and requires, if it is to be understood, a much higher degree of involvement. The noise made by music might affect its *hearer*, but the rich experience of enjoyment music is capable of affording the *listener* is not achieved until he attends to that noise *as* the sound of music. We do not normally say that the enjoyment or relief provided to a person by drugs arises from, and depends on, her understanding of the drugs she takes. But we do recognize a much more intimate connection between the listener's response to music and the understanding she has of it.

Perhaps this conclusion is surprising, given the extent to which the enjoyment of pure music appears to be primarily sensuous (rather than concerning itself with a narrated or depicted content, these being absent). Insofar as the enjoyment of music derives from awareness of its sensuous properties, requires attention to those properties, and is actively pursued, it could be thought that our interest in music is like our interest in ice cream or chocolate. Just as we enjoy the ice cream for its flavor, texture, and coldness, it might be observed, so we enjoy the sounds made by music for their timbres. We take pleasure in the rumbling throb of the organ pedal, the lush fruitiness of the low register of the alto flute, the ethereal character of string harmonics, the piquant combination of piccolo and contra-bassoon, and so on. Properties that present themselves directly to the senses, as do flavors and timbres, are not features calling from the appreciator much by way of thoughtful consideration.[2] The argument might conclude: music is no more to be understood than are other, merely sensuous pleasures.

---

[2] But it can be acknowledge that the experience might be affected by changes in belief in either case. If I do not believe that the cold, sticky stuff I am swallowing is ice cream, I am unlikely to

< 322 >

I do not doubt that an element in the enjoyment of music is straightforwardly sensuous, but I concur with Kivy's position: an interest that stopped
short at a concern with the sensuous properties of musical sounds would be
so impoverished as not to count as an enjoyment of music as such. A person
whose pleasure in Beethoven's Symphony No. 5 is merely sensuous is like a
person who enjoys the sound of a reading of *Pride and Prejudice* though she
does not speak the language in which the book is presented, or like a person
who takes pleasure in the colors of da Vinci's *Last Supper* but who cannot
see that people are represented in the fresco. The first person does not hear
Beethoven's piece as music any more than the second follows Jane Austen's
story or the third sees da Vinci's work. I have argued in previous chapters
that music does not possess a narrated or depicted content, but, just as a
reading of *Pride and Prejudice* is more than a series of noises and the *Last
Supper* is more than a few daubs on a wall, so Beethoven's Symphony No. 5
is more than the succession of timbres its sound presents. Timbre is only one
musical element found in Beethoven's symphony and, besides, the work is
more than the aggregation of its various elements; it takes its identity as
music from the method of their combination. Typically in music there are
hierarchical relationships between the parts (such that their being joined results in units heard as chords, phrases, themes, sections, and movements) and
the succession of elements is to be heard as organized. In brief, the sounds of
music do not merely happen to occur together, or merely to succeed each
other, but to be connected or patterned. To hear these noises as the sound of
music one must listen not solely for timbral (or rhythmic, or pitch) succession
but for organization. If music is organized sound, then someone who cannot
hear sounds as organized cannot be enjoying music as such.[3]

The crucial claim is not that there is nothing to be enjoyed in hearing
merely the sensuous properties of sounds (though I do believe that there is

---

enjoy its taste, even if it does happen to be ice cream. Similarly, if I believe the sounds I hear to
be caused by the screams of dying animals, I am unable to enjoy their timbres. To accommodate
this point, claims about the relevant experiences should be taken as presupposing "standard"
conditions.

[3] For a consideration of attempts to define music in such terms, see Levinson 1990a, chap.
11. I do not think that it is a necessary condition for something's being music that it be organized
sound; neither do I take this to be a sufficient condition. Nevertheless, this feature is characteristic of most music and that is adequate for my purposes. I accept that there are musical works
that take their course as a result, not of organization, but by applications of aleatoric and chance
procedures. I have more to write later in the chapter about the special problems posed by the
appreciation and understanding of such music. In this context I would say only this: I suspect
such music is music only because it comes out of a history of musical practice that aims at
organizing sounds; to hear such pieces as music, one must hear them as presupposing a background of practice to which they stand as a reaction.

< 323 >

less pleasure to be experienced at this crude level than is often supposed). Rather, the point is that a person who listens to music only in this fashion does not enjoy what he hears *as music* (see Kimmel 1992). In the same way, a person who cannot follow the story of *Pride and Prejudice* or who cannot see people depicted in the *Last Supper* does not take pleasure in these pieces *as art* (nor as the artworks they are). I do not deny that he might enjoy the experience he has of them; I deny that he enjoys them under the relevant description or concept, that of being art. The point retains its force even in the case in which, for whatever reason, his pleasure depends on his believing that the pieces *are* artworks, though his interest is not in them as artworks (so that he is like the person who enjoys the taste of ice cream only when he believes that it is ice cream he is eating). A case such as the last shows only that a knowledge of the causal provenance of the experience might shape some of its features; it does not show that cause, recognized for what it is, to be the perceptual *object* of enjoyment. So, the analogy between music and ice cream fails, for, when the pleasure taken in music is like the pleasure taken in ice cream, then that pleasure is not, after all, taken in music as such but merely in some aspect of the sound it happens to make.

I suggested earlier that sometimes the enjoyment of music is primarily sensuous. How can this statement be squared with the argument just offered? This is to be done as follows: The sounds of words are important in poetry and literature. But note that what are important are the sounds of words; sound here is significant in contributing to, or echoing, or providing a counterpoint against, semantic patterns and structures. Correspondingly, color is important in painting in creating or countering elements of content and form, for functioning symbolically, and for its purely sensuous qualities. So, someone who delights in the sound of words, or in the colors of paintings, considers these elements for their place in the wider context rather than being indifferent to, or unaware of, that setting. Such a person might go so far as to abstract sounds or rhythms from the words of a text, or colors and shapes from the depicted content of a painting, to savor their "purely" sensuous aspects. This response is far more sophisticated, however, than the experience of the person who approaches art solely as a source of sensuous experience. Now, music does not differ from the other arts in the respects mentioned. Timbre and other sensuous features of sound, such as subtleties of attack and decay, are important in music not least for the way they mesh or clash with other structurally significant elements within the whole. Instrumental "color" can become a central feature in some styles of music or in the works of some composers (just as the treatment of light and color can lie at the heart of styles and schools of painting). It is so in the techniques of

< 324 >

Klangfarbenmelodie used by some serial composers, as well as in the works of impressionists such as Debussy. Where color becomes of central significance in musical works, this is not because the organization of the sound of the work is irrelevant but because color plays a vital role in achieving that organization.

I have suggested that, if music is organized sound, to hear music as music is to hear it as displaying organization. To hear music as such is to hear it in terms of the principles of order that give it its identity as the music it is. It is to experience the music, in hearing it, as sound organized in accordance with the conventions of style or category applying to it. The relevant conventions differ (to some extent) from one type of music to another and are established by, and within, the music-making practice of the given culture or subculture. In general, the listener should be able to recognize when a significant unit (such as, if the style has such things, a melody) begins and ends and also when previously introduced material is repeated.[4] The listener should hear the completion of the work as an ending, not merely a stopping. When music is coherent, there is a strong sense of the aptness of its progressing as it does, of things fitting together, despite (sometimes) the unexpectedness of the course taken.

I mentioned that musical understanding lies in the manner of hearing rather than being separable from the direct experience of the music. Accomplished listening, no less than accomplished performing, requires spontaneity and unhesitating reactions; if the listener has to think about what is being heard he loses track of the thread. Simply, as a temporal art, music does not give the listener time to work out what is going on in it, because it invites the listener's attention to all its detail as it progresses at the rate of one second per second. If the music never comes naturally to the ear, it probably is not heard as the music it is (just because one is too busy thinking about what one last heard to give due attention to what one is hearing now). So, it is not sufficient for a person's being at home with music that he have a merely intellectual awareness of its conventions (as a result of reading about them in a book, for example).

---

[4] Unless a person can keep a musical idea in mind, he could not understand the many musical forms relying on thematic transformation—theme and variation, passacaglia, chaconne, ground bass—nor could he understand musical structures—sonata, bow, da capo, or rondo forms—generated through repetition. Without such an ability music could make no structural sense; it would appear to be continuous sound, reaching no natural conclusion. It is true, though, that many listeners cannot recall or reproduce melodies after they have heard a work (neither can they recollect a given melody during the work while other themes are being played). The recognition that counts for understanding is "passive" rather than "active"; it requires the ability to

< 325 >

The following comments from Fred Lerdahl and Ray Jackendoff capture much of what I would say about the grounding of musical understanding in the listener's capacity to hear the sound of music as the music it is:

> We will now elaborate the notion of "the musical intuitions of the experienced listener." By this we mean not just his conscious grasp of musical structure; an acculturated listener need never have studied music. Rather we are referring to the largely unconscious knowledge (the "musical intuition") that the listener brings to his hearing—a knowledge that enables him to organize and make coherent the surface patterns of pitch, attack, duration, intensity, timbre, and so forth. Such a listener is able to identify a previously unknown piece as an example of the idiom, to recognize elements of a piece as typical or anomalous, to identify a performer's error as possibly producing an "ungrammatical" configuration, to recognize various kinds of structural repetitions and variations, and, generally, to comprehend a piece within the idiom. (Lerdahl and Jackendoff, 1983, 3).[5]

From what has been said previously, it is obvious that a listener can understand music only if she approaches it in terms of the conventions that shape it as the music it is. A listener who is ignorant of the relevant conventions, or whose knowledge of the conventions is "academic," is in no position to identify the music for what it is through her experience of it, even if she knows that it is music she is hearing. A person who listens to Balinese *Gendèr Wayang*, neither knowing nor caring why the sounds follow each other in the order they do, is someone who interests herself not in the music, but in the noise it makes. Her pleasure is like that of the person who likes eating chocolate. If she is unable to anticipate what might or should be played next, feels no sense of closure on the completion of a piece, is incapable of identifying recurrences of material or of recognizing similarities and differences between parts of a work or between different works, then she does not appreciate the music qua music, though the music causes her enjoyment. This remains true in the case in which, rather than being indifferent to its organization, she radically misperceives the principles governing its generation. This is the position of an Occidental who listens to these Balinese pieces in

---

hear a similarity (or that something has been varied) when it is presented, not to reproduce a similarity at another time.

[5] Among those who share this view and develop aspects of its detail further than I do here are Levinson (1990b) and Raffman (1991).

< 326 >

terms of the musical conventions with which she is most familiar, those of tonal, Western music. She hears the sound as of music in the noises made, but she does not hear the music that is there. She might enjoy what she hears, but it is not the music as such that she enjoys.[6] She would be like a person who listens to Balinese as if it were misspoken English.

A more common experience than these two is that of listening to the music of another culture with an awareness that it is music one is hearing, and thereby with an understanding that what one hears is organized in accordance with some principles, while realizing that one does not grasp those principles and accordingly cannot adequately come to grips with the music as the music it is. The experience in this last case is likely to be one of frustration; it is an experience of the inability, try as one might, to discern the music in its sound.

Chinese opera, or Japanese Gagaku, or Indian ragas, unmistakably sound like music, just as the many languages of these respective countries unmistakably sound like languages, but the musics can be as impenetrable to the uninitiated as the languages are. If music, to be appreciated for the music it is, should be listened to against the background of the appropriate conventions, and if the musical conventions of various cultures can be arbitrarily different, then the music of foreign cultures is inaccessible to us until we learn, if we can, the relevant conventions. And if we are to find the music of alien cultures no less natural than is that of our own, we must absorb those conventions so thoroughly that we apply them unthinkingly, recognizing felicities or mistakes in performance by feeling or sensing what is right and wrong rather than by explicit, intellectual inference. Does this mean that a person from one culture never could understand the music of another? or that a person could never understand the music of some earlier period in her own culture's history?

I speculated in Chapters 1 and 5 that some of the conventions of music structure natural resemblances, though other of music's conventions are arbitrary; I suggested that music has meaning of types B or C more often than of type D. If I am correct in this, it could be predicted that the musics of

---

[6] More likely, because of the inappropriateness of the conventions in terms of which she listens, she will not enjoy what she hears. The music will sound out of tune in general, and the two instruments in each pair of *gendèr* will also sound out of tune with each other. Cook (1990, 149) claims that he does not hear Indian music as if it is out-of-tune Western music (which, according to Cook, Gerald Abraham does). He seems to think that his awareness that he is listening to Indian, not Western, music guarantees that he is appreciating it as the music it is. I do not believe that the relevant guarantee, if one is available, is so simple.

< 327 >

foreign cultures are more readily accessible than are their languages.[7] I believe this to be the case, though I can offer no more than personal observation and anecdote in support of my view. The music of Africa, south of the Sahara, is easily approached by Westerners because it so often employs the equivalent of the major scale for its tonal organization. In addition, anyone familiar with the techniques of repeated motivic variation in folk, pop, and jazz musics, as well as in some "classical" music, will not find it difficult to understand how music for the *mbira* or *likembe* is put together. But to the extent that music *is* conventionalized, not merely natural in its significance, it can be predicted also that the musics of foreign cultures, and of earlier historical periods of one's own culture, are far from transparent. Again, I claim that this is true, at least as my experience reveals it. Few Western listeners will make much sense of Gagaku music on first encountering it, I predict; as a result, they will find there little to enjoy at that stage.

It is possible that, whatever natural elements were once common to the musical ancestors of the styles now found across the world, no common ground remains. It also is possible that we are so deeply embedded in the musical culture we imbibe as children that we can never fully understand the music of cultures foreign to our ways of thinking, or of periods chronologically prior to our own. Nevertheless, I do not believe such things to be the case. Within the dominant Western culture, many listeners, performers, and composers move with ease between different styles or kinds of music—between jazz (traditional, bebop, modern, new wave), rhythm and blues (one style or two?), "classical" (covering mediaeval, renaissance, baroque, classical, romantic, impressionist, expressionist, serial, and so forth), country and western (one style or two?), folk, mainstream popular, church (hymns, incantation, chant), and so on. One or more of these styles has been married to the music local to another culture to produce a hybrid—for example, High Life in Africa, Kronchong in Indonesia, and Pacific island styles of church and popular music. The direction of cultural transmission is not always one-way. Popular music in North America finds its roots not only in Europe but also in Africa. So rich is the cross-fertilization between musical styles and so compelling are the results sometimes produced by the movement toward authentic performance of the music of earlier eras that I am inclined to believe that the cultural and historical barriers separating the musics of the world are superable.

So far I have stressed that, if the object of one's enjoyment is to be music

---

[7] A similar point was made in Chapter 2, where I cited Sparshott (1974) as denying that depiction is arbitrary in the way language is.

< 328 >

appreciated as such, that music must be approached through the conventions giving it its identity. To enjoy the music as the music it is is to hear it in terms of the style or kind to which it belongs. Now, in musical cultures (such as those from which jazz arose) that give the weight to music-making simpliciter rather than to the performance of identifiable works, this might be all that need be said. In many traditions, though, music-making aims primarily at the performance of works that possess and retain an identity independent of that of any one of their performances.[8] Then, to identify the given work not merely as music of a style or kind but as the individual work it is, it is necessary that the listener have some idea of the categories available and what it is that distinguishes one piece from another. To interest oneself in a musical work as an individual, to attempt to understand it for itself, one needs to know what kind of "self" it is, for one cannot sort those of its qualities marking it as of a type from those that are distinctive to it as an individual unless one is familiar with the relevant type. Just as the enjoyment of music as music involves an awareness of its sound such that that sound is heard as the music it is, not merely as the noise made by music, so the enjoyment of music as consisting of works involves an awareness of those works as belonging to a distinguishable musical type. Because of differences between the conventions characterizing suites, symphonies, sonatas, concertos, and the like, hearing a musical work as the work it is involves hearing it in terms of the conventions that apply to it *as a symphony, as a concerto*, or whatever.[9] For example, to appreciate a symphony as a symphony the listener must have some familiarity with the features typical of symphonies, with the place of the work under consideration within the tradition, and so forth.[10]

In the preceding I have outlined some of the "qualifications" required of

[8] I write this in spite of the arguments of Goehr (1989 and 1992). She suggests that the notion of a musical work is a comparatively recent one in Western musical history. If Goehr is correct in her view, then my remarks should be relativized to the period in which works have been written and appreciated as such.

[9] The general point is this: to appreciate a musical work as such is to appreciate it in light of the considerations governing its individuality. Different theories as to the ontological character of musical works take opposing stands on the detail of those considerations. Here I wish to dodge the issues raised in that debate. Simply, whatever is relevant to the identity of the work— be it sound structure alone, or coupled with musical practices that are historically bound, or linked with a specified means for performance, or indexed to the identity of the individual composer—the listener must approach the work with a knowledge adequate to determining its identity if it is to be enjoyed as the work it is.

[10] In the final two sections of this chapter I return to the present topic in considering both how a musical work may be singular as a person is and how the appreciation of a work should take place against the background of an awareness of its category and period.

< 329 >

the listener who aims to understand music as the music it is and, more especially, a particular piece as the work it is. Suppose that just such a listener
attends carefully to a work. It remains to say *what* he understands and *how*
he evidences his understanding. In the next few pages I outline brief answers
to these questions. The remainder of the chapter provides an indirect development of the position sketched here.

What is understood? the organization of the various elements to bring
about the effects heard in the work's sound, these being effects of integration, of tension and release, of balance, of closure, of unity, of expression.
Because the elements of music can be organized in many ways, at a variety
of levels, and with numerous degrees of complexity, musical understanding
is not an all-or-nothing matter but something that comes in many colors
and shades. Inevitably, considering what was done in the work also involves
judging whether that was worth doing—or, at least, whether the time and
effort required of the listener is rewarded to an extent that might draw her
back to the piece in due course.

How is this understanding evidenced? Assuming that the listener is not
herself a performer who might demonstrate to our satisfaction that she
understands a work through her manner of playing it, her appreciation of
the work is displayed in the descriptions she offers of it. I agree, then, with
Kivy(1986 and 1990a): a person does not understand a musical work if she
cannot describe key aspects of its organization when given suitable help and
encouragement.

It might be thought that the line for which I have argued does not entail
so strong a requirement for musical understanding. I insisted that only someone who can hear a musical piece in terms of the conventions applying to it
as a kind or style of music and as the category of piece it is can identify the
work as such—and thereby might understand it as an individual. But I also
allowed that, in practice, the listener's engagement with the work relies on
intuitions and is founded on feelings, rather than being merely intellectual.
So it is open to me to suggest that the relevant information is processed unconsciously. To hold this view is not to suppose that all music is transparent
in its significance, nor is it to assume that children appreciate Bach's music as
well as the experts do. The neurological structures that crunch the relevant
neurons might be culturally acquired rather than built in to the sound-
processing hardware. This is not to claim that any person is aware of learning to listen as he does, or that he could say what he has learned; the attention of consciousness might not be drawn to the formation of such
structures. With all this given, it might then be suggested that the neuron
crunching that goes on results in an output that plugs directly into parts of
the brain dealing with "low-level" motor, somatic, and emotional reactions,

< 330 >

bypassing the "higher," cognitive centers as it does so. According to this view, an understanding of music is shown not in one's ability to describe what one hears but in what one feels, in the music's arousing in the listener a need to dance, and so on.

Appealing though this position is (in that it virtually guarantees that anyone will understand any kind of music provided he exposes himself—mindlessly—to enough of it), I cannot believe that it is correct. Much data processing goes on as one listens, no doubt, and much of this processing is not retrievable by consciousness, I am sure. But I do not think a person could understand music if he could not distinguish one piece from another, or one theme from another, or if he could not tell of a structurally significant section that it had occurred earlier, and so on. Moreover, as Kathy Higgins has reminded me, it is unlikely that this person could dance very well to the music, quite apart from his inability to describe it. And I do not think that a person could be aware of such things without his being able to describe them later (even if he is not aware of being aware as he listens). A person who cannot tell one theme from another is not someone who understands the music at the level of the somatic rather than the cognitive, it is someone who cannot identify the music for what it is and who is in no position, therefore, to comprehend it as such.

As becomes clear, my insistence that the listener be able to describe the music to reveal his understanding of it is not in any way motivated by a desire to argue that musical appreciation is a skill reserved for some cultural elite. Nor is it part of my view that only those with formal training, or those who can read the notations, are capable of appreciating the music to which they listen. I believe that most listeners understand the music they like, though they may not be adept in articulating that understanding. Also, though I maintain that the listener must be capable of describing the music in appropriate terms if he is to show that he appreciates it as the music it is, I do not think that only the technical terms used by musicologists are the appropriate ones. The listener might say "here is the tune again" or "that twiddly bit comes from part of the tune." Or he might note, "though it is the same, it is altered, so that it sounds sadder," whereas a musicologist might say of the same passage that, "whereas the second subject is in the relative major of the tonic key in the exposition, in the recapitulation it returns in the tonic minor."

Enjoyment and Understanding

For the most part I have been considering the conditions under which one's enjoyment might be described truly as an enjoyment of the music as

< 331 >

such. Those conditions are much more demanding than those for the enjoyment of ice cream in the sense that one must bring to the experience of music much knowledge and practical skill (both as listener or performer). For this reason, we might describe the enjoyment of music as much more cognitive than is the pleasure of eating ice cream. The pleasure afforded by music listened to for its own sake is the pleasure of understanding it. To the extent that the process of listening to music as music is a sophisticated mode of perception much refined by experience, the enjoyment of music approached as such is cognitive rather than merely sensuous.

One difficulty that might be seen for my equation of understanding and enjoyment points out that the listener does not always enjoy a work the more for understanding it. As I consider it here, the point of this objection is not that enjoyment and understanding are unconnected but rather that, in understanding a work, the listener may come to realize that it is not worth enjoying. To appreciate or understand a work might involve recognizing that it contains little to enjoy.

This issue has been discussed by Kivy (1990a, 115–118), who suggests that, though it is true that sometimes we understand a work only to discover that it does not reward the effort, the interest we take in music in general presupposes that, more often than not, works are the more enjoyable for being understood. I would develop the point this way: We may not be able to avoid hearing music, but we can avoid listening to it. For the most part we listen to music, not out of duty, nor as a means to practical goals, but for its own sake. This is to say, I think, that we listen for the pleasure that comes from recognizing the music for what it is. The pleasure is not an end to which the music is merely a means, for the pleasure is bound inseparably to the nature of its object. The pleasure just is the enjoyment found in the music through understanding it. I claim that music in general is the more enjoyable when it is understood and appreciated as the music it is than when it is approached on a simply sensuous level as a (possibly) pleasant noise. Accordingly, when we look to pleasure from music we also commit ourselves to understanding it, because it is through understanding it that we gain such enjoyment as it affords. We do not always like what we come to understand, but in that case we avoid that work in the future.

Cognition and Perception

The view I have presented is liable to attract a further criticism: that the enjoyment of music is far less intellectual or cerebral than I have maintained and, hence, is not connected to the pursuit of musical understanding. Indeed,

< 332 >

it might be said, the attempt to grasp the nature of music at an intellectual level *opposes* the listener's enjoyment by blocking or inhibiting that, more natural, response. The version of the objection I consider below is presented by Nicholas Cook. In replying to his points I hope to make clearer the position I have been advocating.

Cook (1990; also see 1987) distinguishes "musical" from "musicological" listening.[11] Whereas a listener of the second persuasion is concerned with regarding and judging a work as a "perceptual object," the first type of listener aims only at the experience of a musical work afforded by listening to it (1990, 152–160). Musicological listening is motivated by a concern to pigeonhole the work, which is measured against typical instances of its type and judged a success if it emulates them.[12] Musicological listening typically involves a concern with the work's form. By contrast, musical listening approaches and enjoys the piece for the sake of its individuality, without first attempting to reduce it to technically describable elements. Whereas Cook regards musicological listening as a legitimate enterprise (for musicologists and ethnomusicologists, at least) as well as a source of pleasure (1990, 166), it is musical listening that is required for the enjoyment of music *as such*. The two kinds of listening, if not strictly exclusive, do not sit comfortably together. Musicological listening inhibits and interferes with musical listening (1990, 174); musicological listening is "unimportant" in an appreciation of music (1990, 46, 55, 147, 165, and 171).

Cook's views have attracted criticism. Ridley (1992) suggests that not everything that concerns musicologists is inaudible and not everything the listener finds gratifying is heard on a first listening. He concludes that there is more compatibility and interpenetration between the two kinds of listening than Cook countenances. Kivy (1992) is more damning. He regards Cook not merely as confused in his evaluation of the relative merits of the two approaches to listening but as committed to something approaching logical incoherence. Kivy suggests that anyone who *listens* to music must take the music (under some description) as the intentional object of percep-

---

[11] The view Cook espouses has always had its adherents. For example, Colin McAlpin says that music "is meant to inspire, not instruct; to solace the heart, not to satisfy the brain. Composers do not reason, they reveal" (1925, 433). He goes on (1925, 440–441) to disparage the intellectual objectivist who, like an entomologist, seeks to pin down for analytic scrutiny what is a plastic beauty. Bujic (1975) is another who believes that musicologists and music lovers no longer speak the same language; he holds that it is technical accounts, rather than ordinary descriptions, that are lacking.

[12] Cook describes pitches and intervals, as well as structural types, as "theoretical constructs" (1990, 217 and 237).

< 333 >

tion,[13] and that even the most untutored makes "judgments" about what she hears. For example, she must recognize that the piece is under way, or that the tune has ended. These two characteristics of the experience—that it is intentional and includes evaluation—are identified by Cook (1990, 154–158) as hallmarks of the listening he despises, the musicological. Now, though, Kivy wonders, what can be left to the kind of listening Cook favors, the musical? He concludes: Cook has described a listener who just does not listen.

I have no doubt that Cook's formulations invite the criticisms Kivy raises. In what might have been an unguarded moment, however, Cook makes this telling observation: whereas music of the late eighteenth century makes sense when played at half-speed, this is not so with Frédéric Chopin's, for at the slower tempo the important distinction in Chopin's music between structural harmonies and chords introduced as splashes of color is lost, so that the texture is muddied. He writes: "Playing [Chopin's] music too slowly, in other words, turns it into nonsense" (1990, 200–201). This suggests that Cook thinks an awareness of the uses of the harmony is important to the appreciation of such music. It is clear, also, that he sees his discussion as revealing the results of musical rather than musicological listening. But the musically sensitive observer who appreciates this feature of Chopin's music must recognize differences in function between the works' harmonies. This involves his taking the music as his perceptual object and making judgments about the various functions of the different chords. Then, it seems that the listener is to approach the work musicologically after all, not musically. Yet this cannot be what Cook means to show. So Cook appears to be confused, at best, about the basis of the distinction on which he rests his whole thesis, that between musical and musicological listening.[14]

I believe that Cook takes his position because he opposes perception to cognition and regards the latter as involving something like an (explicit or unconscious) analytical commentary on what one is doing, and why, as one

[13] Price (1992) misunderstands the point. He takes intentionality to be a matter of directedness, or pointing, and he denies that the musical work points to its formal type, or to anything else. But Kivy's suggestion is not that the form is the *work's* intentional object (whatever that suggestion might mean), rather that the musical work is the intentional object *of the listener's understanding.*

[14] Kivy (1992) holds that Cook mistakes a difference in the *motivation* for listening for a difference in the *mode of perception.* Cook *does* aim to capture a difference in the perceptual character of the two experiences, however. In his view, where the listening is musical the perceptual experience of the music absorbs one's entire attention, but where the listening is musicological at least part of one's mind is devoted to classifying or "describing" the work in formal or other technical terms, and to that extent one's attention to the work is partial.

< 334 >

does it. Such a commentary would distract the listener from the purely per-ceptual experience of listening. Because he does not believe that the ordinary music lover attempts this internal commentary, or that the trained musicolo-gist listens this way unless being self-consciously analytical, and does not believe that commentating takes place in the listener's unconscious (1990, 229–230), Cook holds that listening does not involve judgment. He distin-guishes the aural work, as presented immediately to the musical listener, from the analyst's work, which is visual and intellectual (1990, 58–59). But Cook confuses consciousness with self-awareness, thought with thinking that one is thinking. When I see a sentence in a book, or that the situation is dangerous, or that an argument is valid, or that my computer is switched on, I do not (always) observe sense data which I then interpret. This implies not that cognition plays no part in perception, however, but rather that percep-tion itself is irreducibly cognitive; that seeing or hearing is a thoughtful ex-perience, not in the sense that two separable mental processes often are combined, but in the sense that a variety of thinking that cannot be factored out permeates the perceptual experience. We do not (always) perceive things *before* bringing them under concepts; (usually) we perceive them under con-cepts from the outset.[15] The eyes and ears are educated by experience. We see tables and chairs, not uninterpreted patches of color, even if we do not say to ourselves as we see that it is tables and chairs we see. What a person perceives can depend to some extent on what he believes about his situation, so the relation between perception and belief does not run always or straight-forwardly from the former to the latter.

Because he separates perception from cognition, Cook is unable to ac-count adequately for many features of the listening experience. As he realizes (1990, 150–152), he is compelled to accept that a listener might enjoy a musical work while being unable to distinguish one theme from another, or without knowing when the piece has finished, or without being able to recog-nize another work as in a similar style. Moreover, he cannot acknowledge the extent to which contextual factors of style, category, period, and author-ship affect audible properties of musical works. He cannot allow that a tech-nical description of a piece might be equivalent to a phenomenal account of an appreciative experience of the work. This also means that he cannot ac-cept that a person who listens with ears informed by technical training can

---

[15] I do not say that we are born with the relevant concepts. I maintain, rather, that a condition of our having mastered them is the role they play in descriptions we offer of the phenomenal aspects of perception.

< 335 >

share with the musical listener his understanding and enjoyment. These corollaries of his position are counterintuitive, I believe.

Cook aims to defend the "ordinary" listener by arguing that the technically trained observer is not in a privileged position to understand the music. As becomes clear, I regard that view as laudable. I also agree with Cook that some musicological approaches are almost guaranteed to render nonaesthetic the experience of the work—for example, those that deal with aspects of the compositional process leading to no audible effects. Cook is not wrong to condemn approaches that are dry, sterile, and formulaic in treating the work merely as an instance of a general type while being indifferent to its individuality. But he is wrong to regard all musicological listening as flawed in these ways. He mistakenly equates musicological listening in general with some of its more arcane, specialized approaches, and with some of its more questionable applications. He goes too far in recommending a naïve, mindless approach to music and in denying that understanding and enjoyment can be enriched by formal education. I see Cook as erring in his strategy for defending the validity of the musical experience of the listener who, notwithstanding her lack of tuition in music theory, attends carefully to the work for its own sake. To show that such a listener might understand the music to which she listens he should proceed, not by dismissing as unimportant all the features that concern musicologists, but instead by arguing that "ordinary" perception is more cognitive than is often acknowledged. Even if the listener does not hear the music under the technical descriptions that might be offered by the musicologist, she might hear the music under descriptions that are no less revealing of her grasp of the features salient in giving the music its character.

Many people are leery of talking about musical understanding, as if music were something to be enjoyed without thought or comprehension.[16] The source of their wariness may be that most people do not compose or perform, cannot read the complex notation, and have no grasp of the technical vocabulary employed by trained experts. Moreover, many listeners lack a detailed knowledge of music history and of the development of musical styles. Because they are aware of their areas of ignorance, such listeners would be reluctant to claim an understanding of the music they enjoy, realizing that, in other arenas of life, claims to understanding can be justified only

---

[16] Some music critics seemingly do not recognize the musically unschooled as belonging to their proper audience. Cavell (1977), Kerman (1981), and Tanner (1985) lament the lack of a "humanistic" tradition of music criticism; also see Barzun 1953, Robert P. Morgan 1977, Aschenbrenner 1981, and Kivy 1989.

< 336 >

by the specialist. Nevertheless, these unschooled listeners regard themselves as music lovers, with a full and deep appreciation of the music they enjoy. In my view, they do deserve to be called music lovers because they understand more than they realize.

Knowing How, rather than Knowing That?

If a person understands a musical work, she has knowledge of it. If this knowledge is not a knowledge of technical descriptions, in what does it consist? One appealing possibility is that the person who understand music has practical, rather than propositional, knowledge; that she possesses know-how, without necessarily being aware of what or that she knows. It might be said that musical understanding is evidenced in a skill that need not be expressible in words or in any way other than through its application in producing satisfactory results. The view is attractive for these reasons: it acknowledges that music is the product of skillful activities in composition and performance, and it provides a way of explaining how it might be that those who understand music are not always competent in the articulation of their mastery. Despite its advantages, for which I argue further, I reject this view.

In some cases, the process of composition seems to proceed at an instinctual level. Mozart seems sometimes to have composed in such a fashion. He chose among the ideas that presented themselves those that sounded right or best. Because he did not always labor over his materials, we might suppose that he did not concern himself with analyzing or explaining what the rightness of his choices consisted in; by contrast, Beethoven's notebooks sometimes record a prolonged struggle to shape initial ideas to their final form. Moreover, it might be said, Mozart *could not* have analyzed much of his music, because the theoretical description of sonata form, the structural type given life in his music, was offered by musicologists only after his death. If anyone understood music, surely it was Mozart? Yet his understanding was applied rather than bookish.

Performance, too, involves a mastery of practical skills. It is a commonplace that performing musicians cannot always describe what they do (just as a person adept at tying his shoelaces might be incapable of describing the process accurately). Practitioners do not always make the best teachers, and some skills might not be teachable (by description, or as a formula) except by example. All this is nicely put by Joseph Kerman: "A musical tradition [of performance] does not maintain its 'life' or continuity by means of books and book-learning. It is transmitted at private lessons not so much by words

< 337 >

as by body language, and not so much by precept as by example. . . . The arcane sign-gesture-and-grunt system by which professionals communicate about interpretation at rehearsals is even less reducible to words or writing. It is not that there is any lack of thought about performance on the part of musicians in the central tradition, then. There is a great deal, but it is not thought of a kind that is readily articulated in words" (1981, 196). But, even if a performer cannot describe a work in a way that reveals her understanding, she might show that she understands it by her manner of playing it. Such a performance is convincing; it sounds right; it highlights the elements that need highlighting, balances those that need balancing, and so on.

Composers and performers display their musicality, their understanding, in their mastery of their respective crafts. Perhaps the same is true of the listener. The listener might come to possess the skill of listening without being able to articulate that skill or the understanding achieved through its use.[17] The understanding achieved by the composer and the performer is revealed in the products issuing from their actions, quite apart from what each might say. The listener's understanding should be similar if the analogy is to hold. If listening is a craft, what is its product? The answer might be this: a musical sensibility which, like those of the composer and performer, is revealed in behavioral dispositions. The listener exposes his understanding not so much by what he says as by expressing preferences for some works over others, through his choice of which works to listen to, by his facial expressions, bodily attitudes, and so forth, as he listens with rapt attention.

Now, as previously indicated, I reject the view that understanding music involves know-how unconnected with "knowing that." It is true that we might identify a listener as a musical person, as having a feel for music, as understanding music, on the strength of his listening habits alone. Or we might take his glazed look of otherworldly engagement as a sign of his appreciation. But we do so, I believe, only because we think that, if asked, he could describe the music in a way that indicates his understanding of it. I listed previously the kinds of things a listener appreciates in understanding a work: he hears the various themes as identifiable individuals, he hears patterns of tension and release, he hears an aptness in some continuations (despite their unexpectedness) and the inappropriateness of others. These are things of a kind of which one can be aware of being, or having been, aware. All these things are describable without special difficulty: "that is the tune," "now it has ended," and so forth. A person who is incapable of describing such matters is a person who cannot *hear* them and, hence, a person who does not

---

[17] A sophisticated account along these lines can be found in Levinson 1990b.

< 338 >

understand the music as such. Like Kivy (1990a), I believe that the ultimate test of the listener's understanding resides in his ability to describe relevant features of the music as a result of his experiencing them at first hand.

The descriptions will not always come easily, though. It might be necessary to coax them from the listener. Anyway, they are likely to be peppered with ostensive gestures indicating bits of the music ("there is the tune"), with hummed phrases ("this way, not that"), and with metaphors and analogies ("it is as if it is pulled toward that, rather than pushed from here"). Kivy (1990a, 105–108) accepts that the listener's knowledge might be impossible for her to verbalize without help (because she is "not very good with words"). The help required is not a training in music theory but "something like the midwifery Socrates thought he was giving to Meno's slave boy to bring forth what was already there" (1990a, 108). He distinguishes this type of case from one of more or less pure know-how, such as knowing how to walk. For pure know-how, where crucial aspects of the knowledge have no propositional content, the skill might be indescribable in the strong sense that there is nothing to be brought to light—whereas, in the case of the musical listener, the experience, if indescribable, is so in the weaker sense that the knowledge it captures might be difficult to dredge into consciousness.

Kivy does not generalize the argument, but I would be inclined to do so. I would challenge the view that the performer's or composer's understandings can be of a radically inarticulable type. The reasons given for questioning Mozart's ability to describe his music with understanding are of dubious standing. Mozart may not have thought in terms of "second subject," "false recapitulation," and the like, but he understood the structural function of a second subject, and that understanding could not be entirely beyond articulation. To understand the form of these works is to be able to describe the contribution of the parts to the whole, rather than to be aware of theorist's labels, and there is no doubt that Mozart had this ability.[18] His letters sometimes contain specific descriptions of what he is doing and why, though the comments are not always technical. Mozart is not exceptional in this. The

---

[18] Moreover, apparently Mozart and Haydn expected their audiences to know sonata form (even if the audience could not give a technical account of the form). Their works contain false recapitulations, or other structural twists, as prominent features of the musical foreground. Such devices, which take their interest from delaying or defeating the listener's expectations, are pointless if the composer writes for an audience having no idea of what *should* happen next. These composers had real audiences to please; they did not write for ideal audiences. Even if structural complexities were sometimes curbed in the attempt to make a work more appealing to the popular audience (as with Mozart's Piano Concerto in A, K. 488), the treatment of form in works of the period suggests that the audience then was more musically sophisticated than is commonly supposed.

< 339 >

idea of the mute artist is a myth. Composers usually show themselves to be capable of offering quite detailed accounts of their creative efforts. Of course, this is not to hold that they describe to themselves what they are doing as they do it—to that extent art creation is a practical skill. But it is to suggest that art-making is frequently a self-conscious activity. At its most instinctual, it is unconscious in the way driving a car can be. Even if artists do not have to be aware of what they are doing as they are doing it, what they are doing is the sort of thing they can describe if asked to.

Equally questionable are the reasons given earlier for suggesting that the performer's understanding is radically inarticulable. If we accept a performance as indicating the musician's understanding of the work played, we suppose, I claim, that, if asked and helped, the performer could develop some relevant description of the work and provide some reasons for doing one thing rather than another.[19] It is understandable, given his musical skills and the difficulties of description, that a musician might prefer to play a piece again than to discuss it when asked what it "means," but the evidence suggests that performers are not incapable of discoursing on music. It would be very puzzling to discover a performer who seemed to play a piece with understanding but who could not describe it in a fashion showing that he recognized it for the work it is. In such a case, we might suspect that he is slavishly copying the performance of another rather than playing with understanding; we might suspect that he is the human equivalent of a piano roll or tape recorder. If the piece were by Beethoven, say, we would not predict confidently that he could play other works by that composer convincingly, or works in a similar style written by other composers. Ordinarily, we think that if a musician plays one work with understanding then he should be able to do the same with stylistically similar pieces (given time for practice, and so on). Indeed, we might reasonably regard this as a criterion of musicianship and of understanding in a performer. The person who is inca-

---

[19] Kivy (1990a, 121–122) suggests that performances are descriptions. I think this is silly, though I allow that the character of a performance is often accepted as evidence that, if asked, the performer would be capable of giving a description revealing of her understanding. A performance might stand proxy for a description, but it is not one thereby. Kivy (1990a, 119) excuses himself from considering composition and performance on the ground that they are different activities from listening, which is the topic of his concern. I doubt that they can be so different that we would accept that someone might compose or perform with understanding if she could not also listen with understanding, and that this involves an awareness of a work's expressive character if that is an artistically significant feature of the work (compare Raffman 1991). Cook (1990) argues that performers must listen musicologically in learning how to perform a work adequately, so he distinguishes the skilled performer from the appreciative listener. For further discussion of the performer's understanding, see Mark 1981 and Elliott 1991.

< 340 >

pable of describing the music he plays note-perfectly will be viewed as an automaton who reveals technical facility, but not musical appreciation, I think.

Technical Causes and Audible Effects

I have argued that the experience of understanding a work through listening to it contains a recoverable, describable content, that is, involves knowing *that* so-and-so happens in the music. The listener's understanding is revealed in the descriptions she can offer of the music, these being descriptions of its parts, of how they are combined, of its character, of its expressiveness. The question now to be considered is one about the terms in which such descriptions might be couched. As I wrote before, like Kivy and Cook I believe those not formally trained in music theory to be no less capable of understanding music than are those who have had the benefit of that education. I suggest here that the descriptions revealing of musical appreciation need not be technical in character.

Consider these cases: Of a moment from the last movement of Haydn's Symphony No. 98 (Example 1), one might declare "Here there is an unexpected slide upward, as if the whole piece is lifted by the seat of its pants," rather than saying "Here there is an unprepared modulation from D major to E-flat major." Of a passage in Vaughan Williams's *Job* (Example 2), one might say that it is regal, churchy, somehow very solid; alternatively, one might mention, among other things, that most of the chords are in root position and that the focus is on the Aeolian mode rather than the major key. Or one might say of a melody that first appears in the (relative) major and is recapitulated in the (tonic) minor that it is sadder, somehow, when it returns. Similarly, aspects of performance practice and technique might be described either in technical terms or by their phenomenal character. A listener might nominate a passage in the last movement of Brahms's Symphony No. 4 (Example 3) as involving bariolage (alternation between open and stopped strings, sometimes at the same pitch, for the sake of subtle changes in timbral character), or she might try to describe the subtle difference between the colors of the tones.[20] The listener might describe Stravinsky's *Firebird* as

[20] The account might be analogical: for example, that the difference is like that between someone's saying "oh" and "ee"; or between a flute in its low range and in its middle range; or between a struck hardwood and a struck stone. Changes in tongue position, in register, and in the vibrating medium all affect timbral qualities, so it is possible to indicate the subtle difference in color exploited in bariolage by suggesting other ways of producing similar differences. Alternatively, the describer might turn to synaesthetic analogies.

< 341 >

H.M.P. 79

Example 1

F. Joseph Haydn. Symphony No. 98, 4th movement, bars 200–215 (*Philarmonia,*
Vol. 11, Universal edition. Philarmonia Musikverlag, Vienna, p. 352).

< 342 >

Example 2
Ralph Vaughan Williams. *Job: A Masque for Dancing*, 9 bars before rehearsal figure L (a tempo, Saraband of the Sons of God). (© 1934 Oxford University Press: Oxford, p. 18. Reproduced by permission.)

< 343 >

W. Ph.V. 133

Example 3
Johannes Brahms. Symphony No. 4, 4th movement, bars 77–80 (*Philarmonia*, No.
133. Philarmonia Musikverlag: Vienna, pp. 136–137).

commencing with an eerie sound like the wind in wires or in the trees, or,
instead, he might refer to its beginning with glissandi of string harmonics.

It seems to me that in each of these cases the nontechnical description can
be just as revealing of musical understanding as the technical one. The two
descriptions certainly do not mean the same (no more does "visible light"
and "reflected waves in the band 7000–9000 ångströms" mean the same),
but either they pick out the same effect or one picks out the effect and the
other refers to its immediate cause. Required for understanding is a recognition of the musical effect, and one might have that without also possessing
the vocabulary that would allow for the technical description. To hear
Haydn's modulation with understanding just is to hear the music lifting itself
by its own bootstraps; to hear the string glissandi with understanding just is

< 344 >

to hear the eeriness of the sound. The experiences are brought under different kinds of descriptions, but this does not necessarily indicate a difference in kind or in depth of musical understanding. The listener is not debarred from understanding Stravinsky's music if it happens that he does not know what a harmonic is, or how one is played on a stringed instrument, or how a glissando of harmonics is achieved. The composer and performer cannot be indifferent to such matters because they are concerned not with ends alone but also with the means of realizing them. Thus, that the performer and composer require knowledge of such matters does not show, just like that, that they understand the music better than the listener who can appreciate (and describe therefore) the effect but who is untutored in music theory or in details of instrumental technique.

Indeed, one might suspect that nontechnical accounts of the effect perceived in the music sometimes take precedence over highly technical descriptions as indicating understanding. Where the features are expressive ones, Scruton (1983) identifies the phenomenal, nontechnical description as foundational. This is because a person might know a great deal about technical matters without appreciating the effects (of expressiveness, and the like) to which they should give rise in the listener's experience of the work. A person with no recognition of a work's expressive character might strike us as having only a limited understanding of the piece, whatever technical descriptions she could offer of it. And a skilled performer conversant with the work's structure might not be able to execute the piece convincingly until told to play it as if in anger rather than sorrow.

Now, these examples are ones in which the musical technicalities operate in close proximity to the effects arising from them, so that the person who is trained in music theory and is sensitive to the effects to be heard in the music might regard her technical descriptions as doing duty for a phenomenal account of the listening experience, or vice versa. But musical technicalities sometimes operate at a greater remove than this from the audible effects to which they give rise. Analysts sometimes distinguish between the foreground and background levels of musical works, intending thereby to distinguish those technicalities that can be heard to produce their effects from those that cannot be heard to do so. In either case an audible result is achieved, but the manner of its being realized is increasingly hard to hear as the technical cause retreats farther from the musical foreground.[21] The (allegedly audible) properties that most often are analyzed as depending on

[21] The workings of the background level might be consciously controlled by the composer, or it might be that she deals only with the foreground, choosing what sounds right at that level without concerning herself about the background matters the analyst hopes to bring to light.

< 345 >

background causes are those of musical unity and large-scale closure.[22] Some aspects of performance technique might also be less evident to the listener/viewer than is usually the case. An example might be that of hocketing, where the gestalt the listener is supposed to hear as unitary emerges from the contributions of more than one instrument.[23] Also, some of the acoustic properties of sound could be regarded as part of the physical background of musical tones.[24]

I use Hans Keller (1955) to illustrate the analyst's concern with background technicalities. Sonata form is sometimes described as a tonal drama because a key established at the beginning of the exposition is reaffirmed in the recapitulation after excursions to other keys. Tonal stability is usually at its lowest in the development section. At the start of the development of the last movement of Mozart's Symphony No. 40, K. 550, there are several measures of tonal chaos. According to Keller's analysis, Mozart uses serial treatment to hold the passage together in the absence of a solid tonal base; a three-note "row" appears in several manipulations, including retrograde inversion. Keller is explaining the integration and continuity of the passage as arising from the use of serial procedures, but he does not suggest that Mozart was aware of employing those procedures. Neither does he indicate that the listener who hears the passage as hanging together, despite its tonal disintegration, also hears how that unity has been achieved.

What is the relevance of theories or analyses concerning themselves with musical causes that operate in the background? If what is required for understanding is a recognition of the effect, not an appreciation of the process that brings it to fruition, it might be suggested (see Cooke 1959 and Cook 1990) that such theories can be dismissed as of no importance to the listener. This line is also taken by Alan Tormey (1988). He argues that such analyses pre-

---

[22] Among analysts who see themselves as dealing with the background causes of musical unity are Heinrich Schenker, Rudolph Reti, Hans Keller, and Alan Walker; also note the set-theoretic analyses of Allen Forte. Meyer (1956) might be described as analyzing the background causes (both musical and psychological) of musical expressiveness.

[23] The device is not now much used in Western music, but it was necessary when several nonchromatic instruments combined to play a stepwise melody; for example, several horns, each using a different crook, might combine to play a theme. The device is not uncommon in some non-Western musics, either for the sake of attaining a rapidity that cannot be achieved on a single instrument (as in some Asian musics) or, as just described, where the tunings of instruments are fixed so that not all the notes of the scale are available.

[24] To take a well-known example, timbral quality depends on the distribution and strengths of overtones. One usually hears a note with a certain timbre, not a chord in which the upper notes are markedly more feeble than the fundamental; that is, timbre is an audible quality produced by a combination of tones which, since they are not usually heard as combining to produce the timbre one hears, can be regarded as belonging to the musical background.

< 346 >

suppose that listeners are already secure in their knowledge of the kind of experiences being analyzed. An account of a work's unity referring to background similarities or structures assumes that the listener can already experience that unity, so an understanding of the music is logically prior to, and independent of, such theorizing. Even if the theory, when applied, correctly identifies the hidden causes of the music's unity, this lacks significance to the listener who is already aware of the work's unity; he would not understand the work the more were he to understand and apply the theory as he listens.[25] A knowledge of such theories might make it easier for the listener to explain and justify his understanding, but it does not augment that understanding. This type of analysis stands to musical comprehension in much the way that physiologists' or neurologists' theories stand to the understanding of pain.

The opposite view regards a knowledge of music theory to be essential for musical understanding. Even if the truth makers for technical and nontechnical descriptions might be identical, it does not follow that the two mean the same or reveal the same understanding. Two points might be made in favor of this position: (i) Composers follow, and sometimes deliberately break, rules of musical syntax; for example, the rule against parallel fifths in the seventeenth and earlier centuries was eroded by being broken.[26] The listener must have a technical knowledge of what is happening in the work if he is to understand it, because he can follow the music only if he knows that the relevant rules are followed (or broken) in it. (ii) The language of music theory allows for a more complex and specific description of the music than is available in other terms, so someone whose listening is informed by a knowledge of music theory must gain a more profound understanding, both of the

---

[25] Kivy (1990a, chap. 7) is dismissive of such analytical approaches—especially of the one advocated by Rudolph Reti—but he is so at least partly because he doubts the adequacy of some of the analyses offered in illustration of the theory. Dempster (1991) complains that Kivy focuses on Reti when he should look to the work of Schenker. For a comparison between Reti and Keller and an evaluation of some analyses, see Hutchings 1962. For interesting discussion of some assumptions shared by Schenker and Reti, see Solie 1980; also see Meyer 1991. Skepticism, such as Kivy's, about the possible relevance of musical analyses often feeds on this consideration: Some people might seize uncritically on theories of musical analysis, and might be more inclined to test those theories against their eyes than their ears. Rather than revealing to the listener subtle relationships and structures that otherwise might not be heard, the theory distorts the listening process in such cases. In that way, theorizing about music might become more of a barrier than a help to music appreciation. In the following discussion I assume that some analyses, and some of the theories they illustrate, are convincing.

[26] Kivy (1990a) denies that there is ungrammatical music. His point, however, is not that the rules cannot be broken, and thereby changed, but that deviations from the rule can be known to be deliberate, because it hardly ever is the case that composers "break" the rules through ignorance of them or by accident.

< 347 >

detail and of the wider patterns of overall structure, than an unschooled listener.[27]

Other commentators take a more conciliatory line.[28] Though they allow that a knowledge of music theory is not necessary for understanding, they also accept that a consideration of theory might provide one route to the appreciation of a work's more subtle, complex properties. What a listener can hear in a musical work depends not only on her ears and concentration but also on her familiarity with the given work, with other works by the composer, with the style of the piece, and with independent descriptions of the work. Knowing, as a result of an analysis, to listen for a relationship between two themes might make that relationship audible, whereas otherwise it would be missed. Though it is not a necessary condition of musical appreciation that a person be familiar with music theory and analytical approaches, or that she study particular analyses, her listening experience might be enriched and altered by an awareness of such matters.

On this issue I take the middle ground. Because I believe that there is a close relation between the listener's ability to describe a work and the extent of his understanding of it, I am skeptical of the schizophrenic separation between these two drawn by the view regarding music theory and analysis as irrelevant to the music lover's appreciation. For instance, the experience of hearing a work's unity cannot readily be divorced, I think, from an awareness of relationships between its parts. In the end, someone who hears the unity must be able to describe the parts that constitute the whole as fitting together, and that description, even if it need not delve into the detail an analysis might provide, must go down the same path as is followed by the analyst. Though I accept that there are cases in which a knowledge of theory or analysis affects the listener's experience without increasing her understanding and appreciation of the work—for example, where that knowledge leads the listener to pay more attention than is necessary to the mechanics by which some effect is brought about—there also are cases in which a technically skilled listener understands the work better than another who, while sensing many of the work's features, has only a hazy idea of how those features are realized.

Inasmuch as I believe that a person might cultivate the art of listening to a high level without concerning himself with music theory and that he might describe the style, detail, and overall structure of music in ordinary language (supplemented, perhaps, with ostensive gestures, humming, and the like), I

[27] See Boretz 1970, Sharpe 1982, Dempster 1991, and Price 1992.
[28] See Zuckerkandl 1959, Davies 1983c, Tanner 1985, Budd 1985b, and DeBellis 1991.

< 348 >

also reject the position that regards a knowledge of music theory and analysis as essential for musical understanding. Sometimes it is sufficient that the listener be able to say that some possible continuation of the music is right or wrong, without his being able to articulate the rule he is invoking. In other cases, where musical appreciation depends on a grasp of detail, or of overarching patterns and structures, I do not see that it is necessary in demonstrating understanding that this be revealed by the use of technical terms and concepts. There are many ways through which, by word, voice, or gesture, a person might reveal an ability not only to make fine auditory discriminations but, in doing so, to recognize complex and subtle relationships between the elements he distinguishes. Besides, I see no reason to assume that every kind and level of detail with which music theorists might concern themselves contributes to understanding a musical piece as the work it is. Many things that can be described are not audible in themselves and do not contribute to audible effects.

Two listeners, one of whom approaches a given work with an ear enriched by theory and analysis, while the other knows nothing of such matters, might equally and fully appreciate the music in all its complex profundity, I believe. Both hear those features of the music that are to be recognized if the work is to be understood. For this case I think that the difference between the listeners lies not in the kind or depth of understanding each achieves but merely in the terms each brings to its description. I agree with the first view outlined earlier, against the second: a familiarity with theory and analysis is not necessary for the fullest understanding of music. But, unlike those who hold the first position, I do not think that knowledge of this kind is always irrelevant to musical understanding. Rather, I believe that the understanding that can be expressed in technical terms also might be gained at first hand by those who are ignorant of music theory.

Another Type of Music

The discussion has so far progressed with a certain kind of music in mind—for example, a Schumann symphony. To understand such music is to hear the effects achieved—effects of expressiveness, color, tension and release, unity in diversity. Such effects might be distinguished from the technicalities that generate them. Either the technicalities are inaudible in their operation and, as such, are the business of the analyst, not of the listener, or the technicalities are important not for themselves but for the relationships of resemblance or resolution they produce. Some of these technicalities operate as distant causes distinguishable from their audible effects, as is true of

< 349 >

the causes of musical unity. In other cases the effect just is the effect of some technical device, as the sound of Haydn's modulation in Symphony No. 98 just is the sound of a shift in the music to a new gear. In either type of case, what matters is the effect, rather than the technical means to it, and a person reveals her understanding and appreciation of the music by showing herself to be aware of the relevant effect, which she might do as readily by employing nontechnical as technical descriptions. Music of the type assumed in the previous discussion can be understood through awareness of the musical effects achieved, and an account of those effects need not be technical. It is romantic music, perhaps, that most often is of the type considered so far.

For much music, though, the technicalities are neither hidden nor easily translated into descriptions of expressive or dynamic character and the like. In such music the treatment of the musical material is an end in itself, not a means to something else. No doubt the manipulation of the materials gives rise to musical effects, but one could not appreciate such effects without, at the same time, recognizing them as effects of the treatment used. The effect just is that of a theme played upside down, or whatever. If such music is "about" its own materials, can it too be understood in nontechnical terms? Can the technicalities be dismissed as the analyst's or composer's business, but not the listener's?

As examples I have in mind Bach's fugues and some of Webern's music. To understand such music one must appreciate how it is put together. To follow a fugue or canon, one must hear each voice entering with the same thematic idea. The crab fugues (Nos. 12 and 13) in *The Art of Fugue* must be heard as mirror fugues, for the whole musical point of these numbers consists in this feature.[29] Webern's canons are much more difficult to follow, especially on first hearing, but one should be aware of hearing them (even if they are not traced avidly), I think, if one is to follow the work in the appropriate fashion. It might not be possible to identify the twelve-note row as a unit, but, in the case of Webern's music, the series often comprises recognizable fragments. For example, the row of Symphony, Op. 21, comprises two six-note parts the second of which is a retrograde version of the first; the row of String Quartet, Op. 28, consists of three four-notes motives related by inversion and pitch transposition (aficionados will recognize this four-note kernel as a version of the famous B–A–C–H motive). The listener usually cannot follow the combinations and permutations of a twelve-note row,

---

[29] Cone (1967) upbraids those who produce analyses (including ones of dodecaphonic works) that are no less applicable to an inversion of the work than to the original. Such analyses would imply, wrongly, that Bach's success is guaranteed rather than achieved.

< 350 >

but in this case he can recognize, if not the row as a unit, then the varied repetition of a four-note motto.[30]

Whereas some formal structures, such as sonata form, might lend themselves for use in either type of music, others seem suited to bringing formal considerations to the fore and, for that reason, seem to call attention to the musical material for its own sake. I have already mentioned the formal types of fugue and canon in this connection. Special mention also should be made of the theme and variations.[31] Typically, works or movements in this form have as their primary goal a display of the musical possibilities to be derived from a theme that receives a clear, initial statement. To appreciate such a work, it is necessary that the listener be able to recognize the theme in its various transformations.[32] Similar structures include the passacaglia and the chaconne.

Previously I suggested that there are technical aspects of performance (of how the musical sounds are elicited from the instrument) that need not concern the listener, just as there are compositional matters that need not be known provided that the effects to which they give rise are heard. Equally, though, there are features of performance practice of which the listener must be aware in appreciating some works. If Bach's fugues are "about" the contrapuntal possibilities inherent in his materials, then other works are "about" the techniques required of the performer or "about" musical properties depending on the manner of sound production. I mention two kinds of example.

Some works are "about" the virtuosity they require of the player (Mark 1980 and 1981); it is the difficulty of their performance that gives point to such works. This is true especially of concertos and études, and of vocal pieces such as the display arias for the Queen of the Night in *The Magic Flute*, for typically these take as one of their major artistic goals the explora-

---

[30] Cook (1987) cites experiments as revealing that many listeners do not seem to follow the canonic and palindromic forms of Webern's Op. 21. The interpretation of the results of such experiments is fraught with difficulty, as Kivy (1992) observes, given the varied musical backgrounds and experiences of the subjects, and given also that the listeners are not sure of the point of the exercise, though the strange context and abbreviated musical presentations virtually guarantee that they will take it to have some point other than the usual experience of listening to music.

[31] Musical styles and genres dedicated to versions of this formal type, such as is instrumental jazz, will be musics of the second, rather than the first, kind.

[32] Cook (1987) rightly points out that variations sometimes bear scant relation to their themes. This is likely to be true of only a few variations within an extended set and does not show, anyway, that it is appropriate to be indifferent to the possibility of a connection between variations and their theme.

< 351 >

tion of the limits of instrumental or vocal technique.[33] Such pieces must be heard as difficult to perform (despite being presented faultlessly, one hopes), and that is possible only if the listener has some idea of the relevant limits of instrumental or vocal practice. By contrast, other works are difficult to play not to draw attention to the performers' skills and control but as a means to distinctive aural effects. Stravinsky's *Rite of Spring* makes extraordinary demands on the musicianship of the orchestral performers, but it does so for the sake of conjuring up an aural impression of some strange, wild, primeval society, not to draw attention to the instrumentalists. It is not necessary that one realize that or why *The Rite of Spring* is difficult to perform before one can appreciate the music.

In other cases, significant features of the music, such as expressive or dynamic ones, derive directly from the manner of performance, so that an appreciation of those features requires an awareness of the performance practices involved.[34] For example, what sounds rushed depends in part on the agility of the instrument for which the music is written. A fast passage for the feet in an organ work might be much slower than a fast passage for the hands; what sounds languid on the flute might sound breathlessly rushed on the tuba. Or again, in Bach's Double Concerto in D minor, BWV 1043, the material is often passed from one soloist to the other; such passages should be heard as a dialogue between the solo instruments, but one could appreciate it as such only if one were aware that two violins, not just one, were involved.

Michael Tanner (1985) distinguishes between types of music much as I have done here—between music the point of which is the attainment of some expressive or other effect and music in which the manipulation of the material is the primary end. He seems to believe that, whereas one has no need of a technical vocabulary in describing Schumann's symphonies with understanding, for Bach's mirror fugues a knowledge of some technical factors (and the terms that name them) is required. The musically untutored listener might appreciate music of the first kind but cannot understand music of the second type so well as someone with a grasp of the concepts and the terms

---

[33] The upper notes of the range are difficult to reach for most wind instruments and the voice, but they are not so difficult for strings and are not at all difficult for keyboard instruments. Again, chords can be difficult on the violin, not so difficult on the lute, and not at all difficult for keyboard instruments. Difficulty for keyboard instruments depends on speed, spread, leaps, and the number of simultaneously played notes (except that octave doublings are achieved mechanically on organs and harpsichords). That which is difficult to play depends at least in part on features of the instrument on which it is to be performed.

[34] For discussion of many examples, including some of those I mention, see Levinson 1980 and 1990a, chap. 16.

< 352 >

employed by musicologists. This suggests that some music, if not all, can be fully understood and enjoyed for the music it is only by those with some training (whether formal or informal, imparted by others or mastered on one's own) in musical technicalities (Kivy 1990a approaches this position, I find).

I believe such a view to be mistaken. In Bach's *Art of Fugue*, one must appreciate the musical treatment of the materials chosen by the composer for the light this sheds on their possibilities for combination, and so on. In Schumann's symphonies, the attention should be drawn to effects of expressiveness, mood, or feeling rather than to the mechanics of the process by which such effects are produced. But, as I see it, this difference does not entail that the understanding needs to be conceived more technically in one case than the other, for a person can adequately describe the technicalities appropriate to an appreciation of Bach's music without using the vocabulary favored by musicologists. A person can follow Bach's treatment of his materials, and can reveal through his descriptions of the music that he does so, without resort to the musicologist's terminology. For example, he might say: "This is the same as that, but turned upside down," or "Here the tune is played slowly," or "Here the main bit goes backward," or "Each part starts on the tune as if in a rush, before the last one has finished it." I can see no reason why an untrained person could not hear and describe such works in a manner revealing the fullest understanding and appreciation, while never using such terms as "cancrizan," "retrograde," "augmentation," or "stretto." In these cases, appreciation involves following the treatment of the material, and "following the treatment of the material" depends in practice on recognizing a tune or motive (or rhythm, texture, color, or pattern), so that one is aware of its various incarnations and modifications. That skill can be developed through practice and might be easier to exercise when one knows (as a result of musical training of one kind or another) what to listen for before one hears a piece for the first time, but I can think of no reason for believing that this talent must be absent in those who lack musical training.

My thesis is no less clearly illustrated when one considers the knowledge of performance practice necessary for the appreciation of virtuosic works or for the appreciation of artistically significant properties that depend on the process of sound generation. I do not need to know much about playing the piano or the violin to be aware that much of Liszt's music for the former, and Paganini's for the latter, is demanding. Often, all that is needed for understanding is eyes. It is sufficient for an appreciation of the difficulties that I see the instruments played, or have sufficient experience of seeing them played to have some idea, from the sound, of what is asked of the per-

< 353 >

former.[35] I can see that the two soloists in Bach's concerto exchange musical ideas, and that the organist plays some passages with his feet rather than with his hands.

The point of the discussion is this: A person can hear how the musical materials are treated, structured, and drawn from the instruments without hearing such things in terms of the vocabulary or the more elaborate concepts employed by the musicologist. If that person appreciates and understands the music, he must be able to bring his experience of it under some description that reveals his following the work, but the description need not be technical. Even if a nontechnical description might be metaphoric and to some extent sloppy, there could be a nontechnical paraphrase for each and every technical description that is adequate to display the fullest musical understanding. Thus, I regard the type of description offered as revealing not a difference between kinds of understanding but merely a difference in modes for expressing a single type of understanding.[36]

If Bach's music can be understood without recourse to technical notions, is it after all a different kind of music from Schumann's? I think there is a difference between the two, though I hear it more as one of degree than of kind. The distinction between them does not reside in the type of understanding they require so much as in the object of that understanding. In Schumann's case, expressive and dynamic features are prominent, and it is such properties that are to be appreciated; in Bach's music, it is the way the material is handled, not the supervenient effects achieved through its treatment, that are of primary concern. This said, it is also important to note that one can hear appropriate effects in Schumann's music only if one hears the themes as recognizable individuals, is aware of tonal/harmonic tensions and resolutions, and so forth. So, an appreciation of Schumann's music depends on an awareness of technicalities no less than does Bach's (even if they are not heard under a technical description in either case), though the technicalities of relevance to an appreciation of Schumann's music might lie nearer the musical surface than is the case with Bach's more complex works.

Apart from the point just made, several considerations warn against too

---

[35] Compare this with the case in which a person hears a recording of music played on an instrument with which she is so unfamiliar that she cannot even identify its family affiliation. I predict that it will be difficult for her to make sense of the music heard under these circumstances. In almost all musics, some of the significant properties of the style depend on the possibilities of the instruments used in playing the music.

[36] It is true that those who have the deepest understanding of music very often have taken the trouble to acquire familiarity with some of the musicologist's terms and ideas. As I see it, this is not a requirement for the appreciation they display but instead reflects the interest they have in music as a result of their coming to appreciate it.

< 354 >

sharp a division between types of music by reference to the salience or otherwise of expressive, as opposed to more formal, features. A musicologist might be accepted as showing an understanding of Schumann's symphonies in descriptions cast almost exclusively in technical terms. A significant minority of listeners (as well as most of those who write the notes for programs and for record sleeves) mix technical and nontechnical terms quite freely in their descriptions, referring to modulations, recapitulations, and the like while discussing the expressive tone of the work or developing analogies with nonmusical items, events, processes, or ideas. Though some composers might easily be categorized as drawing attention to their working of the material, and others, by contrast, as aiming at expressive effects, the distinction is not exclusive. Mozart, for example, is often cited as a composer whose music appeals at more than one level and in more than one way (and there is no reason to think that a listener who attends in one way must be deaf to the alternatives).

This discussion completes my argument that the appreciation of music is cognitive, and that the "musically uneducated" listener is capable of the appropriate kind of listening. It is not so, I have claimed, that a person necessarily is hampered in revealing a deep appreciation of music by ignorance of the terminology used by musicologists (or of the notational conventions governing composer's scores, and the like); neither is such a person debarred from appreciating musical works that are reflexive in exploring the formal, rather than the expressive, potentials of their medium. But what I have written here might be read as maintaining that, at base, all kinds of music, all musical works, and all listeners are on a par. This would be a serious misinterpretation of my position.

A first point: Bach's music is harder to understand than Schumann's, I think. It is so because it demands closer and more attentive listening and perhaps also a wider background (but not because it requires a radically different, trained understanding). Bach's music is less accessible than Schumann's because it is more demanding of the ear. Since most listeners do not or cannot muster the time, concentration, and practice that much of Bach's music calls for, his works are likely to be less popular than Schumann's. Nevertheless, fine composer though Schumann is at his most inspired, Bach's music is more profound, offering more for appreciation. Bach's music, like many other of the things affording the deepest, most abiding pleasures in life, yield their delights only to those who work for them. By no means are all listeners prepared to expend the effort of meeting the challenge posed by Bach's more complex works, or by the similarly "difficult" works of other composers.

< 355 >

A second point: An appreciation of music comes in degrees. Many listeners approach music for its own sake and derive considerable enjoyment from what they hear, but their comprehension is comparatively superficial. Usually, they could augment their appreciation by trying harder as they listen or by listening more often. Mostly (here lies the real advantage of a musical training), they would understand more if they had the advantage of knowing what sort of features they should be listening for.[37] Frequently, they would understand more if they tried to learn a musical instrument. So time-and energy-consuming is listening and playing (and so important are other things) that it is not surprising that so many people are content with a level of understanding they themselves would admit to be shallow by comparison with what is possible.

For those who do have the aptitude and inclination, the effort put into understanding music can pay rich dividends in pleasure. It is not the case necessarily that one will enjoy a piece the more for appreciating its character the better, but in general the more one understands, the more enjoyment is to be obtained from music widely recognized as profound.[38] This is likely to be displayed in changes in the listener's predilections. I suspect that not a few listeners whose introduction to instrumental music came through their love of the symphonies of Schumann have since switched their allegiance to the works of J. S. Bach, but I doubt that many listeners have experienced the reverse. (But so many works are there, and so variously enjoyable are they, that the changes are likely to be manifest more through the frequency with which one listens to, or buys records of, the works of the one composer as opposed to the other.) In other cases, the change is one in the features of the work one finds noteworthy rather than in one's liking for the work or the composer.

Technical Features without Artistically Significant Effects

I mentioned earlier that the listener need not concern himself with the mechanics of the compositional process. That remark was made in connec-

---

[37] The danger of a music training is shown in the tendency to listen to works not with an ear to their individuality but with the goal of forcing one's experience into a corset stipulated by theory. As should be clear, I do not see depth of musical understanding as neatly correlated with levels of technical sophistication, as Tanner (1985) and Kivy (1990a) sometimes seem to do.

[38] Dempster (1991) criticizes Kivy (1990a) for failing to explain adequately what is pleasurable about following the detail of a complex musical work; I fear that I am similarly guilty. For a helpful discussion, see Hansen 1971.

< 356 >

tion with the case in which the musical cause of an artistically significant effect, such as the work's unity, might be so distant from that effect as to be inaudible in its causal operation. Then, I said, a person might fully understand and appreciate the music through being aware of the effect realized, while remaining ignorant of the underlying basis of that outcome. Awareness of technical matters might increase a person's knowledge of the composer's methods, or of the compositional process in general, or of a detail of the work's structure, but such knowledge need not augment an appreciation of the given work as the piece it is. Not everything that one might learn about a musical work is used for its appreciation as such.

Now, often composers labor carefully over details of the work which produce no aesthetically significant effects. This need not happen because the composer miscalculates in attempting to achieve a particular effect. Typically it arises from the composer's regulating her approach to the materials as a means of restricting and controlling their otherwise endless possibilities. It comes from the attempt to overcome the blank, unstructured vastness of the empty page so as to get the act of composition underway and to impel it forward. My meaning can be made clearer, I hope, through reference to some examples.

Composers often have used serial procedures for organizing their materials. They settle on some series of intervals (or chords, or rhythmic values, or meters, or instrumentations, or dynamic values, or some combination of these) that are then repeated. These repetitions might be strict or free, depending on the conventions of the style. Under some styles, permutations resulting from pitch-and octave-transposition, inversion and retrograde, are allowed. "Serialization" is usually associated with Schönberg and his followers, who based their compositions on a series of intervals generated from some ordering of the twelve chromatic notes of the octave, but, as Schönberg was keen to emphasize, such compositional techniques have always been used. The techniques are usually applied on a small scale, and it would be possible for the listener to hear the treatment of the material as producing resemblances and relationships. But the extended use of comparatively long series at a level of complexity that makes the process almost impossible to follow with the ear did not begin with the 1920s. In the fourteenth century, isorhythmic motets involved the use of extended serials, for both interval order (*color*) and rhythmic succession (*talea*). And the mathematical complexities of the works of the fifteenth-century Flemish composer Johannes Ockeghem equal the efforts of those 1950s composers (such as Pierre Boulez and Ernst Křenek) who attempted to serialize all the parameters of music, so that everything that is to be written in the score might be determined by

< 357 >

the initial selection of the series to be used and of the manner of their subsequent repetition and variation.

It is not only through the continuing use of extended serials in a work that composers have attempted to tame their medium. In the cantus-firmus masses of the fifteenth and sixteenth centuries, a melodic fragment from plainsong, or from a popular secular song (such as the "L'Homme Armé" tune that came to be used so often), is employed in the tenor part. However, so long in duration is each of the notes sung that the melodic fragment that is their source cannot be heard as such; rather than hearing a theme, one hears a succession of long, pitched tones. As a result, the derivation of other parts from the cantus theme often cannot be appreciated because that theme is not recognizable in the statement it receives. Analysis might reveal much of the music of the mass as deriving from the melodic fragment supplying the notes sung by the tenor, but these connections can be impossible to hear, even where one is familiar with the analysis and with theoretical accounts of this widespread compositional practice.

There is a long tradition of using solmization and codes to derive the notes that are to be central to the work.[39] Sometimes the effect of the treatments is audible—as in the many fugues on B–A–C–H and Schumann's use of ASCH–SCHA in *Carnaval*. In other cases I doubt that it is to be heard as such—for example, in Josquin's solmization of "Hercules Dux Ferrariae" in his mass of that name. The notes derived by the process of solmization are to be heard, but there is no reason to believe that their derivation is also to be recognized. A composer, looking for inspiration, decides to modulate to the keys indicated by the letters that commence his children's names, starting with C major (for Clarence). Then, stuck for the notes with which to begin the first theme, his eye alights on the first two words—"BEEF" and "CABBAGE"—of a shopping list sitting by chance on his desk. . . . There might be a code hidden in Elgar's *Enigma* Variations, a message we may never understand. Nevertheless, we are able to appreciate the work for the music it is.

Here I have concentrated on features that might be discovered by the dedicated analyst in the score, even if they are not to be heard as such. But it is worth noting that much of the creative process might turn out to be *pre*-compositional; I take this to be the case with some of the material recorded in Beethoven's notebooks. Relationships might be inaudible not because they are hidden in the music but because they are composed out of existence during the process by which the first glimmer of an idea becomes the finished work. It can be the case that one musical idea derives from another, as re-

---

[39] For discussion of musical cryptography, see Sams 1980.

< 358 >

vealed in sketches for the work, though the relationship is not apparent in the finished work because the process of thematic development took the relationship beyond breaking point prior to the inclusion of the results of this process in the finished work.

The general point I hope to establish is that the composer must get her notes from somewhere and must settle on a way of proceeding, but not all her reasons are relevant to the listener's attempting to understand her work. Neither is it the case that all her schemes and methods, important though they may be to her in her task, give rise to the artistically significant properties the listener is concerned to understand. Not only is a knowledge of, for example, how much the composer was paid for the work irrelevant to its appreciation, so too is a knowledge of aspects of the composition that have no audible effects when the work is approached as music. If some aspect of the music plays no part (whether immediately or causally, audibly or inaudibly) in establishing the character, mood, or expression of a phrase, melody, or section, or in intimating that one note, chord, rhythm, motive, melody, section, or movement should succeed another, or in shaping the whole so that it begins and ends (rather than merely starts and stops), then that aspect of the music need be of no interest to the listener aiming to appreciate the work as the musical piece it is.

Sometimes it is suggested that compositional techniques of the kind I have been discussing do contribute to significant features of the work, such as its unity, even if they are not usually heard to make that contribution. Schönberg assumes that twelve-tone methods of organizing sounds secure musical unity (just as tonal methods allegedly did in the past). If Schönberg is correct, I should look for other examples. Given the number of arbitrary, bizarre constraints composers might choose to put on the range of continuations available to them, hypothetical cases should not be difficult to construct. But I doubt that Schönberg is correct; no general system for composition, whether it involves composing in twelve tones or seven, makes inevitable the achievement of unity or of a sense of closure. There are as many (perhaps more) disorganized and disunified serial pieces that are scrupulously correct in their application of the technique as there are disorganized and disunified symphonic movements that conform to the standard "rules" for modulation and end in the key with which they commence. This is not to say, though, that composers of the stature of Schönberg or Berg wrote poor works. It is to say, instead, that they did not compose mechanically, relying on the compositional system to do all the work.

Theodor Adorno (1973 [1948]) believed that, as listeners became accustomed to the style of dodecaphonic composition, they would be able to follow the manipulation of the row. For them, noting the treatment of the row

< 359 >

might become no less significant an experience than attending to the vicissitudes undergone by a fugue subject, or of hearing a theme in the variations based on it. The processes of atonal composition would rise to the musical foreground as such music became more widely played, so that children delivering papers in the future might whistle the twelve-tone tunes topping the charts that record the ranking of popular music. Now though, with the hindsight allowed by the passage of half a century since he wrote, Adorno's prediction can be seen to be hopelessly optimistic. Familiarity and the distance of time reveal Schönberg's music to be more lushly romantic and thematic than was suspected by the contemporaries he delighted, as well as those he horrified, but the treatment of the row in his music is far from evident. As I indicated earlier, I believe that the four- or six-note motives in Webern's palindromic rows might be audible, but I do not think that the various, extended series operating in complex pieces can be heard as such.[40]

In denying that all aspects of the compositional process issue (automatically) in aesthetically significant features of musical works, I do not mean to say that musicologists, analysts, students of composition, and psychologists are misguided in studying composers' drafts, sketchbooks, and deletions, or in examining treatises for descriptions of the techniques of composition, or in seeking out reports of how composers discover and mold their materials. My claim, instead, is that the process of composition and the psychology of the creative process are interesting in themselves. And I allow that a person might legitimately ask of a work why it has the notes that it has, not with the aim of understanding it better as a musical work but to see how such things are made.[41] It is not uncommon that people with different concerns might be after different answers to a single question. Both a biologist and an engineer might ask how a creature is put together but, whereas the one is interested in the functional contribution of the parts to the purposes of the whole, the other concentrates on the mechanical relations holding between the parts.

The Crisis of Modern Music?

There is much detail in a musical work and its performance which, quite rightly, does not concern the listener. The listener, in understanding and ap-

---

[40] For discussion, see Lerdahl and Jackendoff 1983, Cook 1990, DeBellis 1991, and Hicks 1991. For criticism of Lerdahl and Jackendoff on this point, see Peel and Slawson 1984.

[41] Perhaps she does so because she wants to make some of her own, or to teach others how to make such things, or because she is the kind of person who feels at ease with computers only when she understands about programming.

< 360 >

preciating the work, focuses on the audible effects achieved. Detail that would not normally be heard as such, and that generates no musically significant audible properties, can safely be ignored.

But now, can this be right, given that many contemporary "classical" works seem to possess no artistically worthwhile audible features? In many cases the compositional process functions—not as a means to producing sounds which, in their structure, expressiveness, or whatever, reward the interest of the attentive, musically informed listener—but as the only end in view. The compositional process itself becomes the point of the musical work, despite the fact that the workings of that process are not audible. To be blunt: if the musical work seems to offer nothing that can be understood at the audible level, and if the composer seems to regard the work's value as residing in the method of his discovery of it, should one not redirect one's attention in the attempt to understand the work?

Works that seem to provoke such questions are the pieces mentioned earlier in which all the parameters are serialized, pieces generated by random processes, or ones using aleatoric procedures constrained by abstract mathematical laws. More generally, any composer who sets out to invent for each work a new musical style and a distinctive musical system as well as give it a content raises this question, for the result can be as puzzling as the vocalizations of a person who attempts to create a new language with every "sentence" he utters.[42] Where the composer relinquishes control of the progress of the work's content, whether to chance or to some predetermined set of series, there is no reason to expect the result to sound musically interesting, no reason to expect it to "say" something worth understanding.[43] If it seems to do so, there is the frustration of not knowing whether this result is an accident of the performance or an attribute of the piece and of being unsure, anyway, if one is hearing the piece in terms of appropriate conventions.

Some such music strikes disaffected concertgoers as perverse. Stanley Cavell (1977 [1969]) lends support to this view in suggesting that neither the audience nor the composer can tell genuine from fraudulent work any longer. Though they may be unable to help themselves, contemporary composers, especially those who pursue total serialization, undermine the trust between artist and audience without which musical appreciation is impossible. As Stephanie Ross (1985) interprets Cavell's view, what is fraudulent is the manner in which such composers shrug off their artistic responsibilities

[42] See Robert P. Morgan 1977 for examples of these various compositional methods.
[43] It is striking that the sound of totally serialized music often cannot be discriminated from that of music generated by chance procedures; see Rochberg 1960 and Meyer 1963.

< 361 >

in choosing to surrender control of the work's contents to an impersonal, mechanical process; what is fraudulent is the claim to have composed the work produced, because the method of composition guarantees that the composer could not *mean* what results.[44]

Ross goes on to criticize Cavell's position. Because he denies the possibility of public tests of fraudulence, Cavell is using the notion in some nonstandard fashion. Nevertheless, Ross does believe that Cavell is correct in rejecting the "philosophy" with which composers who adopt such methods attempt to justify their approach. He may be too quick, though, in dismissing the works they write: the composer might have freely and seriously chosen the notes which, as it happens, were selected instead by chance or by a mechanical working through of the set of series.

I do not find this final point convincing. It is possible that the work freely chosen possesses artistically significant properties that its serial-determined doppelgänger does not. For example, it might contain allusions the other could not. And the one might differ from the other because it belongs in a different genre and because many artistically important properties are genre-relative (see Walton 1970).[45] A change in the circumstances of composition affects the context from which the work derives its properties, so there need be no mistake in insisting that a work produced the one way is fraudulent whereas a piece that is note-for-note identical, but is produced differently, is not. Indeed, differences in compositional processes might so affect the context in which the work is to be located as to play a crucial role in determining its identity (see Levinson 1980). Despite their containing the same notes, there is no reason to assume that the freely chosen piece is the same work as the serial-determined piece.

A deeper sensitivity to ontic issues is shown by Tormey (1974). He argues that the composer who adopts chance procedures cannot thereby succeed in composing herself out of her work, for she retains responsibility for her initial choices and their foreseeable consequences. He also suggests that the composer who seeks total determination cannot succeed thereby in controlling all the properties of a complex work, for some of these emerge unpredictably from the mass of detail. To this one could add that, unless the series

[44] The crucial case is not that in which the composer surrenders a significant portion of the creative role to the performer, as is true in jazz. It is, instead, that in which no human agent directly chooses which notes or sounds succeed which. The ordering of notes is determined by an impersonal procedure and without special regard to the immediate, audible qualities of the music produced.

[45] Serialism itself constitutes a genre, and, let us suppose, the freedom shown by the composer of the first piece pays no heed to serial procedures.

< 362 >

are very long or the work is miniscule, the composer must make many choices about the succession of series. And the composer is responsible for holding to—as opposed to bending, changing, replacing, or abandoning—the "rules" that govern the compositional process, whether the crucial rule is one that says "Let repeated applications of a chance procedure fix the pitches of successive notes" or "Let a prechosen serial determine the sequence of pitches."

Tormey is not much troubled by the fact that many composers opt nowadays for exercising less direct control over the contents of their works than formerly was the case. This is because he believes that there is every likelihood that chance will dish up aesthetic delights; our paradigms of aesthetic objects come from nature and are shaped by the winds and seas, he observes. Cavell, by contrast, is concerned because he doubts that the composer can attract an audience by claiming to aim at an artistically worthwhile result if he renounces direct control over the succession of sounds constituting the work; he thinks that neither chance procedures nor the lawlike rigidity of serialism is likely to result in a musically satisfactory work. Because composers can no longer be believed when they claim to produce pieces deserving consideration as music, they forfeit the trust that brings to their new works the audience won over by the music of Bach, Beethoven, Brahms, and Berg.

Which is better justified—Tormey's optimism or Cavell's pessimism? Personally, I share Cavell's doubts, for I find much of the "classical" music of the 1960s and 1970s arid and empty.[46] Though there are beautiful sounds in nature—in particular, birdsong—the rattle and hum of daily life do not strike me as especially interesting or rewarding when approached with an ear to their coherence, structure, or expression. Simply, I take John Cage to be mistaken in his view that music is all around us while we take an aesthetic interest as opposed to a practical one in the sound of the everyday.[47] Difficult though it is to discern trends, I believe that, with musical minimalism, a concern with non-Western musics, and the reinvigoration of some earlier forms and styles, composers have reasserted their direct control over the material with which they work.

Following Cavell, I have suggested that some compositional techniques are such that they virtually guarantee the absence of artistic interest or merit when the (sound of the) resulting work is approached as (the sound of)

---

[46] I do not mean to condemn out of hand the use of serial techniques or chance procedures. Schönberg, Berg, Webern, and Stravinsky reveal the power and resources of serial composition when that approach is not harnessed to the yoke of ideology.

[47] Nature is described as unmusical not only by Hanslick but also by Cazden (1951), McLaughlin (1970), and Urmson (1973).

< 363 >

music. Robert P. Morgan (1977) apparently would disagree. So long as such music is recognized for what it is—a variety of program music—it can be heard to make sense. He holds that a programmatic work that might be incomprehensible when treated as pure music can often be understood when listened to with the story it illustrates in mind. Similarly, the listener should attend to contemporary works with the composer's explanation of the compositional process in hand, hoping to find in the music an elucidation of that process, because then it will make sense. Morgan suggests that, for such music, the so-called intentional fallacy is no fallacy at all, because the music can be understood only in the light of the composer's account of what she is doing.

Lincoln Baxter objects (1980): It is appropriate to take note of those of an artist's intentions that can be checked against the features of her work. If an artist's intentions are realized successfully in the work, then reference to those intentions can draw attention to properties of the work and, in this way, can be relevant to the work's proper interpretation. But it does not follow from this fact that artists' intentions *determine* the artistically significant properties of their works. An artist's intentions are irrelevant unless they are carried through to the work, and even then they might be ignored in favor of some other reading responsive to the work's features. So, in observing correctly that composer's intentions can be of relevance to the interpretation of their works, Morgan does not disprove the argument that suggests that it is fallacious to treat artist's intentions as determinative of the range of acceptable interpretations of their works.

I think that Baxter is right to challenge Morgan's position, but I believe that his objection misses its target. For the cases under dispute, we can check what the composer said she was writing against what is notated in the work's score, but, if what is in the score does not, on performance, translate into something that can be heard, then it is not clear that the intentions are realized in the work, for the musical work is not the score as such. So, even if anti–intentionalists accept that those of a composer's intentions that are manifest in the work might be pertinent to an appreciative view of her work, they might continue to deny, for the case at issue, that the intentions are revealed in the work (as opposed merely to being apparent in its score). Accordingly, they dismiss as irrelevant to an appreciation of the work and its features a knowledge of intentions. Morgan, by contrast, suggests that the works in question can be understood (only) in light of their creators' intentions. As a result, he concludes that the anti–intentionalist is mistaken (and Baxter's observation is beside the point).

Is Morgan correct, though, in holding that the works in question are ap-

< 364 >

preciable, if not as pure music then as program music that is to be heard with regard to what the composer took herself to be doing? I do not believe so, for reasons I now explain. Sometimes an action appears to be incomprehensible just because that action fails to carry through the agent's intention. The action can be explained as an unsuccessful attempt to execute the intention. This makes sense of the action, though, only to the extent that it explains why the action makes no sense on its own terms. This is a different order of explanation (leading to a different order of understanding) than that involved in explaining how an action is suited, say, to meeting the agent's goals. Now, for the composers with whom Morgan is concerned, it is apparently not that the intention fails, because it is not so that they imagine that the compositional processes will be audible within the sound of the musical work. But, I have claimed, we talk of musical understanding on the supposition that sense can be made of music *on its own terms*; we try to apprehend the sounds of the work so that what happens at any given moment is revealed as coherent in light of what precedes or follows. Even if the composers in question carry through their intentions successfully, Cavell's claim is that it is not plain that an appreciation of this results in an object for musical understanding. To put it crudely, the composer's failure lies, if not in the execution of the intention, then in the goal at which she aims, given that no musical sense is produced. Learning why the music serves no musical point is to understand its pointlessness, which is *not* to understand it as a musical work.[48]

As I read him, Cavell does not mean to deny that totally serialized music and the like *is* music. His claim seems to be that such music is without musical point, and hence that it cannot be *appreciated* as music. Composers are playing a new game, one like that described by Hermann Hesse in *The Glass Bead Game*. They create musical equivalents of the crossword; the sounds are to be taken with clues supplied by the compiler; musical elements, central though they may be, are only one of the media from which the puzzle is created.[49] Cavell's objection, as I see it, is not to the game as such but to its being represented as a continuation of the old one. The objection is to the assumption that the new game should inherit the audience that enjoyed playing the old without attempting to win the audience through its own (largely

---

[48] To use an analogy: I might come to understand why the rattle of pots and pans from the kitchen sounds as it does—because they have been dropped, say—but that would not show that I have understood, or could understand, the rattling as musical.

[49] Robert P. Morgan (1977) suggests that such music requires a new style of analysis. Cavell might agree, while denying that it is *musical* analysis that is called for. Meyer (1963) argues that the work of the avant-garde is "anti-teleological" and, as such, breaks with the earlier musical tradition.

< 365 >

nonmusical) merits. The "programs" of such works might have an interest for us. More generally, we might be concerned with the forces that have led composers in the directions they have taken and in the problems this poses for both them and listeners. Such concerns are distinct from issues of musical understanding, however.

Cavell's challenge to the "classical" music of the 1960s does not suppose that composers are to blame for adopting the styles in which they write. In subscribing to the inevitability and irreversibility of historical change in art, Cavell sees the contemporary composer as driven by forces internal to the practice of musical composition. But, because he finds no evidence of progress in this change, he sees the composer more as victim than as hero in taking his historical place.[50] He recognizes the futility of the composer's attempting to turn the clock back to tonality, and, because he can see no way forward, or no reason for optimism, he writes as if serialism is the swan song of music as an artform.

Ross (1985) agrees with Cavell that there is a predicament facing modern composers and that the same predicament does not arise in other arts, but she disagrees with his diagnosis. Composers can allude to and write in outdated styles, she writes; a contemporary work can be more Mozartian than Schönbergian. If composers cannot do what has been done before, if they cannot reinvigorate past forms, this is because music (unlike other major arts) lacks semantic or depictive content. In music one cannot create new works by filling old forms with new contents; because music lacks semantic or depictive content, new types of work can be created only through the creation of new types of form. Composers cannot say anything new in old styles or forms not because of some metaphysical necessity in historical process but because, in using those styles or forms, they cannot "say" anything that has not already been "said."

As I was previously, I am critical of Ross's insensitivity to the contextualism motivating Cavell's argument. His point is not that history (somehow) prevents a composer writing down notes which, were they to have been written in the eighteenth century, might have been penned by Mozart. It is instead that the historical context affects the properties of the notes in

---

[50] Compare this with Adorno, who is a Hegelian progressivist on the topic of musical history. As Adorno sees it, the survival of music depends not on retrogression but on the amalgamation and absorption of twelve-tone technique by the assumption of its rules through the spontaneity of the critical ear. He writes: "Schoenberg draws the consequences from the dissolution of all binding forms in music, as this existed in the law of its own development" (1973, [1948], 213). For a wider and more recent account of the history of art from a Hegelian perspective, see Danto 1986.

< 366 >

question, so that one cannot now compose music with the power and virtue of Mozart's by writing what he might have written.[51] In addition, I am critical of Ross's positive account of the contemporary dilemma. As this book testifies, I do not believe that, just because it lacks semantic or depictive meaning, music is properly to be regarded as form without content. Simply, it is not true that former musical styles were discarded because their possibilities had been exhausted. So it is not so that what prevents one from "saying" something new in an old style or form is that one could write in that style or form only by repeating what has already been written.

If there is an error in Cavell's approach to musical history, it is not the one Ross imputes. Cavell's fault, as I detect it, lies in his implying that music has no future on the ground that he is unable to read its future.[52] He may have been correct in predicting that serial-determined composition would prove to be an artistic cul-de-sac, but perhaps he was wrong in believing that path to be the highway of music history rather than the byway it now seems to be. The history of music is full of "crises"—such as the erosion of the system of church modes, or the move to equal temperament, or the consequences for performance practice of the development of notations. They were no less traumatic than the overthrow of tonality has proved to be, yet none of these earlier crises spelled the end of music as such.

How Music Is Like a Person

The claim that we attempt to understand music on its own terms deserves amplification. Several writers make the point that understanding a musical work is like understanding a person.[53] Now though, what does that mean? Because so much of this book has been devoted to its consideration, one connection is obvious: the sound of music is like a person's appearance in respect of its expressive character. Another possibility is this: The identity of a person persists through time partly because his actions are unified, and those actions cohere because they are (often) shaped by the will of the autonomous agent with a view to their consistency, to what might be called

---

[51] One could write in an eighteenth-century style, but one's music would be anachronistic in a way that Mozart's is not; one's music would be heard as music written in the post-tonal era and could not help thereby sounding quaint and stilted.

[52] Compare this with Danto 1986. Danto sees the history of art as culminating and ending in his lifetime. Though art will continue to be made, it has reached its posthistorical phase; having fulfilled the destiny toward which its past was a progress, it continues now with nowhere to go. For discussion, see Davies 1992.

[53] For example, see Cavell 1977, Tanner 1985, and Tormey 1988.

< 367 >

their narrative structure. One expects an action to be similar in relevant respects to the agent's past actions. Music is to be understood in an analogous fashion. One striking element in an experience of music is the way the musical progress is "logical," though one could not have predicted at many points what was to come next.[54] The musical ideas fit together—as complementary, or as variations, or as repetitions—so that there is a development or progress of ideas, and the work comes to a close (and does not merely stop). We expect that one musical idea will function as a reason for the next (or at least, that the next will seem, in retrospect, to be a natural continuation). If the juxtaposition of musical events seems not to make sense, we hope that developments yet to come will reveal the aptness of their current proximity. In brief, the music usually strikes us as an integrated whole, with the basis for that integration supplied from within, not without, the work.[55]

Tanner (1985) reminds us that there is another respect in which music sometimes is like a person: both can be inexplicable on some occasions, as well as understandable on others. Sometimes a person I know does something I cannot understand, and neither subsequent events nor his future actions help me to understand him any the better. Sometimes a person acts out of character for no obvious reason. The same is true of musical works. As an example, Tanner cites the opening of Mozart's String Quartet, K. 465 (*Dissonance*). Rather than seeking some elaborate musical explanation of the work's opening where none seems available, we should simply take the passage for what it is, accepting its singularity, just as we take people for what they are, even if not everything they do can be understood.

I take Tanner to be correct in this observation, but it matters, I think, that the phenomenon is one in which a musically inexplicable part belongs to a whole within which musical sense can be made of most of what happens.[56] The musically inexplicable is tolerable within an understandable musical whole; in the same fashion, a person can act out of character only if he establishes a character, which he can do only by acting more often than

---

[54] See Lerdahl and Jackendoff 1983; for a recent article emphasizing the point, see Goldman 1992.

[55] These generalizations apply not solely to pure music of the best kind but to almost all pure music. Telemann's more boring works are no less coherent in their progress than the most sublime of Bach's pieces, but Telemann's ideas are less interesting and their progress is more predictable.

[56] The singularity of a work can consist in the freedom of its overall form from all structural models known to the composer. I take Debussy's *Jeux* and Stravinsky's *Les Noces* to belong to the category of such works. In these cases the singularity encompasses the entire work, but it is apparent in the work's independence of traditional formal models rather than in a lack of coherence.

< 368 >

not in a consistent way. But where nothing in a musical work is musically explicable in terms of what can be heard in the work, then the musical work is pointless (or perhaps has a nonmusical point to make).

Notice that talk of musical coherence need not presuppose that the composer's intentions are always successfully realized. Music is usually designed to be as it is and, given (as I hear it) the widespread absence of musically interesting sounds in nature and society, this is very important. But one does not explain or understand a musical work by direct reference to the composer's intentions and their execution, as one might explain and understand a machine designed to stamp dyes in a factory by reference to its purpose and its designer's intentions. We react to the musical work as if it were autonomous and organic; we expect to find sufficient reason for the work's progressing as it does within the context set solely by its style, form, and content. Thus, "its maker intended it to be so" is incomplete as an explanation of why the music is as it is if no reason internal to the world of the work indicates why the composer had that intention.

The Relevance of History and Style

The analogy between understanding music and understanding a person can be taken further. To understand an individual as a person with a character, a self-structured life, is to presuppose a natural and social history for human beings—a form of life. Our understanding of music is similar. Musical works must be seen as belonging within a history of styles and traditions of composition and performance. An appreciation of musical history is more directly pertinent to an understanding of individual works than is mastery of a technical vocabulary, I feel.

One reason for the relevance of a knowledge of a historically wide spread of works is obvious: musical works can contain quotations, parodies, and other forms of reference to different pieces and styles. But the importance of a historical approach to music runs much deeper than this. As I have noted, the artistically significant properties of any given piece depend in part on when it is written and the style to which it belongs, as well as on its note structure. Also, what is stylistically permissible at one time may not be so at some earlier or later time. Moreover, styles bring with them different possibilities, so that what might be achieved in or appropriate to a given style may not be so in another. In writing at a particular time and in a style, the composer works within constraints. Those constraints need not be burdensome, for they provide the public context in which the composer's treatment of the "problems" posed by her materials can be followed by her audience;

< 369 >

similarly, the "constraint" that one comply with the rules and conventions of one's native tongue in verbally articulating and communicating a thought is unlikely to seem burdensome since such goals can be met only within the context of a public language. In the case of a great many musical works, the fullest appreciation requires an awareness of the "problem" to which the composer's solution is an "answer," and an awareness of that "problem" depends on a sensitivity to the features of the style and genre in which the composer works.

The point can be made, perhaps, when we consider a case mentioned earlier—the singularity of the introduction to the first movement of Mozart's String Quartet, K. 465. The use of an introduction is not itself unusual; that device had already been featured in Haydn's symphonies and string quartets and, anyway, can be traced through the "French overture" to the "Canzona overture" of the early seventeenth century. Other features of the introduction—its slow tempo and lack of thematic connection to the following allegro—conform to the pattern established in these earlier forms. This pattern had already been confirmed by Haydn, Mozart's model. The singularity of the movement's beginning resides, in fact, in the sharpness of the dissonances employed and in the tonal uncertainty to which they give rise. Had the introduction been written by Bartók, however, the harmonies would not have been noteworthy in their tension or instability. The points I have made here are so obvious that they might easily be passed over without comment. But if these points are plain, this is because many listeners have absorbed a sensitivity to historically based styles and procedures. The listener can hear what is singular, and what not, only by locating the work within a history of styles and formal practices.

I now turn to a more difficult case. Suppose a person reads of the finale of Mozart's Symphony No. 41, K. 551, that it is one "where fugue is composed against the background of sonata and, at the same time, sonata against the background of fugue" (Keller 1966, 100). Also suppose that this is a correct assessment of the movement's most significant feature: indeed, the reader goes on to learn that the movement is a masterpiece just by its successful reconciliation of these two structural types. Our music lover, call her Cecilia, wants to understand the movement in such terms. How is she to do so and what is she to understand?

Cecilia might begin by considering textbook descriptions of the formal types fugue and sonata. My guess is that, when she listens to the finale of Mozart's last symphony after reading such characterizations, she will be little the wiser. She will know that the forms are different, but no standard account of these structures is likely to explain to her what a marriage of the

< 370 >

two might sound like, what stands in the way of their union, and what might be gained by the result. Usually musical form is described as a pattern, formula, or recipe. Cecilia, if she is to understand the difficulties of reconciling and combining the two, must consider the sense in which they are opposed. What she needs, then, is a grasp of the artistic functions performed by these structural types and of the contributions made by the parts to the whole.[57] In this case that sense is acquired by considering these various forms in relation to the different styles they display—baroque and classical. To understand Mozart's achievement is to hear how he reconciles these two musical styles in the finale, and to understand why that might be difficult. To put the same point a different way, to understand the music is to hear how Mozart adapts a classical style (and a form, sonata, that had become prominent because it provides such a vivid illustration of classical style) to realize effects that had been thought to depend exclusively on a baroque manner of contrapuntal writing (and on different forms, such as fugue, adapted to the music of that earlier era).

Compare baroque (contrapuntal) and classical styles. In the former, the interest falls on the continuous interplay between several autonomous, equal voices or parts that overlap and crisscross in carrying forward their musical conversation. As a result, there is a high degree of textural complexity in such music. The work progresses through a fluid unfolding of the material, with all the melodic ideas being introduced at the outset. The tension accumulates gradually, peaks, and is discharged near the piece's end. Generally speaking, extreme contrasts in mood or material are avoided, as are modulations that are abrupt and unprepared. The primary mode of contrast involves modification in one or other aspect of the volume of the sound— terraced dynamics, the alternation of solo and ripieno groupings, register changes, and, for the organ and harpsichord, octave couplings and the use of stops, such as flute, lute, or vox humana.

[57] I believe this to be the way musical form is best approached in general. Formalism is sometimes reviled as sterile and academic. Such criticism is deserved when the interest in form leads the listener to treat the work merely as an exemplar of a structural type. But when form is viewed functionally—that is, is considered not as a mold determining the shape of the musical contents but as a set of principles of organization applied in the service of the goal of producing an integrated whole—a listener concerned with understanding a work cannot be entirely indifferent to it. To hear what the composer does as an answer, one must get some idea of the problem. To put the issue at its crudest, the problem is that of ordering the work such that what comes later can be heard to be a natural extension of what went earlier. As Goldman (1992) recognizes, the point of a concern with form is not to comprehend the music as instancing an abstract pattern; it is to have one's listening informed by an implicit grasp of structure, so that one can hear a cadence as a resolution, or a development or a variation as such in relation to a theme.

< 371 >

The material suited to these goals has sufficient character to retain its identity in its various manipulations, but it is not so distinctive that its appearance in any one voice leads that voice to dominate the others; the material is chosen more for its combinatorial possibilities than for its thematic distinction. This means, among other things, that the main melodic ideas do not end with firm cadences (since they should flow on to the next phrase), that often these melodic ideas lend themselves to sequential treatment and other standard approaches to prolongation, and that the phrases of the various voices do not coincide vertically (and may be horizontally uneven and irregular).

The forms that best promote the ideals of this musical style are ones avoiding sectionalization. Because the complexity lies not in the material itself but in the interaction between the voices in their use of it, the exposition is as brief as is consistent with the presentation of the main melodic ideas (neither is there a need for a marked recapitulation as such). Usually, the treatment is developmental throughout. The length of the work is dependent on the interest that can be generated through the combination of voices each of which derives its material from the initial melodic ideas or their development. Given the unrelieved intensity of the treatment throughout the work of its main ideas, considerable concentration is demanded of the listener, who is supposed to follow the interaction between the parts. For this reason, and perhaps also because the permutations and combinations the initial ideas suggest are always limited, movements in these styles and forms tend to be comparatively short.

By contrast, in classical works the main goal is to introduce contrasting ideas, usually possessing considerable melodic character (as well as different tonalities in their initial appearances), and to integrate their disparate natures within a single musical span. One voice, whichever one carries the main theme at the time, dominates the others, which serve merely as its accompaniment. Because several, separate thematic ideas are introduced, each is the focus of attention when it is first stated. Clarity of texture remains desirable throughout, the better to allow the various occurrences of the main thematic ideas to be recognized. This is important because it is at the macro-level of organization that integration is to be realized. The work progresses mainly through the juxtaposition of clearly marked, contrasting segments. Because these segments are "blocked" the one against the other, there is a potential for dramatic contrast as one section gives way to another. Marked changes in melody, key, rhythm, tempo, or instrumentation and alterations in mood or movement consequent on this are often exploited. Equally though, the transition between sections sometimes is made seamlessly. When this ap-

< 372 >

proach is adopted, contrapuntal techniques are often pressed into temporary service; they are most frequently to be found where ideas are developed, as in bridges between statements of the thematic groups or in the section between the exposition and the recapitulation.

The material suited to this approach possesses individuality; it must have a beginning and end as well as sufficient complexity and extension to stand on its own as the target of interest. Its distinctiveness might be harmonic, or rhythmic, but most often it is melodic. These melodies are often in a *cantabile*, or singing, style, and the use of decoration is less prominent than in the baroque style.

In a classical work the form is sectional, with a considerable portion of the movement given over, in the first instance, to the presentation of its various, contrasting ideas and, later, to their restatement. This recapitulation not only counterbalances the exposition but usually displays more tonal stability than is found elsewhere in the movement. Because the aim is to work out, or through, the various contrasts that are presented, and because tonal contrast is almost always present, tonality plays a more prominent structural role in classical than in baroque music. Contrasts between sections can create a pattern of highs and lows, but often there is not a gradual building of tension through the work; insofar as there is a particular moment of release, it falls at the start of the recapitulation (which may be little more than halfway through the movement).[58] Movements structured in this modular fashion can become quite extended, provided that the ideas, or the manner of their presentation, can sustain the audience's interest. In general, such forms call for less concentration from the listener than does the through-composed approach of the fugue, because much more of the piece is given over to exposition than to development. But this allows for a new kind of demand on the listener, who is expected to follow the arrangement of several extended, disparate ideas.[59]

[58] The early nineteenth century saw a prolongation of the development section of sonata form that became, thereby, a truly ternary, not binary, structure. One result of this was to postpone the moment of highest tonal tension (prior to the return of the tonic key with the recapitulation) until later in the movement.

[59] Classical forms did not spring, fully formed, from the godhead. They drew on those earlier forms—especially binary ones—that most readily lent themselves to evolution toward the ideals that were to prevail. Unless the listener is conscious of the models from which sonata form evolved, she is not likely to appreciate the works of such composers as Domenico Scarlatti, J. C. Bach, and C. P. E. Bach. When someone is as explicit as I have tried to be about the difference in styles, he is bound to wonder why the ideal shifted, so that clarity came to trump textural density and did so not because complexity ceased to be valued but because a new type of complexity was created; instead of highlighting subtleties of cooperation between voices handling a common idea, attention now was drawn to the large-scale integration of contrasts and con-

< 373 >

Now, it is only when Cecilia has a feel for the differences between the ideals and practices typically embodied in fugal and sonata writing that she is in a strong position to approach Mozart's Symphony No. 41 with a hope of recognizing the aspects of each style melded in its finale. Only when she has a comfortable familiarity not only with the symphonies of the 1780s but also with the fugal traditions that reach their culmination in *The Art of Fugue* is she prepared for the deepest experience of the last movement of Mozart's final symphony. This comfortable familiarity can be acquired, I believe, only through carefully listening to many works in the relevant styles and by listening to particular works often. Suppose she does this. What does she now find in Mozart's work?

The last movement of Mozart's Symphony No. 41 presents a clear sonata form structure.[60] Nevertheless, there are striking respects in which the material or its treatment is unusual. Instead of a strong, perky, sixteen-bar theme such as might feature as the centerpiece in a sonata rondo, the movement begins with four motives distinguished only by their conventionality. Indeed, the simple figure of the opening four bars had already become a vapid gesture when Haydn used it, twenty-four years earlier, to begin the last movement of his Symphony No. 13 in D of 1764.[61] But clearly Mozart intends the

---

flicts. Why did this happen? This change in musical styles corresponded with important social and cultural upheavals, and these wider patterns might have been reflected in the artistic taste of the time. Moreover, some of these social changes affected the context of music-making: for example, the rise of public subscription concerts eventually freed the composer from dependence on the church and court, contributed to his rising social status, and promoted the domination of works written for professional, rather than amateur, performers. The period in question saw many significant musical changes: the rise to prominence of absolute, or pure, instrumental forms; the final collapse of the modal system in favor of major/minor tonalities; the uniform adoption of equal temperament for keyboard instruments; the replacement of the harpsichord with the fortepiano and the arrival of the modern violin; and the disappearance of the basso continuo as the autonomy of the various instrumental families became more firmly established. Exactly how these musical considerations, or wider social movements, led to the particular alterations seen in the gradual move from baroque, contrapuntal ideals to classical ones is far from clear. For example, one might argue that the greater sustaining power of the fortepiano, as against the harpsichord, explains the shift from ornate decoration to a singing melodic style. Note, however, that decoration was a feature of (some kinds of) vocal and string, as well as keyboard, music in the baroque period, so the connection between the technology of the instruments and the desired sound is far from simple. It is possible that the development of the fortepiano was as much an effect as a cause of stylistic changes.

[60] The first subject group is stated immediately, the second subject group appears at bar 74, the codetta at bar 115, the development at bar 158, the recapitulation at 225, and the coda from bar 360 to 423.

[61] This movement of Haydn's, like Mozart's, combines aspects of the fugue and sonata. Haydn's work, which is charming, witty, and masterly, provides a measure of how impressive Mozart's achievement is.

< 374 >

interest to lie in the contrapuntal development of the material rather than in its melodic beauty. New ideas appear in the first bridge and the second subject, but these are no less fragmentary than those introduced at the outset. Meanwhile, starting with the first bridge, motives from the first subject receive contrapuntal development, including close imitation, and this continues in all sections of the exposition. The two or three ideas introduced after bar 35 are soon associated with the earlier material, and the pace of development scarcely pauses when they make their first appearances. The development section continues the pattern, adding inversion to the contrapuntal techniques already employed and moving more often to minor keys. The recapitulation involves truncation of the first and second subject groups. Modifications and the use of minor keys in the recapitulation of the first bridge recall the development section as much as the exposition, and the use of flattened supertonic harmonies keeps the level of tension high. The arrival of the coda does not lead to relaxation and a cessation of development but, rather, to unexpected complexities. The main motive of the first subject group is easily recognized in retrograde inversion. Soon it is combined contrapuntally with the opening figure of the second subject group and, one by one, most of the movement's key motives are introduced into the contrapuntal mêlée.

By now the force of Keller's observation, quoted earlier, might become clearer to Cecilia. Mozart relishes the integrity and scale permitted to him by his use of sonata form; the important structural points are strongly marked by emphatic cadences and the appropriate sequence of keys is scrupulously respected. But that said, he shapes the detail so that the strengths of fugal writing are highlighted in a manner that would be foreign to most works of the time. Rather than using contrapuntal methods of development merely to fill out the sonata form structure, the movement takes its point (and its structural effects) from the exploration of those techniques.[62] This is apparent in many ways: in the avoidance of characterful, balanced themes; in the extreme economy of materials used; in the preservation of continuity by constant reference to elements that first appear in the initial bars; in the onset of development from the first bridge and in the constant use of imitation and other fugal practices. Also, it is apparent in the general effect, which is one of gradually mounting interest and tension rather than of juxtaposi-

---

[62] So I think that Alfred Einstein is wrong when he writes of the "Jupiter": "This work has been somewhat mistakenly called the symphony with the fugue-finale. For that movement is not a fugue, but simply a sonata movement with fugato passages in the exposition, the development, and the coda" (1966, 235).

< 375 >

tion and overall symmetry. This accumulation of tension and growing complexity is a function of many factors: the second subject is combined with material both from the first subject and from the preceding bridge; the recapitulation has affinities with the development as well as with the exposition; progressively more subtle and complex fugal practices are introduced—imitation, inversion, retrograde, the combination of multiple subjects; the greatest musical drama, a tour de force of contrapuntal complexity and reconciliation, is reserved for the coda. To hear this movement with understanding is to hear it as building steadily to the revelations of the coda. That manner of listening, which more obviously belongs to the fugue than to the final movement of a symphony of the 1780s, is one that will be adopted only by the listener who can hear the movement shaped not only by its sonata form structure but by the contrapuntal tradition on which it reflects.

It might be thought that, in choosing to discuss a work that obviously is designed to provide an overview of two great European musical traditions and styles, I beg the question in favor of my claim that the fullest understanding of music is provided only to those with a sense of the history of changing musical styles. But I believe this allegation to be mistaken, for it is my view that the attempt to understand any work involves consideration of its historical and stylistic context, even if it does not set out to comment self-consciously on those matters. To understand a work is to appreciate why it takes the course it does. Cecilia can do that to the fullest only if she is able to sort those of its features that are unique to it as an individual from those that belong to it, say, as a symphony's first movement, and only if she can sort features that mark it as a symphony from those displayed by concertos, string quartets, opera overtures, and so on. Because these various forms, types, and genres evolved from common ancestors in some cases and from very different ones in others, and because they became what they are gradually, these kinds and levels of sorting presuppose a sense of both the function and the history of the musical practices on which the given work draws.[63]

I agree with the view of musical understanding implicit in this question asked by David A. White: "What elements of the fugue in the first movement [of Beethoven's String Quartet No. 14, Opus 131] are relevant to the fact that this fugue is the first of three movements, each distinct in its formal structure, yet sequentially producing, with gradually increasing tempo, the expressiveness of sadness and gloom?" (1992, 32). I believe, that is, that one

---

[63] I discuss some distinctions between the uses of sonata form in the symphony, the concerto, and the opera overture in Davies 1994, where I also offer functional explanations of these differences.

< 376 >

can and should ask some such question of any work, and that the answer is evident only to a person who has a sense of the work's place within the tradition, because it is that tradition within (or against) which the composer conceives her ideals, projects, and methods. The point of the question is not to pigeonhole the work, not to reduce it to the lowest common denominators it shares with other pieces, but to explore its individuality. That exploration requires of one not only an intimate familiarity with the given work but a knowledge of how it is similar to, and distinct from, other pieces.

One reason I stress the contextuality of musical works is that most of the philosophers who have written recently on musical understanding tend to ignore the importance of the listener's grasp of the history of musical styles and performance traditions as underpinning their understanding of particular works.[64] I am at a loss to explain the approach that treats musical works as if it is appropriate to ignore their cultural and historical location. Perhaps our grasp of the history of musical styles is so practical that it rarely needs to be made explicit; it may be that such matters are not mentioned because they can be taken for granted, not because they are regarded as unimportant. I find this suggestion unconvincing, however, because when large, complex works are the focus of attention, some of the questions most likely to lead to comprehension are ones that do not have the self-evident answers that might be supplied thoughtlessly by the listener's musical intuitions. Alternatively, it may be that there is a reluctance to take the route I favor, since I imply that the fullest appreciation of music might require a dedicated immersion in its works which only a small minority of listeners would aspire to. Those whose aim is to defend the "ordinary" listener against the view that technical training is a requirement for musical understanding might also wish to deny that more should be demanded of the listener than close attention to the given work.

Earlier I suggested that one might understand music without first mastering the technical terms used by musicologists. I also believe that a grasp of the differences between styles, genres, and formal types need presuppose no special training, since what is called for is a sense of the functional possi-

---

[64] Among the few exceptions to this generalization are Lippman 1966 and 1977 and Levinson 1990b. Goldman (1992) uses a well-worn analogy in maintaining that musical styles correspond to types of terrain across which individual works trace a path; only a person familiar with terrain of the relevant kind can negotiate the path successfully. One could develop the analogy in my terms: The work takes the listener on a journey. He can see where he has been, how he got from point to point, and why the path takes the route it does only if he is familiar with the region and with the problems and possibilities it presents to the road builder. Where the "region" is a musical style, these problems and possibilities are as much historically relative as they are inherent in the physical medium.

< 377 >

bilities of musical materials and a grasp of the sonic or structural ideals at which different composers aim, rather than a memorization of formal recipes. But I would not go so far as to deny the relevance of a concern with the intimate relation holding between the properties of musical works and the context in which they are produced. I have argued that formal training is not necessary before a listener might attain a significant degree of musical appreciation, but I have not suggested that appreciation should or would come easily. I see no more reason to believe that great musical works will yield their deepest riches to the casual listener than to believe that the works of Shakespeare or Rembrandt will be revealed fully to the person who takes a passing interest in them and does so with only the vaguest of notions of when, how, or why they were produced or of the cultural and social background that is the intellectual inheritance of the audience for which such things were made. The enjoyment of music might be the work, the hard work, of a lifetime, not least because there can be no substitute for listening carefully and often to many pieces if one is to acquire the practical knowledge needed to inform the listening experience appropriately.

It is important to acknowledge again that an understanding and appreciation of music, like understanding in general, can be both partial and a matter of degree. Indeed, were this not so, it is unlikely that anyone could achieve the understanding I have been discussing; understanding could not begin, as it were, if it could be attained only by those with a grasp of the musical context, given that that grasp would depend in turn on the listener's ability to listen with understanding. The attainment of musical understanding relies on a kind of boot-strapping. One might understand enough about a work to listen to other pieces in closely related styles; this allows one to return to the original work with a richer comprehension of the possibilities it presents; this allows one to refine one's sensitivity to subtleties of stylistic distinction; and so on.

Most listeners master, as part of their general acculturation, a familiarity with quite complex features of the dominant musical style (which, in Western cultural traditions, is diatonic and tonal). Many works are accessible to listeners on the basis of that familiarity.[65] Because we often know much more than we are aware of having come to know, and because much music is written to satisfy those whose sole qualification is this familiarity with the

---

[65] Indeed, sometimes it is possible to follow much of what goes on in a work from a cultural tradition with which one is not at all familiar, provided that tradition shares some basic features with the style most intimately known to one. Some music from south of the Sahara is accessible to Westerners in this way.

< 378 >

(presently) dominant style, a listener might understand much music without taking special pains or thinking very much about what she hears (unless she is asked to articulate her understanding or to justify her enjoyment). But not all (good) music is accessible at this level, and some music that is so might also be approached at other levels. It would not be surprising (given the talents of those who create and perform such works) if the greatest rewards are afforded to the listener mainly by works with a degree of complexity and subtlety that sustains close and repeated attention. In that case, then, neither should it be surprising that the attraction and value of some music is evident only to those who expend the time and concentration necessary to comprehend both what interests and challenges the composer in the production of such a work and why what was written succeeds or not in answering that challenge.

Though I have devoted much of this book to a consideration of the philosophical problems raised by claims about, and responses to, music's expressiveness, the topic of expressiveness has not figured prominently in this chapter. Roger Scruton (1983) suggests that an appreciation of music's expressiveness is crucial to one's understanding of music. This claim strikes me as exaggerated: some music is not expressive and much music that is expressive is so only incidentally. Diana Raffman (1991), by contrast with Scruton, thinks that the appreciation of musical meaning has very little to do with the recognition of expressiveness in music. This view also strikes me as mistaken. There are works the point of which is to be expressive as they are; one can understand why such a piece is as it is only by hearing how its organization contributes to the expressive effect that is its raison d'être. In most respects I agree with the position presented by Kivy (1990a): where expressiveness is a musically significant feature of a work, the listener should recognize what is expressed and what is expressive in understanding the work, but where other features or the treatment of the material are what give point to the work (as often is the case), then it is these matters, rather than expressiveness, that should be the focus of the listener's concern.

I have argued, as have others, that the listener is not precluded from understanding or appreciating music if she lacks formal training in the theory of music. I do so not because I regard as irrelevant the ability to articulate that understanding but because I believe that understanding can be revealed no less clearly by nontechnical descriptions (probably coupled with ostensive gestures, or humming, and so on) than by the use of the musicologist's vocabulary. I hold that the experience of music, where it is concerned with a work not only as music but as the piece it is, is necessarily thought-impreg-

< 379 >

nated. This need not be apparent in thoughts that pass before the listener's mind as she listens, but it is shown by the descriptions she is able to offer (when helped if necessary) of the work and of its distinguishable elements. Unlike those who regard training in music theory as a hindrance to an appreciation of music, I believe that that education, properly applied, can considerably enhance one's understanding.

If my view differs from those of Budd (1985b), Tanner (1985), and Kivy (1990a), it does so in the emphasis I place on the need for a knowledge of the historical and stylistic location of the work one is attempting to understand. For the most part these writers discuss music written in the European tradition that includes Léonin, Machaut, Binchois, Josquin, Monteverdi, Bach, Haydn, Beethoven, Brahms, Mahler, Debussy, Schönberg, and Stravinsky. Music of that kind must be understood against the background of the cultural heritage to which it gives expression, I believe, even if some other, popular forms of music require little more of the listener than a passing familiarity with the main stylistic features of the most widespread music of the listener's society. In general, I take these philosophers to underplay the importance of the listener's attaining musical appreciation and understanding through her working out what is the musical "question" such that what is written might be its "answer."

< 380 >

Works Cited

Ackerman, James S. 1981. "Worldmaking and Practical Criticism." *Journal of Aesthetics and Art Criticism,* 39, 249–254.

Adams, Hazard. 1987. "Titles, Titling, and Entitlement To." *Journal of Aesthetics and Art Criticism,* 46, 7–21.

Adorno, Theodor W. 1973. *The Philosophy of Modern Music.* Trans. Anne G. Mitchell and Wesley V. Bloomster. London: Sheed & Ward. (first published 1948)

Agarwal, Bipin Kumar. 1973. "Langer, Hildebrand, and Space in Art." *Journal of Aesthetics and Art Criticism,* 31, 513–516.

Albersheim, Gerhard. 1960. "The Sense of Space in Tonal and Atonal Music." *Journal of Aesthetics and Art Criticism,* 19, 17–30.

——. 1964. "Mind and Matter in Music." *Journal of Aesthetics and Art Criticism,* 22, 289–294.

Aldrich, Virgil. 1963. *Philosophy of Art.* Englewood Cliffs, N. J.: Prentice-Hall.

Allen, R. T. 1990. "The Arousal and Expression of Emotion by Music." *British Journal of Aesthetics,* 30, 57–61.

Alperson, Philip. 1980. "'Musical Time' and Music as an 'Art of Time.'" *Journal of Aesthetics and Art Criticism,* 38, 407–417.

——. 1992. "The Arts of Music." *Journal of Aesthetics and Art Criticism,* 50, 217–230.

Alperson, Philip, ed. 1987. *What Is Music? An Introduction to the Philosophy of Music.* New York: Haven.

Alston, William P. 1965. "Expressing." In *Philosophy in America,* ed. Max Black. London: George Allen & Unwin, 15–34.

< 381 >

Works Cited

Arnheim, Rudolph. 1974. "On the Nature of Photography." *Critical Inquiry*, 1, 149–161.

Arrell, Douglas. 1987. "What Goodman Should Have Said about Representation." *Journal of Aesthetics and Art Criticism*, 46, 41–49.

——. 1990. "Exemplification Reconsidered." *British Journal of Aesthetics*, 30, 233–243.

Aschenbrenner, Karl. 1981. "Music Criticism: Practice and Malpractice." In Price, ed., 99–117.

Bach, Kent. 1970. "Part of What a Picture Is." *British Journal of Aesthetics*, 10, 119–137.

Ballard, Edward G. 1953. "In Defence of Symbolic Aesthetics." *Journal of Aesthetics and Art Criticism*, 12, 38–43.

Barry, Kevin. 1987. *Language, Music, and the Sign: A Study in Aesthetics, Poetics, and Poetic Practice from Collins to Coleridge*. Cambridge: Cambridge University Press.

Barwell, Ismay. 1986. "How Does Art Express Emotion?" *Journal of Aesthetics and Art Criticism*, 45, 175–181.

Barzun, Jacques. 1953. *Music into Words*. Washington: Library of Congress.

——. 1980. "The Meaning of Meaning in Music: Berlioz Once More." *Music Quarterly*, 66, 1–20.

Baxter, Lincoln A. 1980. "Recent Music: The Intentional Fallacy Restored." *Journal of Aesthetics and Art Criticism*, 39, 77–79.

Beardsley, Monroe C. 1958. *Aesthetics: Problems in the Philosophy of Criticism*. New York: Harcourt, Brace, and World.

——. 1975. "Semiotic Aesthetics and Aesthetic Education." *Journal of Aesthetic Education*, 9, no. 2, 5–26.

——. 1978. "*Languages of Art* and Art Criticism." *Erkenntnis*, 12, 95–118.

——. 1979. "In Defence of Aesthetic Value." *Proceedings and Addresses of the American Philosophical Association*, 52, 723–749.

——. 1981. "On Understanding Music." In Price, ed., 55–73.

Bennett, John G. 1974. "Depiction and Convention." *Monist*, 58, 255–268.

Bennett, Victor. 1936. "The Theory of Musical Expression." *Music and Letters*, 17, 106–117.

Benson, John. 1967. "Emotion and Expression." *Philosophical Review*, 76, 335–357.

Best, David. 1985. *Feeling and Reason in the Arts*. London: George Allen & Unwin.

Binkley, Timothy. 1970. "Langer's Logical and Ontological Modes." *Journal of Aesthetics and Art Criticism*, 28, 455–464.

Black, Max. 1972. "How Do Pictures Represent?" In *Art, Perception, and Reality*. Ed. E. H. Gombrich, Julian Hochberg, and Max Black. Baltimore: Johns Hopkins University Press, 95–130.

Blinder, David. 1983. "The Controversy over Conventionalism." *Journal of Aesthetics and Art Criticism*, 41, 253–264.

< 382 >

Works Cited

———. 1986. "In Defence of Pictorial Mimesis." *Journal of Aesthetics and Art Criticism*, 45, 19–27.

Blocker, H. Gene. 1974. "The Languages of Art." *British Journal of Aesthetics*, 14, 165–173.

Boretz, Benjamin. 1970. "Nelson Goodman's *Languages of Art*: From a Musical Point of View." *Journal of Philosophy*, 10, 540–552.

Bouwsma, O. K. 1950. "The Expression Theory of Art." In *Philosophical Analysis*. Ed. Max Black. Englewood Cliffs, N.J.: Prentice-Hall, 71–96.

Bowman, Wayne D. 1991. "The Values of Musical 'Formalism.'" *Journal of Aesthetic Education*, 25, no. 3, 41–59.

Brown, Calvin S. 1948. *Music and Literature: A Comparison of the Arts*. Athens, Ga.: University of Georgia Press.

Budd, Malcolm. 1980. "The Repudiation of Emotion: Hanslick on Music." *British Journal of Aesthetics*, 20, 29–43.

———. 1981. "Appropriate Feelings." *Times Literary Supplement*, 3 July, 762.

———. 1983. "Motion and Emotion in Music: How Music Sounds." *British Journal of Aesthetics*, 23, 209–221.

———. 1985a. *Music and the Emotions: The Philosophical Theories*. London: Routledge & Kegan Paul.

———. 1985b. "Understanding Music." *Proceedings of the Aristotelian Society*, Supp. Vol. 59, 233–248.

———. 1989a. "Music and the Communication of Emotion." *Journal of Aesthetics and Art Criticism*, 47, 129–138.

———. 1989b. "Music and the Expression of Emotions." *Journal of Aesthetic Education*, 23, no. 3, 19–29.

———. 1991. "Review of Kivy's *Sound Sentiment*." *British Journal of Aesthetics*, 31, 190–191.

———. 1992. "Review of Walton's *Mimesis as Make-Believe*." *Mind*, 101, 195–198.

Bufford, Samuel. 1972. "Susanne Langer's Two Philosophies of Art." *Journal of Aesthetics and Art Criticism*, 31, 9–20.

Bujic, Bojan. 1975. "Aesthetics of Music." *British Journal of Aesthetics*, 15, 329–335.

Burks, Arthur W. 1954. "Icon, Index, and Symbol." *Philosophy and Phenomenological Research*, 9, 673–689.

Burton, Stephan L. 1991. "Novitz on Walton." *Philosophy and Literature*, 15, 295–301.

———. 1992. "Review of Maconie's *The Concept of Music*." *Journal of Aesthetics and Art Criticism*, 50, 82–83.

Butor, Michael. 1968. "Music as a Realistic Art." In *Inventory*. Trans. Michael Brozen. New York: Simon and Shuster, 281–293.

Callen, Donald. 1982a. "The Sentiment in Musical Sensibility." *Journal of Aesthetics and Art Criticism*, 40, 381–393.

———. 1982b. "Making Music Live." *Theoria*, 48, 139–168.

< 383 >

Works Cited

——. 1983. "Transfiguring Emotions in Music." *Philosophische Grazier Studien,* 16, 69–91.

——. 1985. "Moving to Music—for Better Appreciation." *Journal of Aesthetic Education,* 19, no. 3, 37–50.

Carney, James D. 1981. "Wittgenstein's Theory of Picture Representation." *Journal of Aesthetics and Art Criticism,* 40, 179–185.

Carpenter, Patricia. 1966. "But What about the Reality and Meaning of Music?" In *Art and Philosophy.* Ed. Sidney Hook. New York: New York University Press, 289–306.

Carrier, David. 1974. "A Reading of Goodman on Representation." *Monist,* 58, 269–284.

——. 1980. "Perspective as a Convention: On the Views of Nelson Goodman and Ernst Gombrich." *Leonardo,* 13, 283–287.

——. 1983. "Interpreting Musical Performances." *Monist,* 66, 202–212.

Carter, Curtis L. 1974. "Langer and Hofstadter on Painting and Language: A Critique." *Journal of Aesthetics and Art Criticism,* 32, 331–342.

Casey, Edward S. 1970. "Truth in Art." *Man and World,* 3, no. 4, 351–369.

——. 1971. "Expression and Communication in Art." *Journal of Aesthetics and Art Criticism,* 30, 197–207.

Cavell, Stanley. 1977. "Music Discomposed." In *Must We Mean What We Say?* Cambridge: Cambridge University Press, 180–212. (first published 1969)

Cazden, Norman. 1951. "Toward a Theory of Realism in Music." *Journal of Aesthetics and Art Criticism,* 10, 135–151.

——. 1955. "Realism in Abstract Music." *Music and Letters,* 36, 17–38.

——. 1962. "Sensory Theories of Musical Consonance." *Journal of Aesthetics and Art Criticism,* 20, 301–319.

Charles, Daniel. 1988. "Heidegger on Hermeneutics and Music Today." In Rantala, Rowell, and Tarasti, eds., 154–166.

Clark, Ann. 1982. "Is Music a Language?" *Journal of Aesthetics and Art Criticism,* 41, 195–204.

Clifton, Thomas. 1983. *Music as Heard: A Study in Applied Phenomenology.* New Haven: Yale University Press.

Coker, Wilson. 1972. *Music and Meaning: A Theoretical Introduction to Musical Aesthetics.* New York: Free Press.

——. 1983. "Music as Art." In *What Is Art?* Ed. H. Curtler. New York: Haven, 155–173.

Collingwood, R. G. 1963. *Principles of Art.* Oxford: Clarendon Press. (first published 1938)

Cone, Edward T. 1960. "Analysis Today." *Musical Quarterly,* 46, 172–188.

——. 1967. "Beyond Analysis." *Perspectives in New Music,* 1, 33–51.

Cook, Nicholas. 1987. "Musical Form and the Listener." *Journal of Aesthetics and Art Criticism,* 46, 23–29.

——. 1990. *Music, Imagination, and Culture.* Oxford: Clarendon Press.

< 384 >

Works Cited

Cooke, Deryck. 1959. *The Language of Music.* London: Oxford University Press.

Coons, Edgar, and David Kraehenbuehl. 1958. "Information as a Measure of Structure in Music." *Journal of Music Theory,* 2, 127–161.

———. 1959. "Information as a Measure of the Experience of Music." *Journal of Aesthetics and Art Criticism,* 17, 510–522.

Copi, Irving M. 1955. "A Note on Representation in the Arts." *Journal of Philosophy,* 52, 346–349.

Copland, Aaron. 1957. *What to Listen for in Music.* New York: McGraw-Hill. Rev. ed.

Currie, Gregory. 1990. *The Nature of Fiction.* Cambridge: Cambridge University Press.

———. 1991a. "Review of Walton's *Mimesis as Make-Believe.*" *Australasian Journal of Philosophy,* 69, 365–366.

———. 1991b. "Photography, Painting, and Perception." *Journal of Aesthetics and Art Criticism,* 49, 23–29.

Danto, Arthur C. 1981. *The Transfiguration of the Commonplace.* Cambridge, Mass.: Harvard University Press.

———. 1982. "Depiction and Description." *Philosophy and Phenomenological Research,* 43, 1–19.

———. 1986. *The Philosophical Disenfranchisement of Art.* New York: Columbia University Press.

Dart, Thurston. 1980. "Eye Music." In Sadie, ed., Vol. 6, 338–339.

Davidson, Donald. 1978. "What Metaphors Mean." *Critical Inquiry,* 5, 31–47.

Davies, Stephen. 1980. "The Expression of Emotion in Music." *Mind,* 89, 67–86.

———. 1982. "The Aesthetic Relevance of Authors' and Painters' Intentions." *Journal of Aesthetics and Art Criticism,* 41, 65–76.

———. 1983a. "The Rationality of Aesthetic Responses." *British Journal of Aesthetics,* 23, 38–47.

———. 1983b. "Is Music a Language of the Emotions?" *British Journal of Aesthetics,* 23, 222–233.

———. 1983c. "Attributing Significance to Unobvious Musical Relationships." *Journal of Music Theory,* 27, 203–213.

———. 1984. "Truth-Values and Metaphors." *Journal of Aesthetics and Art Criticism,* 42, 291–302.

———. 1986. "The Expression Theory Again." *Theoria,* 52, 146–167.

———. 1987. "The Evaluation of Music." In Alperson, ed., 307–325.

———. 1990. "Review of Kivy's *Music Alone.*" *Canadian Philosophical Reviews,* 10, 368–372.

———. 1991a. "The Ontology of Musical Works and the Authenticity of Their Performances." *Noûs,* 25, 21–41.

———. 1991b. *Definitions of Art.* Ithaca: Cornell University Press.

———. 1991c. "Review of Kivy's *Sound Sentiment.*" *Journal of Aesthetics and Art Criticism,* 49, 83–85.

< 385 >

Works Cited

——. 1992. "The End of Art." In *A Companion to Aesthetics*. Ed. David E. Cooper. Oxford: Blackwell, 138–142.

——. 1993. "Representation in Music." *Journal of Aesthetic Education*, 27, no. 1, 15–21.

——. 1994. "Musical Understanding and Musical Kinds." *Journal of Aesthetics and Art Criticism*, 52, 69–81.

Davison, Archibald T. 1954. *Words and Music*. Washington, D.C.: Library of Congress.

Day, J. P. 1969. "Hope." *American Philosophical Quarterly*, 6, 89–102.

DeBellis, Mark. 1991. "Conceptions of Musical Structure." *Midwest Studies in Philosophy*, 16, 378–393.

Dempster, Douglas J. 1989. "Exemplification and the Cognitive Value of Art." *Philosophy and Phenomenological Research*, 49, 393–412.

——. 1991. "Review of Kivy's *Music Alone*." *Journal of Aesthetics and Art Criticism*, 49, 381–383.

Dewey, John. 1934. *Art as Experience*. New York: Minton, Balch.

Dickinson, George Sherman. 1957. "Aesthetic Pace in Music." *Journal of Aesthetics and Art Criticism*, 15, 311–321.

Dipert, Randall R. 1983. "Meyer's *Emotion and Meaning in Music*: A Sympathetic Review." *In Theory Only*, 6, no. 8, 3–17.

Donington, Robert. 1963. *Wagner's "Ring" and Its Symbols: The Music and the Myth*. London: Faber & Faber.

Dorfles, Gillo. 1957. "Communication and Symbol in the Work of Art." *Journal of Aesthetics and Art Criticism*, 15, 289–297.

Dräger, Hans Heinz. 1952. "The Concept of 'Tonal Body.'" *Archiv für Musikwissenschaft*, 9, 68–77.

Ducasse, Curt J. 1964. "Art and the Language of the Emotions." *Journal of Aesthetics and Art Criticism*, 23, 109–112.

——. 1966. *The Philosophy of Art*. New York: Dover. (first published 1929)

Eaton, Marcia M. 1982. "A Strange Kind of Sadness." *Journal of Aesthetics and Art Criticism*, 41, 51–63.

Einstein, Alfred. 1966. *Mozart*. London: Cassell.

Ekman, Paul, E. Richard Sorensen, and Wallace V. Friesen. 1969. "Pan-Cultural Elements in Facial Displays of Emotion." *Science*, 164, 4 April, 86–88.

Elliott, David J. 1991. "Music as Knowledge." *Journal of Aesthetic Education*, 25, no. 3, 21–40.

Elliott, R. K. 1966/67. "Aesthetic Theory and the Experience of Art." *Proceedings of the Aristotelian Society*, 67, 111–126.

——. 1968. "The Aesthetic and the Semantic: A Reply to Mr. Pleydell-Pearce." *British Journal of Aesthetics*, 8, 35–47.

Epperson, Gordon. 1967. *The Musical Symbol*. Ames: Iowa State University Press.

——. 1987. "Review of Hanslick's *On the Musically Beautiful*. Ed. and trans. Geoffrey Payzant." *Journal of Aesthetics and Art Criticism*, 41, 85–86.

< 386 >

Works Cited

Evans, Martyn. 1990. *Listening to Music*. London: Macmillan.

Farnsworth, Paul R. 1948. "Sacred Cows in the Psychology of Music." *Journal of Aesthetics and Art Criticism*, 7, 48–51.

Feld, Steven. 1988. "Aesthetics as Iconicity of Style or 'Lift-Up-Over Sounding': Getting into the Kaluli Groove." *Yearbook for Traditional Music*, 20, 74–113.

Ferguson, Donald. 1960. *Music as Metaphor: The Elements of Expression*. Minneapolis: University of Minnesota Press.

Finkelstein, Sidney. 1952. *How Music Expresses Ideas*. London: Lawrence & Wishart.

Fisher, John. 1984. "Entitling." *Critical Inquiry*, 11, 286–298.

Fiske, Harold E. 1990. *Music and Mind: Philosophical Essays on the Cognition and Meaning of Music*. Lewiston/Queenston/Lampeter: Edwin Mellen Press.

Frank, Paul R. 1952. "Realism and Naturalism in Music." *Journal of Aesthetics and Art Criticism*, 11, 55–60.

Gärdenfors, Peter. 1988. "Semantics, Conceptual Spaces, and the Dimensions of Music." In Rantala, Rowell, and Tarasti, eds., 9–27.

Garvin, Lucius. 1947. "The Paradox of Aesthetic Meaning." *Philosophy and Phenomenological Research*, 8, 99–106.

Gibson, James J. 1971. "The Information Available in Pictures." *Leonardo*, 4, 27–35.

Godlovitch, Stan. 1990a. "Artists, Programs, and Performance." *Australasian Journal of Philosophy*, 68, 301–312.

———. 1990b. "Music, Performance, and the Tools of the Trade." *Iyyun*, 39, 321–338.

Goehr, Lydia. 1989. "Being True to the Work." *Journal of Aesthetics and Art Criticism*, 47, 55–67.

———. 1992. *The Imaginary Museum of Musical Works: An Essay in the Philosophy of Music*. Oxford: Clarendon Press.

Goldman, Alan H. 1992. "The Value of Music." *Journal of Aesthetics and Art Criticism*, 50, 35–44.

Gombrich, E. H. 1962. "Art and the Language of the Emotions." *Proceedings of the Aristotelian Society*, Supp. Vol. 36, 215–234.

———. 1980. *Art and Illusion*. Oxford: Phaidon. (first published 1960)

———. 1981. "Image and Code: Scope and Limits of Conventionalism." In *The Image and Code*. Ed. W. Steiner. Ann Arbor: University of Michigan Press, 11–42.

Goodman, Nelson. 1968. *Languages of Art*. New York: Bobbs-Merrill.

———. 1970a. "Some Notes on *Languages of Art*." *Journal of Philosophy*, 67, 563–573.

———. 1970b. "Seven Strictures on Similarity." In *Experience and Theory*. Ed. L. Forster and J. W. Swanson. Amherst: University of Massachusetts Press, 19–29.

———. 1970c. "Reply to Lipman's Review of *Languages of Art*." *Man and World*, 3, no. 4, 415–416.

———. 1974. "On Some Questions Concerning Quotation." *Monist*, 58, 294–306.

< 387 >

——. 1978a. "Replies." *Erkenntnis*, 12, 153–179.

——. 1978b. "When Is Art?" In *Ways of Worldmaking*. Indianapolis: Hackett, 57–70.

——. 1981. "Replies." *Journal of Aesthetics and Art Criticism*, 39, 273–280.

——. 1988. "On What Should Not Be Said about Representation." *Journal of Aesthetics and Art Criticism*, 46, 419.

Goodrich, R. A. 1988. "Goodman on Representation and Resemblance." *British Journal of Aesthetics*, 28, 48–58.

Gordon, Robert. 1986. "The Passivity of Emotions." *Philosophical Review*, 95, 371–392.

Grice, H. P. 1957. "Meaning." *Philosophical Review*, 66, 377–388.

Grigg, Robert. 1984. "Relativism and Pictorial Realism." *Journal of Aesthetics and Art Criticism*, 42, 397–408.

Grund, Cynthia. 1988. "Metaphors, Counterfactuals, and Music." In Rantala, Rowell, and Tarasti, eds., 28–53.

Hagberg, Garry. 1984. "Art and the Unsayable: Langer's Tractarian Aesthetics." *British Journal of Aesthetics*, 24, 325–340.

Hall, Robert W. 1967. "On Hanslick's Supposed Formalism in Music." *Journal of Aesthetics and Art Criticism*, 25, 433–436.

Hanfling, Oswald. 1992. "Aesthetic Qualities." In *Philosophical Aesthetics: An Introduction*. Ed. Hanfling. Oxford: Blackwell, 41–73.

Hansen, Forest. 1968. "Langer's Expressive Form: An Interpretation." *Journal of Aesthetics and Art Criticism*, 27, 165–170.

——. 1971. "Thinking about Music." *Journal of Aesthetic Education*, 5, no. 3, 77–89.

——. 1972. "The Adequacy of Verbal Articulation of Emotions." *Journal of Aesthetics and Art Criticism*, 31, 249–253.

——. 1989. "On Meyer's Theory of Musical Meaning." *British Journal of Aesthetics*, 29, 10–20.

Hanslick, Eduard. 1957. *The Beautiful in Music*. Trans. Gustav Cohen. New York: Liberal Arts Press. 7th ed. of 1885. (1st ed. 1854)

——. 1986. *On the Musically Beautiful*. Trans. Geoffrey Payzant. Indianapolis: Hackett. 8th ed. of 1891.

Hare, Peter H. 1972. "Feeling, Imagining, and Expression Theory." *Journal of Aesthetics and Art Criticism*, 30, 343–350.

Harrell, Jean Gabert. 1964. "Issues of Music Aesthetics." *Journal of Aesthetics and Art Criticism*, 23, 197–206.

——. 1986. *Soundtracks: A Study of Auditory Perception, Memory, and Valuation*. Buffalo, N.Y.: Prometheus Books.

Harris, N. G. E. 1973. "Goodman's Account of Representation." *Journal of Aesthetics and Art Criticism*, 31, 323–328.

Harrison, Nigel. 1975. "Types and Tokens and the Identity of the Musical Work." *British Journal of Aesthetics*, 15, 336–346.

< 388 >

Works Cited

Haydon, Glen. 1948. *On the Meaning of Music*. Washington, D.C.: Library of Congress.

Hepburn, Ronald W. 1960/61. "Emotions and Emotional Qualities: Some Attempts at Analysis." *British Journal of Aesthetics*, 1, 255–265.

Hermerén, Göran. 1969. *Representation and Meaning in the Visual Arts*. Lund: Scandinavian University Books.

———. 1977. "Structure, Intention, and Representation." *Grazer Philosophische Studien*, 3, 89–106.

———. 1988. "Representation, Truth, and the Languages of the Arts." In Rantala, Rowell, and Tarasti, eds., 179–209.

———. 1992. "Expression, Meaning, and Nonverbal Communication." In *Understanding the Arts: Contemporary Scandinavian Aesthetics*. Ed. Jeanette Emt and Hermerén. Lund: Lund University Press, 129–146.

Hicks, Michael. 1991. "Serialism and Comprehensibility: A Guide for the Teacher." *Journal of Aesthetic Education*, 25, no. 4, 75–85.

Higgins, Kathleen. 1991. *The Music of Our Lives*. Philadelphia: Temple University Press.

Hindemith, Paul. 1953. *A Composer's World*. Cambridge, Mass.: Harvard University Press.

Hoaglund, Joan. 1980. "Music as Expressive." *British Journal of Aesthetics*, 20, 340–348.

Hospers, John. 1954/55. "The Concept of Artistic Expression." *Proceedings of the Aristotelian Society*, 55, 313–344.

———. 1964. *Meaning and Truth in the Arts*. Hamden: Archon Books.

Howard, Vernon A. 1971a. "Musical Meaning: A Logical Note." *Journal of Aesthetics and Art Criticism*, 30, 215–219.

———. 1971b. "On Musical Expression." *British Journal of Aesthetics*, 11, 268–280.

———. 1972. "On Representational Music." *Noûs*, 6, 41–54.

———. 1974. "On Musical Quotation." *Monist*, 48, 307–318.

———. 1975. "The Convertibility of Symbols." *British Journal of Aesthetics*, 15, 207–216.

———. 1978. "Music and Constant Comment." *Erkenntnis*, 12, 73–82.

Howes, Frank. 1958. *Music and Its Meanings*. London: Athlone Press.

Hutchings, A. 1962. "Organic Structure in Music." *British Journal of Aesthetics*, 2, 338–350.

Hyslop, Alec. 1983. "Seeing-as." *Philosophy and Phenomenological Research*, 43, 533–540.

———. 1986. "Seeing through Seeing-in." *British Journal of Aesthetics*, 26, 371–379.

Ingarden, Roman. 1986. *The Work of Music and the Problem of Its Identity*. Trans. Adam Czerniawski. Berkeley: University of California Press.

Iseminger, Gary. 1983. "How Strange a Sadness?" *Journal of Aesthetics and Art Criticism*, 42, 81–82.

< 389 >

Works Cited

Jacobs, Robert L. 1960. "Music as Symbol: Reflections on Mr. Deryck Cooke's *The Language of Music.*" *Music Review*, 21, 226–236.

Jensen, Henning. 1973. "Exemplification in Nelson Goodman's Aesthetic Theory." *Journal of Aesthetics and Art Criticism*, 32, 47–52.

Jones, Bill. 1970. "Is Music a Language?" *British Journal of Aesthetics*, 10, 162–168.

Kaplan, Abraham. 1954. "Referential Meaning in the Arts." *Journal of Aesthetics and Art Criticism*, 12, 457–474.

Keil, Charles M. H. 1966. "Motion and Feeling through Music." *Journal of Aesthetics and Art Criticism*, 24, 335–349.

Keller, Hans. 1955. "Strict Serial Technique in Classical Music." *Tempo*, no. 37, 12–24.

——. 1961. Deryck Cooke's Achievement." *Music Review*, 22, 34–38.

——. 1966. "Wolfgang Amadeus Mozart." In *The Symphony*. Ed. Robert Simpson. London: Penguin Books, Vol. 1, 50–103.

Kennick, William E. 1961. "Art and the Ineffable." *Journal of Philosophy*, 58, 309–320.

Kenny, Anthony. 1969. *Action, Emotion, and Will.* London: Routledge & Kegan Paul.

Kerman, Joseph. 1981. "The State of Academic Music Criticism." In Price, ed., 38–54.

Khatchadourian, Haig. 1965. "The Expression Theory of Art." *Journal of Aesthetics and Art Criticism*, 23, 335–352.

Kimmel, Lawrence D. 1992. "The Sounds of Music: First Movement." *Journal of Aesthetic Education*, 26, no. 3, 55–65.

Kingsbury, Justine. 1991. "The Expression of Emotion in Music." M.A. thesis, Victoria University of Wellington, New Zealand.

Kivy, Peter. 1980. *The Corded Shell.* Princeton, N.J.: Princeton University Press.

——. 1983. "Sound Sentiment: A Reply to Donald Callen." *Journal of Aesthetics and Art Criticism*, 41, 382–384.

——. 1984. *Sound and Semblance: Reflections on Musical Representation.* Princeton, N.J.: Princeton University Press.

——. 1986. "It's Only Music: So What's to Understand?" *Journal of Aesthetic Education*, 20, no. 4, 71–74.

——. 1987. "How Music Moves." In Alperson, ed., 149–163.

——. 1988a. *Osmin's Rage: Philosophical Reflections on Opera, Drama, and Text.* Princeton, N.J.: Princeton University Press.

——. 1988b. "Something I've Always Wanted to Know about Hanslick." *Journal of Aesthetics and Art Criticism*, 46, 413–417.

——. 1989. *Sound Sentiment.* Philadelphia: Temple University Press.

——. 1990a. *Music Alone: Philosophical Reflection on the Purely Musical Experience.* Ithaca: Cornell University Press.

——. 1990b. "What Was Hanslick Denying?" *Journal of Musicology*, 8, 3–18.

——. 1991. "Is Music an Art?" *Journal of Philosophy*, 88, 544–554.

< 390 >

Works Cited

——. 1992. "Review of Nicholas Cook's *Music, Imagination, and Culture.*" *Journal of Aesthetics and Art Criticism*, 50, 76–79.

——. 1993. "Auditor's Emotions: Contention, Concession, and Compromise." *Journal of Aesthetics and Art Criticism*, 51, 1–12.

Kjörup, Sören. 1974. "George Innes and the Battle of Hastings, or Doing Things with Pictures." *Monist*, 58, 216–235.

——. 1978. "Pictorial Speech Acts." *Erkenntnis*, 12, 55–71.

Körner, Stephan. 1955. *Conceptual Thinking: A Logical Inquiry*. London: Cambridge University Press.

Korsmeyer, Carolyn. 1989. "The Eclipse of Truth in the Rise of Aesthetics." *British Journal of Aesthetics*, 29, 293–302.

Krantz, Steven C. 1987. "Metaphor in Music." *Journal of Aesthetics and Art Criticism*, 45, 351–360.

Kuhns, Richard. 1978. "Music as a Representational Art." *British Journal of Aesthetics*, 18, 120–125.

Kulenkampff, Jens. 1981. "Music Considered as a Way of Worldmaking." *Journal of Aesthetics and Art Criticism*, 39, 254–258.

Kurkela, Karl. 1986. *Note and Tone: A Semantic Analysis of Conventional Music Notation*. Helsinki: Musicological Society of Finland.

——. 1988. "How a Note Denotes." In Rantala, Rowell, and Tarasti, eds., 70–96.

Lamarque, Peter. 1991. "Essay Review of Walton's *Mimesis as Make-Believe.*" *Journal of Aesthetics and Art Criticism*, 49, 161–166.

Lamb, Roger. 1987. "Objectless Emotions." *Philosophy and Phenomenological Research*, 48, 107–117.

Lammenranta, Markus. 1988. "Nelson Goodman on Emotions in Music." In Rantala, Rowell, and Tarasti, eds., 210–216.

——. 1992. "Goodman's Semiotic Theory of Art." *Canadian Journal of Philosophy*, 22, 339–351.

Langer, Susanne K. 1942. *Philosophy in a New Key*. Cambridge, Mass.: Harvard University Press.

——. 1953. *Feeling and Form*. New York: Scribner's.

Laszlo, Ervin. 1967. "The Aesthetics of Live Musical Performance." *British Journal of Aesthetics*, 7, 261–273.

——. 1968. "Affect and Expression in Music." *Journal of Aesthetics and Art Criticism*, 27, 131–134.

Lawrence, John. 1987. "The Diatonic Scale: More than Meets the Ear." *Journal of Aesthetics and Art Criticism*, 46, 281–291.

Leahy, M. P. T. 1976. "The Vacuity of Musical Expressionism." *British Journal of Aesthetics*, 16, 144–156.

Lerdahl, Fred, and Ray Jackendoff. 1983. *A Generative Theory of Tonal Grammar*. Cambridge, Mass.: MIT Press.

Levinson, Jerrold. 1980. "What a Musical Work Is." *Journal of Philosophy*, 77, 5–28.

< 391 >

——. 1981. "Truth in Music." *Journal of Aesthetics and Art Criticism*, 40, 131–144.

——. 1982. "Music and Negative Emotion." *Pacific Philosophical Quarterly*, 63, 327–346.

——. 1984. "Hybrid Artforms." *Journal of Aesthetic Education*, 18, no. 4, 5–13.

——. 1985a. "Titles." *Journal of Aesthetics and Art Criticism*, 44, 29–39.

——. 1985b. "Review of Kivy's *Sound and Semblance*." *Canadian Philosophical Reviews*, 5, 454–459.

——. 1987a. "Review of Hanslick's *On the Musically Beautiful*. Trans. Geoffrey Payzant." *Canadian Philosophical Reviews*, 7, no. 10, 405–408.

——. 1987b. "Song and Music Drama." In Alperson, ed., 285–301.

——. 1990a. *Music, Art, and Metaphysics*. Ithaca: Cornell University Press.

——. 1990b. "Musical Literacy." *Journal of Aesthetic Education*, 24, no. 1, 17–30.

——. 1990c. "Philosophy as an Art." *Journal of Aesthetic Education*, 24, no. 2, 5–14.

——. 1992a. "Musical Profundity Misplaced." *Journal of Aesthetics and Art Criticism*, 50, 58–60.

——. 1992b. "Pleasure and the Value of Art and Music." *British Journal of Aesthetics*, 32, 295–306.

——. 1993. "Making Believe." *Dialogue*, 32, 391–406.

Lipman, Matthew. 1970a. "Review of Goodman's *Languages of Art*." *Man and World*, 3, no. 2, 147–150.

——. 1970b. "A Rejoinder." *Man and World*, 3, no. 4, 417–418.

Lippman, Edward A. 1953. "Symbolism in Music." *Musical Quarterly*, 39, 554–575.

——. 1963. "Spatial Perception and Physical Location as Factors in Music." *Acta Musicologica*, 35, 24–34.

——. 1966. "The Problem of Musical Hermeneutics: A Protest and Analysis." In *Art and Philosophy*. Ed. Sidney Hook. New York: New York University Press, 307–335.

——. 1977. *A Humanistic Philosophy of Music*. New York: New York University Press.

Lissa, Zofia. 1965. "On the Evolution of Musical Perception." *Journal of Aesthetics and Art Criticism*, 24, 273–286.

——. 1968. "The Temporal Nature of a Musical Work." *Journal of Aesthetics and Art Criticism*, 26, 529–538.

Lyons, William. 1977. "Emotions and Feelings." *Ratio*, 19, 1–12.

McAdoo, Nick. 1992. "Can Art Ever Be Just about Itself?" *Journal of Aesthetics and Art Criticism*, 50, 131–137.

McAlpin, Colin. 1925. "Is Music a Language of the Emotions?" *Musical Quarterly*, 11, 427–443.

McClary, Susan. 1990. "Towards a Feminist Criticism of Music." *Canadian University Music Review*, 10, no. 2, 9–18.

< 392 >

Works Cited

———. 1991. *Feminine Endings: Music, Gender, and Sexuality*. Minnesota: University of Minnesota Press.

McDermott, Vincent. 1972. "A Conceptual Musical Space." *Journal of Aesthetics and Art Criticism*, 30, 489–494.

McLaughlin, Terence. 1970. *Music and Communication*. London: Faber.

McMullin, Michael. 1947. "The Symbolic Analysis of Music." *Music Review*, 8, 25–35.

Maconie, Robin. 1990. *The Concept of Music*. Oxford: Clarendon Press.

Malinas, Gary. 1991. "A Semantics for Pictures." *Canadian Journal of Philosophy*, 21, 275–298.

Manns, James W. 1971. "Representation, Relativism, and Resemblance." *British Journal of Aesthetics*, 11, 281–287.

Margolis, Joseph. 1974. "Art as Language." *Monist*, 58, 175–186.

———. 1979. "A Strategy for a Philosophy of Art." *Journal of Aesthetics and Art Criticism*, 37, 445–454.

———. 1981. "What Is When? When Is What? Two Questions for Nelson Goodman." *Journal of Aesthetics and Art Criticism*, 39, 266–268.

———. 1987. "On the Semiotics of Music." In Alperson, ed., 213–236.

Mark, Thomas Carson. 1980. "On Works of Virtuosity." *Journal of Philosophy*, 77, 28–45.

———. 1981. "Philosophy of Piano Playing: Reflections on the Concept of Performance." *Philosophy and Phenomenological Research*, 41, 299–324.

Martin, Richard. 1981. "On Some Aesthetic Relations." *Journal of Aesthetics and Art Criticism*, 39, 258–264.

Matravers, Derek. 1991. "Art and the Feelings and Emotions." *British Journal of Aesthetics*, 31, 322–331.

Maynard, Patrick. 1972. "Depiction, Vision, and Convention." *American Philosophical Quarterly*, 9, 243–250.

Meidner, Olga McDonald. 1985. "Motion and E-motion in Music." *British Journal of Aesthetics*, 25, 349–356.

Merriam, Alan P. 1964. *The Anthropology of Music*. [Evanston, Ill.]: Northwestern University Press.

Mew, Peter. 1985a. "The Expression of Emotion in Music." *British Journal of Aesthetics*, 25, 33–42.

———. 1985b. "The Musical Arousal of Emotions." *British Journal of Aesthetics*, 25, 357–361.

Meyer, Leonard B. 1956. *Emotion and Meaning in Music*. Chicago: University of Chicago Press.

———. 1957. "Meaning in Music and Information Theory." *Journal of Aesthetics and Art Criticism*, 15, 412–424.

———. 1959. "Some Remarks on Value and Greatness in Music." *Journal of Aesthetics and Art Criticism*, 17, 486–500.

< 393 >

Works Cited

———. 1961. "On Rehearing Music." *Journal of the American Musicological Society*, 14, 257–267.

———. 1963. "The End of the Renaissance? Notes on the Radical Empiricism of the Avant-Garde." *Hudson Review*, 16, 169–186.

———. 1973. *Explaining Music*. Berkeley: University of California Press.

———. 1989. *Style and Music: Theory, History, and Ideology*. Philadelphia: University of Pennsylvania Press.

———. 1991. "A Pride of Prejudices; Or, Delight in Diversity." *Music Theory Spectrum*, 13, 241–251.

Mitias, Michael H. 1992. "Dewey's Theory of Expression." *Journal of Aesthetic Education*, 26, no. 3, 41–53.

Moles, Abraham A. 1966. *Information Theory and Esthetic Perception*. Trans. Joel E. Cohen. Urbana: University of Illinois Press. (first published in French, 1958)

Monelle, Raymond. 1979. "Symbolic Models in Music Aesthetics." *British Journal of Aesthetics*, 19, 24–37.

Moravcsik, Julius. 1982. "Understanding and the Emotions." *Dialectica*, 36, 207–224.

Morgan, Douglas N. 1967. "Must Art Tell the Truth?" *Journal of Aesthetics and Art Criticism*, 26, 17–27.

Morgan, Robert P. 1977. "On the Analysis of Recent Music." *Critical Inquiry*, 4, 33–53.

———. 1980. "Musical Time/Musical Space." *Critical Inquiry*, 6, 527–538.

Morris, Charles W. 1939. "Esthetics and the Theory of Signs." *Journal of Unified Science*, 8, 131–150.

Nagel, Ernest. 1943. "Review of *Philosophy in a New Key*." *Journal of Philosophy*, 40, 323–329.

Neander, Karen. 1987. "Pictorial Representation: A Matter of Resemblance." *British Journal of Aesthetics*, 27, 213–226.

Neubauer, John. 1986. *The Emancipation of Music from Language: Departure from Mimesis in Eighteenth-Century Aesthetics*. New Haven: Yale University Press.

Newcomb, Anthony. 1984. "Sound and Feeling." *Critical Inquiry*, 10, 614–643.

Newell, Robert. 1978. "Music and the Temporal Dilemma." *British Journal of Aesthetics*, 18, 356–367.

Newman, Ernest. 1933–46. *The Life of Richard Wagner*. 4 vols. New York: Alfred A. Knopf.

Nolt, John. 1981. "Expression and Emotion." *British Journal of Aesthetics*, 21, 139–150.

Novitz, David. 1975. "Picturing." *Journal of Aesthetics and Art Criticism*, 34, 145–155.

———. 1976. "Conventions and the Growth of Pictorial Style." *British Journal of Aesthetics*, 16, 324–337.

———. 1977. *Pictures and Their Use in Communication*. The Hague: Martinus Nijhoff.

< 394 >

Works Cited

——. 1982. "Pictures, Fiction, and Resemblance." *British Journal of Aesthetics*, 22, 222–232.

——. 1991. "Kendall Walton's *Mimesis as Make-Believe*." *Philosophy and Literature*, 15, 118–128.

O'Neil, B. C. 1971. "Critical Study." *Philosophical Quarterly*, 21, 361–373.

Orlov, Henry. 1981. "Toward a Semiotics of Music." In *The Sign in Music and Literature*. Ed. W. Steiner. Austin: University of Texas Press, 131–137.

Osborne, Harold. 1955. *Aesthetics and Criticism*. London: Routledge & Kegan Paul.

——. 1977. "Inspiration." *British Journal of Aesthetics*, 17, 242–253.

——. 1982. "Expressiveness in the Arts." *Journal of Aesthetics and Art Criticism*, 41, 19–26.

——. 1983. "Expressiveness: Where Is the Feeling Found?" *British Journal of Aesthetics*, 23, 112–123.

Palmer, Anthony J. 1992. "Leonard B. Meyer and a Cross-Cultural Aesthetics." *Journal of Aesthetic Education*, 26, no. 3, 67–73.

Payne, Elsie. 1961. "Emotion in Music and in Music Appreciation." *Music Review*, 22, 39–50.

——. 1973. "The Nature of Musical Emotion and Its Place in the Appreciative Experience." *British Journal of Aesthetics*, 13, 171–181.

Payzant, Geoffrey. 1981. "Hanslick, Sams, Gay, and 'TOENEND BEWEGTE FORMEN.'" *Journal of Aesthetics and Art Criticism*, 40, 41–48.

——. 1986. "Translator's Preface," and "Essay: Toward a Revised Reading of Hanslick." In Hanslick (1986), xi–xvii, 93–102.

——. 1989. "Eduard Hanslick and Bernhard Gutt." *Music Review*, 50, 124–133.

Peacocke, Christopher. 1987. "Depiction," *Philosophical Review*, 96, 383–410.

Pearce, David. 1988a. "Musical Expression: Some Remarks on Goodman's Theory." In Rantala, Rowell, and Tarasti, eds., 228–243.

——. 1988b. "Intensionality and the Nature of a Musical Work." *British Journal of Aesthetics*, 28, 105–118.

Peel, John, and Wayne Slawson. 1984. "Review of Lerdahl and Jackendoff's *A Generative Theory of Tonal Music*." *Journal of Music Theory*, 28, 271–294.

Peetz, Dieter. 1987. "Some Current Philosophical Theories of Pictorial Representation." *British Journal of Aesthetics*, 27, 227–237.

Peltz, Richard. 1972. "Nelson Goodman on Picturing, Describing, and Exemplifying." *Journal of Aesthetic Education*, 6, no. 3, 71–86.

Petock, Stuart Jay. 1972. "Expression in Art: The Feelingful Side of Aesthetic Experience." *Journal of Aesthetics and Art Criticism*, 30, 297–309.

Piechowski, Michael M. 1981. "The Logical and the Empirical Form of Feelings." *Journal of Aesthetic Education*, 15, no. 4, 31–53.

Pike, Alfred. 1970. *A Phenomenological Analysis of Musical Experience and Other Related Essays*. New York: St. John's University Press.

Pinkerton, Richard C. 1956. "Information Theory and Melody." *Scientific American*, 194, no. 2, 77–87.

< 395 >

Works Cited

Pleydell-Pearce, A. G. 1967. "Sense, Reference, and Fiction." *British Journal of Aesthetics*, 7, 225–236.

Pole, David. 1974. "Goodman and the 'Naive' View of Representation." *British Journal of Aesthetics*, 14, 68–80.

Pollard, D. E. B. 1984. "Fictions and Resemblances." *British Journal of Aesthetics*, 24, 156–159.

Pratt, Carroll C. 1931. *The Meaning of Music: A Study in Psychological Aesthetics.* New York: McGraw-Hill.

——. 1938. "Structural vs. Expressive Form in Music." *Journal of Psychology*, 5, 149–156.

——. 1952. *Music as the Language of Emotion.* Washington, D.C.: Library of Congress.

——. 1954. "The Design of Music." *Journal of Aesthetics and Art Criticism*, 12, 289–300.

——. 1964. "The Perception of Art." *Journal of Aesthetics and Art Criticism*, 23, 57–62.

——. 1975. "Abstract vs. Realistic Art." *Journal of Aesthetics and Art Criticism*, 33, 403–405.

Presley, C. F. 1970. "Critical Notice of Goodman's *Languages of Art*." *Australasian Journal of Philosophy*, 48, 373–393.

Price, Kingsley Blake. 1953. "Is a Work of Art a Symbol?" *Journal of Philosophy*, 50, 485–503.

——. 1981. "Review of Kivy's *The Corded Shell*." *Journal of Aesthetics and Art Criticism*, 39, 460–462.

——. 1982. "What Is a Piece of Music?" *British Journal of Aesthetics*, 22, 322–336.

——. 1988. "Does Music Have Meaning?" *British Journal of Aesthetics*, 28, 203–215.

——. 1992. "Review of Kivy's *Music Alone*." *Philosophy of Music Education Newsletter*, 4, no. 1, 11–20.

Price, Kingsley Blake, ed. 1981. *On Criticizing Music: Five Philosophical Perspectives.* Baltimore: John Hopkins University Press.

Putman, Daniel A. 1985. "Music and the Metaphor of Touch." *Journal of Aesthetics and Art Criticism*, 44, 59–66.

——. 1987. "Why Instrumental Music Has No Shame." *British Journal of Aesthetics*, 27, 55–61.

——. 1989. "Some Distinctions on the Role of Metaphor in Music." *Journal of Aesthetic Education*, 23, no. 2, 103–106.

Radford, Colin. 1975. "How Can We Be Moved by the Fate of Anna Karenina?" *Proceedings of the Aristotelian Society*, Supp. Vol. 49, 67–80.

——. 1989. "Emotions and Music: A Reply to the Cognitivists." *Journal of Aesthetics and Art Criticism*, 47, 69–76.

——. 1991a. "Muddy Waters." *Journal of Aesthetics and Art Criticism*, 49, 247–252.

< 396 >

——. 1991b. "How Can Music Be Moral?" *Midwest Studies in Philosophy*, 16, 421–438.

Raffman, Diana. 1988. "Toward a Cognitive Theory of Musical Ineffability." *Review of Metaphysics*, 41, 685–706.

——. 1991. "The Meaning of Music." *Midwest Studies in Philosophy*, 16, 360–377.

Rantala, Veikko, Lewis Rowell, and Eero Tarasti, eds. 1988. *Essays on the Philosophy of Music, Acta Philosophica Fennica*, 43 (Helsinki).

Reich, Willi. 1965. *The Life and Work of Alban Berg*. Trans. Cornelius Cardew. London: Thames & Hudson.

Reid, Louis Arnaud. 1964. "Art, Truth, and Reality." *British Journal of Aesthetics*, 4, 321–331.

——. 1965. "Susanne Langer and Beyond." *British Journal of Aesthetics*, 5, 357–367.

——. 1968. "New Notes on Langer." *British Journal of Aesthetics*, 8, 353–358.

Ridley, Aaron. 1986. "Mr. Mew on Music." *British Journal of Aesthetics*, 26, 69–70.

——. 1992. "Review of Nicholas Cook's *Music, Imagination, and Culture*." *British Journal of Aesthetics*, 32, 91–93.

——. 1993. "Pitiful Responses to Music." *British Journal of Aesthetics*, 33, 72–74.

Rieser, Max. 1942. "On Musical Semantics." *Journal of Philosophy*, 39, 421–432.

Roberts, Robert. 1988. "What an Emotion Is: A Sketch." *Philosophical Review*, 97, 183–209.

Robinson, Jenefer. 1978. "Two Theories of Representation." *Erkenntnis*, 12, 37–53.

——. 1979. "Some Remarks on Goodman's Language Theory of Pictures." *British Journal of Aesthetics*, 19, 63–75.

——. 1981. "Representation in Music and Painting." *Philosophy*, 56, 408–413.

——. 1983a. "Emotion, Judgement, and Desire." *Journal of Philosophy*, 80, 731–741.

——. 1983b. "Art as Expression." In *What Is Art?* Ed. H. Curtler. New York: Haven, 91–121.

——. 1987. "Music as a Representational Art." In Alperson, ed., 167–192.

Rochberg, George. 1960. "Indeterminacy in the New Music." *Score*, 26, January, 9–19.

Rogers, L. R. 1965. "Representation and Schemata." *British Journal of Aesthetics*, 5, 159–178.

Roskill, Mark, and David Carrier. 1983. *Truth and Falsehood in Visual Images*. Amherst: University of Massachusetts Press.

Ross, Stephanie. 1985. "Chance, Constraint, and Creativity: The Awfulness of Modern Music." *Journal of Aesthetic Education*, 19, no. 3, 21–35.

Rowell, Lewis. 1983. *Thinking about Music: An Introduction to the Philosophy of Music*. Amherst: University of Massachusetts Press.

——. 1988. "The Idea of Music in India and the Ancient West." In Rantala, Rowell, and Tarasti, eds., 323–342.

< 397 >

Works Cited

Rudner, Richard. 1951. "On Semiotic Aesthetics." *Journal of Aesthetics and Art Criticism*, 10, 67–77.

——. 1957. "Some Problems of Non-Semiotic Aesthetics." *Journal of Aesthetics and Art Criticism*, 15, 298–310.

Sadie, Stanley, ed. 1980. *The New Grove Dictionary of Music and Musicians.* 20 vols. London: Macmillan.

Sams, Eric. 1980. "Cryptography, musical." In Sadie, ed. Vol. 5, 78–82.

Savedoff, Barbara E. 1989. "The Art Object." *British Journal of Aesthetics*, 29, 160–167.

Savile, Anthony. 1971. "Nelson Goodman's *Languages of Art*: A Study." *British Journal of Aesthetics*, 11, 3–27.

——. 1986. "Imagination and Pictorial Understanding." *Proceedings of the Aristotelian Society*, Supp. Vol. 60, 19–44.

Saw, Ruth. 1962. "Art and the Language of Emotions." *Proceedings of the Aristotelian Society*, Supp. Vol. 36, 235–246.

Schaper, Eva. 1964. "The Art Symbol." *British Journal of Aesthetics*, 4, 228–239.

——. 1983. "The Pleasures of Taste." In *Pleasure, Preference, and Value: Studies in Philosophical Aesthetics*. Ed. Schaper. Cambridge: Cambridge University Press, 39–56.

Schering, Arnold. 1941. *Das Symbol in der Musik*. Leipzig: Koehler and Amelang.

Schier, Flint. 1986. *Deeper into Pictures: An Essay on Pictorial Representation*. Cambridge: Cambridge University Press.

Scholz, Bernhard F. 1972. "Discourse and Intuition in Susanne Langer's Aesthetics of Literature." *Journal of Aesthetics and Art Criticism*, 31, 215–226.

Scruton, Roger. 1974. *Art and Imagination*. London: Methuen.

——. 1976. "Representation in Music." *Philosophy*, 51, 273–287.

——. 1979. *The Aesthetics of Architecture*. London: Methuen.

——. 1980a. "Absolute Music." In Sadie, ed., Vol. 1, 26–27.

——. 1980b. "The Nature of Musical Expression." In Sadie, ed., Vol. 6, 327–332.

——. 1980c. "Programme Music." In Sadie, ed., Vol. 15, 283–287.

——. 1981a. "Photography and Representation." *Critical Inquiry*, 7, 577–603.

——. 1981b. "The Semiology of Music." In *The Politics of Culture and Other Essays*. Manchester: Carcanet Press, 75–79.

——. 1983. "The Nature of Musical Expression." In *The Aesthetic Understanding*. London: Methuen, 49–61.

——. 1987. "Analytical Philosophy and the Meaning of Music." *Journal of Aesthetics and Art Criticism*, 46, Analytic Aesthetics, 169–176.

Serafine, Mary Louise. 1988. *Music as Cognition: The Development of Thought in Sound*. New York: Columbia University Press.

——. 1989. "What Music Is." *Journal of Aesthetic Education*, 23, no. 3, 31–37.

Sharpe, R. A. 1970. "Is There a Language of Music?" *Journal of the British Society for Phenomenology*, 1, 84–86.

< 398 >

Works Cited

——. 1971. "Music: The Information Theoretic Approach." *British Journal of Aesthetics*, 11, 385–401.

——. 1975. "Hearing As." *British Journal of Aesthetics*, 15, 217–225.

——. 1982. "Review of Kivy's *The Corded Shell*." *British Journal of Aesthetics*, 22, 81–82.

——. 1983a. *Contemporary Aesthetics: A Philosophical Analysis*. Brighton: Harvester Press.

——. 1983b. "Solid Joys or Fading Pleasures." In *Pleasure, Preference, and Value: Studies in Philosophical Aesthetics*. Ed. Eva Schaper. Cambridge: Cambridge University Press, 86–98.

——. 1991. "Review of Kivy's *Music Alone*." *British Journal of Aesthetics*, 31, 276–277.

Shephard, Roger N. 1964. "Circularity in Judgments of Relative Pitch." *Journal of the Acoustical Society of America*, 36, 2346–2353.

Sherburne, Donald W. 1966. "Meaning and Music." *Journal of Aesthetics and Art Criticism*, 24, 579–583.

Shiner, Roger. 1982. "The Mental Life of a Work of Art." *Journal of Aesthetics and Art Criticism*, 40, 253–268.

Sircello, Guy. 1965. "Perceptual Acts and Pictorial Art: A Defence of the Expression Theory." *Journal of Philosophy*, 62, 669–677.

——. 1972. *Mind and Art*. Princeton, N.J.: Princeton University Press.

——. 1975. *A New Theory of Beauty*. Princeton, N.J.: Princeton University Press.

Slattery, Sister Mary Francis. 1987. "Looking Again at Susanne Langer's Expressionism." *British Journal of Aesthetics*, 27, 247–258.

Sloboda, John A. 1985. *The Musical Mind: The Cognitive Psychology of Music*. Oxford: Oxford University Press.

Smith, F. Joseph. 1979. *The Experiencing of Musical Sound*. London: Gordon & Breach.

Smith, F. Joseph, ed. 1989. *Understanding the Musical Experience*. New York: Gordon & Breach.

Snyder, Joel. 1983. "Photography and Ontology." *Grazer Philosophische Studien*, 19, 21–34.

Snyder, Joel, and Neil Walsh Allen. 1975. "Photography, Vision, and Representation." *Critical Inquiry*, 2, 143–169.

Solie, Ruth A. 1980. "The Living Work: Organicism and Musical Analysis." *Nineteenth-Century Music*, 4, 147–156.

Solt, Kornél. 1989. "Pictures and Truth." *British Journal of Aesthetics*, 29, 154–159.

Sparshott, Francis E. 1974. "Goodman on Expression." *Monist*, 58, 194–195.

——. 1987. "Aesthetics of Music: Limits and Grounds." In Alperson, ed., 35–98.

Speck, Stanley. 1988. "'Arousal Theory' Reconsidered." *British Journal of Aesthetics*, 28, 40–47.

Stambaugh, Joan. 1964. "Music as a Temporal Form." *Journal of Philosophy*, 61, 265–280.

< 399 >

Works Cited

———. 1989. "Feeling and Expressive Autonomy in Music: A Critique." In *Understanding the Musical Experience*. Ed. F. Joseph Smith. New York: Gordon & Breach, 167–177.

Stecker, Robert. 1983. "Nolt on Expression and Emotion." *British Journal of Aesthetics*, 23, 234–239.

———. 1984. "Expression of Emotion In (Some of) the Arts." *Journal of Aesthetics and Art Criticism*, 42, 409–418.

Stevenson, Charles L. 1958a. "Symbolism in the Nonrepresentational Arts." In *Language, Thought, and Culture*. Ed. Paul Henle. Ann Arbor: University of Michigan Press, 196–225.

———. 1958b. "Symbolism in the Representational Arts." In *Language, Thought, and Culture*. Ed. Paul Henle. Ann Arbor: University of Michigan Press, 226–257.

Stocker, Michael. 1983. "Psychic Feelings: Their Importance and Irreducibility." *Australasian Journal of Philosophy*, 61, 5–26.

———. 1987. "Emotional Thoughts." *American Philosophical Quarterly*, 24, 59–69.

Stravinsky, Igor. 1972. *Themes and Conclusions*. London: Faber & Faber.

Strawson, P. F. 1964. *Individuals*. London: Methuen.

Sullivan, J. W. N. 1927. *Beethoven*. London: Jonathan Cape.

Swanwick, Keith. 1973. "Musical Cognition and Aesthetic Response." *Bulletin of the British Psychological Society*, 26, 285–289.

———. 1974. "Music and the Education of the Emotions." *British Journal of Aesthetics*, 14, 134–141.

Szathmary, Arthur. 1954. "Symbolic and Aesthetic Expression in Painting." *Journal of Aesthetics and Art Criticism*, 13, 86–96.

Tanner, Michael. 1985. "Understanding Music." *Proceedings of the Aristotelian Society*, Supp. Vol. 59, 215–232.

Tarasti, Eero, ed. 1987. "Semiotics of Music." *Semiotica*, 66.

Taruskin, Richard. 1982. "Review of Kivy's *The Corded Shell*." *Musical Quarterly*, 68, 287–293.

Taylor, Frederick E. 1974. "Music and Its Logic." *British Journal of Aesthetics*, 14, 214–230.

Thom, Paul. 1983. "The Corded Shell Strikes Back." *Grazer Philosophische Studien*, 19, 93–108.

Tilghman, Benjamin R. 1984. *But Is It Art?* Oxford: Blackwell.

———. 1991. *Wittgenstein, Ethics, and Aesthetics: The View from Eternity*. London: Macmillan.

Titchener, John M., and Michael E. Broyles. 1973. "Meyer, Meaning, and Music." *Journal of Aesthetics and Art Criticism*, 32, 17–25.

Todd, George F. 1972. "Expression without Feeling." *Journal of Aesthetics and Art Criticism*, 30, 477–488.

Tolstoy, Leo. 1962. *"What Is Art?" and Essays on Art*. Trans. Aylmer Maude. New York: Hespirides. (first published 1898)

< 400 >

Works Cited

Tomas, Vincent. 1952. "The Concept of Expression in Art." *American Philosophical Association Proceedings*, 1 (Philadelphia).

Tormey, Alan. 1971. *The Concept of Expression*. Princeton, N.J.: Princeton University Press.

——. 1974. "Indeterminacy and Identity in Art." *Monist* 58, 203–215.

——. 1988. "Understanding Music: Remarks on the Relevance of Theory." In Rantala, Rowell, and Tarasti, eds., 244–256.

Tovey, Donald Francis. 1972. *Essays in Musical Analysis*, Vol. 4: *Illustrative Music*. London: Oxford University Press. (first published 1937)

Trott, Elizabeth Anne. 1990. "Music, Meaning, and the Art of Elocution." *Journal of Aesthetic Education*, 24, no. 2, 91–98.

Urmson, J. O. 1973. "Representation in Music." *Royal Institute of Philosophy Lectures*, 6, 132–146.

Vermazen, Bruce. 1971. "Information Theory and Musical Value." *Journal of Aesthetics and Art Criticism*, 29, 367–370.

——. 1986. "Expression as Expression." *Pacific Philosophical Quarterly*, 67, 196–224.

Vivas, Eliseo. 1955. "Aesthetics and the Theory of Signs." In *Creation and Discovery: Essays in Criticism and Aesthetics*. Chicago: Gateway, 381–406.

von Morstein, Petra. 1982. "Understanding Works of Art: Universality, Unity, and Uniqueness." *British Journal of Aesthetics*, 22, 350–362.

——. 1986. *On Understanding Works of Art: An Essay in Philosophical Aesthetics*. Lewiston/Queenston: Edwin Mellen Press.

Walker, Alan. 1960. "Aesthetics *versus* Acoustics." *Score*, no. 27, July, 46–50.

Walton, Kendall L. 1970. "Categories of Art." *Philosophical Review*, 79, 334–367.

——. 1973. "Pictures and Make-Believe." *Philosophical Review*, 82, 283–319.

——. 1974. "Are Representations Symbols?" *Monist*, 58, 236–254.

——. 1978. "Fearing Fictions." *Journal of Philosophy*, 75, 5–27.

——. 1979. "Style and the Products and Processes of Art." In *The Concept of Style*. Ed. Berel Lang. Philadelphia: University of Pennsylvania Press, 45–66.

——. 1984. "Transparent Pictures: On the Nature of Photographic Realism." *Critical Inquiry*, 11, 246–277.

——. 1988. "What Is Abstract about the Art of Music?" *Journal of Aesthetics and Art Criticism*, 46, 351–364.

——. 1990. *Mimesis as Make-Believe: On the Foundations of the Representational Arts*. Cambridge, Mass.: Harvard University Press.

——. 1991. "Reply to Reviewers." *Philosophy and Phenomenological Research*, 51, 413–431.

——. 1992. "Seeing-in and Seeing Fictionally." In *Mind, Psychoanalysis, and Art: Essays for Richard Wollheim*. Ed. James Hopkins and Anthony Savile. Oxford: Blackwell, 281–291.

Warburton, Nigel. 1988. "Seeing through 'Seeing through Photographs.'" *Ratio* (N.S.), 1, 64–74.

< 401 >

Works Cited

Wartofsky, Marx. 1978. "Rules and Representations: The Virtues of Constancy and Fidelity Put in Perspective." *Erkenntnis*, 12, 16–36.

Webster, William. 1974. "A Theory of the Compositional Work of Music." *Journal of Aesthetics and Art Criticism*, 33, 59–66.

Weitz, Morris. 1954. "Symbolism and Art." *Review of Metaphysics*, 7, 466–481.

Welch, Paul. 1955. "Discursive and Presentational Symbols." *Mind*, 64, 181–199.

White, David A. 1992. "Toward a Theory of Profundity in Music." *Journal of Aesthetics and Art Criticism*, 50, 23–34.

Wicks, Robert. 1989. "Photography as a Representational Art." *British Journal of Aesthetics*, 29, 1–9.

Wilkerson, Terence E. 1973. "Seeing-As." *Mind*, 82, 481–496.

———. 1978. "Representation, Illusion, and Aspects." *British Journal of Aesthetics*, 18, 45–58.

Wilkinson, Robert. 1992. "Art, Emotion, and Expression." In *Philosophical Aesthetics: An Introduction*. Ed. Oswald Hanfling. Oxford: Blackwell, 179–238.

Wilsmore, S. J. 1987. "The Role of Titles in Identifying Literary Works." *Journal of Aesthetics and Art Criticism*, 45, 403–408.

Wilson, J. P. R. 1972. *Emotion and Object*. Cambridge: Cambridge University Press.

Winn, James Anderson. 1981. *Unsuspected Eloquence: A History of the Relations between Poetry and Music*. New Haven: Yale University Press.

Wittgenstein, Ludwig. 1992. *Tractatus Logico-Philosophicus*. Trans. C. K. Ogden. New York: Harcourt, Brace (1st ed. 1921)

———. 1953. *Philosophical Investigations*. Trans. G. E. M. Anscombe. Oxford: Blackwell.

———. 1974. *Philosophical Grammar*. Ed. Rush Rhees. Trans. Anthony Kenny. Oxford: Blackwell.

Wollheim, Richard. 1964. "On Expression and Expressionism." *Revue Internationale de Philosophie*, 18, 270–289.

———. 1966/67. "Expression." *Royal Institute of Philosophy Lectures*, 1, 227–244.

———. 1970. "Nelson Goodman's *Languages of Art*." *Journal of Philosophy*, 67, 531–539.

———. 1973. "On Drawing an Object." In *On Art and the Mind*. London: Allen Lane, 3–30.

———. 1979. "Pictorial Style: Two Views." In *The Concept of Style*. Ed. Berel Lang. Philadelphia: University of Pennsylvania Press, 129–145.

———. 1980. *Art and Its Objects*. 2d ed. Cambridge: Cambridge University Press.

———. 1986. "Imagination and Pictorial Understanding." *Proceedings of the Aristotelian Society*, Supp. Vol. 60, 45–60.

———. 1987. *Painting as an Art*. London: Thames & Hudson.

———. 1990. "Reply to the Symposiasts." *Journal of Aesthetic Education*, 24, no. 2, 30–36.

———. 1991. "A Note on *Mimesis as Make-Believe*." *Philosophy and Phenomenological Research*, 51, 401–406.

< 402 >

Works Cited

Wolterstorff, Nicholas. 1975. "Towards an Ontology of Artworks." *Noûs*, 9, 115–142.

———. 1980. *Works and Worlds of Art*. Oxford: Clarendon.

———. 1991a. "Artists in the Shadows: Review of Kendall Walton's *Mimesis as Make-Believe*." *Philosophy and Phenomenological Research*, 51, 407–411.

———. 1991b. "Two Approaches to Representation—and Then a Third." *Midwest Studies in Philosophy*, 16, 167–179.

Youngblood, Joseph E. 1958. "Style as Information." *Journal of Music Theory*, 2, 24–35.

Zangwill, Nick. 1991. "Metaphor and Realism in Aesthetics." *Journal of Aesthetics and Art Criticism*, 49, 57–62.

Ziff, Paul. 1960. "On What a Painting Represents." *Journal of Philosophy*, 57, 647–654.

Zink, Sidney. 1960. "Is the Music Really Sad?" *Journal of Aesthetics and Art Criticism*, 19, 197–207.

Zuckerkandl, Victor. 1956. *Sound and Symbol: Music and the External World*. Trans. Willard R. Trask. London: Routledge & Kegan Paul.

———. 1959. *The Sense of Music*. Princeton, N.J.: Princeton University Press.

< 403 >

Index

< 405 >

< 406 >

< 407 >

< 408 >

< 409 >

< 410 >

Index

< 411 >

< 412 >

Index

Orlov, Henry, 124n, 230n, 231
Osborne, Harold, 26, 128, 137n, 170, 178n, 188n, 202n, 214n, 217n, 219n, 268, 270n, 273n, 296

Paganini, Nicolai: *Caprices,* 42n, 353
Paisiello, Giovanni: *Fra i due Litiganti il Terzo Gode,* 94
Palmer, Anthony J., 28
Payne, Elsie, 283
Payzant, Geoffrey, 203n, 204, 208n, 209
Peacocke, Christopher, 52n, 53n, 59n, 65n, 66n, 70n, 71n
Pearce, David, 139n, 140
Peel, John, 3n, 360n
Peetz, Dieter, 61n, 76n
Peltz, Richard 76n, 139n
Penderecki, Krzysztof: *Threnody for the Victims of Hiroshima,* 207
Petock, Stuart Jay, 124n
Photography, 54–55. *See also* Representation
Physiognomic theory. *See* Contour theory of music's expressiveness
Piechowski, Michael M., 124n, 128
Pike, Alfred, 156n, 230n, 239n
Pinkerton, Richard C., 27n
Platonic attitudes, 212–215, 225–226, 251n; as lacking distinctive behavioral expressions, 215, 226, 261, 263; and music, 196–197, 215–216, 261–263. *See also* Emotion; Hope
Pleydell-Pearce, A. G., 52n
Pole, David, 69n, 70n, 71n, 76n
Pollard, D. E. B., 61n
Pratt, Carroll C., 183, 188, 209n, 230n, 232, 234–235, 249, 283, 299n; his theory of music's expressiveness, 134–137
Presley, C. F., 69n, 71n, 76n
Price, Kingsley Blake, 10n, 22n, 81n, 94n, 129n, 131n, 139n, 215n, 261n, 282n, 321n, 334n, 348n
Primary expressions of emotion, 173–180, 225–226; compared to emotion characteristics, 181, 225–226, 261, 264; not involved in musical composition, 179, 182–184, 198, 272. *See also* Expression theory; Secondary expressions of emotion; Tertiary expressions of emotion
Program music, 42, 47–48, 80–83, 93–94, 103–104, 107–109, 111–112, 116–119, 291–292; aspires to the condition of pure music, 102–103, 118; and titles, 82–83, 98–101, 107–114. *See also* Representation; Understanding music
Prokofiev, Sergei: *Alexander Nevsky,* 116; *Lieutenant Kije,* 120; *Peter and the Wolf,* 43n, 116
Putman, Daniel A., 11n, 148, 151, 210n, 213n, 214n, 215, 218, 221, 230n, 268–269, 271n, 308

Rachmaninov, Sergei, 102
Radford, Colin, 193n, 214n, 285, 299n, 301n; on response, 302–305, 308, 311
Raffman, Diana, 4, 6, 276n, 326n, 340n, 379; on ineffability, 159–162
Reger, Max, 40
Reich, Willi, 44
Reid, Louis Arnaud, 17n, 134n, 137n
Rembrandt van Rijn, 243n, 378
Representation: conditions for, 53–79; conventions of, 54–58, 63–64, 71–74, 85–86, 92, 96, 141; as different from assertion, 12–14, 19–20, 76–77, 88–89; versus expression, 104–106, 266; and music, 85–101, 110; speech-act accounts of, 12–14, 19–21, 76–77, 88–89; versus symbolization, 51–52; terminology,

< 413 >

Index

< 414 >

Index

Scruton, Roger, 3, 8n, 11, 12n, 13, 26n, 27n, 54n, 59n, 76n, 104, 107n, 129n, 151, 203n, 206n, 210n, 213n, 229n, 230n, 234, 293n, 294n, 345, 379; on musical representation, 88–104, 109–113, 118–119; on music's expressiveness, 252–254

Secondary expressions of emotion, 175–177, 179, 184, 198, 264. *See also* Emotion; Primary expressions of emotion; Tertiary expressions of emotion

Seeing-in theory of representation, 53, 59–66, 96; applied to music, 82–84, 86–89; versus the semantic theory of representation, 70–74. *See also* Representation; Resemblance

Self-reference and music, 10–11, 22, 41, 81, 93. *See also* Meaning; Self-representation and music; Semantic content

Self-representation and music, 81, 93–95. *See also* Meaning; Representation; Self-reference and music

Semantic content: as absent in music, 3–4, 24–25, 27–28, 39; as presupposing possibility of truthful assertion, 4, 12, 125. *See also* Meaning

Semantic theory of representation, 53, 66–70, 74–77; applied to music, 82–85, 87–89; versus the seeing-in theory of representation, 70–74. *See also* Representation; Resemblance

Serafine, Mary Louise, 237n, 244n

Serialization in music. *See* Total serialization in music

Shakespeare, William, 115n, 293, 378

Sharpe, R. A., 8n, 26, 29n, 153, 164n, 172n, 213n, 214n, 240n, 252n, 277n, 282n, 296n, 348n

Shephard, Roger N., 231n

Sherburne, Donald W., 28n, 29n, 209n

Shiner, Roger, 131n, 203n, 254n

Shostakovitch, Dmitri: *The Age of Gold,* 41; Symphony No. 7, 41

Sircello, Guy, 169, 170n, 179n, 219n, 274

Slattery, Sister Mary Francis, 124n

Slawson, Wayne, 3n, 360n

Sloboda, John A., 4, 98n

Smetana, Bedřich: *Ma Vlast,* 91

Smith, F. Joseph, 156n, 230n

Smith, Jack: *Sea Movement,* 75

Snyder, Joel, 54n

Solie, Ruth A., 347n

Solt, Kornél, 12n

Sorensen, E. Richard, 243n

Sparshott, Francis E., 28n, 73n, 140n, 328n

Speck, Stanley, 185n, 188, 193n, 199n, 268–269, 270n

Stambaugh, Joan, 129n, 204, 230n, 234n, 235n

Stecker, Robert, 169n, 190, 210n, 240n

Stevenson, Charles L., 7n, 130n, 137n, 202n

Stocker, Michael, 217n, 257n

Strauss, Johann, 94

Strauss, Richard, 97n, 102, 282; *Ein Heldenleben,* 45; *Der Rosenkavalier,* 85, 88; *Till Eulenspiegel,* 101

Stravinsky, Igor, 239, 245, 345, 363n, 380; *Ebony* Concerto, 43n; *The Firebird,* 341; *The Nightingale,* 101; *Les Noces,* 368n; *Orpheus,* 24; *Petrushka,* 42, 79; *Pulcinella,* 116n; *The Rake's Progress,* 44, 95; *The Rite of Spring,* 296, 306, 352; Symphony in C, 172; Symphony in Three Movements, 113

Strawson, P., 15–16, 90

Sullivan, J. W. N., 80

Swanwick, Keith, 240n, 249

Symbolism, 7; exemplificational, 137–150, 165–166; iconic, 38, 67,

< 415 >

Index

Symbolism (*cont.*)
123–127, 129–133, 166, 219n; and music, 39–48, 86, 123, 165, 263–264; presentational, 124–127, 129–133, 166. *See also* Meaning; Resemblance; Semantic content

Szathmary, Arthur, 129n, 131n, 134n

Tanner, Michael, 26n, 336n, 348n, 352, 356n, 367n, 368, 380

Tarasti, Eero, 124

Taruskin, Richard, 247n, 275n

Taylor, Frederick E., 28n, 289n

Tchaikovsky, Piotr, 282, 284; *1812 Overture*, 41, 90, 93, 96, 101; *Romeo and Juliet* Overture, 102; Symphony No. 6, 103, 197, 309

Telemann, Georg, 270n, 368n

Tertiary expressions of emotion, 176–177, 180–182; in act of musical composition, 177–182, 272. *See also* Emotion; Primary expressions of emotion; Secondary expressions of emotion

Thom, Paul, 47n

Tilghman, Benjamin R., 161n, 164n, 255–256, 259n, 269n

Titchener, John M., 28n

Titles: and musical representation, 82–83, 98–101, 107–114; and painterly depiction, 62–63, 74–76, 82–83, 109, 112

Todd, George F., 169n, 173n

Tolstoy, Leo, 170n, 293

Tomas, Vincent, 175n

Tormey, Alan, 84n, 173n, 174n, 175n, 178n, 179n, 224n, 289n, 346, 362–363, 367n

Total serialization in music, 360–367

Tovey, Donald Francis, 215n

Trott, Elizabeth Anne, 2

Truth: in music, 14–19; in painting, 12–14, 76–77. *See also* Meaning; Meaning in music; Semantic content

Understanding music: aided by knowledge of technical terms, 348–349, 353, 356, 380; aided by reference to composer's program, 82, 111–112, 364–365; displayed in awareness of musical expressiveness, 314–315, 379–380; displayed in descriptions, 330–331, 338–341, 348, 379–380; does not require awareness of some technicalities, 345–349, 356–367; involves "knowing that" rather than know-how, 337–341; leads to pleasure, 312–313, 316, 332, 355–356; as representational, 98, 101–104, 107; requires awareness of expressiveness sometimes, 169, 177, 198, 312–313, 340n, 342; requires awareness of musical conventions, 325–330, 369–370; requires awareness of musical genres, 113–114, 317, 325, 329, 362, 366–367, 369–370; requires awareness of some technicalities, 349–353; requires cognitive involvement, 321–325, 332–355, 379–380; requires knowledge of musical history and style, 109, 369–379; and the title of the work, 108–114. *See also* Conventions of music; Descriptions of music; Descriptions of music's expressiveness; Value of music

Urmson, J. O., 80n, 91, 95n, 105, 109, 254n, 363n

Value of music, 275–277, 312–314, 316–317, 319; as arising from its expressiveness, 157–158, 173n, 269–276, 310–311. *See also* Expression of emotion in music; Response to music's expressiveness

< 416 >

< 417 >